The Moral Philosophy of Management

D0060798

Studies in Socio-Economics

MORALITY, RATIONALITY, AND EFFICIENCY
NEW PERSPECTIVES ON SOCIO-ECONOMICS
Richard M. Coughlin, editor

SOCIO-ECONOMICS
TOWARD A NEW SYNTHESIS
Amitai Etzioni and Paul R. Lawrence, editors

INSTITUTIONAL CHANGE
THEORY AND EMPIRICAL FINDINGS
Sven-Erik Sjöstrand, editor

THE MORAL PHILOSOPHY OF MANAGEMENT
FROM QUESNAY TO KEYNES
Pierre Guillet de Monthoux

The Moral Philosophy of Management

From Quesnay to Keynes

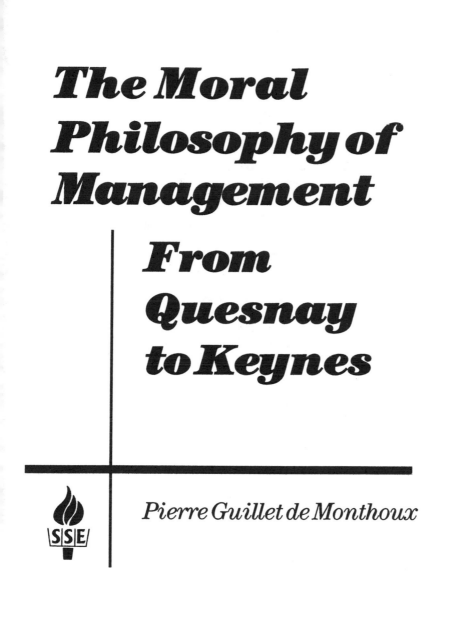

Pierre Guillet de Monthoux

M.E. Sharpe
ARMONK, NEW YORK
LONDON, ENGLAND

Library of Congress Cataloging-in-Publication Data

Guillet de Monthoux, Pierre, 1946–
The moral philosophy of management: from Quesnay to Keynes
Pierre Guillet de Monthoux.
p.   cm.—(Studies in socio-economics)
Includes bibliographical references and index.
ISBN 1–56324–081–5 (cloth) ISBN 1-56324-377-6 (pbk)
1. Industrial management—History.   2. Industrial management—
Philosophy—History.   3. Managerial economics—History.
4. Economics—History.
I. Title.
II. Series.
HD30.5.G85
1993
658′.001—dc20
93–16576
CIP

Printed in the United States of America

The paper used in this publication meets the minimum requirements
of American National Standard for Information Sciences—
Permanence of Paper for Printed Library Materials, ANSI Z39.48–1984.

BM (c) 10   9   8   7   6   5   4   3   2   1
BM (p) 10   9   8   7   6   5   4   3   2   1

To

Albert Danielsson

Contents

Preface

This book is about the foundations of European management philosophy. It is prefaced in a dramatic moment of European history. In this moment we believe the time of the cold war is over and the confrontation between capitalism and communism has ended, and we have seen a monument over closed economies—the Berlin Wall—tumble. Indeed, many of us feel it to be time to reflect on our own heritage—Western capitalism. This need is broadly recognized, not only among students and scholars, but also in the pragmatic quarters of practical businesspeople. My hope is that this book will contribute to an articulate debate on the role of business and management. Its contribution is the result of an archeological and hermeneutical expedition to economic texts: some classics, others forgotten in the dust of libraries. It is a quest for the moral philosophy, or perhaps philosophies, of management embedded in economic thought. When a branch of "moral philosophy" in the early nineteenth century turned into "political economy," which then became "economics" and in the 1920s dropped into the formalism of "econometrics," this managerial message was lost on the way. So was the realism—or, as I will call it, concreteness—of the economic texts that, in early days, often attained literary qualities that made them enjoyable to the practical people they really wanted to persuade.

But what did economists mean when they talked of a business and management? What was an ideal enterprise and its role in society? You are now invited to twelve lectures on the subject. First come two gentlemen in wigs from eighteenth-century France. Doctor Quesnay and the Marquis of Mirabeau, two Physiocrats, long dead, whose views on enterprise had to do with a world of animals and nature. They are followed by Adam Smith, who celebrated the family business of traders and craftsmen. After Smith's lively discourse, we have the honor to hear one of the men of principle, David Ricardo, for whom business was purely a matter of putting money to work. He did not know much about industry, but he did own a large country estate purchased with his speculative profits, and he spent his spare time offering sure tips about dealing on the London Stock Exchange. Ricardo has scarcely left the pulpit before a German with a bushy beard jumps up. It is Karl Marx, who does not mince his words when he expresses his distaste for factories. John Stuart Mill follows Marx to give us a happier picture; he seems to be saying how fine a business venture can be if only we use our common sense. He charms us with illustrations of honest craftsmen and farmers.

The next lecturer has been invited in order that we can enjoy the views of a pure theoretician. It is a lesson to us on how little abstract theories mean in the real world of business. Léon Walras presents business as the happy formula for achieving peace and freedom. The following speaker, Alfred Marshall from Cambridge in England, is indulgent toward his predecessor, despite the fact that his own, immediate concern is that of finding a solution to Britain's economic crisis. Better productivity in more efficient businesses is his message, and this is to be obtained without the loss of a free and good life for the workers! It is again the turn for a German, Professor Doctor Gustav von Schmoller aus Berlin, who has been especially invited to develop his argument against free enterprise and business activity. His is a very special music in the economic chorus, the echoes of which can yet be heard today. Schmoller, however, must soon rush off to some state investigation of the pricing structure. He leaves his place to Charles Gide, who sings the praises of his favorite form of enterprise—cooperative business. If Schmoller and Gide do not appear to have much in common, the next speaker, the young Gunnar Myrdal, is even less in agreement with either of them; his source of inspiration is Léon Walras. Myrdal's meager acquaintance with concrete economics does not hinder him from confident assertions that hold out the promise of monetary control over business enterprise. He brings to life the profit-maximizing manager, dressed purely in monetary clothing! The last of our speakers, tall and distant with a dreamy gaze, holds views that would have pleased both Adam Smith and John Stuart Mill. This is Lord Keynes—Pozzo to the "boys"—who thinks that finance and business enterprise do not go together very well. He should know, because he made his living on the stock market.

I have reserved the last place in this very distinguished company to myself. I shall first provide a concise summary of the central themes that emerge from these lectures. This is the skeleton of a doctrine on business enterprise that shows that anyone who would lead a business in the style recommended by the economists is obliged to perform a skillful balancing act between state and company. He must be constantly on the alert for middlemen who will want tax and interest from his activity. Such aspects are important to a moral philosophy of management. The real manager shall be richly rewarded, not in monetary gains, but rather with the honor of saving the nation from crisis and war. For the business firm is the basic concept of national economics, a view that unites all our economists—with the exception of Schmoller, who gives priority to the state over business—an idea that still tempts a few to repeat the errors of the past.

But one horrible thought intrudes itself: Is business as the economists envisioned it still flourishing or is it just a distant memory? I do not propose to go into a criticism of modern business in this book, but these eleven lectures and the conclusions I draw from them can certainly be used as a point of departure for such an undertaking. We are, however, left with no doubt that the economists had a clear idea about what constituted a genuine business enterprise. Business to them should be a mode of activity that resolves society's crises, not causes them! During the 150 years that separate Quesnay from Keynes, there occurred a process of technical development within business enterprise that increased productivity in the human engagement with nature in a quite spectacular manner. Adherence to the central message of the economists concerning the nature of productive entrepreneurship in increasing the flow of goods and services had helped overcome the basic material shortages that plagued Europe at the time and that had their origins in fiscal policy. The doctrine of the business enterprise not only freed entrepreneurship from the inhibiting burden of taxation but also transformed servants and estate owners into workers and managers.

The productive success of business entrepreneurship, however, was hardly consistent with the notion of a balanced economy that the economists had assumed. Having pulled society out of the state of basic material needs, the business enterprise frequently continued on a process of rationalized expansion that would become a goal in itself. Owners now appeared in the guise of shareholders wielding abstract power, and workers became little more than bureaucrats performing administrative functions in an overarching organization. The earlier ideal of a productive flow of goods and services was transformed into one of organizational control of middlemen in the form of corporations, trusts, and banks. With the administration of industrial funds as its primary object, this form of company capitalism would come to have the same inhibiting effects upon concrete production as had the fiscal policies of earlier times.

The socialists of different denominations, who sought to relieve the crippling effects of stagnation through replacing these institutions with the state, learned a lesson by bitter experience. Conservatives, who would simply reverse the process, make the same mistake. The doctrine of the business that we meet in the classical economists may perhaps enable us to distinguish between the state and company, on the one hand, and genuine business enterprise, on the other. For this genuine entrepreneurship, in the works of the economists from Quesnay to Keynes, was not a contractual apparatus that gave a return in the form of interest nor a convenient hole in the ice from which to fish up taxation. It was rather a concrete way for human beings to work upon nature in order to maintain life and limb, producing adequate housing, clothing, and food so that culture could bloom. On the basis of their concrete experience and realistic philosophy, these economists created their now largely forgotten, lively, and shifting views on management and enterprise.

But look! Here come our Physiocrats. Let's sit back comfortably and enjoy their views on what constitutes "concrete" economics.

Pierre Guillet de Monthoux

The Moral
Philosophy of
Management

1

The Physiocrats' Theory of the Farm

1. France before 1789; *L'Ancien Régime*

Is there such a thing as "concrete economics"? One place to start looking for the answer is among the eighteenth-century French economists who were called Physiocrats. Many of the other eighteenth-century economists in other lands would do as well, since economics at that time was a truly practical subject.[1] Economists lectured on concrete things, and their writings were full of practical advice. While in earlier times economists' advice had often been motivated by questions of morality, the eighteenth-century economists are distinguished by their adoption of a more scientific stance. Their reasonings were accepted as authoritative if they were grounded in natural rather than moral laws. The divine, natural laws were to be discovered through a sharpened sense of observation of economic phenomena, and these were to provide the concrete foundations for the scientific disciplines of economics. A lack of insight into the natural order would result in the failure of a business enterprise. Without knowledge, we stand helpless before our projects, and as Linnaeus once proclaimed, "Knock against the rocks, tear ourselves on the thorns, sink into the mud while the satyrs leer at us as project makers."[2]

The Physiocrats, nevertheless, are regarded as belonging to the discipline of economics in its broadest sense, rather than being more narrowly business economists. I hope to show, however, that their economics would collapse without their notions concerning management and later that this is also true for other schools of economics. To read François Quesnay (1694–1774) is to receive a lesson in what business economics is really about, its social function, and the degree of concreteness with which it should be pursued. François Quesnay was medical adviser to Louis XV at Versailles. His name is immediately linked by modern economists with the work *Tableau économique*, which was printed on the king's press in 1758. The ideas it contained were apparently very popular, since it was reported in the physiocrats' journal, *Ephémérides du Citoyen*, in

3

1767 that it was no longer possible to obtain copies (the publication was sold out!). It was, indeed, the circle around Doctor Quesnay who were busily engaged with interpreting and spreading his earlier ideas concerning the input/output tables on "la distribution des dépenses annuelles d'une nation agricole," the distribution of a nation's annual agricultural costs. The *Tableau* was not Quesnay's first economic work and, from the point of view of concrete economics, by no means the most important. That the *Tableau* remains in the classical memory of modern economists says more about the latter's love for abstraction rather than Quesnay's more generally practical disposition.

In the middle of the 1750s two articles appeared that contained the concrete program of the Physiocrats. They were published in Diderot's *Encyclopédie* in which Rousseau himself, in an article on economics, set out the basic idea that later became *Le Contrat social*. Quesnay's two articles are titled *"Fermiers"* (Farmers) and *"Grains"* (Grain). The first contains the Physiocrats' "theory of the firm," or rather "of the farm," dealing with the productivity of the farm as an enterprise. The second describes the necessary preconditions for the profitability of the farm as a business—the level of prices and sales of grain. The articles were not concerned with any dry systematization of already known facts but were rather concrete analyses seeking to convince and influence. Quesnay pointed out existing shortcomings and argued for legal reforms, and his writings are directed at the entrepreneurs, the farmers, and also at the landowners and the king. With what right did he do this? Was he a "gray eminence" or a secret power holder? The Physiocrats suggested reforms of a nearly "revolutionary character" in a kingdom that we learn in school was despotic and tyrannical. The public distribution of Diderot's *Encyclopédie* was certainly banned. The Physiocrats were constrained to write under pseudonyms or strange initials. Nevertheless, the concrete economic debate was pursued in an often more open and free atmosphere than is the case in today's formal economic journals and business newssheets. What was the status of these economists of *L'Ancien Régime*?

Quesnay was educated as a doctor.[3] As a young and unknown surgeon he had thrown himself into a debate on bloodletting. In 1727 a fashionable Parisian doctor named Silva had published a book on the subject that Quesnay found so lacking that he immediately wrote a "counter book." The two men of medicine eventually held a verbal duel under the expert eye of the Marquis of Noailles. Quesnay was declared the winner after having succeeded in convincing those present of the flaws in Silva's work. He left not only as winner of the learned duel but also with permission to print and spread his "counter book." This was later withdrawn from circulation by the royal censor, but with the support of the Academy of Science the censor's decision was reversed and the book appeared in print the following year.

The royal censor had certainly been impressed by the calculations and learned arguments that the leaders of the Academy of Science gave in support of Quesnay's thesis. Although the censorship was strict, the arguments of the scientists eventually prevailed. By 1737 the now successful Doctor Quesnay had become the permanent secretary to the newly established Academy of Surgeons. He thus became responsible for transforming a mode of employment that was previously more like that of butchering into a professional body. As the secretary to the academy, Quesnay received a practical lesson in how a mode of employment could be endowed with social authority. Later in his life he managed to assemble around himself a circle of competent intellectuals who were interested in his ideas and who were often feared in other circles.

Had Quesnay not been afflicted by gout, he would have continued his career as a surgeon. He turned instead to general medicine and purchased the position as medical adviser to the king, "premier médecin ordinaire du roi." Prospering in his new position, he soon moved into the Versailles palace, becoming a confidant of King Louis XV, who raised him to the nobility. It was in Versailles that physiocracy developed. Around Quesnay there assembled a group, a sect of economists. Here was Du Pont de Nemours, the founder of the American company of the same name, the Marquis of Mirabeau, father of one of the main actors in the French Revolution, Mercier de la Rivière, and many other learned gentlemen and ladies. The king himself called Quesnay "mon penseur" and consulted him often on questions concerning the national economy and welfare. The king's protection provided the economists with the possibility to freely develop their ideas, although to have the king's ear was not the same thing as to have such ideas accepted. The king was, in *L'Ancien Régime*, only one center of power; however enlightened a despot he may have been, there were also other groups who could formulate practical policy.

Versailles itself, where the Physiocrats met, was a forum for different power groupings. Contemporary witnesses describe that enormous construction as a monarchist fairground with the royal family as the main attraction: The carriages run a shuttle traffic between Paris and Versailles bursting at the seams with curious spectators. In the evenings the grand dinners, "le grand couvert," provide a particular attraction, and it is always full in the royal dining hall. Everyone waits with bated breath to see Louis XV perform his special trick. With an elegant stroke of his knife, he decapitates an egg and sends the top sailing through the air in a wide bow. Louis XV knows how to entertain his people. They cheer as he eats more eggs than is sensible.[4] The whole palace is brimful with visitors. Well-dressed Englishmen traveling through shudder over that wide-open, popular palace which is open to everyone irrespective of estate or clothing. It stinks in the saloons, and every corner and alcove is occupied by the court ladies and gentlemen. During Louis XIV's time, it was a duty for the courtiers to attend at court. Those who absented themselves from the round of feasts, balls, and ceremonies were simply "forgotten." To be forgotten was a fate worse than death. From their estates in the countryside, the young move into Versailles, occupying a closet, a stairway, sharing an attic or a tower, laying claim to whatever they find, to remain there for the rest of their lives. The closets provide changing rooms for the grand feasts. It is a special art for the court ladies, who without the benefit of warm or running water, must paint, clothe, and powder themselves as their status and the occasion demanded.

Englishmen are thoroughly bemused by the spectacle. What does the court really do? In England the gentry engage themselves in agriculture and business. In France the country nobility had traditionally farmed the land and provided soldiers. In the France of Louis XV, however, trade and commerce had become a privilege for the bourgeois. The French nobility itself directs its criticism at the neglected feudal duties in the countryside. As one observer of the court remarks: "The nobility provided a bad example in their flight from the countryside."[5] The Marquis of Mirabeau, a Physiocrat, writes of the court to which he belongs that "the court nobility's only profession was that of intrigue."[6] The rich brocades of the dresses and jewelry glitter. Luxury is everywhere apparent, but the true source of wealth is not understood. A perceptive courtier may cry: "Will you be rich? . . . leave the luxury that is degrading you!"[7] But this type of criticism looked back to the old feudal order with its roots in the countryside, village, and family as the sources of a new idealism. In the physiocrats' journal, *Ephémérides*, it was possible to read that the Chinese emperor was a despot. He was, however, a good despot who did not engage in luxurious consumption, but rather in large-scale projects like artificial lakes and the Great Wall.[8] The critics are appreciative of the old landed nobility that held itself home on the estates: "That nobility lived a hard and steady life that was cheap for the state, and which gave more through permanent residence and the manuring of the land than what we give through our taste, our research, our colic and vapours."[9]

At the same time they joke about these "smelly, country bumpkins" who have never been presented to the king, who have never heard of a financial transaction or participated in an exciting speculation of the kind that is increasingly becoming the hobby of the court nobility.

But which among these groups did Louis XV favor? Perhaps it was just these country nobility as, for example, the Marquis of Tubilly, who had invented a ploughing machine. Or was it the Duke of La Rochefoucauld, who had developed a means of efficient milk production? Presumably he also had a sneaking admiration for the Duke of Charost, who stopped demanding a hard day's work from his peasants and instead built a hospital and announced an annual prize for the best essay on farming. Of him, Louis XV is reported to have said: "This was a small, good man . . . who did not appear to be much, but he gave new life to three of my provinces."[10]

It is possible to imagine what subjects were discussed by the king with his closed circle of economists. These discussions were reserved for his private moments, unlike the public performances at the banquets and ceremonies. Among the economists he could talk about topics not approved by the court— and worse still—the powerful provincial parliaments and magistrates of the state. For the latter, the economists, together with the philosophers and others who wrote in the encyclopedias and pamphlets, were the "disturbers of the peace of the public," a peace guaranteed by the magistrates through an infinite number of detailed regulations covering just about every area of human activity. When Louis XIV had declared that it was he who was the state, it was a message addressed to the parliaments that had control of taxation and financing through state loans. Louis XV pursued a royal struggle with these regional governments, "republicans" who hindered all attempts at reformation. At the height of the Physiocrats' period during the 1760s, there were strong conflicts between the king and the parliaments. The king sought to exercise his popular sovereignty and central power against the conservative and decentralized power of the parliaments. The philosophers and economists stood on the side of the king, advocating the idea of a kind of natural order that should reign in economic affairs. It was particularly the economists who provided the ideas that were used in this struggle. These ideas concerned such matters as tax reform and moral regeneration, where the various classes of society would learn to take their responsibility for the functions of a naturally organized state. It was in this situation that the Physiocrats developed their concrete message concerning an effective means of production and distribution. This was the background to their managerial philosophy.[11]

2. Production

Only a productive activity is worthy of being called an "enterprise," and production for Quesnay is identical with agriculture. In actual fact, he never uses the word "production," but rather always talks about "reproduction." The first of the Physiocrats' articles, titled "Fermiers" (Farmers), from 1756, deals with farming as a business enterprise. Quesnay wanted to unveil a number of prejudices about farming and show their destructive consequences for the nation. These prejudices were based upon a lack of concrete observation and detailed knowledge, resulting in a generally "vague" understanding of agriculture that was entirely misleading. This "imparfait" understanding failed to recognize that farming was a business and failed to see the importance of farming activity for the wealth of the state. A widespread prejudice was that "the work of the poor cultivator was as successful as that of the rich farmer."[12]

It was thought that the only thing that distinguished the rich from the poor farmer was the quality of the earth, thus forgetting the working of the farm as a business and the farmer's intelligence and knowledge.[13] The process of reproduction, however, bore rich fruits as the result of a combination of two concrete resources: the earth and the businessman's own input. The farmer as a businessman and manager should be governed by intelligence and knowledge that were within the reach of all careful observers, independent of inheritance and estate. In a very didactic essay, Mirabeau thus gives the following advice to Antoine, a farmer's boy, who is a kind of physiocratic Émile: "The book lies open before you, and you have the same chance as any bourgeois to thoroughly learn this important science that no one should neglect, and which should enlighten all human conduct and the government of the nations."[14]

The concrete economics was created by the farmer, a scientist with his feet in the soil. The speculative scientists, isolated in their towers, were regarded as abstract and dizzy-minded who "observed and noticed all but the land they were standing on and with all their speculations could neither advise themselves nor others."[15]

Quesnay turns immediately to a concrete problem. Should one plow the land with the help of oxen or horses? This choice in the technology of production demanded rethinking because, in the first place, farmers were inclined to retain their traditional usage of oxen and, second, because in the current business climate horses were considered too expensive to purchase. Quesnay, now, investigates this business situation for contemporary agriculture.

The lands were the possession of an owner who could, in principle, choose between allowing them to remain idle or taking them into use. Farming could take one of two forms. One could employ a "Laboureur" plowman who owned no draft animals himself to pull the plow. The plow would be drawn by the landowner's oxen, which also grazed upon the owner's fields. This type of farming was much like the relationship between business and wage labor. In this instance, the owner took his payment in the form of a fixed share of the harvest. If the owner was unable to be present in person to inspect the volume of the harvest, he would demand a fixed sum instead of a share of the harvest. Quesnay does not regard this mode of farming as business in the proper meaning of the term. The agriculturalist becomes a businessman first when he has a tenancy agreement with the landowner and provides his own equipment, plowing animals, and day laborers. His equipment was "une charrue," a plow drawn by at least four horses. The businessman, as distinct from the laborer, invests or "advances" the seed and allows at least two years to lapse before, in August of the second year, he claims his share of the first harvest. Quesnay then continues to describe how this technical advance from plowman to farmer came about and what advantages are implied by the new form of organization.

The argument here centers around the question of the relative productivity of horses as against oxen and takes the form of testable hypotheses. The oxen are slower than horses both in work and in grazing. For example, four horses are capable of doing the work of twelve or even eighteen oxen. That the oxen are stronger than horses is only a prejudice based upon the casual observation that an ox-drawn wagon goes faster than a horse-drawn carriage. More careful observation shows that the horses are drawing a greater weight than the oxen. Quesnay then turns to the question of the quality of the lands. When this is taken into consideration, it becomes clear that the rougher the land and the more clay in it, the more advantageous it is to employ horses. Horses could plow on the average three times the area that oxen could do in the same time. The oxen are owned by the landowner, the horses by the farmer. Since the farmer has learned to handle animals, the landowner now dares to leave his sheep in the farmer's care. The oxen, however, graze in the open, which means that their manure cannot be collected. The horse manure, on the other hand, is gathered in the stalls and contributes to the profitability of horses. A plowman who hires the oxen from an owner would often find it more advantageous to work for a third part than to use the owner's land. The fields become wasteland again, and their price is therefore lower than of the land that is cultivated. Land that is covered with trees is easier to sell because it is purchased for speculation. The money is used in speculation rather than investment in agriculture. The use of oxen, which appears cheaper than the use of horses, becomes in this manner unprofitable. The value of the land sinks. The poor plowmen exhaust the land, but the rich farmers raise its value because, as Mirabeau pointed out, "the large business provides a return in proportion to investment."[16]

Concrete economics, thus, lays weight upon the key role of profitability. The riches of the nation increase when both landowners and land users see that they have an interest in each other's mutual welfare.

Mirabeau lets the farm boy, Antoine, relate a story about a lady of the court who made a quick visit to the estate she had recently inherited. She found there a farmer who obviously made a very good living from his holding. "This rascal is cheating me" was her first thought; and her second was, "When does his lease run out?" Her pleasure was great when she learned that it ran out the same day. She immediately raised the rent sky-high and demanded that the farmer sign the new lease. After failing in his attempt to give her a quick lesson on the profitability of farming, the farmer leaves the estate, refusing to sign the new lease. However, she soon finds another person, a "petit épicier,"[17] without any practical experience, who is willing to take over the holding. But after a few years, he is bankrupt and leaves the estate in an appalling condition. The value of the land now sinks, and the lady is forced to lease it out for a price far below that she would have received from the farmer. It is only true managerial rationality that could help redeem such insane situations.

The mark of a rich farmer is that he can afford to keep horses. A horse with harness certainly costs three hundred livre, while a pair of oxen would go for around four hundred. But a horse can work for twelve years, while the oxen are worn out after only six. Despite the sale of the oxen to the slaughterhouse for meat, the expenditure for them is higher than for horses if it is reckoned that four horses can do the work of twelve oxen. Quesnay then provides the following investment calculation for draft animals: It had been maintained that horses were more sensitive to diseases than oxen. But, assures Quesnay,[18] with twelve oxen the probability of disease is greater than with four horses. Furthermore, the diseases of oxen are more contagious, so that the risk that all the animals would die is also greater. What is the position, then, with regard to the costs of fodder and upkeep? Farming with horses usually produced a third of the production in corn, a third in oats, and the last third in fodder. Production with oxen, on the other hand, usually gave half in corn and half in fodder. It thus appeared superficially that production with oxen gave a greater return in corn than production with horses. But concrete observation had shown that if the land was used only every third year for corn, the annual return was a fifth greater than if it was used every other year. Twelve oxen also eat more than four horses, and the necessity for grazing pastures limits the possibility of cultivating this land. How did it come about, therefore, that six-sevenths of the kingdom's rich lands were still culturated with the use of oxen? Why, moreover, was so much of the land yet covered with trees? This crime against the nation was due to traditional attitudes and abstract prejudices that distanced people from the sound principles of the natural order.

The Physiocrats pointed to three types of prejudice. The first concerned the superiority of town life over that of the countryside. The children of the farmers flock to the towns, attracted by commerce, luxury, and industry. A sign of prejudice, moreover, was to call manufacturing and construction by the term *industrial.* Is not everyone who works industrious? The more people disappear from the countryside, the less was the yield from farming. The landowners, too, have forgotten their feudal, land-related obligations; administration was neglected and the farmers lack leaders and protection. With Versailles and the Paris bourgeois in mind, Mirabeau wrote: "Most landowners, including the largest, believe that it is in Paris and the court that one seeks riches, but there exist here all too many possibilities to waste money on luxuries for one ever to become rich." [19]

The capital disappears to the towns with the landowners; the workers disappear into the factories. In order to finance their life of luxury in Paris, the landowners exploit the farmers in the leasehold negotiations. In this they not only betray the farmers but also neglect the land in the long-term perspective. The Marquis of Mirabeau dared to be much more open on this sensitive question than Doctor Quesnay. The power of the nobility is based on this ability to shield the population and invest in agriculture. The first duty implies that the landowners themselves should pay those who provide protection for the farmers. More clearly expressed, the landowners should pay taxes and not push the costs of such onto the enterprising farmers. The second implies that it is the landowners, and not the farmers, who should provide the necessary labor for the building and maintenance of roads, bridges, canals, and other infrastructure. As soon as the question of taxes and day labor was understood by the farmers, they would immediately recognize the injustice of their burdens, because "a wise farmer should never be burdened with tax payments, either for the land or upon income." [20]

If the farmer takes care of his business, then the landowner should also take care of his. If the landowners do not understand this, then it is necessary to remove the misconception that the use of land is free. [21] The landowners should be made responsible for "societal" investments in land, "les avances foncières," and for the protection of the property of all citizens. When the farmers divest themselves of the burden of tax on to the landowners, it would be time for the latter to ask themselves where all the money from road tolls and the selling of titles and jobs, regulations, and interest had disappeared. Should not this money have been used for the protection of citizens? Did not this money represent a suitable taxation? The landowners would then come to see the importance of a happy revolution, "heureuse révolution,"[22] in the tax question. Mirabeau wrote all this from Amsterdam, and the book was immediately banned.

The other great prejudice was, in other words, the arbitrary taxation that magistrates, because of the failures of the landowners and nobility, felt constrained to visit upon the farmers. Not sufficient that this was unjust, the annual variation in taxation also undermined the farmer's business economic calculations. This was also a negative economic consequence of the third great prejudice: the tax on grain and the price regulations which are the subject of Quesnay's second article, "Grains," which appeared in the *Encyclopédie.*[23]

3. Distribution

One difference between the rich farmer and the laboring plowman is that the farmer must sell his produce on the market. The Physiocrats were, thus, interested in trade or rather free trading. Farming is a case of genuine enterprise, but much effort had been laid down to make a distinction between agriculture, on the one hand, and trade and industry, on the other. Within agriculture, we have seen how the Physiocrats distinguished between the plowman with his oxen, "la petite culture," and the large-scale, "la grande culture," of the farmer, who employed horses. "La petite culture" was not considered to be a genuine form of enterprise. The plowman did not employ labor from outside his own family, except perhaps an occasional worker who carried the produce to the barn. He borrowed the oxen and the sheep; leased the grazing meadows, the house, and perhaps even the equipment from the owner of the estate; and paid for these with a portion of his harvest. The plowman and his family existed on the produce of the soil and were condemned to always remain poor. The only advantage of this system, according to Quesnay, was that he did not have to pay more tax than the tenth of his harvest that was taken for this purpose.

"La grande culture," on the other hand, demanded a businessman, an entrepreneur, who occupied a place between the landowner and the lands and who took care of the yearly costs and investments that arose in connection with the enterprise. For the Physiocrats, being a good manager and businessman was the same thing as being able to take care of such outlays. Antoine, the farmer's boy in Mirabeau's book, is surprised to learn what the Physiocrats actually meant by their notion of "faire fortune"[24] or being rich. In a lesson on bookkeeping, he discovers that all receipts from the sale of grains were swallowed up by the yearly costs: I see with sorrow, Monsieur, from these accounts that all is already predetermined, unchangeably written into the order of nature . . . and therefore there exists no wealth over for the entrepreneur in this business."[25]

But Antoine, do you really believe that profits arise out of nothing? If you take something for yourself from the business, it is not a profit but rather a loan, and all such loans damage the business and its capacity for reproduction. The duty of the entrepreneur is to increase riches. His reward is that of being the leader of a successful enterprise that employs many people. The creation of "richness" is the key to "fortune" and "to become rich and make profits means only to be able to make outlays. "Outlays are the only possibility of enjoying a fortune, and keeping and increasing it."[26]

That person is rich who can contribute to the riches of the nation. Merely to save money in the bottom of a chest is to remove it from useful circulation. Money like blood in a body should be allowed to circulate, to make outlays that increase concrete production.

This concrete economy is based on the notion of cause and effect. The cause, "un accroissement des frais," or an increase in costs, always precedes "celui des produits," an increase in production.[27] Nothing could be physically produced without concrete costs; likewise, all concrete products "sons visibles,"[28] depend upon fully visible, concrete outlays. The idea that some abstract quality, such as "entrepreneurship," could lead to a physical profit was metaphysical nonsense. This is as true for the farmer as it is for the landowner. In an imaginary dialogue with the owner of an estate, Mirabeau allows him to assert that his income from leases are rightfully his because of his title, rank, and blood. But titles and coats of arms provide no physical production, only possibly respect, attention, and ceremonies.[29] The reason that the rents went to him was that he had purchased the lands for money or that his forefathers had confiscated the land with physical force. The estate owner would do well to forget his coat of arms and climb down from his "position de domination," which allows him the false idea that he could isolate himself from society. He should forget his metaphysical abstractions and recall his obligations to hold the estate in good order for the farmers. It was only through the costs incurred here that he had any right to an income, according to the natural order.[30] But, continues Mirabeau, it can be easier for a farmer to understand this concrete economics than for a nobleman who has been corrupted through a life of luxury: "The farmer has a great advantage in getting this into his head over that of the grand nobleman."[31]

In the same manner as the landowner has his duties in the natural order, the plowman, when he became a businessman, would also take his place and social responsibilities. All profits that he gathered into his own pockets were a crime against the nation. There were only three instances where it was justified to include in the farm accounts an entry that we would perhaps today regard as profit.

It was certainly right, for example, for the farmer to make provision against natural catastrophes. Floods, drought, hail, and storms belonged to the natural order of things. Thus, this kind of provision would always be necessary, even in that far-off day when all people would listen to the economists and the ideal natural order of the *Tableau économique* had become reality. In the next two instances, however, this was not the case, as the need for them would disappear with the temporary "vexations" with which man disturbed the natural order. So long as this day had not arrived, it was necessary for farmers to set money aside to cover the contingencies of the existing imperfect order. The second case here involved the question of the necessary provision against arbitrary taxation that could strike like lightning from the heavens. This included "la taille, la dîme, les corvées,"[32] together with the forced recruitment and taxation imposed upon the farmer and his family by the military.

The third case involved the need for providing for the effect of human interference in the natural order of prices in the markets for farm products. Prices were determined through taxes and regulations instead of the natural fact of whether a harvest has been good or bad. In the natural order of things, prices would pose no problems. Antoine scratches his head trying to resolve what this has to do with the farm accounts. Was it not necessary to know the positive price of everything that was included in the calculations? Mirabeau replies that it certainly was necessary to have some idea of prices, but such was obtained through experience of the market.[33] But, he assures Antoine that he can safely forget the problem because, in the natural order, buying and selling are equal so that "you will never come to purchase more expensively than what you sell."[34]

Antoine understands this immediately. If he were to sell his grain more expensively, then it was nothing more than justice that the workers who purchased bread should have higher wages. Then the balance of the accounts would be in order, and the price changes would even things out. It becomes complicated when someone lays a tax on the grain. This is a disturbance of a kind that was necessary to consider so long as humans interfered with the natural order and gave expression to "the human contempt for the general order of the Creator."[35]

It was necessary for entrepreneurs to be on their guard against such disturbances on the market. If trade among states was to become free, it would still be necessary for entrepreneurs to use their intelligence and calculations, but it would be the case, held Quesnay, that their task would be easier, since free prices would stabilize around a natural level. When prices stabilized, when "the good price" had been created, then simple farm boys like Antoine would dare to start their own businesses. They must, however, utilize the only capital they have, skill and intelligence. This is because during the period of the Physiocrats access to credit was highly restricted, so that a new business had to be self-financed. During the years of bad harvest, the new farmer would attempt to benefit from the sale of grain that his large business has enabled him to stock from previous good years. Large-scale farming, however, required a large market. The French population of sixteen million, half of whom died before reaching the age of fifteen, could hardly come to consume half the production of grain that it would be possible to produce through large-scale business methods of farming.[36] One possible solution to this surplus would be free trade; another would be to produce something other than grain, such as meat. If the borders were opened, the French overcapacity in manpower and land could be taken into production. The earth would be put to good use, and the people would develop their intelligence and capacity for concrete observation. It was not only a question that large areas of land still lay under trees but that the education of the children was neglected, which encouraged their flight to the towns. The peasants are, according to Quesnay, regarded as little more than slaves of the state.[37]

In order that real riches could increase, it was necessary for the economist to remove the hindrances that limited the productivity of the natural order. The task of the Physiocrats was not only to point out the real enterprises and their good management but also to unveil the false and point to wasteful methods of production, distinguishing also between entrepreneurs and functionaries.

4. Entrepreneurs and Functionaries

The Physiocrats preached what they considered to be the truth. As economists, they saw themselves as "une ligue," an intellectual sect that spread the word of truth.[38] The truth was to be found in nature, and the process of seeking for the truth consisted of the following steps. The first step is to seek the true human advantages, which were to be found in natural needs. From this point, a source is sought from which to satisfy these natural needs, this source also to be found in nature. The task is then to find the correct means of tapping this source, with work and social rewards providing the pumping mechanism. From this it follows that the true principles of economics are the same as those of nature and that the task of the economist is to re-create the social harmony that would exist in the natural order of things. This implied that the laws of the natural order are self-regulating. When, indeed, Louis XV asked Quesnay what was to be done in a difficult situation, the doctor replied, "Nothing at all." "But who shall then govern?" asked the surprised king. "The laws themselves," answered the unperturbed Quesnay before departing to continue his studies among all the intrigues of court life. Another member of the group of economists, Du Pont de Nemours, wrote as late as 1788 to Adam Smith in Scotland that the black clouds assembling over France brought much good with them because "they cause us to reflect over the interests and rights of man, speeding the development of both the governed and the government."[39]

The economists' intellectual activities went to the very limit that the established society of the time would tolerate. The existence of factions in *L'Ancien Régime* made it possible for them to engage themselves in spreading the principles of the natural order. In an often confused and heated debate, the Physiocrats strangely enough developed a version of those concepts and ideas that were to inform later economic discussion in a more orthodox mantle. Thus, for the Physiocrats, science and its conclusions opened up the possibility to freedom of thought and the development of new concepts.

In his dialogues, for example, Mirabeau distinguished between "class" and "individual." According to the *Tableau économique*, society is divided into three classes: an owning class, a productive farming class, and a "sterile" manufacturing class. The difference between "class" and "individual" implies that one and the same person can be both owner and, in situation of manpower, also a farmer. An individual could thus belong to two classes. The word *class* in this context is perhaps somewhat misleading, since the Physiocrats were not so much referring to arbitrary privilege as to what we would today call social functions. The three groups each had their particular functions necessary for the nation's existence. The task of the state was to safeguard these functions in order that society would act as a whole. It was not the task of the state to protect certain special persons or families that for the moment performed certain functions. As soon as the state concerns itself with individuals, confusing "class" with "individual," there arose privileges and monopolies. In the natural order, an individual is also socially useful by virtue of being a "functionary"; a "functionary" could never be regarded as "isolated and independent." The social world of the Physiocrats was populated by "functionaries" who handled the social relations among people. But it was only in the man–nature relationship that it was justified to use the term *entrepreneur*. When a functionary wrongly maintained that he was an entrepreneur, it indicated that he was laying claim to certain resources for actions in his own interest—that he was about to disturb the natural order. This problem is dealt with by Quesnay in the articles where he also explains what he means by describing industry and craftsmen as "the sterile class."

In 1765, seven years after the first publication of *Tableau économique*, Quesnay wrote an anonymous article in the *Journal de l'Agriculture du Commerce et des Finances*.[40] In this, he allows a merchant to attack the thesis that wealth depended upon agricultural production, and that, although industry and transport were obviously necessary for an economy, they were not in themselves sufficient for the process of creating wealth. In the final resort, the thesis ran, it was out of the relationship of man to nature that wealth was created, and without the farmer, the industrialists and transporters could not exist. Let the nation's production be taken care of by the farmers, holds Quesnay's merchant somewhat abruptly, but do not confuse production and wealth. What is a product without a price? Valueless! It is the payment that is received for a product in good money that is its real value. The price is not created in the meadows, nor in the packaging. The price is created in the market: "The productive class brings forth only the products. . . . The exchange value . . . arises through competition among purchasers. It is also these competitive purchasers who are the class that really produces wealth."[41]

Is it not the trader who pays the farmer for his produce? And what does the farmer pay the tradesman? Nothing at all. The farmers create the produce, but it is the traders who create their prices. Price is identical with value, and value with wealth. Had not Quesnay himself maintained, continues the merchant, that it is necessary to have free trade in order to create a good and stable price for the products of agriculture? This would imply that he also agrees that trade creates wealth.

It is in this manner Quesnay permits his indigent merchant to show that the Physiocrats were not concerned wholly with a one-sided admiration for agriculture. The doctrine of the Physiocrats also contains the notion of a free market economy, although the free market is only a necessary complement to agriculture. Quesnay develops this theme in two dialogues that show that his notion of free trade is something other than a pure worship of commerce.[42] In the real world, merchants would seek to hold up prices and maintain their privileges, and these privileges and monopolies would be legitimized by the claim that it is the merchants and industrialists who create the wealth of the state.

For the merchant, maintains Quesnay, wealth consists of money, valuable metals, and other means of payment. In the course of trading, says the merchant, concrete things are exchanged for money; this is the wealth-creating function of commerce. But is not money a measure of value? Is not money only a means? How could the creation of wealth be identical with the mere collection of money? The merchant's response is that exchange occurs naturally with a profit, and that this profit—a surplus of money—is identical with wealth, which is the goal of the economy. The Physiocrat then asks whether the exchange involved an exact measure in monetary terms of the value of a concrete product? If price and the concrete product were identical in terms of value, then it was pure nonsense to talk of a surplus, and an even greater lie to regard such as a newly created value. Allowing that the purchaser finds a value in possessing or consuming a product, and that the seller finds a value in having money in his pocket rather than the product in store, then these two values are identical. Exchange on the market is proof of identity. It follows that riches cannot be created through exchange, and hence commerce cannot be the source of wealth.

But did not the activities of the merchant lead to the seller's getting a better price and to the purchaser's paying a lower price than would otherwise be the case? No, says the Physiocrat, it is entirely misleading to regard the merchant as an entrepreneur. It is wrong to believe that the trader is the cause of exchange activity. As soon as buyers and sellers come into existence, there appear middlemen, attracted like flies to a pot of syrup. It is not these middlemen, the merchants, who set commerce in motion. The merchants are no entrepreneurs in the sense that they are the arbitrators of prices, because "the causes of prices . . . always exist prior to commerce."[43]

At the most, it could be said that the merchant omitted to actually hinder the exchange and that he thereby avoided a loss. His activity here, however, could not be said to create wealth, since, maintains Quesnay, wealth is hardly identical with the absence of a loss. The negative function of the merchant could not be identical with positive entrepreneurship.

It is necessary, moreover, not to confuse the effects of communication with commerce. The means of communication make it possible for buyers and sellers to meet each other and for goods to be transported from one place to another. But communications take place by way of the roads, canals, and bridges that are provided by the landowners. More precisely, it should have been the landowners who invested in these "débouchés," or channels of distribution. These channels of distribution, which often require large investments, are physical sacrifices that, if anything, gave a right to participate in commerce. It is, thus, the landowners rather than the merchants who should receive thanks for the fulfillment of the trading function in society. Naturally, the merchant is free to become a landowner and in this capacity then possibly claim to be an honest entrepreneur. Beyond this, however, the merchant creates nothing because "the price is always prior to purchasing and selling."[44]

The merchants act in their own cause in seeking privileges. Such privileges are not to be obtained directly but through an alliance with the landowners, who, according to the Physiocrats, would do well to avoid such bad company.

It is only necessary to look at the actions of the merchants in this respect. For example, they want to stop purchases from abroad with the argument that a positive balance of payments creates wealth. But what is the value of money without supply? While the landowner seeks to expand the channels of distribution in order to guarantee a good price for grain, the merchant is looking to stop the flow of goods. Why should we import expensive goods, he asks, and he advocates the local production of goods that neighboring countries are producing more efficiently. The neighboring countries will realize the threat to their markets and respond by closing their borders to imports. The result would probably be that a few millions of textile will be produced at the cost of billions that can be earned from exports of agricultural produce.[45] It is, moreover, necessary that the town workers are maintained cheaply if this luxury production is to be profitable, and this in turn would lead to further regulations on the price of food. The flight from the countryside to the towns is encouraged. At the same time, the neighboring countries would stop the export of the raw materials necessary for luxury production, and these will have to be smuggled into the country at considerable cost. When foreign workers from Savoy seek work on the land, the protectionists object and want to set limits in the flow of money out of the country.[46] It is in this manner that the economy is made abstract in character and the concrete wealth of the nation is eroded. Inspired by Gibbons, Quesnay maintains that the fall of the Roman Empire began with the decline of agriculture and an increase in trade. Carthage was a rich town, writes Quesnay, but collapsed because of its wretched countryside; Spain, which had invested so much in the voyages of discovery, could not save its agriculture with all the gold of Peru.[47]

If the merchant were now to maintain that he at least creates demand, the Physiocrat would reply that this is unfortunately true in relation to luxury and superfluous production. The demand for concrete products such as food, clothing, housing, and tools is a natural demand. Demand would always, with or without the merchant, exceed available resources, and low prices in themselves would never be able to satisfy demand. Exchange would continue "à tout prix," and would stop only if mankind dies out or succeeds in supporting itself without markets as autonomous gatherers in an overabundant forest.[48]

The role of the economist in this scheme of things is to investigate if an activity is a real enterprise or only "une profession particuliaire." In the case of the merchant, the judgment is clear. Trade is useful, but the merchant is a cost that should be minimized, and his interests are often the opposite of that of the nation as a whole. He creates nothing and only takes in money in order to make payments.[49] The status of the merchant depends upon our ignorance of the fact that money in itself is worth nothing. If a merchant thought money is worth so much, writes Quesnay in an ironical vein, he would sell goods worth 1,000 francs for a payment of only 500 just for the sheer pleasure of feeling the coins. This would be pure fetishism and equally as perverse as preferring ornamental flowers rather than useful herbs or preferring parks instead of cultivated land.[50] If the merchant, on the other hand, manages to obtain 1,500 francs for goods worth only 1,000, then he is nothing more than a thief who bleeds the economy of its resources and distorts the "fair price."

Quesnays's judgment is equally hard against craftsmen and manufacturers. If the Physiocrats' basic definition of wealth is accepted, then neither of these groups can be considered anything other than "sterile." The worker only gives form to material that already exists; the shoemaker likewise only assembles together heels, soles, and leather to produce footwear. Even if a pair of shoes costs more than the materials from which it is constructed, it would be wrong to conclude that anything had been created. Likewise, industry creates nothing in a concrete sense but rather adds together existing values. This is something quite different from creating and contributing to the continuous process of reproduction of such materials.[51] The adding of value is not to be confused with the creating of value. Those who imagine that the worker creates wealth would also think that it is only necessary to increase the amount of work done in the nation in order to increase its wealth. Would wealth be increased if ten men were employed to make a drinking glass one man could produce? If craftsmanship were not sterile, the invention of knitting and printing machines would be sheer madness. The obvious usefulness of all inventions including the printing press, maintained Quesnay, attests to the truth of the Physiocrats theory on the sterility of craftsmanship. Industrial employment produces no wealth, but only makes it possible for the worker to survive. Industry pays for the cost of labor that is "always inseparable from the necessary cost for the maintenance of the workers."[52]

From where, therefore, comes the means for the maintenance of the workers? It is obvious that the bread, wine, meat, and vegetables come from no other place than the earth. In the production of these products—real wealth—the factory worker took no part, except where it happened that he made the machines that were used in this agricultural production. In the time of the Physiocrats, however, such machines could be made on the farm.

But how could it be explained, then, that certain products were sold for prices that were much higher than the combined costs of labor and materials? The Physiocrats have two explanations. The first is that the craftsman had a privilege or monopoly that allowed him to live upon the flow of production from agriculture. The second is that the price of the product includes the costs for long studies and training—such as that required to be a master portrait-painter—or other investments of this nature that are difficult to estimate. The function industrial labor performs, it is clear, is not more than the satisfaction of the physical needs of industrial workers, and this is not the same as the creation of wealth. Thus, in this sense, both craftsmanship and trade are sterile.

When this is understood, when the work of enlightenment takes effect, the capacity of the countryside to produce wealth would be more fully utilized. There would be a much greater flow of production to distribute, and this would be assured if the functionaries performed their duties and no one attempted to gain privileges or stuff the wealth into their own pockets. The landowner would certainly benefit from the increased flow of real wealth from the soil, but only if he spent his income on the products of the craftsmen and invested adequately in agriculture. There would be an abundance for consumption rather than for luxury ornaments and trinkets. How was this ideal state to be achieved? For the economists of the Enlightenment, the key lay in good entrepreneurial management education. Those who could read and write had come some part of the way, but it was arithmetic that allowed the farmer to perform business calculations.

5. Calculation for Rational Negotiation

The *Tableau économique* illustrates the relationship between the flow of production and three social functions in the form of a diagram (Figure 1). Here, some five billion pounds worth of agricultural production is distributed in a manner so that two billion goes to the farmers to compensate them for their yearly outlays, two billion goes to landowners as rent and provides the means with which to pay taxes, and one billion goes to the so-called sterile class as a result of the purchases of equipment and tools by the farmers. The landowner allows his two billion to flow further, using half of it to purchase food from the farmers and the other half to purchase goods and luxuries from the sterile class. This sterile class has thus received one billion from the farmers and another from the landowner and uses these two billion to purchase food and raw materials from the farmers. The productive class has with this received back its five billion, and the flow of

Figure 1
Formule du Tableau Économique
Reproduction totale: 5 milliards [liv.]

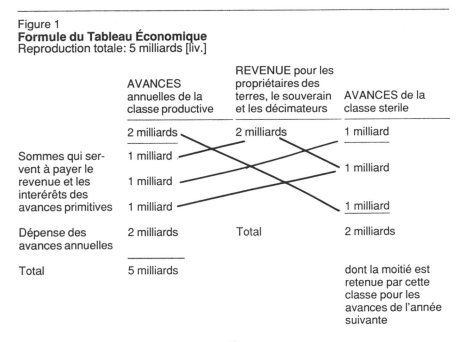

	AVANCES annuelles de la classe productive	REVENUE pour les propriétaires des terres, le souverain et les décimateurs	AVANCES de la classe sterile
	2 milliards	2 milliards	1 milliard
Sommes qui servent à payer le revenue et les interérêts des avances primitives	1 milliard		
	1 milliard		1 milliard
	1 milliard		1 milliard
Dépense des avances annuelles	2 milliards	Total	2 milliards
Total	5 milliards		dont la moitié est retenue par cette classe pour les avances de l'année suivante

Source: Quesnay, *Tableau économique*, p. 58.

economic exchange has by the close of the period returned to its original state and is ready for the next year's flow to begin again. The balance of the ideal economy is an established fact—at least on paper!

Economic balance is a desirable condition, a situation where justice rules and the natural order comes into being. The *Tableau économique* was the utopia of the Physiocrats; it is as utopians that they make their appearance in the history of economic ideas. But it would be unjust to dismiss them only as dreamers, since they also had concrete plans on how the state of economic balance would be realized. The arithmetic of the *Tableau* shows a perfect model of the natural order, but the Physiocrats also use figures in a managerial sense. They need arithmetic not only to model a process but also to influence outcomes through managerial economic calculations.

Mirabeau had described the economists as a league whose mission it was to change an unjust state to an ideal society. The Physiocrats would function as intellectual guerrilla soldiers; they took their duties in this respect very seriously. Mirabeau's dialogues show how the process of enlightenment should proceed. The guerrilla attack would focus on two targets: the landowners and the productive farmers. The task is first to convince these two groups of their correct social functions and then to get them to unite in an active organization that would make the ideas of the intellectual economists a political reality. It is these two groups, according the Physiocrats' theory, that are the most important. It is true, of course, that the merchants wanted nothing better than to ally themselves with the landowners, but the Physiocrats consider such a union harmful. Let us now see how the economist Mirabeau as a physiocratic management consultant attempted to get the landowners and farmers to join a common cause and how he saw the interaction between their respective functions.

First, the landowner and the farmer are being taught their respective functions in the state. This is pursued in two dialogues with an introductory conversation. The farmer's boy, Antoine, who has neglected his father's estate, sits lazily on a bank when Mirabeau suddenly appears:

"Gracious me! Are you not ashamed, Antoine, to waste your time and so ill repay the investment your father has made in you?"

"But I have not voluntarily signed any contract with my father that I must fulfill," replies Antoine.

"Didn't your kind father feed you when you were a small child? Was it not that natural will, your needs, that constituted the basis of the first contract between you and another person—your father? You must learn to fulfill this and all other social contracts so that you can live well."

"If all who were richer than I shared with me, then I could certainly live well," says Antoine and asks Mirabeau how it is that he has so much when a simple farmer's boy owns so little. "Give me half of what you own, and I will give you half of what I own," suggests Antoine. "If everyone did the same, then all would come to possess land and property and the world would become a happy place."

"Certainly," says Mirabeau, "I am willing to exchange with you, but only on the condition that someone who is richer than I will exchange with me on the same principle. But the richest person in the world has then no one to exchange with. It is here that your idea finishes, Antoine, with the proof that such could not be done voluntarily."

"Why not force them then?" asks Antoine angrily.

"Stop there," says Mirabeau. "Now you are angry. That is just how wars begin. All riches are lost and we become poorer than we were before. No, the correct solution lies in cooperation."

When Antoine agrees to accept this line of reasoning, he also accepts his part of the Rousseaunian social contract. It remains now to convince the landowner. He is quickly convinced when he comes to understand that it is his father's concrete investments, and not blood and honor, that have made him into a landowner. His property is worthless without the farmer, and the farmer does not belong to him as some kind of slave. Furthermore, the ownership function and the farming function are inseparably joined to each other, and this is the foundation for the wealth of the nation. The landowner has responsibilities as well as obligations toward the farmer. On hearing this, the landowner becomes afflicted by doubts and remembers that it is often necessary for him to be in the royal capital and also occasionally to travel abroad on the king's business. Therefore,

would it not be better if he left the management of his estates to a hired professional manager that cared for everything in his absence?

"These managers are sharks," maintains the economist. "They poison the
natural relation between owner and farmer. Ownership is a social function, but
the function a vassal performs is not. It would be contrary to the social contract
therefore to set a vassal between farmer and landowner."

With this argument, the landowner, too, is convinced and prepares to sign his
part of the social contract. The alliance between landowner and farmer is now
sealed by the Mirabeau Management School.

The next step in the process is to set this alliance into action. The dialogues
show how the two parties were assigned complementary functions by the Physiocrats. These functions concern relations to the earth, on the one hand, and relations among people, on the other. In the natural order everything is based upon
relations. The relations to the earth are necessary since people die if such relations are not properly cared for, and it is out of these necessary relations to the
soil that riches are obtained. The wise emperor of China has himself said: "If
someone mishandles their farming, it is some other human being that suffers."[53]

Once the social contract is signed, it is necessary that the respective relations
are cared for in the enterprise, and this would lead to a development of the art of
agriculture. Applied agricultural technology, according to the Physiocrats, is an
extension of concrete economics. It entails observation and experiment. Here
both landowner and farmer have large roles to play in reducing the ignorance
that causes people to starve, flee from the countryside, and leave the estates
uncultivated. But who is to bear the practical responsibility for this research in
agriculture? The distribution of responsibility in this question is something that
has to be resolved in the context of free relations. That is, to use modern parlance, it
is to be settled through negotiations. The notion of free relations does not apply to
production but rather to exchange between enlightened and independent farmers and
landowners. It is the method for arriving at this just distribution of responsibility that
is set out in the arithmetic of business economic calculation.

After several conversations that covered these issues, the farmer's boy, Antoine, is sent home to learn how to read and reckon. He returns a year and a half
later, sufficiently mature to learn how to make the calculation. But the
Physiocrats' calculation has little to do with prices, since such were meant to be
set by the natural order of the market. The calculation is meaningless if there is
just one decision maker. It is an activity of a mutual character. As Antoine, who
immediately grasps the point, declares: "Nous sommes deux à compter"—it is
always two who reckon: the farmer and the landowner. With the calculation as a
basis, they establish their respective interests. Then they can negotiate, and the
result of such negotiations would be "un bail," a leasing contract. From the
farmer's point of view, it is necessary to calculate the yearly costs and return on
investments in the personal goods and draft animals that he contributes to the
farm. To this Antoine adds taxes to the church and the king. What is then left

over from the estimated price of the harvest goes to the landowner as a return on his land. With this successfully accomplished, that was the end of the matter.

The calculation appears simple in principle, but the route through its various subheadings entails a complicated debate on justice and distribution. Such a discussion was probably considered to be revolutionary under the conditions of *L'Ancien Régime*—and could even be the case today. Who should pay for keeping the estate in good shape? Who should maintain the roads? Who should pay taxes and in what amount? Mirabeau maintains that these are the landowner's responsibility. It is now time, he says to the landowner, to replace mere fiscal transactions with the natural order that was just to put right the crime of his forefathers in shoving the burden of taxation upon the farmers; if this were not done, there was a good chance that France would collapse as the Roman Empire had in the past. The calculation shows clearly the relations between the landowner and the farmer, who each now know what is expected of him. The farmer would learn to reject the landlord's unprofitable offers that cost more than they appear on the surface. From such negotiations would emerge a recognition of which lands provide the best soil. As farmers expand and rationalize production, they would be encouraged by the landowner who sees it as his duty to finance such increased production. The landowner becomes a kind of working chairman of the board who travels between the estates and Paris. His engagement is to keep a foot in the corridors of power in order to see to the best interests of farmers and the nation. He participates in the capital market where he has a good chance of competing with the industrialists for funds to build canals, roads, and bridges. He would support tax reforms and feel pride in the growing population and increasing wealth of the countryside. The idle drones who live in luxury in their castles and houses would soon disappear. There would instead be a lively traffic between the estates and the markets. Both farmer and landowner have now become good real managers and entrepreneurs. And the trigger that would set in motion this development that the Physiocrats hoped for was an economic calculation based on arithmetic that "created nothing, but settled everything." [54]

Notes

1. Tore Frängsmyr, *Svärmaren i vetenskapens hus.*
2. Ibid., p. 61.
3. Notice sur la vie et les travaux de François Quesnay, in Eugene Daire, *Physiocrates.* Librairie de Guillaumin, Paris, 1846.
4. Frantz Funck-Bretano, *L'Ancien régime,* Vol 1, p. 240.
5. Ibid., p. 165.
6. Ibid., p. 267.
7. Ibid., p. 165.
8. *Ephémérides du citoyen ou bibliothèque raisonnée des sciences morales et politiques.* Paris, 1769, Vol. III, pp 8, 90.
9. Funck-Brentano, *L'Ancien regime,* p. 130.

10. Ibid, p. 184.
11. Ibid. Vol. 2, p. 79.
12. Francois Quesnay, "Fermiers," in Daire, p. 159.
13. Victor R. de Mirabeau, *Les Économiques*, p. 59 photocopy reprint Danstad 1972.
14. Ibid., p. 82.
15. Ibid., p. 106.
16. Ibid., p. 113.
17. Ibid., p. 62.
18. Quesnay, "Fermiers," pp. 164–165.
19. Mirabeau, *Les Économiques*, p. 99.
20. Ibid., p. 134.
21. Ibid., p. 135.
22. Ibid., p. 320.
23. Francois Quesnay, "Grains," in Quesnay, *Tableau économique des physiocrates*.
24. Mirabeau, *Les Économiques*, p. 109.
25. Ibid., p. 113.
26. Ibid.
27. Ibid., p. 198.
28. Quesnay, "Fermiers," p. 190.
29. Mirabeau, *Les Économiques*, p. 183.
30. Ibid., p. 187.
31. Ibid., pp. 194–195.
32. Quesnay, "Fermiers," p. 190.
33. Mirabeau, *Les Économiques*, p. 115.
34. Ibid.
35. Mirabeau, *Les Économiques*, p. 118.
36. Quesnay, F., "Fermiers," p. 172.
37. Ibid., "Fermiers," p. 188.
38. Mirabeau, *Les Économiques*, p. 109.
39. Ernest Mossner, Ian and Ross, eds., *The Correspondence of Adam Smith,* p. 313.
40. Francois Quesnay, "Mémoire sur les avantages de l'industrie et du commerce et sur la fécondité de la classe prétendue stérile," in Daire, pp. 379–383.
41. Ibid., p. 381.
42. Francois Quesnay, "Dialogues sur le commerce et sur les travaux des artisants, "in Daire, pp. 142–218.
43. Ibid., p. 147.
44. Ibid., p. 148.
45. Ibid., p. 141.
46. Ibid., p. 201.
47. Ibid., p. 156.
48. Ibid., p. 159.
49. Ibid., p. 169.
50. Ibid., p. 171.
51. Ibid., p. 188.
52. Ibid., p. 190.
53. Mirabeau, *Les Économiques*, p. 248.
54. Ibid., p. 89.

2

Pleasure and Enterprise:
The Foundation for
"The Wealth of Nations"

1. Scotland Improved

The father of modern economics, Adam Smith (1723–1790), decided in 1764 to leave his professorship in moral philosophy at the University of Glasgow for a well-paid and pensionable post as tutor to the Duke of Buccleuch. The university council expressed regret at the "loss" of the author of "the elegant and ingenious Theory of Moral Sentiments," a work that had made Adam Smith widely known in European literary circles. The students also were no doubt sorry to lose a competent lecturer with "talents in illustrating abstracted subjects, and . . . communicating useful knowledge." [1]

Despite this reputation, it is more difficult than was the case with the Physiocrats to delineate the concrete in the economics of Adam Smith, precisely because he had mastered the art of transforming the abstract into the concrete. Adam Smith fascinated students with his lively lectures on subjects that could easily have seemed both arid and dull. One moment he would be talking with passion and intensity, and the next he would be silent and apparently entirely absorbed in his thoughts. Just as it is difficult to place a finger on the concrete in Smith's work, so is it equally problematical to decide whether he was more philosopher than economist or perhaps even an economic historian. What emerges clearly from a study of the works of Adam Smith, however, is that he was a little of everything, a fact that leads us to conclude how meaningless it is to draw any sharp lines among such present-day disciplines as economics, moral philosophy, and history.

Adam Smith himself certainly appreciated and attached importance to the concrete in the form of the material and the observable. He lived in a Scotland that strived for progress in circumstances that were marked by economic distor-

25

tions and considerable poverty. New factories, banks, and trading houses had come into existence in the lowlands. Here, iron from Russia and Scandinavia was transformed into products for export to the North American agricultural market, augmenting the sales of saddles and harnesses to the plantations of the New World. In a half century, Glasgow had developed from a small town, where shepherds drove their sheep through the streets, to a commercial metropolis of enlightened tradesmen and efficient factories. It was here that the Nailery, the famous nail factory, described in *The Wealth of the Nations,* was to be found.

The exchange of goods went hand in hand with the exchange of ideas. Businessmen and traders mixed intimately with academics and teachers from the university. It was also here that the first "political economy club" was founded, which met to discuss important contemporary issues such as the free import of raw materials from the colonies or the effects of paper money on the metallic monetary system. It was at one of the Thursday meetings at the local "literary society" that Adam Smith lectured on the ideas of his close friend David Hume from Edinburgh with regard to commerce.[2] Associations and clubs where just about anything between heaven and earth was discussed appeared like mushrooms on a summer morning. The dubious exception was religion, the discussion of which was scrupulously avoided for fear that it could undermine the local peace. Not only businessmen, academics, and politicians engaged in these discussions; craftsmen, instrument makers, and engineers also took their part. James Watt, for example, was a member of "the literary society" and a colleague of Adam Smith at the University of Glasgow, where he established an experimental workshop after the local instrument makers attempted to stop his activities outside. The university had an advanced printing workshop that challenged and competed with Elzeviers, the foremost European publishing and printing company, based in Holland. There was also a school for the practical arts such as design and architecture, which provided evening classes for workers with a bent for self-improvement.

The university, almost a town within a town, with its rules and privileges, contributed greatly to both the pleasures of and the lust for debate. Already in the early 1760s the business community of Glasgow was well acquainted with the theories that were later to appear in 1776 in *An Inquiry into the Nature and Causes of the Wealth of Nations.* Its author, Adam Smith, had become the town's "pop" philosopher, and his plaster bust was on sale in the local shops.

Something of the inspiration for Adam Smith's ideas in economics and philosophy seems to have flowed from his teacher, Francis Hutcheson, who lectured at Glasgow College, as Glasgow University was then called, where Smith spent several of his teenage years. In 1740, however, Adam Smith was awarded a stipend and rode southward to take up his academic studies at the Balliol College, Oxford University. There, far away from the bustling and stimulating atmosphere of Glasgow, Adam Smith was to spend the following six years, much of it in solitude studying classics in the university's library. The fact that he was far from home and friends, and surrounded by fellows and professors, many of whom had not given a lecture within living memory, no doubt contributed both to his decision to return to Scotland and to his views on what he considered to be the nature of a good life.

2. Social Interaction in a Friendly Society

When Adam Smith's Oxford scholarship ended in 1746, he returned to Kirkcaldy where he had been born. The special scholarship had originally been intended for candidates to the priesthood, but over the years most recipients had chosen other professions. Smith decided against taking "holy orders" and sought a job as a teacher. When some two years later he still had not managed to obtain a permanent position, he undertook a series of lectures on English literature at Edinburgh, which was the seat of the Scottish Parliament. There was much discussion at that time concerning industrial freedom for Scotland, and through his contact with Kirkcaldy's representative in Parliament, James Oswald, later lord of the Treasury, Smith came to meet David Hume, whose *Political Essays* (1752) attacked mercantilist prejudices concerning the balance of payments and gold reserves. Smith's lecture series proved successful, and the following year he was called to a professorship in logic at Glasgow College. He was not to remain long in this post, however, since a professorship in moral philosophy happened to become vacant. He had perhaps hoped that the chair in logic would go to his friend David Hume, but it was given instead to another lesser-known candidate who is completely forgotten today.

Adam Smith began his career as professor of moral philosophy with a series of popular lectures that were divided into four sections. Popularity was an important ingredient for success, since the professors of the period derived a large part of their income from the entry fees to lectures paid by the students. Several supplemented their income, particularly in years of economic gloom when the number of students could fall drastically, by letting out rooms. There were at this time some three hundred students at the university, and about eighty of them appear to have attended Adam Smith's course. Smith's successful lecture series reportedly provided him with an income of around 170 pounds per year.

His major works originate from parts of this lecture series, which he wrote down for publication. One section was eventually published in 1759 under the title *The Theory of Moral Sentiments* and brought Adam Smith considerable renown as well as a new job with the Duke of Buccleuch. Adam Smith received 300 pounds per year and a promise of a pension of the same order. A second section of the original lecture series under the title *An Inquiry into the Nature and Causes of the Wealth of Nations* appeared in 1776 and was an even greater success. It not only produced a good income from sales but also led to his appointment as a commissioner of customs and to his recognized status as an adviser of statesmen. The remaining two sections of the original lecture series dealt with natural theology—the question of proof for the existence of God—and questions of law, ethics, and justice. Smith's economic ideas in *The Wealth of Nations* are grounded in the social philosophy articulated in *The Theory of Moral Sentiments.*

In this latter work Adam Smith develops the idea of a civilized society as a kind of friendship club that he terms "The Friendly Society." Apparently under the influence of Newtonian concepts, he develops the notion that truly free individuals feel a sympathetic attraction for each other and are thus drawn together to form a society. All human beings, even the most hard-hearted, have a capacity to feel sympathy. Indeed, the book opens with the following lines:

> How selfish soever man may be supposed, there are evidently some principles of his nature, which interest him in the fortunes of others, and render their happiness necessary to him though he derives nothing from it except the pleasure of seeing it. . . . The greatest ruffian, the most hardened violator of the laws of society, is not altogether without it. [3]

This sympathy that links together men in civilized society is also described by Smith as "fellow feeling." By this he means not some kind of distributed collective emotion, but rather that individuals in their isolation observe one another and attribute their own feelings to others: "As we have no immediate experience of what other men feel, we can form no idea of the manner in which they are affected, but by conceiving what we ourselves should feel in a like situation."[4] In other words, our feelings can never carry us beyond our own person. We can never feel what others feel but can only reconstruct such with the aid of our imaginative capacity. That which distinguishes barbarism from civilization is the degree of development of this imaginative capacity. Adam Smith is interested here in investigating the limits of imagination, since such become concomitant with those of sympathy.

At the bottom limit are barbarians who completely lack sympathetic imagination. They are so engaged in the problems of physical survival that they do not have the opportunity to develop relationships that have no direct utility from the point of view of survival. In the condition of barbarism, not only is life nasty and brutish, but there is also very little freedom in human relations. Threatened from both natural and human sources, the life of the individual is bound in, and limited by, relations of necessity. This results in human beings developing a closed and shallow nature that is, moreover, marked by falsehood and lying, which have their origins in the necessity to constantly hide feelings and suppress passions. Before "The Friendly Society" can be realized, it is necessary to satisfy man's basic physical needs, since "before we can feel much for others we must in some measures be at ease ourselves."[5] In both his major works, Adam Smith emphasizes that this minimum needed for a civilized existence is quite easy to obtain.

Once beyond this basic barrier of physiological need, it is possible to develop psychological characteristics, which permit the cultivation of sympathies and fellow feeling. Riches, industry, and other forms of human endeavor require psychological rather than physiological explanations. Why, for example, do people strive to obtain property? "How many people ruin themselves by laying out money on trinkets of frivolous utility? What pleases these lovers of toys is not so much the utility, as the aptness of the machines which are fitted to promote it."[6]

Wealth is a social psychological phenomenon. It is not pursued because of the needs of the stomach or the body. Goods are less useful tools than funny toys. One could sleep just as well, even better, in a cottage as in a castle. The psychological basis for the pursuit of wealth lies rather in the fact that poor people are despised while the rich tend to awake sympathy and be admired. The rich are attractive to others who can never have enough of their company. Progress, wealth, and expansion depend upon an urge to give pleasure to others, and this psychological characteristic is boundless in its nature. As Smith succinctly expresses it, "The eye is larger than the belly."

Adam Smith thus dismisses physiological explanations of the foundations of society as being insufficient. Those statements that content themselves with such physiological explanations would come to fail, even though ideas of this nature may seem plausible when developed in books. To Adam Smith, the Physiocrats, whom he came in contact with when he accompanied the Duke of Buccleuch on his grand tour of Europe, were politically naive. While admitting their intelligence, he considered them to be "men of system" filled with book learning who had fallen in love with a utopia that they hoped to realize by changing human nature so that people would fit together like pieces on a chess board. A statesman of this persuasion

> does not consider that the pieces upon the chessboard have no other principle of motion besides that which the hand impresses upon them; but that, in the great chessboard of human society, every single piece has a principle of motion of its own, altogether different from that which the legislature might choose to impress upon it. If these two principles coincide and act in the same direction, the game of human society will go on easily and harmoniously. . . . If they are opposite or different, the game will go on miserably.[7]

The successful statesman or economist needs to take psychology seriously. That is because psychology is the point of departure for ensuring a coincidence of policy and human nature and for ensuring that the game of human society would go on easily and harmoniously. Psychological assumptions were for Adam Smith a concrete and integral aspect of political economy, and this provides one example of the manner in which he transformed the abstract into the concrete.

The Theory of Moral Sentiments actually contains a psychological model of the process of social exchange that was later incorporated into *The Wealth of*

Nations as a process of economic exchange on markets. As social creatures, human beings are "spectators" and judges of the actions of others. Certain actions are regarded as pleasant, and these awake sympathy in the observer for the actor. Other actions are regarded as unpleasant, and these create a feeling of repulsion in the spectator. There is no easy relationship between feelings aroused in spectators and those experienced by actors. Certain actions may awake no reaction among spectators; on the other hand, an active "agent" may experience "original passions" that are difficult for a spectator to fathom. When communication was successful, however, the spectator could imagine what was involved with the other person concerned. In such situations, says Adam Smith, as observers we "bring home the case to ourselves." If our understanding of the action is positive, if we find such action pleasant, then we are prepared to "go along with someone" and to "adopt the principles of the agent's action."

When we observe our fellow human beings, maintains Adam Smith, we note the consequences of their actions and imagine the purposes for which such actions were undertaken. If we, for example, observe a violent deed, we are affected by both the intentions of the perpetrator and the suffering of the victim. We feel more disgust in the case of a successful crime than if the plan had proved unsuccessful. In the same manner, a good and successful enterprise arouses more sympathy than merely the plan or intention for such. "The world judges by the event and not by the design," adds Smith, and he implies that it is not only the skillfulness with which the action is taken that is important, since opportunity can play a role in coupling intentions and consequences in the realm of the imagination.[8] Thus human beings are pleasant to one another not only because of their nature but also because of what they succeed in bringing about.

In this world of social exchange, both actors and spectators strive to become senders and receivers of socially pleasant messages. Angry and complaining people, even when there may be due cause for their condition, such as physical illness, always tend to awake a repelling emotion. People thus harness their passions and bring them down to a pitch that can be understood by others. Shared pleasures, on the other hand, are doubled pleasures as witnessed by the sense of fellowship aroused by shared jokes and shared readings. It is from this shared fellowship that the rewards, if not the profits, of pleasurable intercourse arise.

The friendly society, thus, develops from the natural propensity of mankind to seek pleasure and avoid unpleasant experiences, and this engine of progress should develop through the spontaneous reactions of individuals to their observations of the actions of others. But it is at this point that an important problem arises for Adam Smith. How is it possible to know that these reactions are spontaneous and not merely simulated or flattering in character? Where lies the border between genuine experience and pure opportunism? Could it not be the case that this market in social exchanges is really nothing but a market in mutual admiration? A vanity fair? More broadly understood, this is the problem of values and their origins that emerges again in *The Wealth of Nations* in connection with the problem of natural, as against market, prices.

Adam Smith begins here by rejecting traditional answers to the question of values. One such answer held that it was laws and rules that determined what was good and bad or right and wrong. But, says Smith, laws and cultural norms are simply judgments that have been made by earlier generations. To point to such is only to refer to the judgments made by our forefathers and provides no guidance with regard to absolute moral values. It is, moreover, no answer to the problem to point to the stabilizing effects of habits and fashions upon thought, for these also build upon judgments.

Adam Smith is also critical of philosophers who while holding that values are not absolute, nevertheless, would offer an anchor for such that would hinder all too sharp and violent swings in judgments. The Stoics, for example, would oppose egoism and teach others that they are always a part of a totality. Melancholics would, on the other hand, oppose egocentricity through teaching pity for others. But, asks Smith, "To what purpose should we trouble ourselves about the world in the moon?"[9]

Adam Smith means by this that we should not trouble ourselves unduly with problems of vanity, for in practice the matter takes care of itself. We are, according to Smith, born with a capacity to judge ourselves in the same manner as we judge others in their actions. In every human being there is an "impartial spectator" that when doubt arises concerning the value of what is being undertaken is capable of standing outside itself and making a definite judgment. This impartial spectator, or "the man within" as he otherwise expresses it, can decide whether the applause received is simply pandering to vanity or whether criticism is motivated by jealousy. When "the man without" has done something, "the man within" emerges to decide if the action involved was praiseworthy or otherwise.

The mechanics of this evaluative process, which lies somewhere near the roots of Adam Smith's social and economic theory, are described by him as follows:

> Nature, when she formed man for society, endowed him with an original desire to please, and an original aversion to offend his brethren. She taught him to feel pleasure in their favourable, and pain in their unfavourable regard. She rendered their approbation most flattering and most agreeable to him for its own sake; and their disapprobation most mortifying and most offensive.
>
> But this desire for approbation, and this aversion to the disapprobation of his brethren, would not alone have rendered him fit for that society for which he was made. Nature, accordingly, has endowed him, not only with the desire of being approved of, but with a desire of being what ought to be approved of; or of being what he himself approves of in other men. The first desire could only have made him wish to appear to be fit for society. The second was necessary to render him anxious to be really fit. [10]

If others did not look upon us, we should ourselves never use such concepts as "ugly" and "beautiful." Someone who merely obtains values from others or from books can never be so pleasant and social as a "man of the world." That the process of adaption stabilizes itself in society depends upon our natural and, in the final resort, God-given capacity to judge the true value of our own actions.

For certain kinds of actions this is easier than for others. One needs only to consider the mathematician who knows that he talks the truth and uses his logic correctly. On the other hand, consider the state of certain artists and other informed persons, such as Voltaire, who decline into intrigues because they are so uncertain about their real value. The rules in the mechanism of valuation can only be obtained from the school of social experience and, in particular, "the great school of self-command." This begins with birth and continues through childhood in contacts with other children which are not necessarily stressful and violent but which, nevertheless, teach the child to "be master of itself." The adult has learned to be "cool" and evaluate himself in the same terms as others. This kind of upbringing occurs best in that environment upon which the adult is eventually dependent, and thus Adam Smith shows his opposition to the custom of sending children to foreign schools and universities.

Despite the fact that *The Theory of Moral Sentiments* and *The Wealth of Nations* lie quite close to each other in a philosophical sense, there was a gap of seventeen years between their publication. Adam Smith had used the interval to collect an enormous wealth of material on a variety of subjects that ranged from commerce and tax policy to political science and history. A considerable amount of this, as well as moral support, he obtained from his home area and friends in Glasgow. Even before *The Wealth of Nations* actually appeared in print, it had already aroused great expectations in many circles. David Hume wrote to congratulate him on writing such an interesting book filled with "curious facts," and on the fact that Adam Smith had finally completed the book that "was a work of so much expectations, by yourself, by your friends and by the public."[11]

Smith had, moreover, the benefit of his discussions with the French Physiocrats, whom he met through Hume's mediation. It is appropriate at this stage to turn to this work to see how his social doctrine reappears in an economic context.

3. The Entrepreneurial Action in a Commercial Society

The very first sentence of the long-awaited work, *The Wealth of Nations*, introduced one of its most central themes: "The annual labour of every nation is the fund which originally supplies it with all the necessaries and conveniences of life which it annually consumes, and which consists always either in the immediate produce of that labour, or in what is purchased with that produce from other nations."[12]

The first chapter of this world-famous book deals, in fact, with the phenomenon of the division of labor in society, the means by which both the "productive power" of workers is increased and a natural distribution of incomes produced takes place among "different ranks of people." It is here that the renowned example of pin manufacturing is to be found whereby ten workers, organized according to the division of labor, succeed in producing 48,000 pins per day. It is this organization that allows a production far in excess of ten workers working independently of each other. Its advantages accrue from the specialization of tasks performed and from the saving of time that would otherwise be needed for workers to change from one task to another. It is interesting that this example constitutes Adam Smith's sole foray into a complete process of production.

Smith places an emphasis on the relationship between the behavior of men and machines. Workers who perform the same actions each day soon come to understand that such can also be performed by a "very pretty machine" and thus may feel inclined to construct such to take over their daily labor. But Adam Smith goes further here in his direct comparison of man and machines: "A man educated at the expense of much labour and time to any of those employments which require extraordinary dexterity and skill may be compared to one of those expensive machines."[13]

Smith's point is that it was necessary for a worker to produce sufficient beyond his daily needs to cover the investment, with interest, in his own training or education. This kind of calculation can be more difficult in the case of persons than of machines because of "the uncertain duration of human life." However, investments in manpower and machines now become directly comparable: "The improved dexterity of the workman may be considered in the same light as a machine or instrument of trade which facilitates and abridges labour, and which, though it casts a certain expense, repays that expense with a profit."[14]

The individualistic strain in Adam Smith's social theory is, nevertheless, strongly apparent. IIis basic idea here is that individuals should have both the freedom and responsibility to act in their own interests. Nations that denied this freedom and responsibility to its citizens made it impossible for people to either create or participate in the production of wealth. Each person and worker should be his or her own entrepreneur, and what the worker sold was not labor but rather the product of his or her labor according to a contract between the parties concerned.

Smith contrasts his ideal here with other forms of organization such as feudalism and slavery. His opposition to slavery, for example, is based upon its uneconomic character. A free worker looks after his own house and family to the best of his ability, but in the case of slaves this responsibility falls upon an often negligent master: "The fund destined for replacing and repairing, if I may say so, the wear and tear of the slave, is commonly managed by a negligent master or a careless overseer."[15]

In contrast to the slave, a poor worker will care for his own family and affairs with all "the parsimonious attention of the poor." Moreover, the free worker may be inspired to invent machines that a slave would never dare to do since he would risk a painful punishment for his laziness.

Adam Smith's opposition to feudalism seems to have been strongly influenced by his experience in the courts and salons of Versailles, Rome, Compiègne, and Fontainebleau. He had met in such places the people who maintained the lower orders not through setting them to work but through the "spending of revenue." The ordinary people in these places were "idle, dissolute and poor" in contrast to those in the English and Dutch trading centers where, "maintained by the employment of capital," the people were "industrious, sober and thriving." In the feudal society it is necessary for the prince to support a large number of people from the proceeds of his estates. He establishes power over them through the distribution of gifts and favors that enable them to exist without working. In return, they merely have to support him in case of war. Such a society, holds Smith, is static and inhibits industriousness. It was, in any case, the clever traders and business interests that had freed the natural entrepreneurial spirit from the dead hand of feudalism.

This development process was set in trail, according to Smith, when the prince was persuaded to utilize his agricultural surplus, which was previously used only for consumption and gifts, to purchase things such as glass beads, "a pair of diamond buckles ... or ... something frivolous and useless." [16] As Smith had already emphasized in *The Theory of Moral Sentiments*, these needs, which could be engendered through "the curiosity of a tooth-pick, of an ear-picker," or of "a machine for cutting fingernails,"[17] had no basis in physiological requirements, but the objects were wanted rather for the pleasure they provided to the senses of their purchasers. It was, nevertheless, the case that these purchases of trinkets and the like by the princes and their courts gradually resulted in their "bartering their whole power and authority"[18] and changing the nature of production in society. The princes were finally forced to diminish their courts and rent out their estates, so that their fortunes became widely spread among the community. Where previously several hundred men had been completely dependent upon him, the prince could now "command and purchase" only a small part of the production of the many handworkers. Smith's consumer was not so much king as citizen of a special kind of republic that was characterized by increasingly interdependent relationships: "In civilized society he stands at all times in need of the cooperation and assistance of great multitudes, while his whole life is scarce sufficient to gain the friendship of a few persons."[19]

In meeting the simple needs of people and households, individuals were placed into relations of mutual dependence upon multitudes of others with whom they had no direct contact or knowledge. They were bound together here by an "invisible hand" that had its origins in the individual pursuit of self-interest and found its developed expression through the division of labor in society. In this new mode of existence envisioned by Adam Smith, "every man ... lives by exchanging, or becomes in some measure a merchant and the society itself grows to be what is properly called a commercial society."[20]

Whereas in "the friendly society" of *The Theory of Moral Sentiments* people lived by exchanging pleasant actions with each other, in "the commercial society" of *The Wealth of Nations* they exchange something more concrete in the form of goods and services. The freeing of what Adam Smith believed to be the natural talent of entrepreneurship among the population had three important aspects. These concern, namely, the means of exchange, markets, and the holding of stocks, which provide the means for the practical realization of his vision of "the commercial society."

4. Enterprise as a Pump of Wealth

4.1 Money

Adam Smith approaches the first of these questions from the point of view of the problems of bartering. A realization of the conveniences and advantages of a common medium of circulation arises from the limitations associated with the bartering of surpluses among producers. In order that such should serve as a satisfactory "instrument of trade," it needed not only to incorporate a sufficient degree of divisibility but also to possess a fair measure of durability. Metals can meet these conditions to a large degree; when bits of metal are stamped by some authority that guarantees their weight, the rudiments of a monetary system come into existence. These metal bits are then awarded names such as "pounds," "shillings," and "pence." It is usually the prince who takes control of this institution in the society, and he sets his own portrait on the money and may begin to fiddle with the metallic content in order to pay his debts with less valuable metals. Beyond this, the currency may be worn by usage in exchange purposes. This necessitates the renewal of the currency from metals obtained from the mining industry. If the exchange of goods in the country increases, this also results in an increase in the demand for currency. Smith uses the model of a "channel of circulation" to describe the function of money in the economy. Money is used to distribute the surplus production, that is, production beyond the needs of the producer and his family, among the community at large, and if these surpluses do not increase, "[t]he channel of circulation, if I may be allowed such an expression, will remain precisely the same as before. . . . Whatever, therefore, is poured into it beyond this sum, cannot run in it, but must overflow."[21]

If the traffic in goods increases, it is necessary to deepen the channel by increasing the supply of money. If there is insufficient water in the channel, there is a danger that the ships of trade will run aground and that circulation will decrease. Leakage from the channel, according to Adam Smith, may occur through wear and tear and the frequent usage of gold and silver for the purposes of decorative objects. The largest problem, however, arises from the stores of currency that are held in chests of tradesmen awaiting to be used. These reserves reduce the flow of the channel and provide an obstacle to economic exchange. Smith regards this, however, as a purely technical problem.

In another of Adam Smith's metaphors, money provides the "great wheel of circulation" with the function of permitting and supporting enterprise, but money itself should never be confused with enterprise because it "makes no part of the revenue of the society to which it belongs."[22] It is in the light of this understanding that Adam Smith can justify the introduction and usage of paper currency. In the same manner as one may purchase new machines if they are cheaper and more economical to run than the old models, so can the same be argued in relation to the introduction of paper currency:

> The substitution of paper in the room of gold and silver money, replaces a very expensive instrument of commerce with one less costly, and sometimes equally convenient. Circulation comes to be carried on by a new wheel, which it costs both less to erect and to maintain than the old one.[23]

The images of the new age of canals, highways, and mechanisms are frequently apparent in the economics of Adam Smith.

The operations of the banking system, which provided this paper currency, were also of great interest to Adam Smith. In Glasgow this system supported a trade that had doubled in volume within living memory, while in Scotland as a whole there had been a fourfold increase. The banks issued, instead of payments in gold and silver, "promissory notes," which were acceptable since they were guaranteed by a parliamentary law that required that such would be exchanged for gold and silver upon demand by their holders. These promissory notes circulated freely as currency, protected by both law and the good reputation of the issuing bank. A further stage evolved when property could be used as security for the issuing of loans in paper money that could then be used for day-to-day payments in business transactions. This development in itself could free the stores of gold and silver in the chests of the tradesmen for the purposes of employing more people or increasing purchases of materials. Traders could now use one and the same bank as a common treasury instead of each maintaining his own.

There was, of course, a danger that with the increase of currency in circulation the channel would overflow if the level of exchange failed to increase. "Overflow" meant quite simply that people who held paper notes that they did not need for their business affairs went to the banks and, in accordance with the law, demanded gold and silver in return. But since the bank also functioned as a common treasury for the gold and silver deposits of the traders, the bank could in practice use its stocks of gold and silver to finance foreign trade. If the water in the channel using the "old wheel" consisted of a hundred thousand coins, when the new "paper wheel" came into existence it would require perhaps only twenty thousand of these to finance the same local trade. The remainder of the gold and silver coinage could then be utilized in foreign trade where the advantages of the "paper wheel," which depended upon the scope of British law, were not available. This surplus thus permitted the purchase of machines and it was these machines that promoted "the quantity of industry." Adam Smith, however, also recognized the increased risks involved with these developments, and his imagery at this point turns to highways:

> The gold and silver money that circulates in any country may very properly be compared to a highway, which, while it circulates and carries to the market all the grass and corn of the country, produces itself not a single pile of either. The judicious operations of banking, by providing, if I may be allowed so violent a metaphor, a sort of wagon way through the air; enable the country to convert, as it were, a great part of its highways into good pastures and cornfields, and thereby to increase very considerably the annual produce of its land and labour. The commerce and industry of the country, however, it must be acknowledged, though they may be somewhat augmented, cannot be altogether so secure, when they are thus, as it were, suspended upon the Daedalian wings of paper money, as when they travel about upon the solid ground of gold and silver.[24]

Adam Smith clearly realized that the major problem of the new mode of circulation arose from the tendency of banks to issue more paper than could be supported by their limited stocks of gold and silver. Difficulties could stem, for example, from providing businessmen with long-term loans for risky capital investments rather than confining loans to short-term purposes concerning current payments. Long-term risk capital, according to Smith, should be obtained from wealthy individuals rather than from the banks, which needed to be very watchful to ensure that their paper issues were actually used for the limited purposes intended and not converted by tricky customers into something else. Not least was the danger that bank money would be used to finance risky projects that could find no other backers. The example of the Ayr Bank, which had gone bankrupt through supporting risky innovators, had clearly made a considerable impression upon Adam Smith, if only because the Duke of Buccleuch, his old student, was among the losers. The great "paper wheel" would pump the waters of commerce satisfactorily only if the bankers resisted all temptations and entreaties to use it for building the channel itself.

4.2 Market

The notion of the market and its expansion, in conjunction with the division of labor in society, provides the second feature of Adam Smith's developmental economics. In the Scottish countryside each peasant tended to be his own butcher, brewer, and baker because when "the market is very small no person can have any encouragement to dedicate himself entirely to one employment."[25]

But even if the division of labor could have been introduced in the countryside, Adam Smith did not consider that this alone would increase productivity in a meaningful fashion if it was not accompanied by an expansion of the area of land employed, either at home or abroad. In agriculture, nature must take its course, but this was not the case in manufacturing, which could proceed largely unruffled by the vagaries of climate and seasons. So long as there was a roadway to the market, production could continue in all weather with the aid of horse-drawn transport. It was even better when there was a waterway, since a ship with a crew of eight could move a cargo between Edinburgh and London that other-wise would require a hundred men, fifty wagons, and four hundred horses. For the sake of such savings, people were more than willing to risk storms and tide waters. Likewise, if there were customs and export prohibitions, people were more than willing to accept the risks of fines, and even the death penalty, in order to obtain the profits, which at the same time extended the market.

Adam Smith was keenly aware of the manner in which the restrictions imposed by authorities limited both the development of the market and the division of labor in society. Customs dues and taxes of different kinds acted as barriers to the free flow "of marketing,"[26] limiting the possibilities of the division of labor and the wealth of the population. France and Spain, in particular, provided models of what should not be done in this respect. The region under the rule of the Duke of Palma, for example, was divided into no fewer than three areas for the purposes of taxes, and under such circumstances it was only the "great fertility of the soil and happiness of the climate [that] could preserve such countries from soon relapsing into the lowest state of poverty and barbarism."[27]

Whereas the situation in Britain was somewhat better, it was yet far from ideal. Each tax or customs duty provided Adam Smith with the material for a critical analysis that balanced the loss of wealth in the economy against the apparent gains to the finances of the state.

Although Adam Smith was a strong advocate of the doctrine of free trade, which flowed directly from his economic vision of an expanding market controlled only through the forces of the "invisible hand," he, nevertheless, demonstrated considerable political realism with regard to the implementation of his viewpoint:

> To expect, indeed, that the freedom of trade should ever be entirely restored in Great Britain, is as absurd as to expect that an Oceana or Utopia should ever be established in it. Not only the prejudices of the public, but what is more unconquerable, the private interests of many individuals, irresistibly oppose it.[28]

Businessmen and manufacturers of different kinds opposed free trade for their own private interests. It was particularly the traders, of all classes, who convinced the "princes, the nobles and the country gentlemen" of the land to provide them with monopoly conditions against foreign competitors and with support in foreign markets. Since governments had so little understanding of trade and industry, they were easily impressed by such stories and acted accordingly. The truth of the matter was, according to Adam Smith, that traders understood their own private interests better than the government understood the public interest; one of the tasks of the economist was to show the limitations of the seductive, mercantilist arguments of such traders.

The destruction of mercantilist notions of economy is usually regarded as one of the larger achievements of Adam Smith, although he was perhaps engaged here more in kicking down an already opening door. Mercantilism was based on the fallacy that the possession of gold and silver was identical with real wealth. The wealth of the country could thus be increased by prohibiting the export of valuable metals of this nature and encouraging their import through a surplus on the balance of payments with other countries. It was particularly the rich traders and manufacturers (who had the ear of the authorities) who benefited from the manipulation of customs and import regulations in the light of such prejudices; meanwhile, the interests of the poorer classes and customers were sacrificed:

> It is the industry which is carried on for the benefit of the rich and powerful, that is principally encouraged by our mercantile system. That which is carried on for the benefit of the poor and the indigent, is too often, either neglected, or oppressed . . . . In the mercantile system, the interest of the consumer is almost constantly sacrificed to that of the producer; and it seems to consider production, and not consumption, as the ultimate end and object of all industry and commerce.[29]

Where one group managed to establish its interests at the cost of other groups, the development of the market was threatened. Smith went so far as to recommend that roads and waterways should not be financed from public funds but should rather be paid for from tolls to ensure that those who actually used them should also pay for them. All state intervention in the form of subsidies and support could only limit the market and reduce the possibilities for each individual to exercise entrepreneurship in response to the price signals that "command and purchase" his work.

Adam Smith's targets were not only the remnants of feudalism and the practice of slavery but also the contemporary form of business organization known as the "joint-stock companies." These had been introduced through an act of Parliament and provided a means of raising capital for the exploitation of trade with foreign parts where the companies were granted monopolies. Merchants and others could purchase a share of a venture planned by such organizations as the South Sea Company, the Royal Africa Company, or the like, which possessed the monopoly, and would then participate in the profits that might derive from the expedition. The purpose of these joint-stock companies was not only to protect trade abroad but also to build fortifications and maintain troops and ambassadors in foreign lands. Smith is curious as to what has happened to the funds provided by the state for the construction of fortifications, whether such companies are truly profitable in terms of their earnings per ship, and whether their real function did not lie in keeping out "private adventurers" from foreign markets. If this was the case, were they any better than the older "regulated companies," which controlled trade with Hamburg, Russia, and Turkey, but which were responsible for their deeds in a manner that was not the case with the joint stock companies? Were not these joint-stock companies simply the old livery companies freed from their previous responsibilities?

Adam Smith's criticism of the closed corporations formed by the old livery and guild companies probably found its origins in his early experience at Oxford: "In the University of Oxford the greater part of the public professors have, for these many years, given up altogether even the pretense of teaching."[30]

In this case, according to Smith, it resulted in too many people obtaining a free education. This could be contrasted with the situation before the advent of printing that enabled the learned to "fix and realize" the product of their studies when *scholar* and *beggar* were "terms very nearly synonymous."[31] In other cases, the corporations and guilds limited the supply of qualified tradesmen through rules governing the number of apprentices a craftsman could employ. A master knife maker in Sheffield or a silk weaver in London, for example, was not allowed to teach more than two such apprentices the arts of the trade. The training period, moreover, was unnecessarily long, not because of any intrinsic difficulties of the trade, but rather so that the master could profit from the cheap labor obtained under the guise of training. Such restrictions not only distorted the market but also undermined the natural entrepreneurship that was the basis of property: "The property which every man has in his own labour, as it is the original foundation of all other property, so it is most sacred and inviolable. The patrimony of the poor man lies in the strength and dexterity of his hands."[32]

Where the market for labor and products had been relatively free from restrictions, the development of the division of labor had resulted in considerable fall in prices. A good quality clock, for example, that cost twenty pounds in 1650 could be purchased for twenty shillings in 1770. The manufacture of clocks had been simplified, and it was possible to learn the trade in a shorter time. The division of labor allowed more people to work for more time with less comprehensive knowledge of the trade.

The corporations and monopolies did everything they could to mystify and hinder the advantages to be obtained from an open-market economy. They stopped the export of machines, weaving stools, and spinning wheels; when it was not these "dead instruments of trade," it was "the living instrument, the artificer,"[33] who was the object of their restrictions. Those who attempted to practice their trade in foreign parts risked being convicted of smuggling. Yet other restrictions stopped the poor from moving to new areas of the country where they might have found better opportunities for work. With the removal of all such limitations, "The trades, the crafts, the mysteries would all be losers. But the public would be a gainer, the work of all artificers coming in this way much cheaper to the market."[34]

It was the task of the economist to oppose all such restrictions on the freedom of labor and the development of the division of labor in order to realize an open-market economy.

4.3 Stock

The third important element in Adam Smith's developmental economics concerned the accumulation of stocks. When the market has been freed from restrictions and the division of labor established in society, it could be considered that human beings had moved beyond "the rude state of nature" and had become "advanced" or "improved." In the savage state, humans are forced into a continuous search for food in order to obtain a precarious existence. While there is in the savage state no productive surplus, there is also no need for products and money, since there is nothing to sell or exchange. Although people are subjected to continuous hunger, the resources of nature are yet free for the taking. The first step toward development is taken through the "appropriation of land," which implies that it is no longer possible to obtain food from nature but that some means of rewarding the landowner for the product of his property is required. The existence of property, thus, provides a prerequisite for the establishment of exchange relations.

But there is still the question of how the producer will survive during the period when he is manufacturing the products that he will later exchange for other goods and services. Adam Smith maintained that a further prerequisite for the development of the division of labor and a market-oriented economy was the existence of a sufficient stock of food, materials, and tools to enable the processes of industry and exchange to be set in motion. Such stocks must either be the property of the producer or have been borrowed by him from some thrifty individual against payments of interest. Thus, the "accumulation of stocks" is essential for industrial development and builds upon the "parsimony" of individuals. This parsimonious and thrifty nature, according to Smith, derives from an inborn urge to self-betterment that continues throughout life: "[T]he principle which prompts us to save, is the desire of bettering our condition, a desire which, though generally calm and dispassionate, comes with us from the womb, and never leaves us till we go into the grave."[35]

It is this deep and usually calm propensity that allows people to overcome the casual hazards of nature and the occasional outbreaks of wastefulness in daily conduct.

The propensity to self-betterment, expressed in the urge to save, however, only becomes meaningful when it is combined with the payment of interest. Without the payment of interest in conjunction with the division of labor and exchange activity, the urge to save would only result in collections of money in mattresses or treasures buried in holes in the ground. But with interest, exchange, and work, savings are recruited to the dynamics of development: the "accumulation of stocks" in this ongoing process possesses something of an autonomous character. Adam Smith, in fact, emphasizes that it is the stocks themselves—not the owners of stocks—that create employment and provide a surplus in the form of interest. It is not a question of a reward for the thrifty owner of stocks or for their successful management. Rather, returns on stocks "are regulated by quite different principles, and bear no proportion to the quantity, the hardship, or the ingenuity of this supposed labour of inspection and direction. They are regulated altogether by the value of the stock employed, and are greater or smaller in proportion to the extent of this stock."[36]

Everything included in these stocks derives originally from the land and the seas—from agriculture, fishing, forestry, or mining. It is through work and exchange that the original gifts of nature are transformed into the products of economic circulation. An inventory of these stocks of circulating capital would include the beef held by the butcher, the pots held by the potter, the material in the loom of the weaver, and the half-finished garments in the possession of the tailor. These stocks held by tradesmen provide a profit in the same manner as their investments in fixed capital. This fixed capital includes such things as seed silos, fences, cow stalls, machines, as well as factory buildings and constructions necessary for production. Beside these forms of stocks and capital, each tradesman or trader possesses a further stored capital in the particular skills that make it possible for his work to "fix and realize itself in some particular subject or vendable commodity."[37] The whole of this stock likewise should provide profits or interest. Finally, there are those stocks held by consumers in their larders and households that have not yet been consumed. Upon such, according to Smith, it is only possible to obtain interest in the form of utility.

Parsimony, stocks, and interest together provide an increased production from the natural resources of land and sea. The obstacles to the release of the industrial potential of the population both at home and abroad are feudal structures, monopoly corporations, and slavery. In such circumstances, the courts of the rich wasted their incomes on bureaucrats, servants, opera singers, and other unproductive types who added little or nothing to the circulation of concrete products in the marketplace. The actions of governments for the most part provide obstacles to the development of the natural entrepreneurship of the population and the "invisible hand" that steers and controls an open-market economy. Smith points out that Edinburgh had become very much more industrious since the wasteful Parliament was moved from there. "We are more industrious than our forefathers," he concludes with some satisfaction.[38]

5. The Concrete in Smith's Management Lessons

The *Wealth of the Nations* is by any standards a lively and practical book, filled with information and examples that illustrate and support Smith's economic theories and judgments. There are many arguments that show that Adam Smith's understanding of the role of the economist is something of a mixture of an enlightened teacher and a prosecutor. As an enlightened teacher, the economist teaches workers, tradesmen, landowners, and statesmen about the management of the relationship between individual action and national wealth. To them, he is a guardian under whose tutelage they will receive the insight and understanding they now lack. For example, the landowners, who had received their position through inheritance, are often indolent and ignorant, since their income does not depend upon "any plan or project of their own."[39] On the other hand, workers are often so pressed that they are in no position to safeguard their own interests without the help of the economist: "His condition leaves him no time to receive the necessary information, and his education and habits are commonly such as to render him unfit to judge even though he was fully informed."[40]

Adam Smith was himself the enlightened adviser of statesmen, being frequently consulted on complex questions of national importance such as that of free trade with Ireland or the policies toward the American colonies. On his last visit to London in 1787, he later remarked: "What an extraordinary man Pitt is, he understands my ideas better than I do myself."[41]

As prosecutor, on the other hand, the economist is the sworn enemy of all those forces in society that transform public interest into private profits. It matters little whether they are the remnants of feudal society or powerful contemporary interests such as those involved in slave trade. Smith was ready to provide business advice when consulted by friends and acquaintances but steadfastly refused to support schemes that involved public funds used for private interests. When, for example, he was invited to support a fund to establish a fishing industry on the Isle of Mull, he politely declined. He believed that the natural entrepreneurship of individuals should be left free to bloom through its own force, unhindered by monopolies, legal restrictions, state subsidies, and taxation.

All this, however, amounts to a certain ethical disposition rooted in a specific view of the human condition, and the question yet remains about the concrete elements of Adam Smith's economics. Wealth is not gold and silver reserves, which are merely the means of promoting economic circulation; nor is wealth to be found in a positive balance of payments with the rest of the world. Wealth for Adam Smith emerges, in fact, from the interaction of two concrete resources: the physical world of nature and the physical population. It is from the organization and activation of the population in relation to the resources of nature that wealth is to be obtained. In an important sense, the circulation of economic activity in this view can be likened to the operation of a gigantic pump that sucks up the resources of nature, transforms them into products, and distributes the products for consumption among the population at large. The role of management is to set this great pump in motion and to force it to function at its maximum capacity. Although the population of Britain (at the time) was only about eight million—as against twenty-four million in France—there were large under- and misemployed human and physical resources that could be freed from traditional restrictions and mobilized in productive economic activity. The "idle" and underemployed resources both at home and abroad would be activated by the freeing of an assumed natural entrepreneurship among the population at large, which, in conjunction with an innate tendency to self-improvement and thrift, would ensure the process of capital accumulation and a rising level of economic welfare.

It is clear that Adam Smith's dynamic conception of an open-market economy differs radically from the notions of the Physiocrats. Smith's emphasis upon the freeing and utilization of human resources means that he can never accept the Physiocrats' theory of value and their ideas concerning the sterile class. While he is appreciative of the intelligence of writers like Quesnay, he considers them all too charmed by paradoxes and empty "metaphysical arguments."[42] Where Quesnay concentrates on agricultural production and considers craftsmen to be unproductive, Smith comprehends both in terms of the ongoing dynamics of a market economy. When Adam Smith seeks to distinguish his position from that of the Physiocrats, he emphasizes the dual nature of economic exchange:

> An artificer, for example, who, in the first six months after harvest, executes ten pounds worth of work, though he should in the same time consume ten pounds worth of corn and other necessaries, yet really adds the value of ten pounds to the annual produce of the land and labour of the society. While he has been consuming a half yearly revenue of ten pounds worth of corn and other necessaries, he has produced an equal value of work capable of purchasing, either to himself or some other person, an equal half-yearly revenue. The value, therefore, of what has been consumed and produced during these six months is equal, not to ten, but to twenty pounds. It is possible, indeed, that no more than ten pounds worth of this value, may ever have existed at any one moment of time. But if the ten pounds worth of corn and other necessaries, which were consumed by the artificer, had been consumed by a soldier or by a menial servant, the value of that part of the annual produce which existed at the end of six months, would have been ten pounds less than it actually is in consequence of the labour of the artificer. Though the value of what the artificer produces, therefore, should not at any one moment of time be supposed to be greater than the value he consumes, yet at every moment of time the actually existing value of goods in the market is, in consequence of what he produces, greater than it otherwise would be.[43]

If Quesnay and Smith were to sit themselves comfortably in some coffee house at the side of a busy market square, Quesnay would be content to note and list all the vegetables and foodstuffs that the traders brought to the marketplace. Smith, on the other hand, would concern himself with the circulation of trading activities. In Quesnay's French farming philosophy, man's hunger sucks physical value out of a well-managed nature. Smith, from barren Scotland, emphasizes how enterprises of pleasant human interaction can pump and circulate a surplus over what farmers and owners would otherwise choose to produce to cover their physiological needs.

Notes

1. John Rae, *Life of Adam Smith*, p. 173.
2. Ibid., p. 95.
3. Adam Smith, *The Theory of Moral Sentiments*, p. 9.
4. Ibid., p. 180.
5. Ibid., p. 205.
6. Ibid., p. 180.
7. Ibid., p. 234.
8. Ibid., p. 104.
9. Ibid., p. 140.
10. Ibid., pp. 116–117.
11. Ernest Mossner and Ian Ross, eds., *The Correspondence of Adam Smith*, pp. 186–187.
12. Adam Smith, *An Inquiry into the Nature and Causes of the Wealth of Nations*, Volume 1, p. 1.
13. Ibid., Volume 1, p. 103.
14. Ibid., Volume 1, p. 265.
15. Ibid., Volume 1, p. 82.
16. Ibid., Volume 1, p. 387.
17. Smith, *Theory of Moral Sentiments*, p. 182.
18. Smith, *Inquiry into the Nature and Causes*, Volume 1, p. 387.
19. Ibid., Volume 1, p. 16.
20. Ibid., Volume 1, p. 24.
21. Ibid., Volume 1, p. 277.
22. Ibid., Volume 1, p. 275.
23. Ibid.
24. Ibid., Volume 1, p. 304.
25. Ibid., Volume 1, p. 19.
26. Ibid., Volume 1, p. 196.
27. Ibid., Volume 2, p. 386.
28. Ibid., Volume 1, p 435.
29. Ibid., Volume 2, pp. 143, 159.
30. Ibid., Volume 1, p. 251.
31. Ibid., Volume 1, p. 134.
32. Ibid., Volume 1, p. 123.
33. Ibid., Volume 2, p. 158.
34. Ibid., Volume 1, p. 125.
35. Ibid., Volume 1, p. 323.
36. Ibid., Volume 1, p. 50.
37. Ibid., Volume 1, p. 313.
38. Ibid., Volume 1, p. 318.
39. Ibid., Volume 1, p. 248.
40. Ibid., Volume 1, p. 249.
41. Rae, *Life of Adam Smith*, p. 405.
42. Smith, *Inquiry into the Nature and Causes*, Volume 2, p. 315.
43. Ibid., Volume 2, pp. 173–174.

3

Men, Food, or Machines:
Entrepreneurs Who Saved Profits
But Destroyed Economy

1. Abstract Arguments in Concrete Debate

When Adam Smith's *The Wealth of Nations* appeared, someone reportedly remarked that a philosopher was as likely to write a book on trade and business as
a lawyer was to write on physics.[1] Dr. Johnson, who came to Adam Smith's
defense, maintained that philosophers had a better overview than did traders,
who were only concerned with their own interests. The remark about the lawyer
and physics later became more appropriate for David Ricardo (1772–1823), who
wanted to understand how national production was distributed and to "determine
the laws which regulate this distribution."[2]

In contrast to Adam Smith, however, Ricardo was a man with practical economic experience. He was a dealer on the London exchange, a profession he had
inherited from his father, a Dutch immigrant to Britain. Before starting work
helping his father on the exchange at the age of fourteen, David Ricardo had
received a little training in trade but had never studied philosophy. He was soon
to break with his family and his Jewish faith and embark on his own business.
Ricardo dealt successfully with large-scale transactions; it was not long before he
became a very wealthy man, married, and left the exchange for an estate in the
country and a seat in Parliament.

The young David Ricardo had used his free time to study mathematics. As he
became wealthier, he had equipped a laboratory in which he experimented in
chemistry and mineralogy. He never developed, however, any penchant toward
systematic study until he happened to read *The Wealth of Nations* during a visit
to the health resort of Bath in 1799. It was then that he began to display his
surprising quickness at figures and calculation in investigations of the prices of
gold and silver that were quoted daily on the exchange. From this, he proceeded

to play with assumed figures for those concepts that then existed in economic thought—profits, interest, and wages. He cared little that these figures were "assumed . . . and probably very far from the truth,"[3] but concentrated upon manipulating them according to set rules that he himself constructed. It was the gradual changes in the figures that interested him. Having considered both the utopian Physiocrats and the historically minded Adam Smith, we now come to an economist who is more in line with contemporary economic model builders and marginal analysts.

Under the initial "R," Ricardo published his first debate article in 1809, in the *Morning Chronicle*. It was titled "The Price of Gold" and contained an unusual analytical explanation for the record-high gold prices that were the subject of much contemporary speculation. It was then the general belief that the high prices were due to an increase in the demand for gold, an explanation that was in line with Adam Smith's theory of market behavior. Ricardo, however, noted that a gold bar weighing a pound was usually minted into 44 ½ guineas that according to the Bank of England was the equivalent of £46 14s 6d in paper money. It was, nevertheless, possible to purchase a pound of gold on the market for paper money worth £55 16s 0d. Ricardo, who daily mixed with buyers of gold, found it difficult to believe that these people were so eager to obtain gold that they were willing to pay 1.2 times its value in currency. It was more probable that the paper money had sunk in value and thus caused the discrepancy. Ricardo found support for this notion in the Bank Restriction Act, a provisional measure introduced in 1797 during a panic rush by holders of paper money to the bank to exchange paper for gold. The law was retained on the statute books and served to limit the responsibility of the Bank of England to accept currency notes in exchange for the legally fixed value in pure gold. How was it in any case possible to say that gold had a high value if the paper money was not separated from gold? The gap between the prices of gold and notes, moreover, was increased by the illegal activity of melting down gold coins to sell at the higher price obtaining for gold bars.

In his article "The Price of Gold," Ricardo displayed his manner of thinking on a miniature scale. Prices were the expression of deeper-lying factors and not merely the result of an agreement founded on market conditions. The article is spiced with the political consequences of the discovery. It would be necessary to put an end to inflation to limit the freedoms of the bank directors, to provide security for small savers, and to formulate economic policy on the basis of strictly scientific thought:

> It would then be evident that all the evils of our currency were owing to the over-issues of the Bank, to the dangerous power which it was entrusted of diminishing at its will, the value of every moneyed man's property, and by enhancing the price of provisions, and every necessary of life, injuring the public annuitant, and all those persons whose incomes were fixed, and who

were consequently not enabled to shift any part of the burden from their own shoulders.[4]

The article provoked a debate, and a House of Commons committee that was appointed to investigate the matter called in diverse authorities to provide their views on the subject. Despite the fact that none of these gentlemen actually named his explanation of the phenomenon in this context, Ricardo's conviction remained undiminished. In the margin notes to the Bullion Committee's 1811 report it is possible to read something of his tired resignation about these practical men's ignorance of the fact that it was a surplus of paper money, and not a shortage of gold, that lay at the root of the problem. Ricardo held that they had probably been misled by Adam Smith, and he believed it could only lead to a monetary surplus if people were forced to use paper money. The general confusion reigning on the subject resulted in the provisions of the Bank Restriction Act being retained until 1821, when they were rescinded more for practical political reasons than in deference to any Ricardian theoretical reasonings. But even the more theoretically minded found it difficult to swallow Ricardo's arguments, although they appreciated his efforts to find a scientific explanation behind the economic phenomenon. As a result of the debate following the gold question, Ricardo was in 1811 to come in contact with one of these skeptical gentlemen with whom he continued to correspond on scientific questions throughout his life.

2. Malthus as a Source of Concrete Inspiration

Thomas Robert Malthus (1766–1834), the famous author of *An Essay on the Principle of Population*, goes directly to the point in his first letter to Ricardo, to say that while he did not share the latter's explanation of the gold question, he felt that they were "mainly on the same side of the question,"[5] since they were both seeking after "the just principles of political economy." It is interesting to note that Ricardo in his reply declares rather that he is interested in "the just principles of science." So began a correspondence stretching over many years with Ricardo's attempt to convince Malthus that his "doctrine respecting the exchange"[6] and ideas concerning the surplus of paper money were correct. Following an involved discussion concerning the meaning of "surplus," Malthus recommends that Ricardo read Hume, Smith, and Huskisson. Ricardo, however, refuses to give ground and decides to "humbly retain that opinion notwithstanding the high authorities against me."[7]

That which most separates Malthus and Ricardo is the importance they assign to the market in economics. That which unites them is the search for deeper truths, together with a mutual tolerance for the different paths that may be chosen by the seeker after truth. The Reverend Thomas Malthus was famed for his 1798 study based on the idea that the population, driven by "the passion between the sexes,"[8] necessarily grew with a geometrical progression. Food supplies, on the other hand, could only increase arithmetically. The true philosopher must look this question straight in the eye and understand that only an increase in food production could free the factory workers from "unhealthy occupations of manufacturing industry"[9] and offer work in the fresh air instead of the "close and unwholesome rooms."[10] But complete freedom from the problem of the relationship between population and food supplies was not to be obtained. The true philosopher must also give up the utopian idea of "unlimited progress" for a more marginal and realistic idea of progress through "partial improvements."

It must be understood, according to Malthus's view, that social institutions do not cause the troubles of the world but rather attempt to relieve such problems. Marriage and ownership are examples of social institutions of this nature. There are, however, exceptions such as the Poor Laws that compensate lowly paid individuals from the parish funds through charity, instead of letting employers and workers find a solution to their problems through confrontation with the difficulties of nature. Only dreamers and prophets whose "beautiful fabric of the imagination vanishes at the severe touch of truth"[11] refuse to see that there exist natural boundaries and absolute material limits. These false philosophers would deceive us into believing that physical growth has no boundaries, and that it is possible to produce food in infinite quantities. They maintain that human reason would conquer passions, but the true philosopher, relying only on personal experience, knows that muscles set a limit to our wandering despite our intentions. The body is the tortoise that always in the longer run takes the soul.[12]

The task of the true philosopher, according to Malthus, is to ignore the casual and random occurrences of everyday existence and to seek instead general laws because "the constancy of the laws of nature and of effects and causes, is the foundation of all human knowledge."[13]

On this point the two correspondents were in complete agreement, but from there on their views take quite different directions. Malthus gave out his work in six increasingly large volumes in which he laid out the demographical facts on the development of populations in all the various countries that he had visited and observed. Ricardo, on the other hand, chose to build his position on logic. He saw it as his task to investigate the general laws from his writing desk and thereafter considered the different courses of action that lay in the interests of the various social classes to pursue, as a result of these laws. If empirical facts of human behavior showed that people did not act in their own interests according to such general laws, this was no argument against the priority of economics as logical analysis, but rather showed that they should change their behavior. Political economy was for Ricardo a question of postulating and clarifying the rules of the economic game and studying their implications. This was a point of view that was to have profound effects upon the future development of economic theory as perhaps the following quotation illustrates:

The first point to be considered is, what is the interest of countries in the case supposed? The second what is their practice? Now it is obvious that I need not be greatly solicitous about this latter point: it is sufficient for my purpose if I can clearly demonstrate that the interest of the public is as I have stated it. It would be no answer to me to say that men were ignorant of the best and cheapest mode of conducting their business and paying their debts, because that is a question of fact not of science, and might well be urged against almost every proposition in Political Economy.[14]

In the almost normative priority of science over fact in this sense, Ricardo influenced the development of contemporary economic thought to a degree that certainly exceeds that of Malthus and possibly even that of Adam Smith. This was the beginning of economics as an "as if" irrefutable science.

3. Production of Value

After several entreaties from his friend James Mill, the historian and father of John Stuart Mill, Ricardo wrote a major book on political economy with the title *The Principles of Political Economy and Taxation*, which was published in 1817. The first chapter deals with the theory of value. The exchange value of a product or good is defined as "the power which a commodity has without any reference whatever to its absolute value."[15]

Adam Smith had earlier maintained that the value of a product, given the relevant conditions of demand and supply in the market, should tend toward stabilization at a natural level "to which the prices of all commodities are continually gravitating."[16] This is a formulation that evoked considerable interest among those who, like Ricardo, preferred "the grand and consistent theory of Newton" rather than "the wild eccentric hypothesis of Descartes."[17] It implied the existence of more general values beneath the fluctuations of market prices, perhaps even an absolute value that could explain the causal origins of exchange behavior. The field was open to further speculation precisely because Adam Smith himself refused to adopt a definitive point of view on this question. The market prices of commodities, according to Smith, tended to move toward their natural levels, which reflected the underlying real value; by way of a circular argument, he defined this underlying real value as "the quantity of labour" which made it possible "to purchase and command."[18]

Ricardo sought after long-term and general rules and saw the market as the regulating mechanism that guaranteed that prices always returned to their natural levels after temporary fluctuations, which could have psychological causes. Just as Malthus argued that the body, the natural physique rather than psychology, provided the ultimate grounds, Ricardo now argues that there must exist a fixed and absolute foundation for the problem of exchange values: "In speaking, then, of the exchangeable value of commodities, or the power of purchasing possessed by any one commodity, I mean always the power which it would possess if not disturbed by any temporary or accidental cause, and which is its natural price."[19]

Ricardo did not, however, seek this natural foundation through observation of the practical activities of agriculture, industry, or trade, but rather withdrew himself from the exchange to write down the rules of value.

3.1 Quantity of Labor—The Major Rule

In the long run, value does not depend upon "changing fashions" or "accidental and fluctuating causes"; yet utility is an all too subjective and psychological concept to serve as a measure of value among different commodities. Everything we might consume can be regarded as being in some sense useful, but this does not imply that such, therefore, has value in an economic sense. That value also has little to do with wealth is clear to all who live in the flood of products from the industrial society, which through rationalization has become increasingly less valuable or cheaper. Ricardo points out that trade does not provide "more valuable objects, but more useful ones."[20] He also notes that "improvements in the means of abridging labour . . . in the mode of manufacturing cloth, linen and cotton goods, iron steel, copper and stockings . . . in husbandry all. . . . tend to lower the value of these goods and the produce of the soil."[21] It is true of such developments in all these areas that "[e]conomy in the use of labour never fails to reduce the relative value of a commodity.[22]

With the support of statements of this kind, Ricardo is then in a position to state his general rule for the absolute value of a commodity or product: "the proportion between the quantities of labour necessary for acquiring different objects seems to be the only circumstance which can afford any rule for exchanging them for one another."[23] Ricardo then suggests that the rule could be used for practical investigations of questions concerning value.

Suppose, for example, that we have two products: fresh salmon and venison. Suppose also that yesterday we were required to pay four salmon for a steak of venison and that today the price has fallen to two salmon for a steak of the same quality. Did the change in the exchange value depend upon a fall in the absolute value of the steak? Alternatively, is it the case that the value of salmon has increased? It is also possible that there have been changes in the prices of both salmon and venison. In order to investigate the cause of the change, suggests Ricardo, it is first necessary to compare the prices of salmon and venison of yesterday and today with the prices of "shoes, stockings, hats, iron, sugar" from yesterday and today. If it proves that it is only one product that has changed its exchange value with all the others, "we may then with great probability infer that the variation has been in this commodity."[24]

As a second step in the investigation, we should, according to Ricardo, make a careful "description of labour" for that product which we now believe to have changed its exchange value. If it is now found that more labor today is "bestowed on" or "realized in," for example, salmon rather than venison, then the matter is settled. "Probability is changed to certainty"; it is the salmon that has become more valuable. The rule also serves to discover the true causes of fluctuations in value.

The rule as formulated here, however, is only applicable to products the quantity of which could be influenced by "human industry." The high exchange values of old wines and rare works of art are the result of arbitrary valuations of taste in the market, as are also all other products and goods that are "monopolized either by an individual or by a company."[25] But all other commodities that are manufactured in free competition and without secrets, protection, or patents should follow the general rule concerning prices with only small exceptions: "the rule which determines how much of one [commodity] shall be given in exchange for another, depends almost exclusively on the comparative quantity of labour expended on each."[26]

This rule, which was widely accepted among early economists, provided what became known as the labor theory of value.

3.2 Return on Capital—The Secondary Rule

Consider the case that when seeking for the cause of a change in exchange value of salmon and venison it is discovered that precisely the same quantity of labor was expended upon these commodities yesterday as today. What then could the change be dependent upon? Ricardo suggests that in such cases it is necessary to investigate the part that capital played in the costs of production. If it is found, for example, that deer were always shot with a bow and arrow, while it required an expensive net to catch the salmon, the mystery is solved. The value of the fish has increased because the costs of the instruments of production have been "transferred to" the value of the commodity. Capital is to be regarded as stored-up labor; if two products are produced with equal amounts of labor but different amounts of capital, then a "modification to the rule" should be entertained that included "a just compensation for the time that the profits were withheld."[27] In other words, a return on the capital employed is also to be taken into consideration in the calculation of exchange values.

Ricardo rejects in the strongest terms Adam Smith's supposition that "the reward of the labourer" determines exchange value. There are as many different wages as there are products, and it is the quantity of labor rather than its price that constitutes the major rule. But, on the other hand, if the wages for the production of a commodity that demanded a certain capital should change, this would be reflected in the exchange value relative to some other product that is produced with less capital. The costs of production consist of both the quantity of labor and a return on the amount of capital employed. The return on capital, in its turn, consists of the exchange value minus the amount of wages that an entrepreneur had to pay for labor. While an economy to Smith mainly seems to consist of self-employed enterprising laborers, Ricardo assumes the existence of hiring capitalists. Thus the higher the level of wages, the less remained to the entrepreneur as a return on capital. Moreover, since this return is to be calculated as a percentage on the whole of the capital employed, a fall in a given year would reduce the percentage for the whole capital. If wages went up, then the return on capital went down, and this implies a fall in real production costs, and in exchange value, relative to such goods that could be produced without capital.

Changes in wages could yet in a further manner affect exchange values. This is through the more efficient use of labor resulting from the increased employment of machines. Ricardo supposes that an engineer in the course of a year develops and builds a machine that could do the work of a hundred men. The engineer asks a price of 5,000 pounds for his machine, since each man costs 50 pounds per year to employ. Now when the wage level suddenly rises so that the hundred men now earn 5,500 pounds per year, the entrepreneur naturally becomes interested in an investment that would reduce the yearly production costs by 500 pounds. The machine is, thus, purchased, and the workers are dismissed; this results in a fall in exchange value relative to other products that are manufactured with less capital but more labor. Wages do not affect exchange values directly but rather indirectly as a result of this kind of innovation.

The engineer in this example is in no position to raise the price of his machine to 5,500 pounds when the price of labor rises. This is because he, like all other entrepreneurs, makes his profit from sales. When he sets the price of the machine at 5,000 pounds, he takes into consideration that it is necessary to employ 85 men on the building of the machine during the year so that his wage costs came to 4,250 pounds (50 x 85 = 4,250). This leaves him with a profit of 750 pounds. When the wage rate increases, the engineer is affected, as are all other businesses. His new wage costs come to 4,675 pounds per year (55 x 85 = 4,675), which reduces his profit to 325 pounds. Since all businesses are affected by the new level of wages, the general level of profits is reduced in proportion to the increase in wages. If the engineer demands a higher price for his machine, then capital would be attracted by the higher level of profits into the production of machines. This would result, through the logic of the market, in the pressing down of this temporary increase to "the common rate of profits."[28] Rising wages always create an incentive to replace labor by machines: "We see here why it is that old countries are constantly impelled to employ machinery and new countries to employ labour."[29] It was the profit mechanism that provided the engine of economic development.

3.3 Foreign Trade—The Supplementary Rule

In the determination of the exchange value of products between two individuals, it is necessary, according to Ricardo, first to take into consideration the major rule concerning the quantity of labor and then to complete this with the rule concerning profits. But this has to be borne in mind: "The same rule which regulates the relative value of commodities in one country does not regulate the relative value of the commodities exchanged between two or more countries."[30]

Ricardo emphasizes in an antimercantilist spirit that foreign trade in itself does not bring more value into a country than what it costs, since every exchange must be balanced. It was, however, possible to obtain more of a product through exchange with other countries than through confinement to the home market. The same product can be produced at different costs, in terms of the capital and quantity of labor employed, in different countries. It is, thus, necessary to introduce a supplementary rule for foreign trade. This rule could be formulated in the following manner: Two identical products have different exchange values in relation to another product if produced in different countries as the production and capital costs are different. The rational capitalist naturally prefers to establish production where costs are lowest, Ricardo points out, but he is tied to his home country and wants to maintain control over the use of his capital. Each country, therefore, retains the industry for which it is best suited. This explains, maintains Ricardo, why Poland and America produce corn for industrialized Britain, which specializes in the manufacture of "hardware and other goods." Ricardo illustrates the logic of this position with the aid of the following famous example:

> It will appear, then, that a country possessing very considerable advantages in machinery and skill, and which may therefore be enabled to manufacture commodities with much less labour than her neighbours, may, in return for such commodities, import a portion of corn required for its consumption, even if its land were more fertile and corn could be grown with less labour than in the country from which it was imported. Two men can both make shoes and hats, and one is superior to the other in both employments; but in making hats he can only exceed his competitor by one-fifth or 20 per cent, and in making shoes he can excel him by one-third or 33 per cent; will it not be for the interest of both that the superior man should employ himself exclusively in making shoes, and the inferior man in making hats?[31]

So long as the price of a commodity, reckoned in gold, is lower abroad than at home, it could be imported with profit if some other product could be exported for the same profit. Trade among countries is dependent upon prices rather than production costs, as is the case between individuals. Such could continue as long as the price of gold remains stable, so that the price differences remain unchanged.

4. Distribution of Produce

Having expounded the rules for the evaluation of production, Ricardo turns to the question of the distribution of national production among its three classes: landowners, capitalists, and workers. To Adam Smith, distribution was primarily a simple question of the sale of products on the market. Subsequent distribution, in turn, was dependent upon the functions of the labor, land, and capital markets. Ricardo, on the other hand, reduces the role of the market to that of a control function. On the question of distribution, he also prefers to propose general and scientific explanations concerning regulations for the distribution of incomes. That part of production that goes to capitalists in the form of profit on their capital is under constant pressure from that part that is distributed to labor in the form of wages. The return to farmers, on the other hand, is under constant pressure from the landowners who seek to raise rents. All social classes, in turn, are pressed by the state, which imposes taxes "for the support of unproductive labourers ... taken from the productive industry of the country."[32] In other words, Ricardo regards distribution as the result of three types of institutionalized interactions, which follow—or rather logically should follow—three rules governing such interactions: the rules for rents, wages, and taxes. Ricardo considers that this question of distribution is not to be confused with that of producing values. It is not through changing the price of a product that capitalists can increase their profits. The distribution of the economic cake depends rather upon the action of these rules.

Ricardo's ideas concerning distribution first made their appearance in his correspondence with Thomas Malthus and had matured into a definite form early in 1815. In February, he had written two pamphlets on the question of imported corn, and, toward the end of the month, he sat down to write, in a matter of a few days, "An Essay on the Influence of the Low Price of Corn on the Profits of Stock." This proved to be an argument in favor of free trade, with particular reference to corn imports, which was founded upon his logical model for production and distribution. The 1773 Corn Law had been replaced by that of 1804, and the time was now ripe for a further review of the import restrictions.[33] The February pamphlets had examined the question from the debate in the House of Commons and two official inquiries into the matter. The harvest of 1813 had been a record, Napoleon was still confined safely to Elba, and farm prices were low. The farmers' lobby maintained that it was necessary to protect the home production of corn through an import duty that would ensure the benefits of large-scale production and thus a volume of corn that would hold down food prices. The cynics maintained that the secret desire of the large landowners was to eliminate the small farmers during the years of bad harvests and then fix prices a hairbreadth under that border where hunger riots would force a lowering of tariff barriers. A protected agriculture, moreover, it was maintained, would provide farmers with greater profits.

Malthus, in the main, supports the protectionist position, but largely for the reason of ensuring that the national food supply is not threatened through a foreign blockade. Others want to protect agriculture, which they consider to be more sensitive to market fluctuations than is manufacturing. A farmer must take the price that is offered, as it was claimed by a farmer politician, because "he is different from the common manufacturer who calculates all his expenses in producing an article and charges accordingly for that article."[34]

Yet others remember that it was Adam Smith himself who had pointed out the advantages of large-scale production in industry, but they seem to have missed the point that large-scale production also had its advantages in agriculture. Certain farmers bear witness that small farms employing "high farming" and "curious cultivation"[35] methods are both expensive and difficult in practice. Outside the House of Commons, riots break out when at last agreement is reached on the new import restriction on corn. The small businessmen of the bakers' guild are not much happier when it is decided in April of the same year to abolish the price lists for bread in order to increase the demand for flour. The pleasure of the farming and landowning interests, however, proved short lived as a result of the falling prices on the home market and the obvious overproduction.

Any short acquaintance with the issues of contemporary debate at that time shows that there was an almost complete lack of any overall perspective on causes and effects in the economic chaos that ruled. The aim of the politicians was to attempt to normalize the British economy following the long years of war, but in this they adopted arguments that suited their causes of the moment and as little then as now followed any general economic doctrine. Not before 1821 did Ricardo's ideas on the subject happen to prove convenient. By that time, however, he had already (1819) taken himself a seat in Parliament and there sought the aid of logical reasonings to bring some order to the general chaos that had become something of a public issue.

4.1 Rents

Table 1 is Ricardo's famous illustration of the growth of rents on arable lands.[36] Behind this model and its rules of calculation lies a small story—or a theory if you will—concerning the manner in which landownership arises. The rent on land is defined as "the compensation which is paid to the owner of the land for the use of its original and indestructible powers."[37]

The rent is paid in corn by the farmer to the landowner, but at the beginning of time there was no landowner—only a number of human beings with a large amount of arable land. If food was required, it was only necessary to cultivate the land that happened to be convenient. This meant that people lived in a condition of simple but sound happiness, which, according to Malthus's theory, implied that they would increase in numbers at a very considerable rate. The food that could be produced from the local land then no longer sufficed, and it was necessary to travel ever farther in order to find uncultivated land. The cost of transport and labor involved rose to a degree that correspondingly reduced the return on the distant lands employed. Land, moreover, was not a homogeneous entity but was better or worse for arable purposes according to its innate qualities, requiring different inputs of labor and capital to obtain a given return. It was

Table 1

Table showing the Progress of Rent and Profits under an assumed Augmentation of Capital

Capital estimated in quarters of wheat	Profits per cent	Neat produce in quarters of wheat after paying the costs of production	Profit of 1st portion of land in quarters of wheat on each capital	Rent of 1st portion of land in quarters of wheat	Profit of 2nd portion of land in quarters of wheat	Rent of 2nd portion of land in quarters of wheat	Profits of 3rd portion of land in quarters of wheat	Rent of 3rd portion of land in quarters of wheat	Portion of 4th portion of land in quarters of wheat	Rent of 4th portion of land in quarters of wheat	Profit of 5th portion of land in quarters of wheat	Rent of 5th portion of land in quarters of wheat	Profit of 6th portion of land in quarters of wheat	Rent of 6th portion of land in quarters of wheat	Profit of 7th portion of land in quarters of wheat	Rent of 7th portion of land in quarters of wheat	Profit of 8th portion of land in quarters of wheat
200	50	100	100	none													
210	43	90	86	14	90	none											
220	36	80	72	28	76	14	80	none									
230	30	70	60	40	63	27	66	14	70	none							
240	25	60	50	50	52.5	37.5	55	25	57.5	12.5	60	none					
250	20	50	40	60	42	48	44	36	46	24	48	12	50	none			
260	15	40	30	70	31.5	58.5	33	47	34.5	35.5	36	24	37.5	12.5	40	none	
270	11	30	22	78	23	67	24	56	25.3	44.7	26.4	33.6	27.5	22.5	27.6	12.4	29.7

	When the whole capital employed is	Whole amount of rent received by landlords in quarters of wheat	Whole amount of profits in quarters received by owners of stock	Profit percent on the whole capital	Rent percent on the whole capital	Total produce in quarters of wheat, after paying the costs of production
1st Period	200	none	100	50		100
2d Ditto	410	14	176	43	3.5	190
3d Ditto	630	42	228	36	6.5	270
4th Ditto	860	81	259	30	9.5	340
5th Ditto	1.100	125	275	25	11.5	400
6th Ditto	1.350	180	270	20	13.25	450
7th Ditto	1.610	248.5	241.5	15	15.5	490
8th Ditto	1.880	314.5	205.5	11	16.5	520

Source: Sraffa, 1951. Volume IV 17.

in these differences, the "difference between the produce obtained by the employment of two equal quantities of capital and labour,"[38] that a new landowning class arose.

This new class originated from the insight of the farmer with the better land that, although his neighbor worked as hard as himself, he only obtained for his efforts a harvest that was considerably less than his own. It then strikes him that he could maintain his right to the prime land and live well on the difference between his own fine harvests and the poorer harvests obtained by his neighbor on lands of secondary quality. Landownership emerges when the farmer decides to find another person to work his land who is willing to pay him this difference in the form of rent. As the population increases even further, it proves necessary to take into use third-class land that requires yet larger inputs of labor and capital to obtain a given return. In this situation, the original farmers of secondary lands soon see their opportunity of becoming landowners themselves and of living off the rent of their land without working. The landowners of the primary lands now wait in expectation for the leases on their lands to expire so that they can contract new leases at yet higher rents, as it has been clearly demonstrated that a farming entrepreneur is prepared to settle for an even lower return and "there cannot be two rates of profit."[39]

With the new negotiations concerning the lease, the landowner would maintain that the lowest profit, corresponding to the return on the worst land, should be the profit norm for the whole agricultural society.

Ricardo completes his theory with a further explanation of why all farming entrepreneurs must accept the worst estates' profitability as the norm in leasehold negotiations. The farmer who already has a lease can, during its period, invest a small amount of capital in order to obtain a marginal increase in harvests. A farmer would be prepared to make such marginal investments to that point where he is certain that the price of corn is exactly "sufficient to replace his expenses and his profits, for he knows that he shall have no additional rent to pay."[40]

This is because he knows that the leasing agreement has several more years to run. It is thus the last small bit of cultivated land upon which no rent is paid that reveals the exact value on the corn market. And since Ricardo, in the rules of exchange values, had decided that the value of a commodity should be determined by "costs of production including profit," it is not possible to raise the price or profit margin. Of two rates on profit, it was presumably the lower that was valid, and therefore the landowner has "the power, at the expiration of his lease, of obliging him to pay."[41]

It is against this background that we can understand David Ricardo's rather materialistic view of business profits:

> Profits of stock fall because land equally fertile cannot be obtained, and through the whole progress of society, profits are regulated by the difficulty or

facility of procuring food. This is a principle of great importance, and it has been overlooked in the writings of Political Economists. They appear to think that profits of stock can be raised by commercial causes, independent of the food supply.[42]

It is, thus, in the final analysis, inequalities in the use of land for the production of food in relation to the demand for food by the population that determines the special place of rents in Ricardo's scheme of thinking.

4.2 Wages

Wages are determined by a contract that "should be left to the fair play and free competition of the market and should never be controlled by the interference of the legislature."[43]

Both Ricardo and Malthus were against the notion of charity as a means of compensating workers for high food prices. If wages were too low to feed a worker's family, the raising of wages could only lead to yet further rises in the price of food. If wages are insufficient, this is an important signal that something is wrong with "the real funds for the maintenance of labour." Ricardo regrets in this question that such inroads have been made in the principles of free regulation and cites approvingly a certain Mr. Buchanan, who has held the following: "In this, we act much in the same manner as if, when the quicksilver in the common weather-glass stood as *stormy*, we were to raise it by some forcible pressure to settle fair, and then be greatly astonished that it continued raining."[44]

In the short run, wages are determined by a mixture of the supply of "funds" with the available liquid capital resources. If there is a particularly large demand for labor, the level of wages could be pushed upward in the short run. But in the longer perspective, the good fortune of these workers would soon find expression in increased numbers of children, who, entering the labor market, quickly press wages down again to their natural "subsistence level."

This regulating mechanism, which forced wages to assume their natural level in covering the costs of subsistence, nevertheless, required time for its operation, since "labour is a commodity which cannot be increased and diminished at pleasure."[45]

But even before an increase in population succeeded in reducing real wages, it was probable that rises in the price of food would have reduced the value of the increase in wages. Malthus's investigation had shown the need to hold a watchful eye on the development of population and "regulate the increase of their numbers and to render less frequent among them early and improvident marriages."[46]

The problem of food is often a more difficult question to resolve; Ricardo thought that the only guarantee against the catastrophe of hunger lay in the industriousness and inventiveness of the population that, through finding new machines and products, continuously increased demand. In countries where the population had few demands and was content with the cheapest of foodstuffs, the threat of hunger appeared with even small downturns in the annual harvest, for in such countries there were no industries that could produce anything that could be exchanged for bread with neighboring countries: "The friends of humanity cannot but wish that in all the countries the labouring classes should have a taste for comforts and enjoyments, and that they would be stimulated by all legal means in their exertions to produce them."[47]

If the population is encouraged to be rich rather than merely to cover the necessities of life, they would demand more of such products as "tea, sugar, soap, candles," even if their wages are insufficient to purchase "bacon, butter, cheese, linen, shoes, and cloth," which increase in price in the long run as more land is brought under cultivation. In this longer perspective, however, Ricardo thought that since landowners must receive an increasing share of the economic cake in rents, the real wages of workers were bound to fall.

4.3 Taxes

Adam Smith would activate as large a proportion of the population as possible to participate in economic life. He attracted them with the possibility of creating wealth under the protection provided by the institutions of money, markets, and capital against the state and "the frequent visits and odious examination of the tax gatherers."[48]

Taxes had the effect of reducing the industriousness and inhibiting the entrepreneurial activity that provided the means of maintaining and employing a larger population. This is a point of view shared by Ricardo, who considers that "taxation under every form represents but a choice of evils."[49]

Smith had grounded his analysis of taxes upon several rules concerning the general nature of taxation that would serve to shield the productive forces and reduce the number of unproductive state bureaucrats. A good tax, according to Smith, should have the following characteristics: A tax should affect all individuals equally, i.e. in relation to the income that they had managed to earn under the protection of state institutions. A tax should be clearly fixed and not arbitrary in relation to its amount or time and method of payment. A tax should be taken at that time that is convenient for the tax-payer. A tax should land in the state treasury without hindering entrepreneurship more than necessary, without creating smuggling, and without creating income for ineffective tax gatherers.

Ricardo's examination of taxation followed in the footsteps of Adam Smith's. Taxation on agricultural products, for example, would affect consumers and raise the level of wages, which means that the ultimate burden of such a tax would fall upon businesses. The tax on land rents needs to be carefully calculated so that the return on buildings is not also affected, since that is a tax upon capital. A badly managed tax upon land rents would place a burden upon capital and hinder entrepreneurship. Ricardo also maintains, using his land rent theory, that a tax on harvests would fall mainly upon farmers if they did not succeed in raising the price of corn and so pass it on to consumers. The landowner would escape the burden of such a tax, since the lease on his property would have been signed beforehand and would not be changed by the tax. The tax on luxury articles that are used by drones and for mischievous purposes falls quite rightly upon those who consume them, as distinct from a tax on foodstuffs that would first burden workers and thereafter business profits. All tax on wages, according to Ricardo, is "wholly a tax on profits."[50] Moreover, where taxation is used by the state to purchase unproductive manpower, it drives up the price of labor, which further burdens profits. In his discussion of taxation—as with the questions of rents and wages—Ricardo concentrates upon the problem of business profits, a perspective that has a clear relation to business economics.

5. Machines That Rescue Profits But Destroy Economy

The major long-term problem with which business leadership must always struggle, according to David Ricardo, is that "profits can never be increased but by a fall in wages and that there can be no permanent fall of wages but in consequence of a fall of the necessaries on which wages are expended."[51]

In the short-term perspective, it does no harm that the industrial entrepreneur is clever and quick in harvesting a little extra profit as a reward for his suitable reaction to a sudden rise in demand. But the logic of the market soon attracts competitors to the honey pot; when floating capital finds its way to the temporary source of higher profits, marginal investments soon press down the rate of return again to its normal level. If the profits prove all too low, capital then flows into other branches until the level of profits stabilizes itself in each branch, depending upon its conveniences, cleanliness, and so on.

The situation is, however, somewhat worse for farmers. If they were to respond to the market in the short run and increase supply, it would be necessary to increase wage costs with increased production, as poorer land is taken into use. The farmer produces foodstuffs and also pays out his wage costs in foodstuffs, so that as wages rise his workers come to eat up an increased proportion of the harvest. Each year, thus, there would be proportionately less of the harvest left over in the barns for making profits. The wages of workers would tend to increase together with the rents paid to landowners, but the prospects for profits could only be bleak. According to the rules of the game set up by David Ricardo, the day must surely come when

> there must be an end of accumulation; for no capital can yield any profit whatever, and no additional labour can be demanded, and consequently population will have reached its highest point. Long indeed, before this period, the very low rate of profits will have arrested all accumulation, and almost the whole produce of the country will be the property of the owners of land and the receivers of tithes and taxes.[52]

This long-term problem of safeguarding profits cannot be solved through higher prices, new products, or new markets, because it is primarily a question of distribution. In the first place, advises Ricardo, the prices of foodstuffs should be held low since profits would be higher with lower wages, and the level of wages is dependent upon the price of foodstuffs that are in short supply. All other commodities, on the other hand, could be produced in abundance. In order for food production to be secured, it is necessary, paradoxically enough, to liberalize the trade in agricultural products and, beyond this, to encourage all improvements in agricultural productivity. This is to be achieved, on the one hand, through growing new crops, for example, "turnip husbandry,"[53] and using new methods of farming and new sorts of fertilizers; on the other, through reducing the numbers employed on the land through technical improvements like "the plough, and the thrashing machine, economy in the use of horses employed in husbandry and a better knowledge of the veterinary art."[54]

In the best case, these changes could work to eliminate the differences between good and bad soil, so that the level of rents would fall. Ricardo also refers to Malthus, who had likened agriculture with its different qualities of land to a machine park:

> The land has, as I before said, been compared by Mr. Malthus to a great number of machines, all susceptible of continued improvement by the application of capital to them, but yet of very different original qualities and powers. Would it be wise at a great expense to use some of the worst of these machines, when at a less expense we could hire the very best from our neighbours?[55]

The striving to rescue business profits would lead to improvements and rationalizations, and it is at this point that Ricardo makes his most interesting observations from the point of view of business economics.

In the third edition of *The Principles of Political Economy and Taxation*, Ricardo has included a chapter, "On Machinery," where he makes a definite departure from Adam Smith's optimism that had regarded the division of labor as something beneficial to all classes of society. Through rationalization, the prices of industrial products would fall, the landowners would be able to purchase more for their land rents, and the inventors of new machines and methods would earn an extra profit in the short time it took for their new machines and methods to spread throughout the economy. The machines and inventions that are not shielded by patents or monopolies of knowledge would be free for all to exploit because for the "materials . . . pressure of the atmosphere [and] . . . elasticity of steam . . . no charge is made . . . because they are inexhaustible and at every man's disposal."[56]

Since machines could not become a monopoly of a new owning class, they would lead to price falls, so that the whole population could purchase more goods and commodities, expanding the arsenal of things that satisfied the infinite number of psychological desires. This, writes Ricardo in his new chapter, is an all too optimistic view. Landowners and capitalists may well gain from the use of the new machines, but the working population at large, all those whom Adam Smith would attract with the activities of his pump of wealth, would lose in the process that would result in a condition where "population will become redundant and the situation of the labouring classes will be that of distress and poverty."[57]

Optimism changes to pessimism as a result of a mistake that Ricardo thought he had discovered in Smith's reasoning. The machines have their price, and when the businessman invests his capital in such machines, he ties up a large part of his capital in fixed assets. That part of his capital that remains untied, "the one fund . . . upon which the labouring class mainly depend may diminish."[58]

If, for example, a businessman has 20,000 in capital, of which 7,000 is tied up in buildings and machines, he is left with 13,000 for foodstuffs that could be paid out as wages to workers in the course of the year. The yearly gross production for this business is 15,000 and (since $15,000 - 13,000 = 2,000$) 2,000 is the net production. The profit of the business on its capital of 20,000 is 2,000 in the form of products. At this point, the businessman decides to make an improvement through the introduction of a new machine. During the following year he arranges for half the work force to construct the new machine while the other half continues with its usual activities. During the year in which the machine is built, the company earns only 7,500 gross (half of 15,000), since those engaged in this task cannot contribute to the production of commodities. At the close of the year, the businessman, thus, stands with his machine and a capital of 7,500 from which he substracts 2,000 as profits. The result is that he now has only 5,500 in untied capital with which to employ workers. If now the new machine and the reduced number of workers can produce for him a net profit of 2,000, the businessman should be reasonably pleased. But a number of people now find themselves outside the house that pumps the wealth. They no longer participate in the economic circulation, since they are unemployed. Ricardo admits that the machine could produce more than 2,000 in profits and that the increased profits could be used to employ more workers. He admits, furthermore, that businessmen in reality rarely would invest half their capital in machinery during a single year, as his calculations had assumed, but rather would spread their investments over a number of years. Nevertheless, argues Ricardo, international competition would in any event make it necessary to invest in machinery, so the matter cannot be ignored. Many of those who became unemployed in the direct production could also possibly find employment in machine building or services. However, Ricardo is quite convinced that mechanization would come to reduce the demand for labor, although he does not have much to say on the matter. As a warning he provides an example of what could happen if this mode of attempting to rescue business profits were to be adopted.

The day could come when rationalization and innovation would so reduce employment that economic circulation would stop. The cloth manufacturer in a mechanized textile industry is uninterested in procuring more food from the farmer or landowner than what he and his family can consume. On the other hand, he has no workers to feed; since he operates in a competitive branch of industry, there is no way in which he can raise the level of profits beyond the normal without it being forced down again by the market prices. The farmer or landowner who wants cloth must invest in his own cloth-making industry, using agricultural capital for this purpose. The price of food would have sunk so far through rationalization and savings in labor costs that those who had use for cloth would have to produce it themselves. The institutions of market, money, and stocks would cease to function, and the pump of wealth would be reduced to a small automatic pump for the satisfaction of entrepreneurs' own needs and the exclusion of the majority. The feudal system would be re-introduced, and the unemployed population would once again become dependent upon what landowners provide from their harvests for unproductive labor or luxurous consumption. According to Ricardo, economic development has culminated in a negative process because of the entrepreneurs' attempt to rescue net production (2,000), while the preservation or expansion of gross production (15,000) lay neither in their interest nor in that of the nation: "The employing a greater number of men would enable us neither to add a man to our army and navy, nor to contribute one guinea more in taxes."[59]

Such is the fate that would befall the economy from an unremitting attempt to rescue profits at the expense of production in the Ricardian school of thought.

6. The Concrete in the Abstractions

Drawing his inspiration from Malthus, David Ricardo came to take a position somewhere halfway between Quesnay and Smith. He accepted the institutional reality described by Adam Smith, but he rejected Smith's social psychology in favor of a more physiocratic-inspired worldview where population and food provide the concrete limits of the economy. The market was a temporary phenomenon that needed to be taken into consideration in economic calculations, but the greater challenge lay in long-term development that obeyed rules of a less subjective and psychological nature. Ricardo does not deny that the businessman lives according to a market logic that drives him toward upholding the level of profits in his branch: "It is then the desire, which every capitalist has, of diverting his funds from a less to a more profitable employment that prevents the market price of commodities from continuing for any length of time either much above or much below their natural price."[60]

The logic of the market explained why prices tended to move toward their natural level, which Ricardo, in turn, attempted to explain through the logic of production in business life.

In the rules for distribution and value, Ricardo often included elements of knowledge drawn from the nature of physical reality. If it is known how many quarters of corn ten men can produce, and how many quarters ten additional men would produce, then it would be known how much the price of corn was likely to change if the corn production was handled by twenty men rather than ten. If it is known how many quarters of corn a worker and his family eat up in a year, and how much of industrial products they purchase, then it could be calculated how much the worker's wage would rise if agricultural production increased. If the wage increase of the workers is known, then it would be possible to calculate what would be left over as profits for farmers when they had paid their workers and the rent to the landowners. It is against a background of the realities of physical production that Ricardo seeks to show how the situation of value, measured in money, could lead to changes.

This concretization, however, was founded upon the abstract supposition that the quantity of labor employed provided the ultimate measure of value and that this absolute value, in turn, determined the relative exchange values of commodities in the market. The entrepreneur's logic of production would lead eventually to a reduction in the value of his products. Ricardo maintains that decisions concerning rationalization and innovation are taken on purely physical grounds, the change from the use of manpower to the use of machines occurring when the entrepreneur believes that the machine could produce that physical surplus that he had previously enjoyed as profits. That the value of production sank did not imply that objects had become less useful or that those who used them felt less rich. The only thing that this means is that objects are no longer the building blocks of economic circulation, that they do not function as receipts for inputs of labor and thereby as proof of participation in national production.

Ricardo shows the shortcomings in Adam Smith's vision of "the commercial society" as an overarching solution for the questions of distribution and production. But what does he offer instead? The lack of work could hardly be expected to be hailed as a newly won freedom, but rather condemned as unemployment. Keynes described Ricardo as the supreme of abstract thinkers:

> Ricardo offered us the supreme intellectual achievement, unattainable by weaker spirits, of adopting a hypothetical world remote from experiences as though it were the world of experience and then living in it consistently. With most of his successors common sense cannot help breaking in—with injury to their logical consistency.[61]

The question of whether David Ricardo really was a concrete economist must naturally depend upon how far we could consider that he succeeded in capturing a physical reality in his suppositions, and an institutional reality in the rules he postulated in his models of economic processes. Perhaps there was something a trifle more concrete in his abstractions than Keynes had allowed.

Notes

1. John Rae, *Life of Adam Smith*, p. 288.
2. David Ricardo, *The Principles of Political Economy and Taxation*, p. 3.
3. Piero Sraffa, ed., *The Works and Correspondence of David Ricardo*, Volume IV, p. 15.
4. Ibid., Volume III, p. 21.
5. Ibid., Volume VI, p. 21.
6. Ibid., Volume VI, p. 63.
7. Ibid., Volume VI, p. 39.
8. Thomas Malthus, *An Essay on the Principle of Population as it Affects the Future Improvement of Society with Remarks on the Speculations of Mr. Godwin, M. Condorcet, and Oher Writers*, p. 11.
9. Ibid., p. 325.
10. Ibid., p. 313.
11. Ibid., p. 189.
12. Ibid., p. 229.
13. Ibid., p. 159.
14. Sraffa, *Works and Correspondence*, Volume VI, p. 64.
15. Ibid., Volume IV, p. 398.
16. Adam Smith, *An Inquiry into the Nature and Causes of the Wealth of Nations*, Volume I, p. 60.
17. Malthus, *Essay on the Principle of Population* p. 159.
18. Smith, *Inquiry into the Nature and Causes*, p. 60.
19. Ricardo, *Principle of Political Economy and Taxation*, p. 51.
20. Ibid., p. 176.
21. Ibid., p. 15; Sraffa, *Works and Correspondence*, Volume IV, p. 374.
22. Ibid., p. 15.
23. Ibid., p. 6.
24. Ibid., p. 9.
25. Ibid., p. 262.
26. Ibid., p. 6.
27. Ibid., p. 23.
28. Ibid., p. 26.
29. Ibid., p. 26.
30. Ibid., p. 81.
31. Ibid., p. 83.
32. Ibid., p. 160.
33. Boyd Hilton, *Corn, Cash, Commerce, the Economic Policies of the Tory Governments 1815–1830*, p. 6.
34. Ibid., p. 120.
35. Ibid., p. 19.
36. Sraffa, *Works and Correspondence*, Volume IV, p. 17.
37. Ricardo, *Principle of Political Economy and Taxation*, p. 34.
38. Ibid., p. 36.
39. Ibid., p. 36.
40. Ibid., p. 220.
41. Ibid., p. 36.
42. Sraffa, *Works and Correspondence*, Volume IV, p. 13.
43. Ricardo, *Principle of Political Economy and Taxation*, p. 61.
44. Ibid., p. 143.

45. Ibid., p. 105.
46. Ibid., p. 61.
47. Ibid., p. 57.
48. Smith, *Inquiry into the Nature and Causes*, Volume II, p. 312.
49. Ricardo, *Principle of Political Economy and Taxation*, p. 106.
50. Ibid., p. 140
51. Ibid., p. 80.
52. Ibid., pp. 71–72.
53. Ibid., p. 43.
54. Ibid., p. 44.
55. Sraffa, *Works and Correspondence*, Volume IV, p. 34.
56. Ricardo, *Principles of Political Economy and Taxation*, p. 34.
57. Ibid., p. 266.
58. Ibid., p. 264.
59. Ibid., p. 235.
60. Ibid., p. 50.
61. John M. Keynes, *The General Theory of Employment, Interest and Money*, p. 192.

4

Karl Marx: A Ricardian Management Scientist

1. The Call of the Critics

The German poet Heinrich Heine wrote of his friends, the "doctors of revolution," as follows: "The more or less secret leaders of the German Communists are the great logicians, the strongest of which have their background in the Hegelian school. These are without doubt the most talented and energetic heads in Germany."[1]

Among these "doctors of revolution," Karl Marx (1818–1883) became the best known. Heine and Marx had, in fact, met in Paris in the early 1840s at the time when Marx began his voyages of discovery into the literature of political economy. Marx had come to Paris from Cologne after having published a series of articles in the *Rheinische Zeitung für Politik, Handel und Gewerbe* concerning the social conditions of the Moselle peasants. This had proved the drop that caused the cup of the Prussian censor to run over. Already in his first political article, Marx had attacked censorship and ridiculed its stated policy of liberalization. He was then in Bonn where he had come from Berlin after writing a doctoral thesis on the difference between the philosophies of nature in the Democritian and Epicurean schools of ancient Greece. The thesis, however, had been presented in the University of Jena since Marx had considered it below his dignity to allow the reactionary ideologists at the University of Berlin to judge his work.

He had come to Berlin from Bonn in 1836 with the intention of studying law. His father, a high court judge, considered that young Marx had displayed a good head for studies during his schooldays at Trier and would secure a safe future in a successful legal career. When Karl during his first term decided to study no fewer than nine different subjects—everything from art and cultural history to legal subjects—his father began to worry for his son's future. Following problems of drunkenness and dueling, Heinrich Marx decided to send his son to Berlin instead of continuing his studies in Bonn. Marx junior increasingly gave up legal studies in favor of philosophy and tried to cover up the change and calm his father's fears in the letters he wrote him. Kant, Fichte, and particularly Hegel—a Berlin professor who had died five years earlier—provided the foundations for Karl Marx's intellectual development and left clear marks on his work that can be traced through to *Das Kapital*, which appeared some thirty years later.

Karl Marx trained his special talent of translating abstract philosophical arguments into powerful and concrete political polemic upon his radical, middle-class student friends in the so-called Doctors' Club.[2] These critical discussions presumably dealt with such subjects as the role of the state, the implications of law, and the law's capacity to control conduct. It is in this atmosphere of legal criticism that Karl Marx glides ever further away from his father's wish that he study to be a lawyer. Having failed to obtain a position at the University of Bonn following receipt of his doctoral degree, Karl Marx opts for a career as a political journalist. Now began his serious life work, which found expression in a series of newspaper articles and books, together with a flood of draft manuscripts and other material that was reproduced word for word in the MEGA (Marx-Engels Gesamtausgabe) series in Berlin. During his lifetime, however, Marx's newspaper series attracted only limited attention, while his books were in the main subjected to "the nagging criticism of the mice." The first of the three volumes of *Das Kapital*, which appeared in 1867, the only part completed by Marx himself, contained much of the thinking on political economy that had been developed in innumerable earlier manuscripts and had its philosophical roots grounded in his doctoral thesis. It is particularly with this section of *Das Kapital* that we are concerned in this chapter.* It is where Marx develops a concretization of Ricardo's abstract theory   a Ricardian theory of business economy and management.

Karl Marx's major work, *Das Kapital*, was given the subtitle *Criticism of Political Economy*. Marx maintains that contemporary Europe could be described in terms of a certain form of economic reality, namely, the capitalist mode of production. Its purest form, according to Marx, was to be found in England, where he had arrived in 1849 and would spend the rest of his life as a writer, pamphleteer, and political organizer. He lived a meager existence on the sale of articles, collection from socialist friends on the Continent, gifts and support from his friend Friedrich Engels, and occasional loans from a rich Dutch uncle. While he by no means belonged to the working class whose misery he describes, he certainly knew from his own experience what it was like to live in poverty where there was frequently no food for the day. During his most difficult time in the Soho district of London, he lost three of his daughters. Nevertheless, he fought on with his writings and newspaper articles, which were published, among other places, in an American newspaper. Marx remained for the rest of his life a German refugee who mixed for the most part with other German

*All english quotes were translated by the author.

refugees. The England that he criticized was known to him only as an outsider and observer, as a reader of newspaper articles, and from a seat in the British Museum. He made clever use of the contemporary official investigations and social reportage concerning industrialization that reached the general public.

Friedrich Engels had written in 1844, after two years as a traveling salesman for his father's cotton factory in Manchester, one such study that had been published under the title *The Condition of the Working Class in England*. It was with Engels that Marx had first visited England in 1845. The reality of economic conditions in Britain was easier to grasp than that in Germany, since as distinct from the latter country there already existed in Britain a fairly developed system for the collection of social statistics. Parliamentary commissions were appointed to investigate conditions in the factories, and laws were passed concerning maximum working hours and public health. These were enforced with the aid of factory inspectors and doctors whose detailed reports made "the contemporary process of change understandable"[3] even for the German doctor of philosophy sitting in his seat in the reading room of the British Museum. The reports and legislation of the British state provided Karl Marx with a keyhole through which he could peer out on economic reality and compare what he saw with that which he gleaned from studying the works of the political economists. Not least with the help of the reports of the factory inspectors, Marx attempted to show that management and business life followed rules that were formed through conflict between different social groups or classes. This was held to be true for earlier forms of economic organization but it applied also to the contemporary nineteenth-century industrialized scene, which was something that the political economists had chosen to ignore:

> The economists go to work in a strange manner. It appears as if for them there are only two kinds of institutions, the artificial and the natural. The feudal institutions are the artificial and the bourgeois are natural. In this manner, the economists are like theologians who also distinguish two kinds of religion. Every religion that is not their own they characterize as a human invention, while their own religion is a revelation from God.[4]

Marx appears to have been cross and hopeless in dealing with people who held ideas differing from his, and he placed most of the political economists in this category. Either they were "dwarf economists" or idiots and "sycophants" with "limited brains," or they were "vulgar economists" and capitalist ideologists who through their "kretinismus" could never make an honest attempt to understand the real rules of the capitalist society in a critical spirit. The vulgar economists were "Masters of Plagiarism" who changed economics from a science to a "bourgeoisie duty." They merely repeated what the "agents of the bourgeoisie mode of production" themselves maintained was the truth. They were engaged in systematizing and rationalizing these myths which were finally declared to be eternal truths.[5] All were idiots with the possible exception of Adam Smith and

David Ricardo, whose theories, Marx considered, were marked by an unusual "lack of prejudice and love of truth."[6] It was Adam Smith who had clarified the ideological basis of the rules of capitalism, but since he lived in a nonindustrialized world his analysis had its limitations. It was rather in the abstract theories of David Ricardo that the rules of capitalism were best reflected. Marx thus took the Ricardian theory of how the pump of wealth functioned as it stood, but with a serious reservation concerning the interest on capital. The business economics of Karl Marx arose, as we shall see, from a hunt for the concrete cause of interest on capital.

2. The Abstract Theory of the Market

Both Ricardo and Marx considered that a scientific theory was an abstract explanation that depended upon the scientist's ability to find the logic underlying economic reality. Marx emphasizes, however, that this perspective implies a difference between a science of nature and social conditions because "with the analysis of economic forms can neither the microscope nor the chemical reagent be of use. The power of abstraction replaces them both."[7]

With this background in German philosophy of history, it is also natural for Marx to adopt a more relativistic view of logic than Ricardo. The economic logic that explained capitalism was, for example, something different from the functional logic that explained feudalism. Every epoch had its own form of logic that controlled human actions: "The formula quite obviously belongs to a form of society where the process of production rules over men, and not men over the production process."[8]

The difference between Ricardo and Marx consists also in the experience of a further fifty years of intensive economic debate. Marx could now pick and choose among the literature, selecting those contributions that he thought provided a correct logical description of the functioning of the pump of wealth in capitalist markets. He read the works of the political economists in something of the same spirit as a sociologist of religion may approach the Bible. The task was to chart a comprehensive industrial worldview with both moral and material consequences.

Marx is particularly impressed by Ricardo's labor theory of value, and it was this that he had in mind when he wrote, "A scientific analysis of competition is possible only when the inner nature of capitalism has been understood, precisely in the same manner that the movements of heavenly bodies only become understandable for those who know their real movements which are not observable through the senses."[9]

The concrete economy that it is possible to observe with our senses—the useful objects, the craftsman's goal-directed activity, tools, and techniques—is treated by Marx entirely in a Kantian spirit as forms of the perception of physical phenomena. It is these *Erscheinungsformen,* "apparent forms," that it is the duty of political economics to penetrate beyond to the deeper-lying logic. Knowledge of the physical aspect of the economy, thus, had little to do with the science of political economy: "The usefulness of commodities belongs to its own discipline: the knowledge of commodities."[10]

Abstract economic theory is regarded by Marx in his Kantian analogy as the attempt to find the essential nature of things, their meaning as components of the pump of wealth.

Das Kapital begins with the following sentence:

> The riches of the society in which the capitalist mode of production dominates, express themselves as an "enormous commodity collection" of which the elementary form is the single commodity. Our investigation, therefore, begins with the analysis of the commodity.[11]

As distinct from other economists, Marx begins with an analysis of objects rather than values and human evaluations. An object that possesses an "apparent form" of a useful object in its everyday appearance is regarded by economists as an exchange phenomenon and becomes a commodity or "das Ding an sich." When Marx begins his analysis of commodities and their exchange values, he does not choose beavers, fish, or deer as examples. He allows rather a coat and twenty yards of cloth to meet and be exchanged on a market. He dramatizes his examples by allowing his objects to think and talk to each other, because it is only as a market phenomenon in exchange relations that an object becomes a commodity imbued with value: "One can turn and twist an isolated commodity as long as one will, but she yet remains uncomprehending as a value-object."[12]

"Miss Linen" considers herself good enough to be exchanged on the market for "Mr. Coat" in whose "buttoned up appearance" (*zugeknöpften Erscheinung*) she recognizes a beautiful kindred value-soul.[13] To the economist who correctly understands their market nature, these objects as commodities will come to whisper: "[O]ur value in use interests human beings. . . . As objects we interest ourselves in our own value. We reveal this for you in the manner that we relate to each other as commodity-objects. This relation to each other can be described as exchange value."[14]

Within the pump of wealth, objects circulate as commodities. An object becomes a commodity as a result of an independent contribution of labor. Adam Smith's division of labor was a necessary but insufficient precondition since, for example, Indian villages, too, possessed a division of labor, but products there were not exchanged as commodities in a market. Even within the factory, objects remain as use-objects. They are not purchased and sold as commodities among different production departments. It is in the market that objects are transformed into commodities and begin to babble their "exchange language" in dollars and cents.

But Miss Linen's romance with Mr. Coat is not something private or incomprehensible for outsiders. Two commodities are exchanged for each other because they have something in common; this common denominator has nothing to do with their physically useful properties. The coat is exchanged for linen because they both contain the same quantity of labor. In a poetic formulation of Ricardo's theory, Marx declares that the coat and the linen are a "jelly of labour."[15] How different is the tailor's craft from that of the weaver, yet the efforts of both contribute to the "productive flow from the human brain, muscle, nerve, hand, and so on, and in this respect are they both human work."[16]

Two objects, different in use, are comparable as commodities with equal amounts of "abstract labor." Obviously it can happen that the weaver does not get that price in the market that his personal calculation had led him to expect, even when he had been particularly careful to reckon up his labor costs per yard of linen. The abstract work that determines the exchange value of a commodity is not a question of the personal work of the individual weaver, but rather the socially determined average labor that is fixed by the competitive market. The value of a commodity, in other words, is determined behind the backs of the commodity producers. If the weaver does not keep up with the technical developments that are definitive for determining the average labor value, he would find himself unable to compete with more effective producers. It is, thus, competition and labor value that determine exchange values in capitalist markets.

Following in the footsteps of Adam Smith, Marx considers that the first step in the economic process lies in the observation that both the tailor and the weaver have their respective crafts and that they produce cloth and coats, not for their own use, but rather for exchange on the market. In order that trading could move beyond simple barter, cloth against coat, money is introduced as a general means of exchange, a public or social equivalent form. The property of money in being exchangeable for all other commodities on the market "clings fast to certain kinds of commodities or crystallizes itself into a form of money."[17]

With the introduction of money, which is the second step in economic development, the circulation of commodities begins. The weaver now sells his cloth on the market for money and then appears as a buyer of, for example, an attractive bible. The money now goes to the bible seller, who perhaps drinks it up in the nearest tavern, thus exchanging it for wine and spirits. When the cloth, bible, and alcoholic beverages are worn out, tattered, and consumed, respectively, they no longer exist in their physically natural skin (*Naturalhaut*), although thanks to money they survive in their exchange value form or gold skin (*Goldhaut*).[18] The suction of the pump arises when a commodity is consumed and thus removed from circulation, and someone sees the chance of obtaining the desirable coins that remain. This someone produces for this purpose a commodity of exactly the same value as the coins. The reason is this: "He can take out of circulation only money against which he has set in commodities."[19] The market is the great social retort into which everything is sucked in to emerge again crystallized into a money form.

The retort also has a small hole through which the gold and silver of money could be let in, but Marx emphasizes that money comes into circulation "as a commodity with a given value." When the businessman purchases cotton for a hundred pounds and sells it for a hundred and ten, it appears as if something mystical has happened in the social retort that cannot be explained in terms of the law of circulation of equal exchange. Through the supposition of the given value of money, in the footsteps of Ricardo, Marx rejects the theory that the amount of money can influence commodity values. How is it then possible for businessmen to create value if they operate in markets where everything is exchanged equally against other things?

3. The Enterprise as a Creator of Value

3.1 The Mystery of Value

On what grounds could it be held that a profitable business creates additional value for society as a whole?

First, it could be argued that it is an "inexplicable privilege" for all sellers to dispose of their commodities at prices 10 percent higher than they had paid for them. But if all sellers in the market had such a privilege, then all prices would rise, and this would mean that businessmen would be forced to pay the higher price for their purchases. The privilege, thus, cannot explain profits.

A further possibility is that there exists a special social class that only consumes. This consumer class is responsible for purchasing commodities at prices above their value. But, asks Marx, from where does this class obtain its money? In a market economy all money must come from the owners of commodities. If such a consumer class exists that obtains some part of resources without payment, then a profit would appear that was at the cost of the owner of commodities.

A third possible explanation is that buyers and sellers in the market are "smart" (*pfiffig sein*)[20] as individuals. A clever salesman fools a buyer into paying 50 pounds for a commodity that is only worth 40 pounds. Such cleverness, however, maintains Marx, cannot explain profits as a social phenomenon. Despite the seller obtaining 50 pounds and the purchaser 40 pounds, the total value in society is only 90 pounds, and this is not a pound more than before the theft was perpetrated.

Such explanations are clearly inadequate, according to Marx, who holds that, although value is created in society, it is not possible to explain this phenomenon from the point of view of the political economists' theories of circulation. On the contrary, such theories serve only to mystify the true situation. That Adam Smith, the honest economist, had suffered no pangs of conscience (*Gewissenskrupeln*) in proposing his theory of profits, which was in contradiction to his theory of value, was understandable because he had had so many confused notions. Ricardo, on the other hand, had touched upon the problem several times but had been blinded by his bourgeois background: "The classical political economy touches several times upon the truth of the matter without, however, formulating it consciously. This it cannot do so long as it is a prisoner of its bourgeoisie skin."[21]

Marx accepted, in other words, that profits had something to do with value. He also accepted that Ricardo's labor theory of value was correct. From this point, he takes over the notion of the Physiocrats concerning the creation of physical values through agriculture, and transfers this eighteenth-century idea to nineteenth-century conditions of industrial manufacturing. The physiocratic farmer had seen the surplus value of his labors with his own eyes, perhaps as it lay in the barn to be sold on the market. Everyone could see how the farmer divided his labor between the landowner's farms and his own kitchen garden, where he farmed for his own use. In the factory, the situation is more difficult to see:

> The worker in manufacturing does not increase the physical mass, but rather only changes its form. . . .In manufacturing one does not see, in any case, how the worker produces his means of life, nor the surplus over his means of life that is produced. The process is negotiated through buying and selling, through circulation's different phases, and requires an analysis of exchange value itself in order to be understood.[22]

What the Physiocrats could concretely see in agriculture, Marx would now make visible in the case of industrial manufacturing with the aid of Ricardo's abstract theory of value. In the pump of wealth, according to Marx, value is not determined by physical mass but rather through "a determined existing social mode of activity";[23] that is, through work. All profits arise from the market, but the laws of the market do not explain how this occurs. The capital "could also not arise from circulation, and at the same time could equally not arise without circulation. They must arise both within and outside it."[24] This paradoxical mystery finds its logical solution when it is realized that a commodity, which according to market rules was purchased for money and was in the possession of a business, is consumed in a purely private manner outside the market, and this gives rise to surplus value. Now the only commodity that according to the theory of Ricardo had this property was that of labor: "[T]he owner of money finds such a commodity on the market—the capacity to work or manpower."[25]

The worker appears in the market as the free owner of his own physical and psychological powers, which are placed at the disposal of the businessman, in return for money. The businessman then uses this labor power to create value just as the Physiocrat's farmer did on agriculture. It is in the management of business enterprises, not in the market, that it is possible to see how this process of creating value proceeds. Marx begins his study of management with the following words:

> The consumption of manpower, like all other commodities, draws it out of the sphere of market circulation. Let us also leave this lively, shallow sphere that

is open to the gaze of all, and follow the owner of money and owner of labour in the veiled home of production where it reads on the entrance: "No admittance except on business."[26]

It is, thus, this veiled world of management that it is necessary to penetrate in order to resolve the mystery of profits.

3.2 The Exploitation of People in Production

Suppose that all commodities are worth their labor. Then the labor itself is worth the period of work that it takes to manufacture what is necessary for the upkeep of the worker and his family. This period of work is what Marx calls "the necessary working time." If the worker's wife slaves away at a spinning machine and his children draw loaded trucks in the coal mines, the worker does not require the same amount of wage to maintain his family at the existence minimum. His necessary working time is reduced. When, moreover, the worker's food is cheapened through the use of chemicals, such as when the baker mixes "Alum, Soap, Ashes, Chalk . . ."[27] in the bread, the businessman could reduce the worker's wage level even further. It should not, however, be imagined that the worker could go home earlier because of these factors. On the contrary, the employer's major concern is to hold the worker at the workplace as long as possible. The more work that is laid out in the factory, the more the value that is created, and the more earned by the businessman from the sale of the commodities that contain this labor. This is, of course, dependent upon the businessman using a technology that is not more expensive in practice than that of his competitors. The difference between what he pays for labor and what he receives from sales is surplus value. Surplus value, according to Marx, is to be regarded as unpaid labor that, because of the market situation, falls into the pockets of the businessmen rather than of the workers.

In the market it is necessary for both businessmen and workers to follow the laws of the state, but behind the factory walls the businessman is free to construct his own penal code. It is he alone who decides how machines, raw materials, energy, and manpower are to be consumed. He minimizes the prices at which he purchases and maximizes the returns from sales, driven by an evil, vampirelike rationality. With a crafty, knowing glance (*schlauem Kennerblick*)[28], he picks out the means of production and manpower for the purpose of satisfying his passion (*Heisshunger*) for surplus value. The workers are, for example, sent to the cotton mill where they stand before a mountain of raw material and rows of machines. The cotton sucks up their labor power, which, together with the stored-up work in the machines, transforms the raw material into yarn and cloth. The percentage profit is a poor measure of the creation of value, which should rather be calculated in terms of the size of the surplus value. For this purpose it is essential to investigate the difference between the workers' necessary working time and the actual time they are forced to work in the factory under the despotic business economic regime. With an example drawn from the cotton industry, Marx demonstrates how such an investigation should be undertaken:

> Take a spinning mill with 10,000 spindles, that manufactures yarn no 32 from American cotton with a pound of yarn per spindle. Material lost is 6%. Each week 10,600 pounds of cotton are used to manufacture 10,000 pounds of yarn, and 600 pounds disappear as waste. In April of 1871 this cotton cost 7¾ d per pound, so for 10,600 pounds the cost was about 342 pounds sterling. The 10,000 spindles, inclusive of prespinning machines and steam engine, cost 1 pound sterling per spindle, i.e. 10,000 pounds sterling. The yearly depreciation is reckoned at 10%, i.e. 1,000 pounds sterling or 20 pounds per week. The hire of the factory building is 300 pounds sterling or 6 pounds sterling per week. Coal (4 pounds per hour and horsepower, for a 100 horsepower (indicator) and 60 hours a week inclusive of heating) 11 tons per week at 8 sh 6 d per ton costs 4 ½ pounds sterling per week; gas 1 pound sterling per week; oil 4½ pounds sterling per week. Altogether, energy 10 pounds sterling per week. The constant value part, thus, is 378 pounds sterling per week. Wages for labour are 52 pounds sterling per week. The price of yarn is 12¼ d per pound so that 10,000 pounds equals 510 pounds sterling, and surplus value is thus 510 − 430 = 80 pounds sterling. Deducting the constant portion of the value of the product, which plays no part in the creation of value, we have 510 − 378 = 132 pounds sterling, as the value created weekly. Of this 52 pounds represents variable capital and 80 surplus value. The rate of surplus value is therefore $80/52 = 153^{11}/_{13}\%$. In an average ten-hour working day this implies that: Necessary labour time = $3\ ^{31}/_{33}$ hours and surplus labour = $6\ ^{2}/_{33}$ hours.[29]

Marx maintains that value could be created in one of two ways in a business. He talks of what he terms the absolute and the relative surplus value. Surplus value increases absolutely when people are forced to work longer in a factory. The workers are locked in, forbidden rest times, and forced to eat while operating machines; they sleep on the factory floor and work in day-long shifts. The reports of the factory inspectors provide evidence of how the absolute surplus value is increased through such theft of people's labor. When the absolute surplus value cannot be increased any further, the businessman then attempts to increase the relative surplus value. With a fixed length for the working day, surplus labor time could be increased through a reduction of the necessary labor time. This could occur through a reduction in wages, although Marx also saw another possibility here that is through the "intensification" of labor.

3.3 Working Time

In order to satisfy the needs of existence for one day, a human being requires commodities that take six hours to produce. Nevertheless, workers are required to work twelve hours in the factory. The results find expression in the form of diseases, epidemics, as well as in small and physically weak beings who are worn out after ten years of factory labor. This is evident not only from the factory inspectors' reports but also from the official statistics, which show, for example, how height declined among recruits to the army. The working situation had become considerably worse than in the previous century, and the working week stretches out to its utmost moral limit, which leaves only Sunday free. It is such obvious abuses that led to the various reforms that Marx regarded as being an integral part of the capitalist system rather than as political actions to stop the economic exploitation of labor. He reviews, for example, five laws that were passed between 1802 and 1833 for the purpose of limiting working times, but he claims their effect to be nil because they lack the means for any effective enforcement of them. Marx bemoans the fact that people no longer are outraged by child labor or by the terrible working conditions of women, and he is indignant at a legal system that allows minors to be bound by contracts and parents to sell their children as slaves in the so-called era of freedom. When a ten-hour working day is proposed, it is opposed not least by professors in the pay of businessmen with a rather confused argument. In 1837 the cotton manufacturers of Manchester called in an economics professor from Oxford to provide scientific arguments against the ten-hour working day. This professor made, according to Marx, a very confused calculation, dividing the sum of the annual fixed and working capital and its annual profit, by the number of hours worked. The working day was 11½ hours, whereas the professor had assumed that the profit of the business was earned in just the last working hour. On this false premise, he had argued that any shortening of the working day would prove to be catastrophic.

Marx points out that the calculation has two large errors. The first is that the capital costs are transferred to the product via human labor in the factory. If fewer hours are worked, then the capital costs in the factory would also decrease and consequently less cotton and fewer machines would be used during the year. The reduction in working hours thus results in savings on raw materials and the means of production. Second, it is always necessary to take wages into consideration and compare a day's wage against the sales value of a day's production. It would then be seen that the surplus labor time is much greater than one hour. The shortening of the working day to ten hours would certainly reduce the businessman's surplus value, but it would hardly transform a profit into a clear loss.

Heroic factory inspectors fought an uneven battle with both factory owners and ministers. The factory owners did everything in their power to hinder an effective control of working hours, and the ministers preferred to reckon with the votes of factory owners in the House of Commons than with the number of hours worked in the factories. Marx is, nevertheless, convinced that the capitalist factory owners would in the end be forced to give in to public opinion, which would demand a shorter working day. The consequence would be that businessmen would have to give up their demands for absolute surplus value and concentrate instead upon more sophisticated methods of increasing the relative surplus value.

3.4 Work Organization and Working Machines

The manager would first and foremost attempt to reduce the wages and the necessary labor time. Surplus value consists of unpaid labor. If the wage cannot be reduced, the manager would resort to a kind of experiment in the nuclear physics of value. Marx explains it as an attempt to condense the degree of labor in the "porous" working hours through "compressing together a larger mass of work" so that the worker gives out more energy (*mehr Kraft*) in the same time period.[30] This intensification of work would mean that the workers become exhausted in a shorter time. It would increase production without lowering the value of production despite the working time remaining unchanged. Marx, who is anxious to show that the businessman's clever exploitation of labor always leads to an increase in surplus value, is forced at this point to an obvious departure from David Ricardo's labor theory of value. Management, according to Marx, uses two methods to manipulate time in this respect: organization and mechanization.

Adam Smith had already pointed to the division of labor as an important starting point for the new economic society. Even so, he devoted only 2 of the 800 pages of his economic teachings to the now famous example of the pin makers. Marx believes that it was probably a mistake for Adam Smith to see the division of labor in the market and firm as one and the same natural process. In the market the division of labor into different trades and crafts is dependent upon chance, whereas in the factory it occurs under the command of the capitalist and in accordance with his plan of organization. In the market, work is divided among categories that sell commodities to each other, but in the factory there is no market and work is distributed in a single process of production.

But all businesses are not, according to Marx, capitalist organizations. When a businessman has so many workers employed that the total surplus value he obtains exceeds a normal working wage, the business assumes a capitalist character. When the businessman has become a capitalist, he no longer regards his employees as craftsmen and individuals but rather as an amount of labor with a certain average laboring capacity. This capitalist mode of equality has its origins in the Christian religion. When the businessman becomes a capitalist and increases the number of employees, he could either assemble different handworkers under one roof as, for example, the wagon manufacturer assembled "the tailor, locksmith, beltmaker," or he could like the papermaker or pin manufacturer bring together several handworkers of the same kind. When this occurs, it is not long before each worker is assigned a limited and particular element in the overall process of production. Different specialities arise, and Marx provides the following untranslatable example of all the special operations that would develop if clock making became a factory process:

> Aus dem individuellen Werk eines Nürnberger Handwerkers verwandelte sich die Uhr das gesellschaftliche Produkt einer Unzahl von Teilarbeitern, wie

Rohwerkmacher, Uhrfedermacher, Zifferblattmacher, Spiralfedermacher, Steinloch- und Rubinhebelmacher, Zeigermacher, Gehäusemacher, Schraubenmacher, Vergolder, mit vielen Unterabteilungen, wie z.B. Räder-fabrikant (Messing-und Stahlräder wieder geschieden), Triebmacher, Zeiger-werkmacher, acheveur de pignon (befestigt die Räder auf den Trieben, poliert die facettes usw.), Zapfenmacher, planteur de finessage (setzt verschiedene Räder und Triebe in das Werk), finisseur de barillet (lässt Zähne ein-schneiden, macht die Löcher zur richtigen Weite, härtet Stellung und Gesperr), Hemmungsmacher, bei der Zylinderhemmung wieder Zylinder-macher, Steigmacher, Unruhemacher, Requettemacher (das Rückwerk, woran die Uhr reguliert wirt), planteur d'échappement (eigentliche Hemmungsmacher); dann der repasseur de barillet (macht Federhaus und Stellung ganz fertig), Stahlpolierer, Räderpolierer, Schaubenpolierer, Zahlen-maler, Blattmacher (schmilzt das Email auf das Kupfer), fabricant de pendant (macht bloss die Bügel des Gehäuses), finisseur de charnière (steckt den Messingstift in die Mitte des Gehäuses etc.), faisseur de secret (macht die Federn im Gehäuse, die den Deckel aufspringen machen), graveur, ciseleur, polisseur de boîte usw., usw., endlich der repasseur, der die ganze Uhr zu-sammensetzt und sie gehend abliefert.[31]

Specialization leads to increased productivity but also to psychological de-struction and "idiotization." The more the businessman controls and organizes the factory, the greater the problem he has with disciplining the workers. It is now that the need for a subject of "management" occurs. A corps of overseers and managers becomes necessary to maintain the internal order through such means as observation, fines from wages, dismissal, and quality control. But, construes Marx, it is only possible to deal with the disciplinary problem when "self acting mute agents" are employed, when the workers are replaced by ma-chines in the ongoing process of mechanization.

Marx divides the machines into three categories: tools, power machines, and those that negotiate the power from the latter to the tool. The specialization of manufacturing had already given rise to a large number of specialized tools. Marx calculated that there were no fewer than five hundred different kinds of hammers in use in the metal workshops of Birmingham. In the beginning of the era of steam, the small cottage industries had joined together, each household paying a share of the common "engine house." But soon these small businesses were forced to integrate into factories or were pushed out of business, and the "engine room" became the heart of a large factory. To start with, the machines were used to reinforce the activities of weaker humans. Women and children minded the new equipment that helped raise the level of productivity, as attempts had even been made to obtain better results through dosing them with opium. But so long as wages were low, many of the machines that had been invented in Britain were used only in America. It was often cheaper to let women and children, working in the home at starvation wages, perform routine tasks such as sewing or the plaiting of straw hats. And as long as children could be packed together in "natural schools" and forced to work from the age of three upward, there was no incentive to invest in expensive machinery. When, however, the pressure of public opinion began to mount and focus itself upon these rat holes of home industry, the time was ripe for the introduction of machinery. The sewing machine was then introduced, throwing large numbers out of work in "the wearing apparel" industry, and the children who had dipped matchsticks in the sulfur mixture were replaced by "dipping machines."

The machines made it possible for businessmen first in with the latest advance to raise their profits temporarily over those of their competitors. However, they were soon forced to raise the intensity of the work of the remaining work force. Machines that had perhaps been intended to help lighten the burden of work now served to increase the pace and intensity of work in the factories. The faster the machines were driven, the more accidents occurred. Although well-meaning public opinion often demanded safety and hygienic laws, the demand usually went no further, held Marx, than regulations concerning "white walls" and the like. The level of investment in new machines was also forced upward through the introduction of new models that made the older machines obsolete. In the cloth industry developments had moved so quickly that machines were often old-fashioned even before they had been installed in the factories.

Mechanization led also to an increased demand for raw materials, together with a new class of mechanics, machine builders, and engineers. The ring spread out on the surface and gave rise to new forms of activity. By 1861, Marx points out, 15,000 people were already employed in the gas industry, 2,500 in telegraphs, equally many in photography, 3,500 on steamships, and 70,000 on the railways.[32] Machines demanded more machines, which were themselves built by machines.

3.5 Wage Strategy

Besides working times, organization, and mechanization, a strategy on wages was an important concern of the management of a business. Wages that were always paid retroactively consisted of either time payments or piece rates. The time rate was the commodity price for manpower divided by the number of working hours, something that was set by the businessman himself. A system of rewards forced workers to work more than was necessary and at the same time distracted the workers, who were concerned about the level of wages, from a realization of unpaid working time. When the businessman had reckoned out an hourly wage, moreover, it was then possible to employ people for an hourly rate, without even taking into consideration the covering of their necessary working time. Standardized time payments also made it possible to pay a person the same rate, even to those who perhaps worked sufficiently "for two" persons.

Piece rates, according to Marx, are even more confusing than time payments, not the least because they give the impression that a market price is being paid for a commodity. That this was pure illusion can easily be seen when one understands how piece rates are calculated. This is done with the same division as for the wage rate, but now with the normal number of products per working day also arbitrarily set by the employer. Piece rates, however, had an important advantage for the businessman, who could combine it with quality control and refuse to pay for products that were defective. When a miserly cotton manufacturer saved money through purchasing poor quality raw material that frequently snapped, the cost was passed on to the workers. Piece rates also made it possible for the manager to make internal contracts concerning quantity directly with the workers. Through this means he could avoid paying the costs of middlemen in the production process, and he could give the workers a false sense of freedom and individuality. This, in turn, increased the internal competition among workers and further raised productivity.

3.6 The Factory—Marx's Enterprise Model

Marx's business economics deals almost exclusively with the economics of factory production. Of the 20 million inhabitants of Great Britain in 1861, Marx calculates that some 8 million were employable. He excludes women, children, old people, vagabonds, and criminals, together with lawyers, priests, and the military and civil servants who belonged to "the ideological estate." Of the 8 million, Marx considers only some 4 million to be real workers. There were 1.2 million employed in the mines, equally many in agriculture, and a further million who were "house slaves" in the service of the capitalists. *Das Kapital*, however, deals with the other 4 million, who were employed in large-scale industry and manufacturing; it has little to say concerning those employed in trading and the financial world as "funktionierenden Kapitalisten."[33] Marx's favorite example is the factory and particularly the textile factory of that kind that was owned by the family of his friend Friedrich Engels.

The factory was still a new phenomenon in Marx's time. It became the usual form of industrial organization only after 1835. By 1861 there were about 3,000 businesses in the English cotton industry that employed some 450,000 workers, who worked approximately 400,000 stream-driven weaving frames and thirty million spindles.[34] The numbers employed had sunk to 400,000 by 1868, and the number of weaving frames was 20,000 less. Many of the businesses had been founded by speculators who supplied yarn, machines, and space to an overseer who lacked funds but had experience from employment in a larger factory. These small factories often went bankrupt after a struggle that was painful for all involved. Workers were often employed on a part-time basis at a minimal wage, and through the piece-rate system they were often to take the blame for poor quality that often resulted from the employers' efforts to maximize profits. The American Civil War stopped the import of cotton between 1862 and 1863, and few factories could work the full sixty-hour week. About 60 percent of the looms and spindles stood idle. In a long catalogue of events tracing the development of the cotton industry from 1815, Marx depicts the difficult struggle between, on the one hand, increased demand with the establishment of new businesses and technical development and, on the other hand, falling demand, the abolition of the Corn Laws, strikes, the flight from the countryside, and the American Civil War, which he called a "complete collapse."[35] A detailed analysis or even any clear criteria concerning the causes and implications of this crisis situation, however, are lacking. Nor is there any discussion concerning the conditions that are essential for the establishment of businesses. Marx's supposition is that the factory business exists in a kind of anarchistic competition with other businesses where only the strongest survive to impose their own law. It was not by accident that Marx wished to dedicate the English version of *Das Kapital* to Charles Darwin. The honor, politely declined by Darwin, transferred in the end to a certain Wilhelm Wolf, a German immigrant in Manchester, who in his time had been spokesman for the Silesian weavers during the revolt of 1844.

4. The Pump of Wealth as a Treadmill

The business organization in its capitalist form has a long history behind it, and the factory system is the culmination of this course of historical development. The individual businessman's struggles to increase surplus value both extensively through longer working hours and intensively through greater control were strategies in a vast play where the overarching rules had been made up behind the backs of the actors. In the course of the nineteenth century, furthermore, the base had been laid for different kinds of financial transactions that made it possible to centralize capital ownership and increase surplus value through the integration of already existing businesses. It was through this that great projects such as the building of the railways had been made possible. The discipline of the business and new modes of finance guaranteed both interest and growth of existing capital, but since capital accumulation presumed the existence of capital, it could not explain how capital as such had come into existence. It was to clear up this mystery that Marx provides his theory of "original accumulation."

To Marx the stories provided by the political economists concerning capital accumulation were idiotic old wives' tales. The stories assumed as given that certain people were born industrious and others lazy. This to Marx was part of the mystification of bourgeoisie religion, whose attempts to explain capitalism he ridicules by attributing to them the analogy of Adam Smith biting on the apple of knowledge in the Garden of Eden and thus turning paradise into enterprise. While priests preached that we have to work by the sweat of our brow, economists are attempting to justify why certain people should not be required to work for their daily bread. The true story of the origins of capital must explain why all property tended to concentrate itself in the hands of certain people, while others possessed nothing but their own labor. The polarization between the owners of the means of production and the propertyless workers was, according to Marx, the outcome of a long process of historical development that was characterized by "immediate violence outside the economic realm" (*ausserökonomische unmittelbare Gewalt*).[36] It all began in the countryside.

In Britain, the classic home of the bourgeoisie, there had existed during the Middle Ages a mode of social organization that could be likened to that existing in Japan.[37] Under the English feudal system, it was the number of subjects that was the measure of power, rather than the amount received in land rents. These subjects were peasants who each had his own bit of land and as yet owned his own means of production. Although the king and Parliament had opposed this feudal system, its real death blow had come from the wool manufacturers of Flanders. The increase in the demand for wool from this source, maintains Marx, resulted in the feudal lords beginning to replace the peasants with sheep. Villages were torn down, peasants driven off, and meadows transformed into grazing fields.

The lawmakers had attempted during the fifteenth and sixteenth centuries to dampen the effects of this expropriation, which had created a new class of propertyless vagabonds. Laws were passed that set a maximum limit upon the size of sheep herds and that required that at least four acres of land should be attached to each peasant cottage. But the trend of development nevertheless continued, and the lawmakers slowly began to concern themselves more with the new propertyless vagabonds. If a person was caught without work, he was whipped and sent back to his place of origin to find employment. If he was caught a second time, he could lose an ear, and a third time his life was in danger. During the time of Henry VIII, a vagabond could be made into a slave by anyone who claimed to have "found" him; under James I, vagabonds were imprisoned. In France they were forced to become galley slaves under a "grossly terroristic" ordinance. As late as 1825, reports Marx, the Duke of Sutherland had replaced 15,000 people with 130,000 sheep; a relative of the duke, who lived on rents and created wage slaves, had had the temerity to arrange a fashionable reception for Harriet Beecher-Stowe, the author of *Uncle Tom's Cabin*, when she visited London in 1853. By this time, however, the sheep, in their turn, had been thrown out, and the countryside transformed into a hunting territory for the aristocracy.

At the same time as the feudal peasants had their lands appropriated by the lords, the Protestants had utilized the Reformation to lay their hands on the great properties of the Catholic Church. Cloisters were torn down and monks set to work, and funds that had been contributed for the support of the poor and needy were withdrawn in order not to undermine the latter's will to work. William of Orange had in the course of his Glorious Revolution sold off the property of the towns for a pittance to the new owning class.

There now arose also a new class of leaseholders who obtained long leases on the property that during the fifteenth and sixteenth centuries provided profits when the price of silver and gold fell as a result of the discovery of the American mines. According to Marx, these leaseholders created the original capital that could be transferred to the waking industry. But this required that the guild organizations with their regulations concerning the size of workshops and other barriers to establishment be eliminated. When this had occurred, the agricultural capital was free to seek new modes of use and the employment of workers. During the sixteenth century demand for labor was greater than supply, which led to maximum wages being set by law within both agriculture and industry. These laws were not abolished in Britain until 1813 when, according to Marx, regulation could be left to the businessmen's own private lawmaking. As one of the many proofs that the law was written according to the interests of the businessmen, Marx points out that a breach of contract on the part of an employer was regarded as a civil case, but a breach on the part of workers was treated as a criminal offense.

Capital was obtained, however, not only from home sources. Foreign trade made it possible to obtain initial capital through speculation in slave trade and opium. When the guild system had been abolished, such trading profits with other exploitive gains could also be channeled into industrial activities. Capital for industry was now also provided by the states, which began to increase their national debts. This development, in turn, gave rise to a credit system for loans and a tax system for their repayment. The burning of witches stopped, and the currency forgers were hanged instead. This was the true source of capital, according to Marx, and also the beginnings of the first capitalists.

As with all other courses of development, however, this history of capital was not a simple process, but was marked by contradictions and tensions. Older traditions and customs embedded in law created opposition to the introduction of the new, and Marx attempted to show that this accelerated the pace of development rather than hindering or even actually stopping it. When, for example, child labor was opposed on moral grounds, the response, it is suggested, was accelerated investment in machines. When public opinion, together with Marx, was outraged about women and children having to work half naked in the mines, the reaction took the form of new regulations that only increased unemployment. It was in this manner that the pump of wealth developed, according to Marx, without ever returning to the original treadmills.

5. The Collapse of Management

Adam Smith saw the pump of wealth as a means for obtaining a goal in the form of the economic well-being of the population. The pump of wealth would provide rewards for labor that was worth while in character. Ricardo, on the other hand, constructed an abstract model of a logical nature, which he allowed in his world of thought to develop toward its collapse. Marx attempts to clothe Ricardo's theory in concrete human terms and conditions drawn from the contemporary world of factory production. He showed that rising land rents, sinking real wages, and falling profits would have concrete consequences in practical political terms. But in contrast to Ricardo, who had never openly maintained that the pump of wealth was the only possible system, Marx supposes that this is the case. The pump of wealth would become a treadmill and must necessarily collapse. There was no possibility of either repairing the machine or creating an alternative path of development for production and distribution, and this is the terrible vision that the bourgeois economists attempted to hide at any price. They did this by supposing that economic problems could be solved by methods outside of economics. Through this, they became, according to Marx, the lackeys of the capitalists in the same manner that the lords during mercantilism had conspired with the merchants. Marx rejects all suggestion that reform and liberal political initiatives could alleviate the economic condition of the working class. No strivings on the part of trade unions could reduce the human costs of the treadmill. In *Das Kapital*, Marx does not bother so much as to comment upon possible reforms of the state system of taxation and other state action that could influence production and distribution in the nation. The nation was a reflection of the interests of businesses, and if anyone thought differently, he was naive. Finally, Marx turns against not only the economists and businessmen but even the British working class:

> ...the ultimate aim of this most bourgeois of lands would seem to be the establishment of a bourgeois aristocracy and a bourgeois proletariat side by side with the bourgeoisie.... the revolutionary energy of the British workers has oozed away... .[38]

Marx believes that it is only in undeveloped countries that it is possible to find well-being among the population. The richer the nation, the greater the misery of the population. The pump of wealth does not have the welfare of the population as its goal, rather it uses people as its tool. All this misery in the nation is caused by the state, under capitalism, acting as an interest organization for business and for businessmen. This would become clear from a look at how the original accumulation of capital had actually occurred.

When a business expands, it is the surplus value created by labor that produces that part of capital that is nonfixed. The larger the volume of production and the greater the number of employees, the larger is this surplus value. When a new machine is invented or a chemical process discovered, it is necessary for businessmen to adopt the new process quickly so that it soon gets converted into a new technology. This changes the relationship between fixed and nonfixed capital, even as it changes the need to employ a certain number of people. The result of this is unemployment. This unemployment had, according to Marx, an important role as a potential threat. Through its existence, it made the workers more willing to work harder and longer for lower wages, since the "industrial" reserve army of unemployed regulated the level of wages in the factories. It was not necessary, as Malthus and Ricardo had believed, to wait for an increase in population before wages would fall. The existence of the reserve army was sufficient for this purpose. When economic conditions were bad, workers were sacked and wages reduced; when things improved, a wandering gang of navvies or underaged children were hired. In certain industries characterized by fast change, the reserve army was also changeable; but in agriculture, which was marked by the depopulation of the countryside, it was constant. The threat of the reserve army also made it possible to raise the rents of the monstrous housing in the slums, forcing workers to a state of undernourishment and a life worse than that of prisoners. Many workers, therefore, preferred either to emigrate or to go to prison. Businessmen did their best to stop emigration, particularly of craftsmen, since it reduced the reserve army and the power of the potential threat. At the same time, the wealth of the capitalists and their luxury consumption continued to increase with surplus value, and the capital became concentrated into all fewer hands.

Marx uses various sources in his attempts to justify his theory. He investigates, for example, the tax returns of individuals and comes to the conclusion that for every million-pound fortune between 1815 and 1825 there were four between 1855 and 1859. He also investigates the relation between land areas and ownership and concludes that between 1851 and 1861 the number of plots under a hundred acres had reduced by some 5,000, because of incorporation into larger holdings. Through Marx one also learns that there were only some 300,000 income taxpayers among Britain's 24 million inhabitants. All those who earned more than 60 pounds were liable to pay income tax, and the total value of these payments was 95,844,000 pounds sterling. He calculates the total production of coal and steel in the realm, together with the miles of railway track, which had increased from 8,000 to 12,000 between 1854 and 1864. Other figures he offers cover imports and exports, the number of the poor—which according to official figures had increased from 800,000 to a million between 1854 and 1864—and the housing conditions of workers, which were worse than the conditions in military barracks. Undernourishment was worse than in the prisons.[39]

It was, in the colonies, Marx assures us, that the accumulation of capital could most clearly be observed. The native inhabitants refused to follow the bourgeois moral of work and capital accumulation, but the new masters set a price on land and used the money they received from its sale for the import of a "lumpen" proletariat from the homeland who were then forced to work for their daily bread. It is through political action, Marx asserts, that the businessmen managed to control economic development, and all talk of natural laws governing population and economics is, according to him, pure mystification. The whole of the capitalist project, both at home and abroad, would finally collapse, predicted Marx. The pump of riches would become a treadmill, since it is so expensive in action that it consumes more energy than it produces and distributes. Whole populations are exploited in such a manner that there eventually would be no place for individual consumption. Human beings and machines are integrated in a single organization that becomes increasingly cheaper in practice, the only difference between the humans and the machines being that the former sleep at home rather than in the factory. The workers, moreover, are further pressured by the ten-year economic cycles of expansion and growth followed by decline and depression. The businessmen would finally have to force-feed the workers in the same manner as the mine owners in Peru force-fed the Indians, who actually preferred bread but could bear heavier loads if they were fed on beans. In the final reckoning, as Ricardo had supposed, the factory would be reduced to a completely automatized stronghold where the businessman sat shielded from the hungry masses outside. But these masses would grow so large that no stronghold could be safe, and it was only a matter of time before it was stormed. The era of capitalist privilege would then end. "The expropriators would be expropriated ... by the mass of the people," wrote Marx in *The Communist Manifesto*, which he and Engels produced in 1848.

In his later years Marx is reported to have stopped searching newspaper articles from the financial and business world for evidence of the imminent collapse of capitalism that he had predicted. He was indirectly responsible for the dissolving of the First International. He began to study Russian in order to better understand his growing number of disciples in that peasant economy who had as yet not experienced anything of the pump of wealth in full action. Did he begin to suspect the existence of a political reality beyond economics? Was this the difference between business and national economics?

Notes

1. Heinrich Gemkow, *Karl Marx, eine Biographie,* p. 74.
2. Isaiah Berlin, *Karl Marx, His Life and Environment,* p. 69.
3. Karl Marx, *Das Kapital, Kritik der Politischen Ökonomie,* Vol. 1, p. 15.
4. Ibid., p. 96.
5. Ibid., p. 95.
6. Ibid., p. 461.
7. Ibid., p. 12.
8. Ibid., p. 95.
9. Ibid., p. 335.
10. Ibid., p. 50.
11. Ibid., p. 49.
12. Ibid., p. 62.
13. Ibid., p. 66.
14. Ibid., p. 97.
15. Ibid., p. 72.
16. Ibid., p. 58.
17. Ibid., p. 103.
18. Ibid., p. 129.
19. Ibid., p. 147.
20. Ibid., p. 177.

21. Ibid., p. 564.
22. Karl Marx, *Zur Kritik der Politischen Ökonomie*, Vol. 2, p. 341.
23. Ibid.
24. Marx, *Das kapital,* p. 180.
25. Ibid., p. 181.
26. Ibid., p. 189.
27. Ibid., p. 189.
28. Ibid., p. 199.
29. Ibid., p. 233.
30. Ibid., pp. 432, 434.
31. Ibid., pp. 362–363.
32. Ibid., p. 469.
33. Ibid., p. 470.
34. Ibid., p. 458.
35. Ibid., p. 478.
36. Ibid., p. 765.
37. Ibid., p. 745.
38. Berlin, *Karl Marx,* p. 239.
39. Marx, *Das Kapital,* pp. 678–682.

5

Good Management in Harmonic Stagnation: Business Economics and Ethology in John Stuart Mill

1. "To Be a Reformer of the World"

For John Stuart Mill (1806–1873) the philosophical analysis of society was something of a family business. He was the son of James Mill, who had been Jeremy Bentham's fellow warrior in the struggle for utilitarianism; it had been James Mill who had encouraged Ricardo to write his important work on the principles of political economy. James Mill had persistently searched for philosophical principles that could show the British that their traditional institutions and way of thinking lacked any rational grounds. He had been born in Scotland and, like Adam Smith, had first studied to become a priest. But his studies led him away from Scottish Presbyterianism with its belief in the Bible as the revelation of God's truth. Nor was he able to find any rational basis for deistic notions that a good God created the universe. He had noted that different gods, through time, could assume the characteristics of human "wickedness,"[1] whereafter they functioned more as an excuse for man's wickedness than as moral guardians of the world of goodness. James Mill finally concluded that the answer to the question, Who was the creator of the universe? always springs from man's own conditional wishes. Emotionally loaded questions of faith that had no possible rational answer should be avoided. With great energy and following "the principle of losing no time," he constructed a rational doctrine on morals that he hoped would make it possible for people to do good rather than merely feel the divine. Most important were human actions or outer "conduct." "Feelings, emotions, passions," or "conscience" led only to undesirable exultation, mysticism, and meaningless ceremonies.

It followed that emotions and passions were to be replaced by knowledge and logical reasonings in every human undertaking. The intellectual content of this

90

program was taken by James Mill from his own and Jeremy Bentham's reflections that had their roots in Scottish notions of enlightenment and classical philosophical sources. For those who placed emphasis upon action and enterprise, it was not sufficient to be content with philosophical speculations of a private nature. There was the duty of spreading ideas in a convincing manner in contemporary debate. When John Stuart Mill was born, therefore, James Mill reared him from the beginning as a warrior in the service of radical philosophy. The education of John Stuart Mill began soon after James Mill had become personally acquainted with Jeremy Bentham.

Each day father and son would work together at the same writing desk. On one side sat James Mill, who was writing the history of India, and on the other, John Stuart Mill, who studied Xenophon, Herodotus, and Plato's dialogues. Since there unfortunately existed no English–Greek dictionary at that time, the three-year-old John Stuart Mill would ask his father the meaning of an unknown word if he could not find the answer in the Greek–Latin dictionary. The evenings were devoted to the study of arithmetic. Before breakfast father and son would take long walks during which the young Mill would conscientiously relate what he had read of Hume, Gibbon, or Burnett the previous day. Reading for pleasure was also allowed, but only to a limited extent, and mostly dealt with the lives and adventures of important and powerful men. Occasionally John Mill would receive a children's book, such as *Robinson Crusoe*, as a present from friends of the family. When he was eight years old, having learned Greek and Latin, he was set to work teaching languages to his younger sister. At the same time he studied the works of Horace, Lucretius, and Livy, and other Latin classics.

His reading then began to approach philosophical subjects, and he also practiced the art of writing through summarizing or making continuations of the works he had read. His father encouraged him to write in verse, in the mode of the classical poets: "Some things could be expressed better and more forcibly in verse than in prose. . . . People in general attached more value to verse than it deserved."[2] Modern poets, and even Shakespeare, however, were not highly rated by James Mill, who preferred Sir Walter Scott's metrical romances.

John Stuart Mill began, moreover, to take an interest in the natural sciences. This interest was "in the theoretical, however, not the practical sense of the word; not trying experiments—a kind of discipline I have often regretted not having had—nor even seeing, but merely reading about them."[3] He read everything he could concerning physics and chemistry. The morning discussions with his father dealt increasingly with thought itself rather than the logical manner of thinking, and reading material was selected for its philosophical content. Demosthenes' speeches, for example, concerned the institutions and laws of Athens and the ability of rhetoric to influence the minds of citizens. These speeches demonstrated the skills of the speaker and "how everything important to his purpose was said at the exact moment when he had brought the minds of his audience into the state most fitted to receive it; how he made steal into their minds, gradually and by insinuation, thoughts which if expressed in a more direct manner would have aroused their opposition."[4]

The younger Mill began exercises in logic, and his father drilled him in the art of drawing correct conclusions from premises. This form of argument, the so-called syllogism, or "ratiocination," was not merely a question of forms for James Mill and his radical friends. Jeremy Bentham had written a "book of fallacies" that had been inspired by parliamentary debates, carefully noting their logical faults in argument. John Stuart Mill lived in a world where Plato's dialogues demonstrated not only the practical power of the Socratic method but the need to seek always clarity and precision in the vague abstractions of "popular phraseology." The training in logical thought would sharpen his critical faculties and ability to argue:

> The first intellectual operation in which I arrived at any proficiency, was dissecting a bad argument, and finding in what part the fallacy lay: and though whatever capacity of this sort I attained, was due to the fact that it was an intellectual exercise in which I was most perseveringly drilled by my father, yet it is also true that the school logic, and the mental habits acquired by studying it, were among the principle instruments of this drilling. I am persuaded that nothing, in modern education, tends so much, when properly used, to form exact thinkers, who attach a precise meaning to words and propositions, and are not imposed on by vague, loose, or ambiguous terms. The boasted influence of mathematical studies is nothing to it; for in mathematical processes, none of the real difficulties of correct ratiocination occur."[5]

In 1818 James Mill's large work on the history of India appeared, containing a radical criticism of the British constitution and law in general, and an analysis of the privileges of the East India company in particular. It is perhaps a mark of the open-mindedness of the times that the following year James Mill was appointed correspondent with the company. John Stuart Mill was to hold a similar appointment from 1823, it being considered suitable for someone "not being of independent circumstances" who would "devote a part of the 24 hours to private intellectual pursuits." His rich authorship was combined with this appointment, which he held until 1858 when the company was wound up.

But before he began this thirty-five-year daily acquaintance with the social organization of a foreign culture and its manner of understanding both politics and economics, John Stuart Mill had already obtained a considerable knowledge of contemporary political economy. This had begun in 1819 when James Mill had provided him with a copy of David Ricardo's *Principles of Political Economy and Taxation*, which had recently appeared. James Mill wrote his own book, *Elements of Political Economy*, which was proofread by John Stuart Mill on his return from France in 1820. This journey to France provided his first flight from the utilitarian circles that surrounded his father. He lived with Jeremy Bentham's brother, Sir Samuel Bentham, who had been stationed at Toulouse after the peace. During this journey, John Stuart Mill came into contact with French economists such as Jean-Baptiste Say and caught a glimpse of Saint-Simon. Moreover, he discovered the beautiful French countryside and the pleasant manner in which people conversed. In England, he now thought, one treated others as either "an enemy or a bore." It was to France that he often was to return in the future for inspiration in both philosophy and economics; in his old age he retired to a cottage at Avignon where he spent the remaining years of his life.

By this time, however, he had long been a quite different person from the one who had been "made or manufactured" by his father and utilitarian philosophical circles. John Stuart Mill himself carefully dated the year of his break with the past to 1826. Up to that time he had lived in a whirl of utilitarian writings, discussion clubs, rhetorical performances, and verbal duels where the aim was to obtain advantage through "fluency, decision, telling sentences," and "serré confutations." The technique of debate was sharpened in the Cambridge Union and the Oxford Debating Society where the battle was waged against Owenites, Whigs, and Tories in favor of a rational liberalism. One day, without warning, he was struck by this thought: "Suppose that all your objects in life were realized; that all the changes in institutions and opinions which you are looking forward to, could be completely effected at this very instant: would this be a great joy and happiness to you? And an irrepressible self-consciousness distinctly answered, 'No'."[6] From this time, John Stuart Mill's days as an orthodox utilitarian were numbered.

2. Understanding Human Enterprise

John Stuart Mill's philosophical approach to social research has exerted considerable influence among English-speaking economists, not least through John Maynard Keynes and his friend Bertrand Russell, who was the godson of Mill. This philosophical approach had its origins in the manner that John Stuart Mill found the solution to his personal crisis of 1826. This crisis, which aroused such doubts about the integrity of utilitarianism, was a matter of great seriousness to him, since he had been raised to judge every human action from the utility principle of "the greatest possible happiness for the greatest possible number." He now found that when you "ask yourself whether you are happy . . . you cease to be so."

Mill had been taught to question and analyze all arguments, whether of a public or private nature. The point of this upbringing was to link positive feelings to actions that were meant to be good in a logical sense, and negative reactions to those that analytical rationality had shown to be bad. The purpose of both upbringing and education was to link psychological reactions to logical goals. When the crisis hit John Stuart Mill, so that he now no longer felt pleasure in that which had been proved to be happiness, he thought that he had been cheated by analytical reason into dismantling his own mental construction. He knew that he should feel happiness with regard to certain situations but that the intellectual proof of such, nevertheless, left him quite unmoved. All was finished, and the joy in life had passed. It was in this state of deep melancholy that he began to read poets such as Coleridge and Wordsworth, who were disapproved of by the utilitarians, but from whose mystical experience he obtained some satisfaction. One day he happened to read certain lines that "moved him to tears", and this experience itself was sufficient to revive his spirits. It proved at least that his feelings remained in his body, that he was not just "stock or stone." He had received proof of this not through philosophical intuition but rather through his tears. Emotions were a concrete reality instead of an illusion: "a fact as real as any of the other qualities of objects; and far from implying anything erroneous and delusive in our mental apprehension of the object, is quite consistent with the most accurate knowledge and most perfect practical recognition of all its physical and intellectual laws and relations."[7]

From this point began the laborious task of integrating psychological experience with those parts of the old doctrine that could yet be valuable in the light of the new revelation.

John Stuart Mill maintained that for his own part now happiness was not something that could be strived after as a final goal, but rather something that arose spontaneously and "en passant" during daily activities. Mill began to develop another philosophical position that was yet different from "the German or apriori view of human knowledge . . . enabled to dispense with the obligation of justifying itself by reason . . . devised for consecrating all deep-seated prejudice."[8] This was the purpose of Mill's large work, *A System of Logic*, which appeared in 1843. This book contains the germ for several different schools of economic thought, a notion of what is realistic upon which many economists were to base their faith that what they pursue is in fact a concrete and empirical science whose truths can be proved starting from logical premises.

According to this way of thinking, the search for truth begins with propositions. Such propositions, which could take the form, for example, of "Wellington is a man," according to Mill, are a "call for belief." Realism says that our knowledge concerning what the proposition is about determines whether we accept or reject the proposition. We always know something about something. The proposition concerns not only our ideas, as had been maintained by the so-called conceptualists. Mill also rejects the notion that propositions concern only the significance of the name or word as the nominalists usually assert. A consistent nominalist would accept the proposition "Wellington is a man" only if Wellington's parents had thought of the word "man" when they gave him the name "Wellington," and if the name "Wellington" is generally associated with the word "man." A realist, on the other hand, regards words and language as reflections of concrete things, although the term *concrete things* here must be interpreted as covering both mental and material objects. Things, thus, could include a person's thoughts and feelings as well as what that person experiences through the senses, sensations. Whether what we perceive really exists and if in this case our perceptions correctly reflect the real nature of that which exists are things we cannot say with certainty. While these metaphysical questions are interesting, Mill believes it is unnecessary to mix them up with the search for truth. It is sufficient for everyday knowledge and beliefs that we rely on our capacity. It is unnecessary to make reference here to some intuitive and uncontrollable form of knowledge of the nature of the thing itself. The word "is" in the proposition "Wellington is a man" does not call for an existential interpretation. We ought to be able to distinguish between what is true and what is false without having to resort to "apriorism." Thus, Mill attacks those who maintain that there exist eternal truths that are uncontrollable. The mathematician who maintains that the concept of a circle is an absolute truth has forgotten that which lies beyond the figures and symbols of mathematics.

All knowledge is constructed from observation and experiment. It is the task of education to sharpen the alertness of our senses and our capacity for observation. Logic comes into it once man has with language formulated his experience and reached his propositions through induction. Several propositions can now be combined so that established knowledge, through deduction, can lead to new knowledge. This happens, for example, in the use of syllogisms where two premises result in a conclusion such as the following: "All humans are mortal." "Wellington is human." "Wellington is, therefore, mortal." Such inferences, arrived at through induction and deduction, are the grounds for the development of human knowledge. But all human beings are not equally capable of formulating their thoughts and observations in beautiful words and syllogisms. The painter's skillful handwork shows that he can combine colors and create new tones, but it requires a schooled logician to formulate in words what the painter does in deeds. Logic could carefully lead us toward greater precision and sharpness of thought. It should never force itself upon the language of the practical observer, which is based on observations of, and inductions from, reality. The logician is, nevertheless, of value, particularly in unveiling the charlatans and others who "employ the commonplaces of philosophy to justify their practice."[9]

The syllogism functions, thus, as a mode of control rather than a source of truth in itself. With the aid of Euclid's geometry, Mill shows how it is possible to pursue a deductive proof with a minimum number of inductive propositions. Following on Kepler's observation concerning the elliptical orbits of the planets, Newton combined propositions relating to physical laws into a new deductive science on the movements of heavenly bodies. A similar combination of propositions relating to regularities or laws obtained through induction could be combined into a science concerning human beings. Mill maintains that it is thus possible to discover the laws of what he calls the "moral sciences." A law entails a determined relationship between initial "causes" and the results following in time. He attempts to show, however, that belief in the existence of a law concerning human conduct is not the same thing as a belief in an absolute determinism.

On the one side, John Stuart Mill cannot accept what he terms "the German school of metaphysical speculation,"[10] while, on the other, he rejects Comte's doctrine that only external causes could account for human actions and thoughts. The Germans apparently believed that it was possible neither to explain human action nor to change the human situation. Auguste Comte leaned toward a total determinism. Both positions, according to Mill, constitute an "aberration from the true scientific spirit." He rather prefers to call himself a "necessitarian," and explains his position in the following manner: "Necessity is simply this: that, given the motives which are present to an individual's mind, and given likewise the character and disposition of the individual, the manner in which he will act might be unerringly inferred."[11] People who know us well can predict what we would do, although many people understand such propositions as "humiliating to the pride and even degrading to the moral nature of man,"[12] which, says Mill, depends upon a serious misunderstanding.

It is obvious that it is possible to show that certain traits of character necessarily "cause" certain kinds of actions. The term *causes*, however, only means that we note that something had preceded something else in the course of time. It is necessary to free ourselves from all compulsive thoughts around words such as *cause*, *effects*, and *laws*. A mental disease is just a state where certain character traits are linked with a certain type of behavior. Healthy individuals form their own character, so that to be a necessitarian does not imply a belief in fatalism. Character is formed through practical experience where influence is exerted daily for us to change our actions. If character has been formed by ourselves, it is not degrading for us that others know how we intend to act. Their knowledge how I intend to act builds upon their knowledge of my good qualities. Knowledge of the logic of the mind is not in conflict with the idea of the freedom of will.

It is from the laws of psychology that one derives the premises that could contribute to a deductive knowledge concerning human character, a so-called ethology. But both character and conduct must be studied in the social reality where we can observe empirical relations where the true nature of this relationship is hidden by the chaos of reality. Human beings are influenced by an infinity of different sources that reinforce certain laws and weaken the effects of others. If we were forced to base our knowledge of people only upon observations of others, without the aid of logical deduction, we could never obtain a knowledge of ourselves. Pure empiricism, held Mill, allows no recourse to insight. It must be admitted, on the other hand, that our logical deductions from psychological observations only provide us with knowledge of certain "tendencies" rather than with any absolute certainties. There are, moreover, two fallacious methods that should be avoided in social research.

The first of these, which often arises in political debate, could be called the *experimental or chemical method*. A truly experimental approach to human behavior would involve the controlled and separate upbringing of individuals and the study of the consequences upon their behavior. Himself being something of the victim of such an approach, Mill rejects this course as being open only to an oriental despot. It would in addition be impossible to subject a whole society to such an experimental approach. Suppose, for example, we compare two nations with regard to the effects of free trade upon wealth. If one country with free trade is wealthier than another without free trade, the cause of this difference could lie elsewhere than in free trade. If it were to be maintained in debate that it had been scientifically proved that free trade is the only thing that wealthy nations have in common, it would be a faulty argument. How could we know that two countries are completely different in everything but free trade? If all the imaginable causes of wealth are discounted, what remains, according to this use of the experimental method, must depend upon free trade. But how is it possible to guarantee that there is not an unknown cause? It is clear that the experimental method is not possible in a human context. In any case, chemistry, which earlier had been purely experimental, had now become a science through the transformation of an uncertain empiricism into a deductive form of knowledge.

The second methodological fault, according to Mill, is that which he terms the *geometrical*. It is here that Bentham and Mill's own father made their error in imagining that it was possible to deduce all social phenomena from one general law. Human actions, it had been maintained by the utilitarians, were always determined by their interests. The principle of "worldly self interests"[13] was believed to be the foundation of human conduct, and it had been held that this was true for all people, the governed as well as the governing. It was, nevertheless, necessary, in the view of the utilitarians, for the governing to pursue the interests of others in their accounting methods and democratic principles. Such a simplistic perspective ignores the influence of ideas and feelings upon human behavior. This simplification is probably not even a good explanation of the actions of the unimaginative and puritanical Englishmen. It was clearly the case, held Mill, that "so sweeping a proposition is far from being universally true." In defense of his father, however, Mill explains that the utilitarian principle had been originally devised for "serving the cause of parliamentary reform" but that unfortunately it had subsequently been blown up into "a complete theory."[14]

The utilitarians were, nevertheless, correct in their use of the deductive method. If they had fastened upon mechanics instead of geometry, their contribution would without doubt have been more fruitful. Not only are the different principles of geometry not integrated with each other, but

> geometry affords no room for what so constantly occurs in mechanics and its applications, the case of conflicting forces; of causes which counteract or modify one another. In mechanics we continually find two or more moving forces producing, not motion, but rest; or motion in a different direction from that which would have been produced by either of the generating forces.[15]

But how then should social science be pursued? Mill would combine observation with deduction in a social science "by a convenient barbarism . . . termed sociology."[16] His visionary view here is the notion of a sociology that through historical studies would delineate the dynamics of social development. It would then be possible to discover how different historical periods were the causes of other periods, even as they were also the effects. Social statics—how consensus existed in the legal, intellectual, and national orders of society during a certain period—was to be complemented by social dynamics. The path to insight was now open for realism, while metaphysics and religion had been pushed aside. Within general sociology, however, John Stuart Mill saw two different social sciences.

The first of these was political ethology, with the task of researching the traditions and character of various countries at different times. In this new science, Mill was probably influenced by his own experience of foreign travel, together with his work as correspondent for the East India Company, which gave him almost daily contact with the social order of India. A political ethology would enrich the rather limited views of the British and Americans as to what constituted correct human conduct.

The second science involved was that of political economy, which was concerned with "mankind as occupied solely in acquiring and consuming wealth."[17] It was to study the production of wealth and its protection through the institution of property, how competition distributed production, and how this distribution was effected through the instruments of money and credit. A basic proposition of economy is that people always prefer "a greater portion of wealth to a smaller one."[18] But like mechanics, political economics should deal with two forces: the positive industriousness and the negative laziness. Sometimes, however, other forces make their appearance and complicate the deductive argument, such as Malthus's population principle. The development of the science of political ethology would, in time, come to complement political economy through encouraging the study of situations that did not concur with the suppositions of the latter discipline. It happened, for example, that production was not always divided among three classes but was concentrated by tradition and custom in the hands of a ruling class. One of the most important limitations of political economy is the assumption of competition when reality often consists of customary regulations:

> In political economy for instance, empirical laws of human nature are tacitly assumed by English thinkers, which are calculated only for Great Britain and the United States. Among other things, an intensity of competitions is constantly supposed, which, as a general mercantile fact, exists in no country in this world except those two. An English political economist, like his countrymen in general, has seldom learned that it is possible that men, in conducting the business of selling their goods over a counter, should care more about their ease or their vanity than about their pecuniary gain. Yet those who know the habits of the Continent of Europe are aware how apparently small a motive often outweighs the desire of money-getting, even in the operations which have money-getting for their direct object.[19]

On the other hand, Mill is careful not to accuse political economists of being particularly narrow-minded or parochial. No honest economist had ever "pretended to give advice to mankind with no lights but its own."[20]

Good economists do not exaggerate or pursue the results of their deductive reasonings to the limits. Even if Ricardo's argument concerning unemployment was correct, they could see that the implementation of such large projects as the building of the railways would hold unemployment down. Although they may believe in "the law of diminishing return" in agriculture, they also know that invention and discovery provide a counterforce that make it possible for this true law to be temporarily stopped or to be "stretched out to the utmost."[21] In this manner, it was possible to combine Ricardo's hypothetical abstractions with the social philosophy of Adam Smith. When John Stuart Mill wrote his book *Principles of Political Economy* in 1848, he did it with a view to updating *The Wealth of Nations* with "the best social ideas of the present time."[22] Let us now turn to what he wrote about business economics and ethology and what he considered to be "good management."

3. The "Matters of Fact" of Enterprise

3.1 Physical Production

In contrast to other economists who began their discussion of economic principles from the theory of value, Mill begins his work from the point of view of production. A realist must accept that production follows regularities in which there is "nothing optional or arbitrary."[23] People set things in motion through their work and make it possible to utilize physical powers in production. People and nature work together in both country and town. This is equally true for the fields of the Physiocrats and for the spinners and weavers who produced with the spinning jenny or steam-driven weaving frame. It is the instruments of production that constitute the real "wealth of nations," together with all the knowledge that makes it possible to add products to the nation's store. A tailor works and sells his product, and a coat is exchanged for money. An Italian may sing an aria, a German may take a job as a governess, while a Greek could hold philosophical lectures. These provided three instances where only money and services were exchanged. It is what leads to useful products that is productive, but what is good in itself—food, housing, and clothing—does not increase the production of things that are distributed and sold. When Mill writes about increasing the wealth of the nation, he thinks more in terms of the instruments of production rather than of the necessities of life.

Mill emphasizes the enormous productive capacity of the pump of wealth. England's existing riches, he held, had in fact been produced during the previous twelve months. We are surprised to note how quickly war-destroyed nations reconstruct themselves. Properly managed, the misfortune of war could lead to an increase of wealth. This could be seen, for example, in the case of the Napoleonic Wars where Britain had hired foreign mercenaries at its own expense. This led to a reduction in the flow of capital, yet there were the same number of mouths to feed at home. Wages sank, while production and profits increased. On the other hand, Napoleon, who did not understand economics, had Frenchmen fight the wars but let them be financed by the states he conquered. Mill points out that in France there now exist few workers, but much capital, so that as wages increase production falls.

But is there not a risk that production could be too large? Could it be useful to produce without limit? Mill considered that those who already in his time maintained that overproduction was a reality were guilty of a logical error. Everyone who undertook something and produced more than their household needs did so because they "want something." Supply was, thus, logically identical with this desire, and through exchange this desire was realized as "effectual demand."[24] It was the case, thus, that "All sellers are inevitably and ex vi termini buyers."[25]

Mill could then postulate an equation where SUPPLIED QUANTITY = DEMANDED QUANTITY. Individual producers could naturally make mistakes in their "business" of adapting their production to demand, but where this happened it meant that demand was directed toward another existing product in the market. Nor did the individuals who produced need to consume the production themselves. These could be capitalists who invested their earnings in production. The wages of the workers made it possible for them to realize their desires as capitalists, and the fact remained that demand was always identical with supply. The supply of products is thus ensured through the desires of capitalists and through the workers who guaranteed that the wheels turned and the money flowed. There is, however, a second "matter of fact" on which economy rests, and this is the question of thrift.

3.2 Thriftiness

If we would obtain economic well-being, we should not ask ourselves "how a market can be created for produce, or how production can be limited to capabilities of the market."[26]

Those who imagine that demand and consumers create our wealth reverse the logic of economic welfare. Rich and wasteful consumers can only contribute through pushing up market prices and stopping poorer people from purchasing expensive products. Even better, however, these rich "spendthrifts" fail to note that they are being continuously "cheated and robbed on all quarters, often by persons of frugal habits."[27] Against their will, thus, the wasteful rich became a source of useful capital.

If a rich person wastes his income on gold-embroidered lace, he creates the demand for an existing business that produces this luxury product. Should he suddenly tire of this interest, the turnover of this business would fall, and the businessman would have to reorient his capital in some new activity that coincides with the changing tastes of the rich. This does not lead to any increase in consumption, as the mercantilists had maintained, but only to a re-allocation of capital to another activity.

If now the rich man decides to build a house instead, his activity here changes from wastefulness to an investment in the wealth of the nation. Through this decision "in the mind of the capitalist—in his will to employ them (the money) for one purpose rather than another,"[28] new capital is created that would keep the builder employed with the construction of the house. It could be thought that the rich man had suddenly become interested in construction work and displayed a certain business talent. Should he not like the house when it was ready, he could sell it and make a profit on his capital that consisted of a reward both for refraining from wastefulness and for his business talent. The money that he obtained from the sale of the house could now be lent to some other enterprising person in return for interest payments. If there was difficulty in finding a person who could be depended upon, it is possible to become instead a "sleeping partner" in a joint-stock company that is managed by "hired servants." Whichever course he decides upon here, he had in any case become a thrifty capitalist, and the time was past when he used his income "in supplying his personal consumption and that of his family, or in hiring grooms and valets, or maintaining hunters and hounds, or in educating his children, or in paying taxes, or in charity."[29]

In the same manner as the rich man's character had been changed in the direction of thrift, Mill maintains that the English character had undergone a drastic change since the time of Adam Smith. It was no longer possible, held Mill, to find happy spendthrifts and pleasure-seeking idlers in Great Britain and America. In these countries it was now difficult to believe that there really existed strange native peoples who were only interested in the production of what was good in itself. Only savages could think that machines and stocks had no significance for the future. It was, maintained Mill, only through hard discipline and control that the Jesuit missionaries in Peru had succeeded in introducing investment and production among the Indians. Even so, no sooner were their backs turned than the latter would slaughter and consume the livestock.

It was possible that the lack of thrift among native peoples depended upon their living in a state of natural abundance or upon their being constantly threatened by the plundering raids of their enemies. Thrift in Europe had presumably increased when plundering had been reduced and when law, together with "manners and opinion," provided protection for private property against the arbitrary actions of individuals and state taxation. Moreover, craftsmen and traders had succeeded, as Adam Smith had shown, in increasing the range of desires among the uncivilized peasants and farmers. Certain aspects of this experience were made use of by the English colonizers in their plans for urbanization, which utilized the wealth-creating mechanism of the town–countryside relationship as their model. In the English-speaking world, considered Mill, thrift and abstinence had presumably reached its peak. Work and saving "has become the habit of the country; and life in England is more governed by habit, and less by personal inclination and will, than in any other country, except perhaps China or Japan."[30]

The character of the English is dull, and the real problem is not so much to encourage thrift but rather to awake feelings for "the nobler interests in humanity." Among people in Britain and America there is only work and "ennui." But even if Frenchmen and natives were more interesting to deal with, this mania for thrift brings with it certain essential advantages.

If we accept, as Mill is inclined to do, that Ricardo's vision of declining profits is realistic, then we have reason to fear that economic development and capital accumulation would one day stop. But perhaps habitual English savers did not need to be enticed with the offer of higher profits. In England, points out Mill, people were already willing to invest their capital for a return of between 3 percent and 4 percent, while in Burma it was necessary to offer between 30 percent and 40 percent return for the same investment. Industrialization had perhaps led to a situation where investment is reduced to a habit. Production had been transformed from an adventurous entrepreneurship to an accepted social routine. This change is clearest when Mill analyzes Adam Smith's critique of the joint-stock companies.

3.3 Cooperation

Production in society could well enough be handled by state businesses, although for ideological reasons John Stuart Mill believed that the shareholding company was a better alternative. It was preferable to obtain the necessary capital through the voluntary purchase of shares than forcibly through the tax system. An increasing number of activities were now financed in the form of the shareholding company, and the force of Adam Smith's criticism of the same had begun to weaken. Businessmen who were not made responsible for their actions with the whole of their fortunes, Smith had maintained, were liable to have less interest in the success of the business. When the owners themselves, moreover, did not participate in the running of the business but employed managers or "hired servants," this led to corruption. Mill holds, on the other hand, that the hired managers could be controlled through careful legal regulation but could hardly be encouraged by this means to undertake large and adventurous projects. Large businesses were perhaps also less inclined to make small savings. These large businesses, however, have a considerable advantage in industrial activities by reason of their size, which make them more profitable. The small business has to pay a high price for its freedom before being finally struck down by the "underselling" resorted to by its larger competitors.

The shareholding company is the ideal form of organization for large-scale production on a routine basis. How would it be possible for a small postal company to manage several deliveries each day? With the use of bonuses and participation in profits, the motivation of hired business management could be maintained. High salaries would result in large-scale businesses being managed by

> persons of a degree of acquirement and cultivated intelligence which more than compensates for their inferior interest in the result. Their greater perspicacity enables them, with even a part of their minds, to see the probabilities of advantage which never occur to the ordinary run of men by the continued exertion of the whole of theirs; and their superior knowledge, and habitual rectitude of perception and of judgment, guard them against blunders, the fear of which would prevent others from hazarding their interest in any attempt out of the ordinary routine.[31]

The problem of business management could thus be solved. But the most important precondition for the success of the shareholding company, according to Mill, is a radical change in the character of the ordinary workers that is already perceptible to some degree. The quality of products had recently become better, and buyers now dared to purchase large quantities of goods of which they had only seen samples. Cheating with weights and quality had become unusual. Cooperation and dependability would seem to have spread itself to the working class.

This new morality made it possible to take advantage of the division of labor. Adam Smith had, according to Mill, overlooked the major advantage of the division of labor, which lay in the possibility of fitting jobs to individual talents. The "right man in the right place" also needed to be extended to the "right woman" who had as much a right to a good job as a man. When special jobs were introduced in a business, there were further factors encouraging large-scale production. It was necessary, for example, to introduce as many machines as required to keep a specially trained mechanic fully occupied throughout the day.

John Stuart Mill's ethological analysis of society leads him to emphasize the importance of thrift and cooperation. He continues from this point to consider how morality and economy could be integrated in a reformed society.

4. The Goal—A Condition of Education and Activity

4.1 Welfare and Zero Growth

We have seen how Mill's personal crisis cured him of the belief that the goal of life was to reach the ultimate destination of happiness. Now he is convinced that it is activity in itself that is the correct form of human life. Suffering should naturally be avoided, but true happiness is something that occurs randomly along life's way. The inner life of the mind is for Mill equally as important as the outer world of human conduct. He has nothing against the notion of a quiet environment filled with lonely reflections. It was possibly this that led him to accept

Ricardo's vision of a stagnating society in a far more positive manner than did most of the contemporary economists, who were filled with fear by the thought of a necessary fall in the rate of profits:

> This impossibility of ultimately avoiding the stationary state—this irresistible necessity that the stream of human industry should finally spread itself out into an apparently stagnant sea—must have been to the economists of the last two generations, an unpleasing and discouraging prospect; for the tone and tendency of their speculations goes completely to identify all that is economically desirable with the progressive state, and with that alone.[32]

Wealth is not boundless, and expansion or "progress" must come to an end.

The time would then be right for real "improvements" in the human condition. When the period of struggle and competition is over, the new period could begin:

> I confess I am not charmed with the ideal of a human life held out by those who think that the normal state of human beings is that of struggling to get on; that the trampling, crushing, elbowing, and treading on each other's heels, which form the existing type of social life, are the most desirable lot of human kind, or anything but the disagreeable symptoms of one of the phases of industrial progress.[33]

In the stagnating society there would be neither poverty nor any violent material desires. The elbowing and pushing could stop, and a more humane life would become possible. But even if the threatening economic stagnation was already apparent, there yet remained a long and difficult passage to the eventual quiet harmony.

In somewhat the same manner as Marx, John Stuart Mill is deeply concerned by the poverty and injustice of contemporary English society, although unlike Marx he offers a way out of the dilemma. Mill rejects all efforts to better the lot of the poor through charity and fellow pity. The would-be protectors of the poor were themselves dependent upon the threat to the weak in order to play their roles as saviors. The poor themselves, through agitation and the spreading of literacy, had begun to analyze and change their own situation. Need forced these people to a clear-sighted realism that gave their analyses a concrete content. The poor should be given the opportunity of helping themselves rather than being dependent upon charity. Such a possibility for self-help exists already in the institution of ownership.

4.2 Ownership and Self-Help

The rights of ownership were often referred to, but their correct interpretation and understanding as an institution had, according to Mill, been confused through various laws of inheritance. The children of the rich inherit the fortunes of their parents, while the distant relatives of childless capitalists ensure that wealth remains in the family long after the death of those who had created it. Naturally the children of the rich have a right to live, and it would be irresponsible for either rich or poor people to bring children into the world without giving them a chance to survive. On the other hand, it is not necessary that the children of the rich inherit enormous fortunes. Mill suggests that the norm applied for the support of children born out of wedlock should also be applied to children born in wedlock and that any remaining funds should become public property. He points to America where rich people donate money to public institutions. The right of the dead to decide things long after they had departed should be limited. The original inspiration of the institution of ownership was that individuals should have during their lifetime the right to the results of their work. This insight, however, not only implied that the laws of inheritance should be reformed but also that land itself should never be owned: "No man made the land. It is the original inheritance of the whole species. Its appropriation is wholly a question of general expediency. When private property in land is not expedient, it is unjust."[34]

It was also wrong to own a public appointment or profession. Together with the earth, such positions can only be administered rather than owned, held Mill, whose sympathetic inclination toward the socialistic ideas of 1848 are evident in his book that appeared in the same year. Mill takes up here the arguments of Saint-Simon, Fourier, the Owenites, and the Communists, which he knew well as a result of his youthful discussions. He rejects the popular notion that socialism would lead to the undermining of industriousness, since control under socialism is exerted by fellow workers rather than managers or owners. It is just in the effectiveness of such control that Mill finds socialism's only negative aspect: "[N]o society in which eccentricity is a matter of reproach can be a wholesome state."[35]

But, on the other hand, if the choice is between the injustices of the existing situation and socialism, such shortcomings are "but as dust in the balance."[36] It was, however, Charles Fourier's happy vision of a hopeful common activity in which both public and private ownership existed side by side that seemed to suit Mill best. Like Fourier, Mill now began to consider what form of enterprise would be most suited to the future harmonious society he envisioned.

5. The Means—Ideal Enterprises

5.1 The Ideal Farm

John Stuart Mill carried on a long correspondence with Auguste Comte, the French philosopher and sociologist. They shared an interest in the possibilities of positive science, but the friendship ended when Mill came to understand that Comte was attempting to use his philosophy to construct a new type of total system—a despotism of the worst kind that had ever sprung from a human brain.[37] His last letter to Comte contains the following comment on the Irish famine: "You are aware of the deplorable economic condition of that country, the division between a multitude of hungry and idle peasants and a small number of unmoved and debt-ridden large landowners who press as much as they can out of the peasants, not through brute force, but through encouraging competition among them."[38]

Ricardo and Malthus had shown what was involved with the growth of population when the large estates were owned by the "landlords." The situation of the poor land workers in Ireland was far worse than that of the slaves on these plantations. No landowner in Ireland was prepared to give up the competitive system where "free" people vied with each other for starvation wages and, nevertheless, looked after themselves and the land without the control of the slave owner. The Irish were so debt-ridden that any good harvest went immediately to pay off these debts. They were exhausted through extra work in home manufacturing, fishing, and hunting. Their only protection lay in the hope that neighbors would maintain solidarity in not undercutting one another in leasehold negotiations. But for most, this hope was not fulfilled. They lived, increased in numbers, and died like animals.

It had been, however, the French Physiocrats who had wished to improve the situation of agriculture through "grande culture" and competition with leasehold negotiations. John Stuart Mill was interested in investigating the situation from the point of view of his Indian experience. During the period of Hindu control, land rents were paid by the ryot, the peasant or tenant farmer, to the princes who owned the land. These peasant families had by tradition, however, the right to use their piece of land. The land rents were fixed by law or tradition and not through competitive leasehold negotiations as in Britain, so that they were the same for all tenants and for all types of land. This traditional system existed until the arrival of the British, who decided to introduce competition and large-scale production on estates. It now became necessary to find estate owners, and this function was assumed by the zamindar who had previously collected the land rents. These had been functionaries without responsibility for the land or right to any share in the profits they gathered in for the princes. When they became landowners, the zamindars abolished traditional rights at the same time as they fell into debt through living over their means. The land soon ended in the hands of the town bankers, who proved to be even harder in leasehold negotiations. The traditional system was now completely destroyed, but estate ownership and large-scale production had been introduced in accordance with the ideas of the political economists.

According to Mill, political economy had made two basic mistakes when dealing with agriculture as a business enterprise. The first concerned a belief in the virtues of large-scale operations. It was the Physiocrats who had rejected the *métayer* system and argued for large-scale agriculture and competition when the real problem of prerevolutionary France was the burden of taxation. When the French Revolution had swept away the old tax system with the monarchy, although the size of farms was still small, the level of production had increased. That English economists preferred large scale operations in agriculture was simply a matter of prejudice. The Continental economists who had observed small-scale agriculture in practice were better informed. The Italian métayer system in the Piedmont divided the harvest according to tradition and "fixed usage" between the landowner and the farmer. In Toscany, it was possible to witness the efficiency of harvesting and threshing, together with the thrift of the peasants when they used their *vinella* or *aquarolle*—wine mixed with water—for everyday consumption. But they lived and dressed well, and their women had large dowries. Through traditional rights to the land, they possessed a detailed knowledge of the fields and did not act in the same manner as casual leaseholders or in accordance with some general but shallow regulations. If one traveled to Switzerland or Belgium, it was possible to see small farms whose owner-farmers were well-off. It was possible to live there on a six-acre farm with a cow and a fat sow. This farm could produce thirty-nine bushels of corn and forty-nine of potatoes, which was sufficient for the year, and this still left three and a half acres over on which to grow products that could be exchanged for tools and other necessaries in the market.

These small farmers, moreover, lived thrifty and sensible lives. The younger generation never married before they had obtained a farm and did not bring too many children into the world. The houses of the Swiss farmers were tastefully decorated, and they jointly manufactured large fat cheeses. In Belgium it was possible to find farmers who managed to get almost pure sand to bloom, in small holdings. English economists did not need, in fact, to travel farther than the Channel Islands of Guernsey and Jersey to witness how small farms flourished and how the bank accounts of the farmers were increasing. All this demonstrated how "the magic of property turns sand into gold."[39]

Englishmen had forgotten what it meant to be a free farmer. It was only in Cumberland and Westmoreland that it was possible to meet free human beings who had inspired Wordsworth—Mill's favorite poet—to write of them:

> . . . a perfect republic of shepherds and agriculturists, proprietors, for the most part, of the lands which they occupied and cultivated. The plough of each man was confined to the maintenance of his own family, or to the occasional accommodation of his neighbour. Two or three cows furnished each family with milk and cheese. The chapel was the only edifice that presided over these dwellings, and the supreme head of this pure commonwealth; the members of which existed in the midst of a powerful empire, like an ideal society, or an organized community, whose constitution had been imposed and regulated by the mountains which protected it.[40]

It was, thus, clear that there was little to be said for the preferences of the political economists for large-scale agriculture.

The second mistake of the economists, however, was the belief that agriculture could ever be a market controlled by free competition. Not only was the land in the possession of a small number of landowners, but its productivity could not be increased "ad libitum." It was, therefore, necessary to stop regarding agriculture as a market. The Irish lands, Mills suggested, should be given over to the peasants against fixed rents and leases regulated by tradition. This should preferably occur as the result of an act of Parliament that expropriated the lands from landowners in exchange for a reasonable compensation. Mill understood well enough that such a law would never come into being in Ireland, even if certain Continental countries, like Prussia, had carried out land reforms. A more realistic proposal would be that the state purchased unused land and divided it up. Mill noted that companies were formed for the purchase of land, the so-called freehold Land societies,[41] which hired out land against fixed rents for farmers. It was obviously necessary to stop any speculation in such land rights. Beyond this, however, emigration and the colonization of foreign lands should be encouraged to relieve the pressure of population in Ireland. On the other hand, charity was to be rejected. If money was simply given to the poor without property, it would be used to support wives, and it would "people down" wages to an existence minimum by producing even larger families. The money would go to food, and wages would fall still further when the children were forced by hunger to compete for work.

5.2 The Ideal Firm

John Stuart Mill was more favorably disposed toward large-scale industry, even if he was skeptical about categorical assertions concerning falling costs with increased volume of production. In the case of products whose manufacture was not limited by natural limitations, competition would without doubt be a sound principle to apply. According to Mill, the unsound element in contemporary large-scale business is that the capitalists offend the institution of ownership through taking what actually belongs to the workers. It is, however, possible to come to rights with such problems without losing the advantages of large-scale production.

On American ships trading with China, the crew received part of the profits, whale fishing was pursued as a collective endeavor, while in the Cornwall tin mines, miners worked on a weekly contract for a share of the value of the sold ore. Around 1849, there had come from France many reports about employers who allowed their workers to be part owners, this resulting in busy enterprises in place of the idleness and drunkenness that had reigned previously. More than a hundred "associations" were formed in Paris during 1848. A certain Mr. Leclaire, a housepainter, had experienced difficulties with his workers since they were paid the same wage irrespective of their performance and frequently changed jobs. He had decided already in 1842 to give his painters part of the profits, contenting himself with a fixed return on the capital and a fee for his service. His 200 painters became much more industrious, stopped changing jobs, and received a regular profit bonus of 300 francs per year beyond their annual wage of 1,200 francs.

Mill refers to Charles Babbage who describes how one sets about starting an "association" business. The basic principle is that wages are entirely determined by the results of the enterprise and that all improvements developed by the part owners result in maximum advantage when used in their own business. Beyond this, it is but necessary to assemble a group of skilled craftsmen, together with a little capital, for example, about 800 pounds, which they had saved. Half of this sum would go toward the hire of a workshop and the purchase of tools, and the remainder would be used to purchase materials and establish a wage fund. Wages are fixed at the common level of a pound per week per man. The capital is also treated like a man, having the right to a pound per week. As production got under way it would be necessary to keep a careful control over the economy. Each week the wages to both men and capital are distributed, while further sums are set aside for the repair of tools and as a reserve. What was left over is then distributed equally among all employed, with capital still being counted as one person. The advantage of this system, according to Babbage, is its considerable efficiency, although it also suffers from the disadvantage that disagreements could arise among the part owners. With a little goodwill, Babbage held, it is possible to reach agreement in these situations.

Mill referred to several examples where the participants lacked any starting capital. One such was the case of the workers who wanted to found an association for the manufacture of pianofortes and asked for a loan of 300,000 francs from the French government for this purpose. It would be quite impossible, they stubbornly maintained, to begin work with less than this sum. Their request was rejected. Some of these workers had then assembled their own tools that were worth about 2,000 francs, and others managed after much difficulty to raise a starting capital of 10 francs per man. Friends lent a further 230 francs, and on March 10, 1849, the manufacture of the first piano began. The first sale was made on May 4, and after they paid all debts, there remained the sum of 6 francs and 61 centimes per man. Each then received 5 francs in wages, and the remainder was spent on a large feast to celebrate the establishment of the company. For the first time in a year, the fourteen part owners and their families were in a position to drink proper wine. Thereafter, they lived on 5 francs per week up to June, when a baker purchased a piano for which he paid under the counter, in bread. By 1850, the business had 40,000 francs in assets, cash, materials, and tools.

Mill also discusses the consumer cooperative at Rochdale where poor people could for the first time make their purchases without fear of being cheated. Here were people who before "never knew when they put good food in their mouth, whose every dinner was adulterated, whose shoes let in water a month too soon, . . . whose wives wore calico which could not wash."[42]

Mill warned that this cooperative would need to hold fast with its principles if it was not to become transformed into an anonymous shareholding company. Rochdale lived and flourished from 1848, but by 1870 had "degenerated." It is necessary to have competition if such an idea is to survive, maintained Mill. He was against all socialists who, not understanding economics, blamed competition for all ills. In order that the cooperatives and associations should flourish, it was also necessary that they meet the competition from capitalist businesses, which were often more efficient. It was only under such circumstances that new forms of business could develop and gain public confidence. Enterprises that produce anything that could be manufactured with labor should always be "an affair of competition instead of custom."[43]

5.3 The Ideal Bank and Commerce

Society needs not only new forms of business in agriculture and manufacturing but also in trade and finance, which keep business activity alive in the face of Ricardo's threat of stagnating profits. The function of these businesses is either to reduce the supply of capital so that the return in interest payments increased or to reduce wages and increase productivity, which influences profit margins. Wages and the productivity of labor are controlled by two kinds of businesses.

The machine builders and inventors transform scientific ideas into productive equipment. Mill observed that it was very profitable to be a machine builder for industry. New equipment would also increase the return from agriculture; so would methods such as the use of guano fertilizer or the introduction of sugar beet. Despite the fact that Ricardo's geometrically precise theory showed unmistakably that it was against the interests of landowners to introduce innovations that reduced the rent of the land, many inventions had come into usage. This provided for Mill a further proof of how one social law could be opposed by another: the law of reduced profits against the law of increasing population. Since more mouths required feeding, the innovations were tolerated, and the total area under cultivation did not decrease. Profits were temporarily maintained.

The other kind of business that saved the profits was concerned with foreign trade in cheaper goods from abroad. Ricardo had shown that the exchange values among the products of different lands were not determined by their respective costs of production. If Englishmen were willing to exchange ten yards of broadcloth for fifteen yards of linen, and Germans in their home market received twenty yards of linen for the same amount of broadcloth, the situation was set for a useful trade between the two countries. It is in a discussion of the exchange relations between two countries, using the example of broadcloth and linen between England and Germany, that Mill introduces his major and only contribution to theoretical economics. He maintains that the cause of exchange relations should be sought in the balance between the quantity of broadcloth supplied by England and the quantity of linen demanded from Germany. Broadcloth, measured in linen, would cost between fifteen and twenty yards so that both parties stood to gain in terms of quantity from the business. Mill stops short of defining the exact position for the exchange relations, stating that such depend upon other factors. The sale of silk handkerchiefs, for example, will certainly increase when the price falls, but the market for steam engines is less sensitive. Should the attempt be made to establish an exact theory concerning what people desired, it would lead back to the same narrow geometrical modeling of the type he had earlier rejected: "The circumstances on which the proportionate share of each countryland more remotely depend, admit only of a very general indication."[44]

We shall soon see how a coming generation of economists was to ignore Mill's reservations on this point.

Mill's general thesis was that industrialism changed the character of people in the direction of thrift and work and that one result of this was that there would never be a shortage of saved capital. On the other hand, it could be thought that profits would sink as a result of a surplus of capital. But the lower the rate of profits in percentage terms, the more willing people would be to take risks. Speculators provide a "ready ear" for questionable large-scale projects. They willingly place their savings in the shares of railway companies or mines of a very risky nature. These very seldom give a profit and frequently collapse before the project has even come into operation. Following bankruptcy, further capital is lost in the rusting machines, unemployed persons, and useless factory buildings. It is just these destructive consequences of the capitalist system that are the social function of failed enterprises.

Mill finally emphasizes that speculative business enterprises are necessary in order to set liquid capital to work and stop sudden falls in prices. When speculators make profitable business, they serve a social function in holding up the level of prices in the circumstances of a temporary fall. But could it not be that these speculators drove up prices and lived at the cost of society? No, maintains Mill. If all speculators gained from their dubious affairs, it was a certain sign that they had only speeded up a price rise that would have come into existence even without their actions. If speculators themselves caused the rise in price, it was not possible for them all to make profits from the situation. Some might profit, but others would lose, and speculators as a group would pay for the operation. No one suffers from the activities of speculators, but all benefit from their function of balancing out price fluctuations. Speculators, like other groups such as trade unions and middle men, help to maintain the market in action. Society needs the speculators in the daily struggle of competition against the forces of tradition:

> The market rate is not fixed for him by some self-acting instrument, but is the result of bargaining between human beings of what Adam Smith calls "the higgling of the market"; and those who do not "higgle" will long continue to pay, even over a counter, more than the market price for their purchases.[45]

6. The Functions of the State

6.1 Financing Reform

How should these ideas be put into practice? During Mill's time there was certainly no lack of proposals for reform, and he himself complained about these reformers with their notions concerning how the Corn Laws should be abolished, taxation reduced, small denomination notes spread, the church revived or abolished, or the aristocracy eliminated. The trouble with all these reformers was that they failed to listen to Mill's own ideas. It was, nevertheless, difficult for Mill to complain too much, since his own analysis of democracy and freedom, together with his advocacy of the equality of the sexes, was an important contribution to contemporary political debate. He himself sat at one time in the House of Commons, but it was, however, as a writer that he most exercised his considerable influence upon the work of reform in nineteenth-century Britain.

Mill held in principle to the doctrine of laissez-faire, but he qualified this with certain reasonable exceptions. People in general knew what was best for themselves, and the state should be a helper in need although not a source of charity. People should be encouraged to self-help where this was possible; the underaged, sick, aged, and insane should certainly be protected. It was, however, necessary to be on guard that such protection was not misused as, for example, by avaricious relatives who were only interested in getting their hands on the property. The more that human actions concerned the future and complex interactions of others, the more difficult it became for the individual to comprehend the situation. Eternal contracts, either in business or marriage, should not receive the sanction of the state. People also hardly knew their own best interests when it came to questions of education and culture, although this was not to be taken as an argument in favor of a state monopoly in schooling. The rule of the majority under democracy was always a potential threat against the individual, but without the initiative of the state, certain useful enterprises would never have come into being. The geographical expeditions, for example, would not have been equipped, not to mention hospitals, colleges, roads, harbors, or the "printing presses" that would not exist without the initiative of the state. It was also the duty of the state to put the administration of land into the hands of the industrious small-holding farmers. How should this be financed?

Since there existed no shortage of capital, the state could afford to expropriate the large estates to pay for public education, which would extend literacy to the population in general. This could be financed through three honest methods, plus one that was of a criminal character.

It was possible, in the first place, to utilize indirect taxation, but Englishmen disliked "seeing the face of the tax collector"[46] and fiddled the books or avoided indirect taxation by other means if they got the chance. One possible solution is to tax only visible objects, as, for example, a certain tax upon horse-and-carriages. In the case of agriculture, it would be necessary to distinguish land rents from the income from farming. Double taxation should be avoided, and sufficient income should be left for existence and the necessary investments for old age and the maintenance of children. All financing through taxation, even through indirect taxes, involves intricate judgments concerning justice.

A second possibility is for the state to borrow money if it has the necessary security, although this is only justifiable if it is intended to use the money for some productive activity. In this case, it does not matter as long as it does not force people to save more than they otherwise would have done. If the rate of interest rises after the issue of a loan, it is a certain sign that the state has through its borrowing swallowed up the nation's capital instead of increasing it. In this case the state borrowing has no effect.

A third method of financing reforms is through establishing a state bank or creating state enterprises through borrowing on the open market or through issuing shares. Mill suggests that it makes no difference if a company is in private or state ownership. Particularly in the case of monopolies, state ownership is preferable. This is because monopoly profits are comparable with compulsory taxation, and only the state has the legal right to tax its citizens. Mill suggests, for example, that the three companies that provide London with its water supply should be amalgamated. They did not, in any case, compete with each other and only lowered prices in order to stop new companies from establishing themselves in the business. Those who imagined that it was not possible for taxpayers to control business managers in the same manner as private owners were guilty of an unrealistic worship of private business. A politician who badly misbehaved was equally difficult—or easy—to get rid of as an incompetent business manager. It could be argued here that a business manager has more interest in the business than a politician has in the state, but in the same way as a manager could own shares, a politician or bureaucrat pays taxes. The fault with state enterprises lies on another level, and it is rather for reasons of public morality that the state should encourage the financing of private businesses.

The fourth, and criminal, method of financing reform is through issuing notes that have no reserves to back them. Notes should be secured either with precious metals or through property. This, according to Mill, is as applicable to states as to companies and individuals.

6.2 Legislating for Ethology

The difficulty with state action is that it does for its citizens what they should learn to do for themselves. Business enterprise is, for Mill, something of a school for the general public. It is in the successes and failures of business enterprise that people learn to be thrifty, industrious, and realistic. It is an ethological school of—as Adam

Smith said—self-command. It is also the arena for social experiment and change:

> Every theory of social improvement, the worth of which is capable of being brought to an experimental test, should be permitted, and even encouraged, to submit itself to that test. From such experiments the active portion of the working classes would derive lessons, which they would be slow to learn from the teaching of persons supposed to have interests and prejudices adverse to their good; would obtain the means of correcting, at no cost to society, whatever is now erroneous in their notions of the means of establishing their independence; and of discovering the conditions, moral, intellectual, and industrial, which are indispensably necessary for effecting without injustice, or for effecting at all, the social regeneration they aspire to."[47]

It is the duty of the state, through new laws and institutions, to make this possible. If an inventor would exploit his product commercially, he could, following the abolition of the usury laws, obtain a loan even if his security is limited. If he completely lacks any security, he could seek a companion and begin a "partnership." The companions could then found a "joint-stock company" on the basis of their respective contributions of money and knowledge, hoping to participate in future profits. Disputes that could arise concerning the distribution of profits should be settled according to simple rules and practices that could soon settle the matter. What would happen, however, if there were only losses to distribute?

Before the law of "limited liability" was introduced in Britain in 1855, the companions were held fully responsible for all their debts. If a creditor demanded payment, he could take any property they owned, either privately or in the company, for this purpose. The result was that those who lacked a private fortune, or the ability to impress people that they were rich, could forget any ideas they might have had about entering business. The inventor was forced to sell his patent as a product to some rich businessman. It was also not possible for ordinary people to test their business abilities in the marketplace.

The 1855 law provided British citizens with the same opportunities as French people already had on the other side of the Channel. Each inventor could now sell parts of the company to shareholders who hoped to share in the profits and knew that they only risked their contributed capital in the event of bankruptcy. So functioned the French *société anonyme*, which provided the model. Perhaps the inventor had his own ideas about how the company should be run. He himself could then become a full partner and offer others a more limited participation in the risks. In such enterprises, the management is in the hands of the owners, which makes it possible for the inventor to retain control in his own hands. If, however, the new forms of business organization were not accompanied by a better understanding of the laws of business economics, the result would be to undermine rather than encourage entrepreneurship among the population.

6.3 Legislating for Economy

Critics of the new laws had maintained that limited liability led to a lack of responsibility. It was as a safeguard against this that the new law required that the bookkeeping should be open to inspection. The old type of company had obtained credit on the basis of the good reputation of the owners. If they were wealthy people with fortunes, they could obtain credit on everything down to their clothing. It was nevertheless possible, as Mill pointed out, for owners of part of a company to hide away their fortune or to obtain even further credit through bluff and, in the event of a crash, drag others down with them. Now, an association that wants credit must show its books, and if these have been "cooked," it could expect punishment in the event of bankruptcy. Mill, in fact, complains that these punishments had generally been too mild, allowing creditors only access to the owner's property. In earlier times, the latter had ended up in the debtors' prison where a period on bread and water would often serve to dislodge the hidden assets. The milder regulations that made it more difficult to accumulate debts are a further argument in favor of limited liability and the excellence of associations. Moreover, the requirements that the other financiers of the company should be shareholders provided an increased security for a creditor, since there were fewer problems now concerning the priority of debt payments if things should turn out badly.

Mill advises the British government to adopt a tough line as the French had done with rogues, swindlers, and those responsible for messy bankruptcies. In the business-minded state, it is essential that economic order prevail. Enterprise goes hand in hand with sound and careful common sense. A brief look at the investigations into the causes of bankruptcy shows that carelessness is the most common reason for the misfortune: "Many insolvencies are produced by tradesmen's indolence; they keep no books, or at least imperfect ones, which they never balance; they never take stock; they employ servants, if their trade be extensive, whom they are too indolent even to supervise, and then become insolvent."[48]

Good business ethology goes hand in hand with careful business management, and when the ground for this is established the harmony of the business-minded state would bloom. According to Mill, it is only necessary to consider the example of New England in America where every town is "incorporated" so that churches, schools, universities, banks, and libraries are run, like industry and agriculture, with limited liability. In that society, there is no longer a special working class, and no political economist is necessary to calculate what is productive work rather than luxury and momentary pleasure. Everyone possesses a just and equal chance to both the necessities and the pleasures of life.

Notes

1. John S. Mill, *Autobiography*, p. 41.
2. Ibid., p. 15.

3. Ibid., p. 17.
4. Ibid., pp. 20–21.
5. Ibid., p. 19.
6. Ibid., pp. 133–134.
7. Ibid., pp. 151–152.
8. Ibid., pp. 225–226.
9. John S. Mill, *System of Logic Ratiocinative and Inductive*, Vol 2, p. 479.
10. Ibid., Vol 2, p. 446.
11. Ibid., Vol 2, p. 422.
12. Ibid., Vol 2, p. 421.
13. Ibid., Vol 2, pp. 482–483.
14. Ibid., Vol 2, p. 486.
15. Ibid., Vol 2, p. 480.
16. Ibid., Vol 2, p. 488.
17. Ibid., Vol 2, p. 496.
18. Ibid., Vol 2, p. 496.
19. Ibid., Vol 2, p. 501.
20. Mill, *Autobiography*, p. 237.
21. John S. Mill, *Principles of Political Economy with Some of Their Applications to Social Philosophy*, p. 188.
22. Ibid., p. xxvi.
23. Ibid., p. 198.
24. Ibid., p. 445.
25. Ibid., p. 558.
26. Ibid., p. 562.
27. Ibid., p. 73.
28. Ibid., p. 56.
29. Ibid., p. 55.
30. Ibid., p. 105.
31. Ibid., p. 141.
32. Ibid., p. 746.
33. Ibid., p. 748.
34. Ibid., p. 233.
35. Ibid., p. 211.
36. Ibid., p. 208.
37. Mill, *Autobiography*, p. 213.
38. Lucien Lévy-Bruhl, ed, *Lettres inédites de John Stuart Mill à Auguste Comte*.
39. Mill, *Principles of Political Economy*, p. 278.
40. Ibid., p. 257.
41. Ibid., p. 335.
42. Ibid., p. 786.
43. Ibid., p. 794.
44. Ibid., p. 587.
45. Ibid., p. 937.
46. Ibid., p. 864.
47. Ibid., p. 906.
48. Ibid., p. 912.

6

From Bookkeeping to
General Equilibrium:
Management in the Doctrine
of Léon Walras

1. A Family Firm

Who was Léon Walras (1834–1910)? A reasonably well educated economist would probably answer that he was the person who first developed equilibrium theory in economic analysis, complete with the diagrams and equations that are so pleasing to modern economists. Léon Walras is also of interest to us in this our present endeavor, because his ideas concerning management and business economics coincide with modern views on these topics.

Despite the diagrams, equations and symbols, Walras did not derive the notion of economic equilibrium from mathematics or geometry. Rather, he had worked as a business manager, and the inspiration for his idea of economic equilibrium had come from his experience in balancing the accounts of the company. It was by the method used to balance debts against assets, income, and costs to show the company's financial situation that he seems to have obtained the idea of attempting to demonstrate in a "scientific" manner what had already been maintained by the classical economists. When the natural price of goods equals the price obtaining in the market, these economists had held, the quantity of goods in demand would be the same as that supplied, and the sale price would be equal to the costs of production. Where such a state existed, Walras now maintained, there was a situation that was characterized as an economic equilibrium.

Léon Walras's work *Éléments d'économie politique pure ou la théorie de la richesse sociale* appeared in 1874. He considered this to be a very important work for having raised the subject to the level of a pure science that had global implication. Having "proved" the scientific truth of free trade and competition, he went so far as to suggest himself as a candidate for the Nobel Peace Prize in 1909. This was because "[i]t is impossible for two peoples to subsist on each other if they are engaged in war; and reciprocally, it is also very difficult for them to begin a war if they obtain a large part of their subsistence from the other. In a word, free trade not only supposes and demands peace, but also maintains and assures it."[1] International interdependence was, thus, the guarantor of the peace.

Léon Walras was a Frenchman who held a newly established professorship in political economy in the faculty of law at the University of Lausanne between 1870 and 1892. He had first visited Switzerland during the 1860s in connection with a competition concerning the topical subject of taxation. The competition was actually won by another Frenchman, Pierre-Joseph Proudhon, whose ideas had already been criticized by Léon Walras in his first economic writings in 1860. Walras obtained only the fourth prize in the competition but returned home with good contacts among the young radicals in Switzerland who were later to nominate him for the professorship, which he obtained with a majority of a single vote. The more conservative minded were long dubious about allowing this socialist the opportunity of lecturing in public. Having obtained his professorship, however, Léon Walras saw it as his duty to attempt to bridge the divide between conservative and radical economic theorists.

The economists in France competed not only for the three professorships and few more academic posts that then existed in the country but also in ideological terms. A considerable debate existed between socialists who sympathized with thinkers such as Fourier, Saint-Simon, Proudhon, and Blanc, on the one hand, and liberals under the leadership of Guillaumin, Passy, Garnier, and Baudrillart, on the other. [2] The liberals defended their laissez-faire position through the *Journal des économistes,* where Léon Walras, encouraged by his father, Auguste Walras, made repeated efforts to obtain acceptance. When more of his articles were rejected than accepted, his father comforted him with these words: "What does it matter about a herd of sheep like economists who huddle together under Daddy Guillaumin. You can let them graze in peace and quiet. It is better to go round or fly over the herd."[3]

Auguste Walras was also an economist, although his relation to his son was hardly of the nature that existed in the Mill family. Léon Walras rather saw himself as developing and refining the ideas of his father whom he held in the highest regard. The students at Lausanne noted with pleasure his small idiosyncrasy of always lifting his skull cap when he mentioned his father's name during lectures.

Auguste Walras had studied at the Ecole Normale Supérieure together with Augustin Cournot, who was another important influence upon the development of Léon Walras. The school was, however, closed in 1822 with the restoration of the monarchy, as it was considered to be a source of revolutionary ideas among the students. Léon Walras himself made two unsuccessful attempts to enter the Ecole Polytéchnique, which was another elite school with revolutionary connections. He followed, instead, the lectures given at the school of mining, Ecole des Mines, although he had little enthusiasm for the thought of a career as a mining engineer. He wanted rather to be a novelist, and he actually succeeded in publishing one novel before promising his father during a visit to the family home that he would concentrate upon "social and political economy and not literature in its proper sense."[4] His father who now saw that he had a heir, burst out, "You are my future and pride!" although his mother, who had seen the family fortune melt away in financing Auguste Walras's writings, was less enthusiastic. "Are you also thinking of doing political economy like your father?" was her only doubting question.[5]

His father actually worked as an inspector of schools and universities, although he was almost entirely engaged by the so-called property question. Already as a young student, Auguste Walras had been annoyed by legal theories that explained property rights by reference to custom and tradition. Where was the rational explanation of property ownership? was the question that bothered him. He could find no satisfactory answer here among the economists. Jean-Baptiste Say, for example, had maintained that economics was a question of utility and interests and was not concerned with the question of the distribution of property, which properly belonged to law and morals. Auguste Walras saw his task in terms of developing economic theory as the foundation for a rational theory of property ownership, something that could then be used to fight reactionary notions based on tradition, together with the idea that society was founded upon contract. The social was rather something born in mankind and was that which separated men from animals. This became clear, Léon Walras was to maintain, in economic behavior. When an animal is hungry, it simply finds something to eat. When a man is hungry, on the other hand, he makes a pair of shoes, which are then sold. Economic behavior, like other social phenomena, was a natural aspect of human rationality. The social scientific problem is to find the rational plan underlying the social facts. It was against this background that father and son developed a theory of property ownership for use in the problem of taxation.

From time immemorial, Walras held, people had lived by hunting and fishing, and even among herders there existed no contracts for land and the earth. It would, nevertheless, be wrong to maintain that property did not exist, since it did in the form of communal ownership. It was only during relatively recent times and the advent of industrialization that people had begun to divide up the lands and a class of landowners had come into existence. The next course of development lay in a movement beyond the stage of industrialization toward the era of commerce characterized by international trade. It was necessary, thus, for the agricultural sector to support not only the industrial class but also the growing numbers of merchants, traders, and functionaries that were now becoming increasingly important. The time was ripe for a return to common ownership of the land, and the theory of natural rights showed the way toward a reform of land laws that would leave the state as the sole owner.

When this reform had been carried out, the state could then finance the public sector from its income from land rents. This would make it unnecessary for the state to burden individual ownership with taxation and forced savings, and thus this reform would provide a solution to the tax problem: "[T]he state should own the land and from the rents obtain both its income for its existence and the necessary capital. Through giving the land to the state, the tax question is solved, or more correctly, abolished."[6]

It was this message that Léon Walras presented to the tax conference in Lausanne, mentioned earlier. Walras, however, had no inclination in all this toward a communistic equality in the division and distribution of wealth such as was advocated by the Fourierists and others. Ownership and distribution were not to be likened to the division of food between two brothers by an authoritarian father at the dinner table because "it was obvious that in this case the two exchangers were not even."[7]

Neither was it possible to distribute property according to the principle of friendly gifts to the deserving poor. This was something Walras had himself experienced as a schoolchild when the children of the wealthy were required to spread their jam on the bare slices of the poorer children: "Shortly stated, society was not a picnic. Concessions which could be accepted as friendship if voluntary would become a humiliation if imposed by law."[8]

People are not altruists, and they work primarily to satisfy their own needs. Beyond the question of land, Walras emphasized the rights of individual ownership: "For my part, I am very individualistic, and with regard to the terrain of individualism, I am inclined to consider that right [of private property] to be absolute."[9]

The ownership and inheritance of capital in general were not the targets of Léon Walras.

2. Combining Liberalism with Socialism

Auguste Walras had opposed Jean-Baptiste Say's method of separating economics from law, and his son had attempted to develop a theory that covered the question of private property. Toward the close of the 1860s, Léon Walras provided a series of public lectures on the contemporary economic situation, deeply regretting the decline of the true and classical doctrine among political economists: "Yes, gentlemen: in earlier times political economy, free competition and free exchange were synonyms, but today there exist economists of control and protectionism, economists who defend privileges and monopolies."[10]

What a division now existed between, on the one hand, the English economists with their "genie liberale," and on the other, the French socialists with their communistic notions. How was it possible for certain economists to limit themselves to utility value theory when it was obvious that there was much that was useful which yet lacked value? How could others maintain that work was the only source of value without being able to explain how work itself has a value? And then there were those lax-minded liberals who preached "laissez-faire" but never bothered to prove that their ideas were correct! They rejected all proofs on the grounds that such was dogmatism and petrified doctrine because, according to these free thinkers, everything was movement, feelings, and self-organization. Such a liberalism, warned Walras, threatened to break down into anarchy in ideas, since it ignored everything that was not strictly individual in character. On the other hand, those who advocated the labor theory of value were not much better. They raised their value theory to a moral doctrine about property that was grounded in the value of work. When they then sought to apply their moral doctrine, they met difficulties that they attempted to resolve in a desperate resort to violence and tyranny. The socialists, moreover, could not understand how an economy actually functioned. A good example of this, held Walras, was the collectivist Marxists' attempt to solve the problem of distribution in society.

When the Marxists had abolished profits and interest and had handed over all businesses to the state, the workers would be rewarded with products on showing a receipt for their contribution to production. Besides smaller problems, such as meeting the costs of depreciation and accounting for the real contributions of work, the state-owned business would be confronted by the workers who demanded products for their receipts. Even if human needs were known, there arose here an unavoidable problem that was not possible for the Marxists to resolve. There existed useful products that would not be sufficient for all if they were distributed according to the promised work-value price. It would not be impossible to imagine, for example, that the workers could demand a million bottles of the Château-Lafitte wine. It took perhaps only an hour of labor to produce one such bottle. But this fine vintage only existed in an annual harvest of some 20,000 bottles. How was this to be distributed, Walras asked of the Marxists, through lottery or through an underhanded distribution among members of the government and their friends? An alternative solution would be for the Marxists, who despite everything were considered by Walras to be at least honest, to pull up the grape vines and plant apples or hops instead. Cider and beer production was easier to regulate than production of a special wine according to the principle of the quantity of work. The labor value theory, thus, led to the conclusion that commodities that could not be produced in quantities that would be demanded at the work-value price should not be produced at all. Walras considered that such commodities existed to a far greater extent than the classical economists had allowed. Both Mill and Ricardo, held Walras, had given the false impression that goods could be reproduced in infinite quantities with the help of manpower. When they discussed commodities that could not be infinitely reproduced, they took up extreme examples such as diamonds and wine, continued Walras, forgetting the fact that he himself had used one such example.

The value of a product or commodity depended rather on the fact that it was not infinitely reproducible. Value, in other words, depended on the shortage of products and services, which in turn was a function of the quantity owned and the human need for it. So ran Auguste Walras's formula for value. If the socialists understood the theory of value, they could soon make very good business with the state-owned vineyards when the latter had been nationalized. They could sell Château-Lafitte at high market prices to rich individuals who had earned their money honestly through their personal talents. The state would profit from the shortage of suitable vineyards, while persons who possessed a monopoly of some talent—such as the writer Alexandre Dumas or Mario the popular singer—could wet their throats with the wine and thereby contribute to the state treasury to the benefit of the greater public. It was, thus, possible to combine socialism with a liberal marketing system. Injustice and distorted distribution were not the result of the functions of a market economy. It was only necessary here, maintained Léon Walras, to consider the fortunes of American millionaires, which were rather the result of monopolies and speculation than the operations of a free market.

Léon Walras, nevertheless, experienced considerable difficulty in convincing both liberals and socialists of the validity of his arguments. He related how, following a difficult discussion with Saint-Simon, he had come to understand that he must find a better form for his argument if he was to succeed in convincing socialists that free-market prices would certainly lead to the greatest welfare. It was then that he was struck by the idea that would guide him to the pure theory: "Obvious! It was necessary to prove that free competition procured the maximum utility. I thus came to approach mathematical economics."[11] Given his mathematical background in mining engineering, this would not be difficult. Léon Walras himself describes this moment as being that when he saw his Newton apple fall.

3. Firms in Pure Economy

3.1 Bearers and Exchangers

Walras was convinced that human thought and ideas serve to formulate the world. Had not the French Revolution, for example, been prepared through reflection and set in motion through feelings? Doctrine, the purified teaching, preceded action as life itself preceded thought. Léon Walras came to believe that his basic task in life was to construct the doctrine of pure economics. He was the first systematic builder of economic models, and his gigantic system of formulae was presented in a series of forty-two lectures. With a magnificent display of mathematical equations and geometrical diagrams, he sought to cement into place the ideas to which the classical economists had given expression in their texts. He by no means attempted to hide the fact that the notions of the market and free competition had already been developed by his predecessors, but rather saw that his task was to confirm these ideas through exact scientific argument. Walras saw himself as the mathematical housecleaner among the distorted notions of the contemporary economists in their different camps. If the pure doctrine was to provide a backbone for economics as a discipline, it must appear as an authoritative contribution to the debate in favor of free markets:

> Few of us are in a position to read Newton's Mathematical Principles of Natural Philosophy or de Laplace's Celestial Mechanics; but we nevertheless rely on competent judges and believe in the description of the astronomical facts that is made with the aid of the principle of universal attraction. Why should we not, in the same manner, rely upon a description of economic facts of the world in conformity with the principle of free competition?[12]

In his efforts to present the pure doctrine, Walras felt constrained to introduce certain simplification of the ideas held by earlier economists. These simplifications also had relevance to his views on business and business enterprise.

3.2 Exchange

Walras set to work to "demonstrate" that which economists had already maintained, in particular, that the market price implies that the quantity supplied is identical with that demanded. The market for Walras is an assembly of individuals who approach each other as bearers (*porteurs*) with the intention of becoming exchangers (*échangeurs*) in the light of their individual abilities and capacities. Here comes a man bearing a quantity of oats, and there comes another dragging a sack of bread corn, and between them in the middle of the market stands the crier (*le crieur*) whose task it is to bring about a price that is "completely natural . . . under the influence of competition."[13] The market price that emerges in these circumstances is a natural phenomenon rather than something that arises out of the negotiations or contracts between different people. It is only necessary to observe how easily the crier on share or commodity markets raises and sinks prices until the supply and demand of sellers and buyers is equal one to the other. When supply is equal to demand, the market price is fixed, which is precisely what other economists had been arguing for the past fifty years.

Walras now seeks to make a more thorough investigation of "exchange value as general phenomenon."[14] The market price is so fundamental that he refrains from explaining the price mechanism from the example of the stock market, which presumes the existence of both capital and stock market institutions. Money and the stock market, as all other relevant institutions, are the result rather than the cause of the phenomenon of exchange. Walras, thus, allows two persons to exchange two commodities against each other without the intervention of money. The supply of the one commodity is set against the demand of the other, and the demand of the second commodity is set against the supply of the first. This mirror imaging made it possible for Walras to apply his method of demonstration "that from given assumptions and conditions [one could] formulate an equation system with an equal number of equations as unknowns whose roots are the assumed quantities."[15] The simplified picture of the market is, thus, to be transformed into a mathematical model.

It was now necessary to work out those demanded quantities and the prices at which these would be identical with their respective supplies. The man with the oats consequently provides oats against bread corn, and the man with the bread corn provides bread corn against oats. It is then possible to set up equations for these two exchanges that must be like the double entries of a bookkeeping account. The two accounts for the men with the oats and bread corn would, using Walras's symbols, depict the respective demands and supplies for the commodities in question thus:

Oat Owner's Account		Corn Owner's Account	
Demanded Corn	Supplied Oats	Demanded Oats	Supplied Corn
Db which can be written as Fb (pb)	Oa which can be written as DB (pb) or Fb (pb) pb	Da which can be written as Fa (pa)	Ob which can be written as Da (pa) or Fa (pa) pa

Demand (for oats Da, corn Db) was regarded by Walras as a function of the price (Fa (pa) and Fb (pb) resp). Supply (Oa resp Ob), on the other hand, he regarded only as a result of demand at a given price (Db (pb) and Da (pa), resp). Thus, when oats are exchanged against corn, the supply of oats in relation to corn depends on the amount of corn demanded multiplied by its price in oats. In the exchange market, it is clear that the mirror image—i.e., the exchange of corn against oats at the same time—is valid. Supply can even be expressed with those symbols that were used for demand: Supply of oats Oa = Fb (pb) pb and the supply of corn Ob = Fa (pa) pa, respectively. Beyond this, it was clear that the price of oats in terms of corn multiplied by the price of corn in terms of oats must always be equal to 1. With the help of these symbols, Walras was now in a position to provide his demonstration in the form of equations which showed the balance between the two accounts.

It can now be seen what Walras meant by a "demonstration." He did not show how market dynamics produced the equilibrium price, but rather he formalized the static relationship that would obtain when that price had been achieved. Given that supply was identical with demand, he showed how this could be formalized with the aid of symbols. Given that equilibrium arose under certain conditions, he showed with a formal and static argument of a circular nature the conditions under which this state would obtain. He himself remarked rather laconically after this demonstration that "[t]his law would appear to be so simple that we could have formulated it directly following the study of the share market, but a rigourous demonstration was necessary."[16]

The deductions to be drawn in the pure doctrine provided no new knowledge. It formalized without explaining or providing any understanding. It could, on the contrary, be held that such an approach filtered out the odd cases that did not meet the suppositions. If figures are adopted in the respective accounts for oats and corn instead of equations, it is immediately possible to see the practical difficulties Walras was forced to ignore in order to maintain the pure doctrine pure.

Let us suppose that the crier one fine day opens the market with the bid, "2 bushels of oats against 1 of corn." The oats owner responds in this case with the demand, "12 bushels of corn," which means that he is willing to supply 2 x 12 = 24 bushels of oats. The owner of corn answers in the same moment that he demands, "16 bushels oats," which implies that he is willing to supply 16/2 = 8 bushels of corn. The crier now understands that the supply of oats is 24 bushels while demand is limited to 16 bushels, and that the supply of corn is 8 bushels while there is a demand for 12 bushels. He thus makes a new bid. He will, according to the marketing method, raise the value of corn in terms of oats so that the supplies of corn and oats approach their respective demands. The new bid is perhaps, "3 bushels of oats to 1 of corn." But on an exchange market, where commodity is exchanged against commodity, it is not at all certain that such a rise in price reduces the gap between supply and demand. If the oats owner will still demand 12 bushels of corn, he may well now supply 36 bushels of oats. If the cheaper oats attract the owner of corn to purchase these 36 bushels for 12 of corn, then the required equilibrium is obtained. But the cheaper oats could also perhaps only increase the demand to, say, 18 bushels since the owner of corn possibly has not more horses than could devour the 18 bushels. In this case, the new price would lead to an increased demand for oats but a reduced supply of corn (earlier 8 against 12, now 6 against 18 with the new bid of 3 to 1). Such effects, which would tend to show that a certain single price was hardly a natural phenomenon on exchange markets, were to a large degree ignored by Walras. The advantage that the exchange case had of lending itself easily to demonstration with the aid of equations does not extend to proving that a single, in some sense natural, market price was the necessary outcome of free exchange markets.

Léon Walras was, however, more interested in establishing a pure economic doctrine and thus ignored such problems. With this law—his Newton's apple—in mind, he rushed on to consider the fundamental causes of value.

From the example of accounting with physical transactions in exchange markets, he moved on to the very heart of economic metaphysics.

3.3 Individuals—The Pump of Demand

Walras postulates that supply is a result of demand, and thus it is now relevant to penetrate into the causes of demand. Demand as a function of price could be depicted with the aid of a curve that shows how much of a commodity a buyer would be willing to purchase at different prices in the market. Such are known as demand curves and generally slope downward from left to right, showing that more will be demanded as price falls and less as it rises. But what is it that determines the shape of these curves? What is it that determines these listed quantities at different prices?

The curve's lower end could show how much of a commodity would be demanded if it were (very nearly) free of any price; its upper end could show how little of the commodity would be purchased if the price were very high. In order to obtain such a curve for any given person, it is necessary to know how much this individual would purchase at some range of prices between these points. For both Léon Walras and his father, the phenomenon depicted in these curves emerged from something they called intensity of need, which was essentially individual in character. Léon Walras emphasizes that shortage or insufficiency provides the absolute basis for the fact of relative exchange values. Nevertheless, "these shortages, which are absolute and not relative, are subjective or personal, and hardly real or objective. They exist in us and not in the object."[17] If this is the case, however, the question is likely to arise as to how it is possible to construct the pure economic doctrine on the basis of something so subjective and personal. Walras is content to avoid the question:

> This analysis is incomplete, and it would seem not possible to pursue it further since the absolute intensity of utility does not vary in time and space in a directly measurable form. . . . Oh well! (Eh bien!) This difficulty is not insurmountable. Assume that such a relation exists."[18]

Walras now adopts the model of the economic man. All individuals in the marketplace are assumed to know the shape of their own subjective utility curves, which for every market price would provide a constellation of purchases that would maximize satisfaction. Whichever price is called on the market, the exchangers would know their own best interests and continue to exchange goods and services in such a manner that their utility maintains a relation among them as with prices. Walras found here an argument that he had lacked in his earlier debate with Saint-Simon.

Following the publication of his pure theory in 1874, Walras received a letter from William Stanley Jevons, the English economist, which mildly pointed out that the notion of shortage was very much like his own theory of exchange. There was, furthermore, Walras discovered, a German by the name of Herman Heinrich Gossen who had also played with the idea of the intensity of needs. The difference was that while Gossen considered all human satisfactions to be equal, which led him among other things to advocate an equal distribution of commodities without regard for private ownership, both Walras and Jevons emphasized that the quantities owned would provide the basis for the calculation of need.[19] In such a distribution system, it was clear that everyone would not experience the same need satisfaction, although they would all come to experience satisfaction in the same proportion as prices. Walras' distribution system also retained the gap between the rich and the poor and did not seek to level out the differences. The communistic exchange model, on the other hand, demanded the use of the authority of the state for its leveling operations, since it was considered that such operations could never be achieved on a voluntary basis. When Gossen recommended that two owners who possessed, for example, 100 kg meat and 200 kg bread, respectively, give each other 50 kg meat and 100 kg bread, respectively, so that each ended up with an equal amount of both commodities, Walras and Jevons considered it just that the meat owner should exchange 70 kg meat for 60 kg of bread. The quantities should not be equally distributed, according to Walras's theory of proportionality. It was more important that the owned quantities following the exchange correspond to the intensity of need in proportion to price. If the price of meat against bread was in the ratio 1 : 2, the owner of meat could have 30 kg left after having purchased 60 kg of bread, and the bread owner could have 140 kg bread left over after having exchanged the rest for 70 kg meat. The price proportion 1 : 2 corresponded, thus, to the ratios meat: bread: : 30 : 60 and bread : meat : : 70 : 140. This, in short, is Walras's view of the origins of demand and the determination of value. We can now turn to the role of business in Walras's economic doctrine.

3.4 Firms as the Passive Suppliers

The suction of the pump of wealth, according to Walras, stems entirely from the demand from individuals, and business functions as a kind of pressure gauge in the pumping system. In the exchange theory, individuals appear as "bearers," "owners," and "exchangers" of commodities, the existence of which is taken for granted. The commodities have simply appeared as a result of the active demands from individuals, and Walras stubbornly opposes all suggestions that individuals, through investing labor and capital in production, could increase the national wealth. Whereas in his theory of exchange he deals with individuals, in his theories of production and capital he turns to the role of the firm in the market.

Against the active suction of demand in the pump of wealth from the land-, labor-, and capital-owning individuals, Walras poses a passive supply from business. All commodities emerge through a combination of work, capital, and the products of the earth. This combining process takes place in businesses that, in contrast to individuals, lack needs and will, passively adapting to the signals from the market. It is here that Walras differs radically from other economists, such as Mill, Smith, and Ricardo, who conceived the market as a unit where people as producers met with people who were consumers. Walras avoids the problem of market interaction by assembling all causes of marketing activity under the demand side of the question so that the supply side appears largely as an effect from this source. Production is an effect of demand; the transition in the cause/effect relationship here is achieved with the aid of two concepts.

Walras felt, in the first place, that it was necessary to replace the notion of the active individual as producer, seller, and saver in the market with "the entrepreneurs whose goal was to realize profits through transforming production services into products"[20] Walras thus discovers the entrepreneur whose role or function is to be clearly distinguished from those of workers, capitalists, and landowners: "Let us now call this fourth role the entrepreneur, being entirely distinct from the foregoing [worker, capitalist, landowner], and whose task is to hire land from the landowner, personal qualities from the worker and capital from the capitalist, combining these three production services in agriculture, industry and trade."[21] One and the same person could play several roles. A shoemaker, for example, could be a worker when he stands with his last and an entrepreneur when he visits the bank or sells shoes over the counter. When the business makes a profit, the shoemaker earns wages as a worker and profits as an entrepreneur.

Walras's second innovation is to divide the concept of the market into two separate markets for the services of production and products: "One can here, in order to better understand the phenomena, represent two markets, instead of one: a market for services [of production] where services are supplied exclusively by landowners, workers and capitalists, and where the demand . . . for the productive services comes from entrepreneurs; and a product market where products are supplied exclusively by entrepreneurs."[22]

This, however, is only the beginning of the process of subclassification of markets. As water in a canal system may be dammed, divided into different channels, and guided through locks, Walras divides and guides the economic flood of the services of production—capital, land, and personal qualities— through various markets in the economy. The land leased by the businessman gives its return in terms of land rent. The personal qualities are the source of labor that is hired by the businessman and paid for in the form of wages. Likewise, he pays in the form of interest for the use of the capital that contributes to his profits. The entrepreneur who senses suction from the product market makes his calculations and offers his products at different prices based on a knowledge of the prevailing conditions in the market. When equilibrium prices are reached, the purchaser obtains contracts (*bons*). In the period following, they are then fulfilled and the goods produced and delivered under the leadership of the entrepreneur. The products arise from the application of a technical formula that expresses the relationship between the productive factors of labor, profits, and interest. When the proportions in the formula change, a technical development takes place. The reduction of the role of land rents relative to that of capital, according to Léon Walras, is a definition of economic development.

The role of profits in business is to measure the suction of the market. In a situation of pure equilibrium where demand is equal to supply and price is equal to costs, there are not profits. This state of equilibrium is an ideal condition that is never realized in practice. Walras compares the markets to the behavior of the seas, which on occasion may be whipped up by the winds and at other times may be quiet but yet never achieve a condition of complete rest. The entrepreneur who seeks profits would at the same time contribute to the reduction of profits through guiding work, capital, and land toward a larger supply of the product in demand. Profit is measured through the instrument of bookkeeping. The company is for the entrepreneurs only an account, a balance sheet that provides the results over a given period. The most concrete aspect of Walras's pure theoretical doctrine shows how the entrepreneur enters the economic waters to determine the situation at a given point in time.

3.5 The Task of the Entrepreneur

The adaptation of the business to the market through the increase or reduction of the quantity of supply is something, according to Walras, that happens naturally when conditions of free competition prevail. Walras's formalization of production functions was not intended to inform businessmen about what they should do or the like, but rather, as in the case of the exchange theory, to demonstrate how that which happens de facto in the markets could be conceptualized in mathematical terms. Walras had already made the following important distinction between practical and theoretical solutions in his discussion of exchange theory:

> The practical solution is quick and certain, leaving nothing more to desire. One can see how the great markets function without dealers or criers, how the equilibrium price is determined within a few minutes, and how considerable

quantities of merchandise are exchanged at this price in two or three quarters of an hour. The theoretical solution, on the contrary, would in most cases be absolutely impracticable.[23]

Just as Newton had declared that he had no intention of controlling the stars with his celestial mechanics, so did Walras disclaim any aspirations to developing his equilibrium theory into a guide for practical management training. The pure doctrine, with one exception, was never intended as an instrument. This exception concerns business bookkeeping.

Walras considered it possible for the entrepreneur to measure the pressure in the pump of wealth through consulting "the books and the condition of the raw material and products in stock."[24] It is here that Walras provides the only practical lesson in the whole of his pure doctrine of economics. It concerns the manner of bookkeeping and maintaining inventories according to

> [t]he mode taken from ordinary practice which was in full accord with the preceding [theoretical] conceptions, which therefore proved that our theory of production was well grounded in reality. I begin with a few short words to describe the principles of double bookkeeping.[25]

The entrepreneur's tool is his cashbox. In order to keep a check on its contents, he takes a sheet of white paper and writes "Cash" as the title. He then draws two columns and writes down all the sums of money he had received in the left-hand column and all the sums he had paid out in the right-hand column. The left-hand column he titles "Debits," being that which the business owes to those who have paid money; the right-hand column he titles "Credits," being that which had been used. Curious as to where all the money comes and goes, the entrepreneur allocates accounts to his capitalist friends from whom he has borrowed money, as well as to the factors of production he has purchased from other businesses, or for production services he has hired in the market for such services. Besides his cash account, he has his capital account, cost account for products, recurrent account like wages, interest, and so forth. He records all these business transactions in two registers: first in the day book in chronological order and then in the main book in the appropriate account.

Take, for example, a cabinetmaker, who sets up business with an initial capital of 10,000 francs. He contributes 3,000 francs of this sum from his savings and borrows the remaining 7,000 francs at 5 percent interest from friends and relatives who are concerned about him and trust him. He has, thus, 10,000 francs in his cashbox, and a new company sees the light of day. He now leases for 500 francs per year a piece of land on which he builds a workshop, which, together with the equipment, costs a further 5,000 francs. He enters this as credit in the cash account and as investment in the cost account. Wood and material for furniture he purchases for 2,000 francs, which he credits in the cash account and debits in the product account. When he has sold furniture for 6,000, this is debited from the cash account and credited to the product account. He then decides that it is time to assess how the business is progressing. After making an inventory, he discovers that there is no furniture in the store. He has a surplus from sales of 4,000 francs (6,000 francs income minus 2,000 francs for wood and materials), which he uses to pay wages of 2,000 francs and rent of 500 francs, and a further 500 francs as interest on the loan to friends and relatives. The profit from the period is, thus, 1,000 francs. Walras depicts this situation as follows:

> When the period is completed, the accounts are balanced in the following manner:
> The cash account has received 16,000 fr and paid 10,000 fr. That is a debit of 6,000 fr.
> The company account has received 10,000 fr. This is a credit of 10,000 fr.
> The investment account for establishment, has received 5,000 fr. This is a debit of 5,000 fr.
> The product account has received 6,000 and paid 6,000. It is, thus, balanced.
> The cost account has received 3,000 fr and paid 3,000 fr. It is, thus, balanced.
> The profit and loss account has received 1,000 fr. It is credited with 1,000 fr.

The balance is summarized as:

ACTIVE (composed of all debit accounts)

Cash	6,000 fr
Investment costs	5,000 fr
Total	11,000 fr

PASSIVE (composed of all credit accounts)

Company	10,000 fr
Profit and loss	1,000 fr
Total	11,000 fr[26]

It would naturally be somewhat more complex in reality, adds Walras. Payments are spread out over time and are often not made in cash but through exchange. Suppliers often give credit, and customers are also often granted credit. The largest problem of modern bookkeeping—that of valuation—is not, however, touched by Léon Walras. This is because in the world of pure theory, prices are set by the market and no bookkeeper needs to bother about valuations, since this is taken care of automatically.

The entrepreneur's rewards for his efforts come in the form of profits. His efforts lie, however, in the realm of bookkeeping. The example where the cabinetmaker appears as manager, worker, and capitalist is typical for Walras, who believes that it is just this combination of roles that marks the genuine firm, a point that he had made in a debate some ten years before the appearance of the pure doctrine.

4. The Genuine Enterprise

4.1 Cooperative Action

Walras's life was marked by his involvement in controversy, and his equations were often contributions to discussions and arguments rather than destined for the bookshelf. He had when younger thrown himself into the tax debate in order to float his father's radical notions concerning the state ownership of land and the abolition of income and business taxation. Some five years later he had published his *Les associations populaires de consommation, de production et de crédit*, which dealt with the great French debate concerning the cooperative movement. Walras as usual offered his contribution from the point of view of a social scientist who would convince through the weight of rational arguments. He had hoped for a better response in the cooperative debate than he had. met in the question of taxation, and he held that it was just in the cooperative movement that there "opened a terrain where political economics and democracy were united in their destinies."[27]

Being of democratic persuasion, Walras accepted the idea that workers should get together in a cooperative in order to become entrepreneurs; moreover, he regarded the notion as being rationally acceptable from a theoretical economic point of view. He was also careful to point out that cooperation was not a threat to other forms of business enterprise or to private property as an institution. Cooperation was rather an important but small part of the national economy. The heart of his message was the demonstration that economic revolution was unnecessary because "nothing was sillier than to make a revolution when it was sufficient with a reform."[28]

French economic law needed reform because it had been written under the influence of more or less widespread economic prejudices. The law, however, was now for many economists a house that should be demolished, whereas lawyers regarded it as a beautiful monument that should be preserved. Walras, for his part, meant that it was sufficient, with a small addition to the great monument, to cater to the needs of cooperative forms of business.

There already existed three major forms of business organization: the "société anonyme," the "société en nom collectif," and the "société en commandite." These forms were distinguished from each other by the degree of responsibility of the participants. The responsibility was complete in the case of the "société en nom collectif"; limited in proportion to the amount of the capital contributed in the case of the "société anonyme"; and in the case of the "société en commandite," limited for certain individuals and unlimited for others. The "société en nom collectif," according to Walras, was well suited for trading companies where the full responsibility of the owners provided adequate security to the suppliers. The "société anonyme" was a suitable form for an industrial business, a factory, or a railway that required large amounts of capital to set in operation. It could not provide the same security for third parties as the "société en nom collectif," but it ensured that the owners would not lose more than their contributions. It was possible that one or more of these three forms of business organization could be suitable for cooperative enterprises, although there existed a clear problem with regard to law. Both the number of part owners and the amount of capital should be flexible in a cooperative business. Thus, the law should be changed to allow new members to come and go on the condition that the names and addresses of members and the total capital were made public each month. With regard to the inner organization of cooperatives, Walras considered, as was the case with other forms of businesses, that state control was to be avoided. Cooperative enterprises—whether of the English consumer model or the French producer model, or in the form of the German credit cooperative—should be allowed to function under conditions of the maximum possible freedom.

This freedom implied that businesses would function in a market, which for Walras was an assembly of individuals competing with each other as buyers for supplied quantities of commodities that could originate in either state or private businesses. Prices would be determined through open competition, and for this reason, Walras opposed forms of cooperative enterprise that rewarded their members with cheaper goods, higher wages, or lower interest rates on loans. A cooperative should, as with other businesses, make profits that could, in turn, be saved in order to serve as a source of insurance and investment for its members.

Freedom within the company means that it should be free to organize its activities according to its own order. This should cover both the raising of funds and the disposition of profits, together with the administration that would be under the control of a committee or someone who is in charge of the employees. Cooperation is built upon brotherly feeling, but this is something that cannot be guaranteed through the proclamation of revolutionary laws and regulations. The order within the company must be allowed to develop freely according to the principle of self-help. In this way, charitable organizations such as philanthropic housing schemes, insurance, and cooperative enterprises could utilize the general climate of freedom.

4.2 Cooperative Capitalism

Suppose now that there is a man with two empty hands who seeks a place at the pump of wealth. He could contribute with his knowledge and skills, such tools or equipment that he may own, and the sums of money that he may have saved. But if he lacks both equipment and funds, how could he obtain the means to hire the capital necessary to begin his own business? He could offer no real security to obtain a loan beyond perhaps his personal assurance that, if he obtained funds, he would work industriously to ensure the success of the business. In Germany, however, Ferdinand Lasalle had suggested a passage to the pump of wealth via the general right to vote. The idea was that when this right had been achieved, it could be used to pass a law that would provide interest-free loans from the state, which would place capital in the hands of the industrious workers who lacked property. Since Walras disliked taxation, he praised the German *Vorschussbanken* for having fought against poverty and unemployment in a much more effective and free manner. These cooperative credit banks had come into existence during the 1850s, and by 1862 Walras reckoned that there were 511 such institutions. In order to become a member, it was necessary to pay a fee of about four French francs and thereafter to save between 30 and 60 centimes per month. An investigation of the accounts of 243 of these banks showed a total membership of 70,000 with a paidup capital of 5 million francs. Beyond this, however, they had control over a further 23 million francs of which 10 million francs had been borrowed from members and the rest from other institutions. Each member could borrow directly that sum he had himself saved, and if more was required for some particular business enterprise, he had to ask other members to stand as security. These cooperative banks, thus, functioned as both saving and credit banks, providing a route, according to Walras, through which the emptyhanded man, with the help of his comrades, could obtain the necessary capital without security.

Walras describes two similar French cooperatives. The one named "Société du crédit au travail" was a credit and loan bank for workers. The other, the "Caisse d'escompte des associations populaires," in the administration of which Walras himself had participated, was a bank that had been started by the economist Léon Say, who was the grandson of Jean Baptiste Say. This bank specialized in providing help for already established associations and groups. As distinct from the "Société du crédit au travail," it lacked any individual savings or lending activities. Walras considered that these banks increased the possibilities of beginning new businesses, but this capacity could be improved if the state accepted his proposal for a change in law, particularly in relation to the form of responsibility, "garantie mutuelle," which he suggested. This mutual guarantee already existed in certain insurance companies that calculated their premiums so that the yearly sum of the damages paid out was distributed in proportion to the insured amounts of the members. If a large catastrophe should occur, it is then possible that the premium would rise to the sum of the insurance, although naturally it could not exceed this amount. The adaptation of such a principle of responsibility in the case of cooperative credit schemes would, held Walras, combine the principles of full and limited liability in such a manner that would encourage both the willingness to bear risks and the building of capital. Transferred to the credit market, the insurance principle would mean that if any of the bank's customers got into difficulties and could not repay his debts, the other borrowers would contribute toward the repayment in proportion to their respective credits. A reform to the advantage of cooperative enterprises would involve an increase of individual capitalism, greater economic democracy, and an important step on the road toward the union of liberalism with socialism.

5. A Dogmatic Doctrine

Walras is regarded as the father of modern economic equilibrium analysis. His manner of formalizing economic arguments has greatly influenced contemporary economists. It is, therefore, of interest to ask in conclusion what all this has to do with concrete economics and management.

Walras, in fact, only dealt by way of exception with concrete business economic conditions, although it is significant that these exceptions are concerned with bookkeeping and the forms of business organization. On practical economic action, Walras had little to say that was new. Behind his equations, formulae, and symbols there was a politico-economic manifesto that was hardly original in content. The economic proof of the maximization of happiness under the condition of free competition was received with skepticism by his contemporaries. The vice-rector of the University of Sorbonne, for example, rejected his offer to lecture on the philosophy of the social sciences with the excuse that it was necessary to obtain the permission of the archbishop before such a message could be delivered.[29] Certainly, Walras never presented himself as having some kind of religio-economic mission, although he did have a tendency to regard himself in terms of a doctor dealing with the ills of society, someone who was doing for economics what Newton and Darwin had done in the realms of physics and biology. He was succeeded in his professorship at Lausanne by Vilfredo Pareto, an Italian who considered that Walras's ideas on economic equilibrium were interesting but thought that they were bedded in a metaphysical reasoning that bordered upon the absurd. Modern commentators have considered that the emphasis upon mathematics tended to push out the concrete elements and hide Walras's important message concerning the interdependence of different markets.

But for Walras himself, economics was a science that could be fully compared with mathematical physics,[30] and mathematical research most probably represented for him the attempt of thought to obtain certain clarity. Walras seems in this to have been influenced by elements of the Socratic doctrine that marked Galileo and Newton, namely, that knowledge of the world already exists in the world if only we would learn to see it clearly. Galileo's work, for example, did not derive from observable physical objects and the famous experiments from the Leaning Tower at Pisa but rather from ideal mathematical objects such as spheres and planes. Had not physics found the general laws of motion with the help of geometry and algebra? When these abstract notions prove to be in agreement with concrete physical reality, it is easy to be taken in by a mystical belief concerning the power of pure thought. This would be particularly true, as in the case of Walras, when supported by a somewhat oversimplified view of the manner in which scientific research is actually pursued. Strangely enough, Walras himself seems to have had rather limited mathematical talent. He had failed in his attempt to enter the Ecole Polytéchnique, and his ideas in mathematical mechanics appear to have been obtained from Antoine-Agustin Cournot, the mathematician, a friend of his father. In the light of Cournot's attempts to combine mathematics with economic questions, Walras's novelty cannot be rated particularly high.

Cournot had written two theses in physics dealing, respectively, with the theory of bodies and the movements of heavenly bodies. He was an intellectual child of the rationalist movement of revolutionary France, where mathematics was developed as a tool for both engineers and the state administration. After 1789, mathematics had become more a subject for popular education than a hobby for learned gentlemen. Textbooks were written that could easily be grasped by students who had little understanding of philosophical issues. It was in this spirit that Walras pointed out that his pure theory was suitable for schoolchildren with only a basic knowledge of geometry and algebra. Mathematics provided one means of attacking the inherited burden of traditional classical education. Cournot, for example, considered that the advent of political economy made historical analysis old-fashioned. Smith and Say had said everything that was worth saying, and it was now time to direct attention to the future with mechanics leading the way. From 1789 onward, held Cournot, the world would come to develop, to an ever greater degree, a likeness with the ideal model of mechanics. The introduction of universal measurement systems and well-functioning credit institutions was a clear sign that frictions would come to be successively reduced in economic reality:

> The extension of commerce and progress in commercial arrangements tends to approach successively in reality the abstract world in which theoretical reasonings are based; even as a clever mechanic approaches the conditions of calculation as a result of polishing surfaces and the precision of cog wheels which reduces the friction.[31]

Cournot is the observer who thinks he can perceive a process of social development, while Walras takes on the role of the planner and advocates an active policy. If equilibrium prices presume free competition, it can be argued, for example, that this is an unrealistic assumption on which to base economic theory; but Walras argues that the theory rather provides a challenge to remove all barriers to free competition. Mathematics makes it possible, he maintains, to demonstrate which conditions must prevail in order that the benefits of free competition can be realized. He realizes that the picture of the ideal market provided does not always coincide with reality:

Besides these [ideal] markets there are others where competition, despite being regulated somewhat, functions acceptably and satisfactorily: these are vegetable, fruit and poultry markets. The streets of a town where stores and shops such as bakers, butchers, grocers, tailors and shoe makers exist that function in an even more defective manner with regard to competition, but where it nevertheless makes itself felt.[32]

Walras is also conscious of the fact that he is not really saying anything new, but he holds that he is providing the precise conditions under which free competition is possible, namely, where individuals themselves make decisions with regard to products of private interest. The argument for free competition is not meant to be valid in the case of "des services publics."

When Walras was attacked on the grounds that his model was based in free will and that such decisions were not amenable to calculation, he replied: "We have never attempted to calculate the free decisions of human beings, but only expressed mathematically their effects."[33]

Cournot, for his part, held that utility could never be calculated or evaluated. Questions concerning need and utility were "questions of judgment and not questions that were resolvable through calculation or logical argument."[34]

Cournot was not in agreement with Walras's notion that only a few people could understand Newton although many believed in him. Writing for students of "une école célèbre"—probably the Ecole Normale Supérieure—Cournot apologizes that the mathematics in his book may appear banal to a professional geometrician. While he is primarily interested in banishing the ignorance that he felt lay at the back of a dislike for mathematics, Walras is of the opinion that all opposition to mathematics is founded in an opposition to progress. Cournot was careful, thus, to emphasize that he used only mathematical functions and that his method should not be confused with elementary algebra or banking arithmetic. Mathematical analysis, he maintained, provided only a lead toward more positive studies that could be grounded in empirical customs and trade statistics. It was such that would be necessary when people became tired of all too general economics arguments. It was, however, just this general systematic ambition that moved Walras: a system where the theory of exchange led on to the theory of production, which, in turn, led on to the theories of capital and money. It was founded, moreover, on assumed measures of individual decisions that were immeasurable in principle and on a rather political promise not to tamper with the existing order or the institution of private property.

In conclusion, it would be interesting to cite a statement from Cournot that shows the deep division between his positive economics, which uses mathematics as an instrument, and Walras's use of mathematics as an abstract debate tool "I refrain from writing with a systematic ambition, under the banner of a party, since I consider there is an immense gulf between theory and its governmental applications."[35]

Notes

1. Léon Walras, *La Paix par la justice et le fibre échange.*
2. Marcel Boson, *Léon Walras fondateur de la politique économique scientifique.*, p. 74.
3. Ibid., p. 77.
4. Ibid., p. 47.
5. Ibid., p. 30.
6. Léon Walras, *Etudes d'économie sociale*, p. 218.
7. Ibid , p. 210.
8. Ibid., p. 211.
9. Ibid., p. 222.
10. Ibid., p. 47.
11. Boson, *Leon Walras fondateur*, p. 97.
12. Léon Walras, *Eléments d'économie politique pure ou la théorie de la richesse sociale*, p. 428.
13. Ibid., p. 44.
14. Ibid., p. 48.
15. Ibid., p. 427.
16. Ibid., p. 65.
17. Ibid., p.153.
18. Ibid., p. 74.
19. Walras, *Etudes d'économie sociale*, p 209.
20. Walras, *Eléments d'économie*, p. xii.
21. Ibid., p. 191.
22. Ibid., p. xii.
23. Ibid., p. 65.
24. Ibid., p. 198.
25. Ibid., p. 198.
26. Ibid., p. 204.
27. Leon Walras, *Les Associations populaires de consommation, de production et de crédit*, p. xvii.
28. Ibid., p. 104.
29. Boson, *Leon Walras fondateur*, p. 78.
30. Walras, *Eléments d'économie*, p. 29.
31. Ibid., p. 232.
32. Ibid., p. 38.
33. Ibid., p. 232.
34. Augustin Cournot, *Recherches sur les principes de la théorie des richesses*, p. 6.
35. Ibid., p. xi.

7

Enterprise against Stagnation: On Management of Productivity and Risk in Alfred Marshall's Theory

1. England in Crisis?

World War I was not long ended before the former Cambridge professor Alfred Marshall (1842–1924), and his beloved wife, Mary Paley, daughter of a priest and economist, decided to seek peace and refreshment on an alpine holiday. They chose to visit the South Tyrol of which they were both very fond, but it was not until 1920, with their baggage delayed by a railway strike, that they finally sat on the train that puffed its way from Verona up toward the Alps. Recalling their earlier holidays, they wondered if the old couple who ran the inn where they had stayed was still alive. They remembered Frau Filomena who had cared for them in earlier summers and improvised an elegant tea party for their Austrian economist colleagues such as von Wieser and Böhm-Bawerk in the bedroom of the inn.[1] The landscape that met them through the train windows was certainly the same, but the Italian station signs witnessed that Europe had basically changed. The old professor perhaps recalled his youth when he had proudly climbed Grossglockner with only a guide to help. Perhaps he also thought of how he and the liberal professor Henry Sidgwick had taught the first women students—among them Mary Paley—at male-dominated Cambridge.

Although Marshall was now old, he had just recently published a new book titled *Industry and Trade*, which had appeared the previous year, 1919. Its major theme concerned the decline of British industrial leadership, and the ability for "doing things, which other countries with similar economic problems will be doing a little later, but are not ready and able to do yet."[2] British economic production before World War I was nothing to grumble about, but industrial improvements, the new "methods of industry," were in an ever-increasing degree coming from other countries. The striving after industrial leadership had become a normal aspect of national ideals on the European scene. It was in trade between states, the character of what was imported and exported, that this leadership was made clear. The ability to make unique and desirable products was not sufficient in itself for a nation to be regarded as an economic leader.

The high cultural standards of the Greeks, for example, depended upon their social freedom. But they had used this freedom wrongly, held Marshall, who himself had been forbidden by a strict father—a cashier of the Bank of England[3] —to play chess and study mathematics, having instead been forced to learn Hebrew in preparation for a coming career as a priest. The Greeks unfortunately lacked "self mastery and persistent resolution,"[4] and while the pleasant Mediterranean climate was suitable for intelligent thought, it also encouraged a certain "frivolity." The Romans were certainly somewhat more industrious, but they spent most of their energies upon politics and war, leaving economics and production in the hands of slaves. Trade, moreover, was only a means of obtaining gold and silver. The sword rather than exchange provided the Roman strategy. According to Marshall, the Saracens were a quick-thinking race who appreciated learning for its own sake, as distinct from the Christians, but it was not until learning and ideas had reached the Teutonic race that they were applied to business, trade, and industry. The Teutons were a trifle slow in the head, but were strong in body and faithful in their habits.

The vicissitudes of migratory movements fortunately resulted in the British Isles being "peopled by the strongest members of the strongest races of northern Europe; a process of natural selection brought to her shores those members of each migratory wave who were most daring and self reliant."[5]

Climate, race, and immigration had created during the seventeenth and eighteenth centuries an industrious middle class with a demand for goods that could only be met through continuous hard work. The court and ruling class, however, were so idle and incorrigibly corrupted that not even that clear-minded Adam Smith could believe that there could exist honest, social-minded "civil servants" who, according to Marshall, were to be found not only in Germany and America but also in Britain, in the late nineteenth century.

The early British entrepreneurs soon became bemused by their own successes and began, in the name of individualism, to fight blindly against all state intervention in business affairs. At the same time, the country was struck by a number of non-economic misfortunes, such as the Napoleonic Wars and the Corn and Poor Laws; meanwhile distorted growth and an incredible system of taxation had led to regrettable social conditions. Many began to imagine that it was industrialism as such that inevitably led to ruin. Marx, together with others of goodwill, believed somewhat too hastily that they could demonstrate how the factory worker was deprived of his portion of the surplus from production. But it was not industry, held Marshall, that was to blame for these conditions. Children who worked at home were often driven harder by their parents than in the factories that competed with each other for labor. In the labor market, competition forced wages up, so that at least a part of surplus production ended in the pockets of the workers. More effective industries produced more and cheaper products, which also gave the consumer—that is, the worker as a buyer—some part of the benefits. If the price of a pound of tea was 20 shillings, the worker perhaps purchased a pound. If it fell to 14 shillings, he would perhaps increase consumption to 2 pounds. For 28 shillings he then experienced the utility that should really be the equivalent of 34 shillings (that is, 20 shillings for the first pound and 14 for the second). The increased efficiency of tea production, thus, had given the consumer a benefit of at least 6 shillings.[6]

The most important advantage of industrialism, however, was that the British on their small islands, which were subjected to Ricardo's principle of diminishing agricultural returns, now produced goods that increased returns in ever more effective industrial businesses. Workers should be grateful to these businesses whose products could be exchanged for food and raw materials that supported the growing population: "If he can make his labour more efficient in producing things which can be exchanged for imported food, then he will get his food at less real cost to himself, whether the population of England grows fast or not."[7]

How then was productivity to be increased? In earlier times Britain had imported more effective methods from abroad. Textile techniques had been imported from France, wool from Flanders, banking and shipping from Holland. Easily repaired ships with standard components, crewed by only nine men, were in production in Holland when British ships required a crew of thirty for a similar vessel. While Dutch industry was based on wood, that in Britain got under way with iron and coal. When this process came into full swing, the rich son of a factory owner could be destroyed overnight by "rugged but powerful men"[8] who found some means of increasing the efficiency of production and had the full confidence of the banks.

British inventors perhaps lacked the ingenuity of French engineers who were interested in design and directed themselves to the individual demands of an aesthetic ruling class. The British were rather interested in producing goods "needed by strong well-to-do people, and which made them stronger and more well-to-do."[9]

Alfred Marshall and his wife would sometimes spend their summer vacation visiting factories and wandering around working-class areas. He recalled here the example of a French silk weaver from Lyon, who rejected the use of steam powered looms because a few drops of oil from the machine could destroy the expensive material that cost 130 francs per meter. The work of a whole day could be ruined! In Britain, on the other hand, craftsmen were only too willing to invest in machinery, and the skills employed, thus, tended to be transferred to the machine manufacturers. Moreover, if French workers went into the factory, they could not expect to be very well paid. It helped somewhat that their women were such excellent housewives who could conjure up appetizing meals on limited budgets. The French industrial tradition was different from that of the British, and the French frequently failed when they imported British machinery in order to imitate the factories of the latter. The French companies were continuously dependent on new ideas. Their designers created products that were then copied and marketed by English and German businesses.

The construction of machines was a contributory factor to early British industrialization. The younger German industry, according to Marshall, rested to a large degree upon chemistry. The whole of the German Empire rested upon, if not science, academic foundations. It was in the universities that the state had been grounded like an "empire in the air."[10] But the Germans had also taken to imitation, and the state had financed the purchase of foreign machines that were then dismantled and copied. With a special talent for organization and Bismarck's iron will, an industry had been created that was in many ways more efficient than Britain's. The Germans worked hard without high wages, placing much weight upon their children's schooling, something that was seen as a duty in preparing them for a hard life in the factories. In America, maintained Marshall, the same respect for schooling was to be found, although here it was modified by the notion that practical experience provided the best education. Examinations were a help, but the final proof was "the money test." America was a melting pot of different races that formed a giant market where all appeared to purchase the same kinds of clothing, equipment, and furniture. It was only a few blacks who refused to accept the common pattern of consumption. Italian immigrants picked fruits in California, and central European Slavs worked in the steel industry. Business was led by people of British, German, and Scandinavian stock who had the necessary "resolute will" and "self control."[11] At the level of foremen where previously the Irish had dominated, an ambitious central European or two was now to be found.

The immigration of trained craftsmen from Europe had now largely stopped and had been replaced by a stream of "poor and backward people" who were only too willing to adapt to routine labor in the large companies. Marshall emphasized that it was fortunate that immigrants from all countries were industrious. That all worked was a security that ensured that economic power would not come to rest in the hands of inferior races, something that would be threatened if white men despised work and preferred to remain unmarried, and if they were too poor to live off the work of others:

> [O]n the Pacific Slope, there were at one time just grounds of fearing that all but highly skilled work would be left to the Chinese; and that the white men would live in an artificial way in which a family became a great expense. In this case Chinese lives would have been substituted for American, and the average quality of the human race would have been lowered.[12]

Thus, according to Marshall, it came about that Britain in the beginning of the twentieth century was surrounded by industrious nations. What had happened to puritanical Anglo-Saxon energies? These had created so much well-being, together with "cheap underclothing, without which cleanliness is impossible for the masses of the people in a cold climate: and that is perhaps the chief of the benefits that England has gained from the direct application of machinery to making commodities for her own use."[13]

The world was still a long way from that happy condition where it was possible to rest at ease without work. The goal of life was to enable people to develop their higher abilities, and for this purpose material well-being was necessary, even if it was not sufficient. Britain must become younger and increase its productivity. The recipe for the cure is given by Marshall in his theory of development where the businessman is the key figure.

2. Business Management and Economic Development

2.1 From Newton to Darwin

Alfred Marshall's father, who hoped that his son would become a priest, would certainly have preferred that his son had attended the University of Oxford, which specialized in the humanities. But Alfred Marshall, already tired of dead languages, had become increasingly interested in mathematics and geometry. These were subjects that his father neither understood nor appreciated, so that they provided for Alfred Marshall an area where he could develop his own thoughts. His studies at Cambridge were, in fact, financed by a relative who had happened to become rich during the Australian gold rush as a result of employing only handicapped people on his farm. They remained at work when all the able-bodied men had exchanged the plow for the gold pan. Marshall studied mathematics at Cambridge and was considering specializing in molecular physics when he came into contact with the circle around Henry Sidgwick, who was then teaching moral philosophy. Discussion in these circles ranged around the philosophical grounds of knowledge, with emphasis upon theological questions. Marshall now gave up not only his plans to become a physicist but also the more dogmatic aspects of his Christian beliefs. Lord Keynes,[14] who later became both his student and his biographer, emphasizes that Marshall always combined science with a certain ethical disposition. The transition that now occurred was rather a giving up of the static, the fixed, and the dogmatic, in preference for a fascination for movement and change.

When Marshall married, he could no longer hold his fellowship at Cambridge. In 1876, therefore, the young couple moved to Bristol where they taught economics to students and trainees. Following this period in Bristol, they moved to Oxford where Marshall's duties included special lectures for students who were intending to take up a career in India.

In 1884, however, Marshall was elected as professor of political economy at his old university, Cambridge, and the following year his installation lecture, which dealt with his view on "the present position of economics," was published. [15] In this lecture Marshall asserts that earlier nineteenth-century economists had been fascinated by mathematics and physics, but since they had seldom actually studied physics, they had missed the point that physics was constant and unchanging even in different countries and even at different times. Man was, for them, a coldly calculating "city man" who was regarded "so to speak [as] a constant quantity," and economists were hardly interested in human change: "Their most vital fault was that they did not see how liable to change are the habits and institutions of industry."[16]

Marshall, on the other hand, knew his Hegel and Goethe and had learned from them that human beings and their institutions were in a constant state of flux. Laws or principles that were useful for understanding tendencies in a certain period were unsuitable when applied to another period when conditions had changed. Economics should study change, not sudden changes, but rather the gradual and continuous. The motto he chose for his *Principles of Economics* was, in fact, "Natura non facit saltum"[17] (Nature makes no jumps).

In his *Origins of the Species*, Darwin had posed the question to biologists as to whether they really believed that all species had been created for all time according to a "plan of creation" that displayed a "unity of design." Darwin suggested the hypothesis of natural selection as the basis of a dynamic view of the development of forms of life. Marshall now held in the foreword to his *Principles of Economics*, which appeared in 1890, that a kind of economic biology provided the future for the discipline of economics. It was necessary to use the mechanical concept of equilibrium with care, appreciating its limits, in order that the dynamic aspect of economic development was not lost from sight. Darwin's theory had shown how it was possible to understand that the beak of a bird had become an efficient instrument for extracting worms, why South American ducks had stunted wings, and how the beetles from Madeira had become wingless. Those beetles that had flown best were blown out to sea by the winds, so that only the wingless survived! Both the beak of the bird and the wings of the South American duck had developed because they were characteristics that were the most economically useful to these species in their given situations. That Marshall should turn to Darwin in this respect was not so surprising in the circumstances, for Darwin had received much of his inspiration from Malthus, who was regarded as an economist. Darwin himself had written the following:

> Hence, as more individuals are produced than can possibly survive, there must in every case be a struggle for existence, either one individual with another of the same species, or with the individuals of distinct species, or with the physical conditions of life. It is the doctrine of Malthus applied with manifold force to the whole animal and vegetable kingdoms.[18]

Economic phenomena are formed from human intentions and motives but are becoming increasingly collective in character. Human beings are not isolated atoms, but rather individual members of a species. The process of development for Darwin could be likened to a tree where the healthiest buds grow into strong branches and where geologists search for fossils of long-dead species among the roots, as evidence of missing links with the past. Marshall adapted this picture to management:

> Thus the rise and fall of individual firms may be frequent, while a great industry is going through one long oscillation, or even moving steadily forwards; as the leaves of a tree ... grow to maturity, reach equilibrium, and decay many times, while the tree is steadily growing year by year. [19]

The fate of the tree, for Marshall, was something different from that of its individual leaves.

2.2 The Businessman's Psychology of Balance

When Marshall made an important decision, it was his habit to write out a list of advantages and disadvantages on a piece of paper and then give points for their relative importance.[20] Before he and Mary moved to Bristol, for example, he carefully weighed the advantages of a fixed salary against the disadvantages of administrative duties that hindered his scientific interests. Such a psychology where reasons for and against an action were assessed in terms of points, honors, or money provided for Marshall a generally valid model or "organon" on which the understanding of all economic action rests.[21] Every attempt to measure the "motor force" of action could only be indirect, since it is not possible to talk of deeper human reasons or spiritual nature. Marshall's basic view with regard to the question of quantification is well expressed: "When you have found a means of measurement you have a grounds of controversy, and so it is a means of progress."[22]

The task of the economist is not to be confused with that of the philosopher. The economist is to investigate human beings "in ordinary life" with the aid of the "common sense" of everyday language. Whether a mother knits socks, a worker accepts a job, or a businessman begins a new project, all the actions of everyday people form the economy. Marshall, indeed, spent much time in discussions with workers and businessmen. He purposefully avoided mathematical formulas in his books, setting out more complex points in appendixes, in order that practical people could more easily understand what he was writing about. Marshall believed that businessmen knew in a practical manner that which economists struggled hard to articulate in their writings. But the balancing psychology of the everyday businessman is not to be confused with a calculating arithmetic. Without "unlimited intelligence and wisdom," for example, the farmer knows that he should not waste time and energy in excess upon his fields or unnecessarily wear out his equipment. With quite normal "business ability," and with only knowledge concerning market prices, businessmen successfully manage to make difficult business decisions:

> When we speak of the measurement of desire by the action to which it forms the incentive, it is not to be supposed that we assume every action to be deliberate, and the outcome of calculation. For in this, as in every other respect, economics takes man just as he is in ordinary life: and in ordinary life people do not weigh beforehand the results of every action, whether the impulses to it come from their higher nature or their lower.[23]

Economists should, therefore, utilize with care the notion of a psychology of balance. In itself, the balance model contains no concrete economic knowledge. It is only "an engine to discover a concrete truth."[24] With this notion at the back of their minds, however, economists could discover how such diverse phenomena as the habits of Hindus or the behavior of medieval people, together with the actions of modern businessmen, became economically understandable.

Economists who attempted to make overrefined causal distinctions in the use of such models had failed to understand their task. Marshall is, in fact, critical of all those who had attempted to do this in relation to the theories of Smith, Ricardo, and Mill. How meaningless it is to argue as to whether demand or the costs of supply determine the value of a product. Any intelligent reader know that Ricardo saw demand and supply as columns in a vault or the two sides of a pair of scissors. The columns bear up the vault jointly, and both sides of the scissors are necessary in order to cut something. In the short run, value is raised by demand, but in the longer run, labor and capital are attracted to the area that increases supply and affects the costs of production. An all too simple theory, however, is always wrong: "You can't afford to tell the truth for half a crown."[25]

Marshall is certainly true to this principle, taking some twenty years to compose his *Principles of Economics*, where he provides the following advice to his colleagues:

> In this world therefore every plain and simple doctrine as to the relations between costs of production, demand and value is necessarily false: and the greater the appearance of lucidity which is given to it by skillful exposition, the more mischievous it is. A man is likely to be a better economist if he trusts to his common sense, and practical instincts, than if he professes to study the theory of value and is resolved to find it easy.[26]

There are no simple solutions to be found to the problem of value.

2.3 Business Power

To study a firm that pumps wealth is like watching an engine at work or reading the measures on a weighing machine. The scale shows the weight of a given object even as the steam emerging from a vent demonstrates the pressure in a certain pipe. When an economist sees that a businessman has purchased new machines or employed more people, he is in a position to consider that "there is a margin through which additional supplies come in after overcoming the resistance of a spring, called 'cost of production.' "[27]

When the businessman with his balance psychology understands that further "agents of production" cost more than they give, he stops the inflow of purchases and "the valve remains shut."[28] Marshall again emphasizes that marginal analysis is an observational method that in itself does not contain any concrete knowledge. An economist, therefore, should never maintain that marginal costs determined the value of a product. Such a model could not dictate a reality but only serve as a point of departure for the study of the observable consequences of business power.

Marshall's businessman is also responsible for pumping in capital to the business and keeps himself well-informed of the relative efficiency of the different factors of production. As soon as he sees an opportunity to increase efficiency, his balance psychology comes into play, leading him to experiment with the marginal substitution of one resource against another. In this manner, "the law of substitution—which is nothing more than a special and limited application of the law of the survival of the fittest—tends to make one method of industrial organization supplant another when it offers a direct and immediate service at a lower price."[29]

The businessman, thus, according to his best ability, combines the inflow of capital and labor in a proportion that gives a profitable outflow of products for the market. The volume of the inflow comes to "be driven up to a valve which offers to it resistance equal to its own expanding force."[30] When the businessman, however, is faced with investing in a new machine, a new factory building, or a new "line of production," he is forced to make judgments concerning the future marketing situation. That is to say, he must make judgments on inflows and outflows that do not at present exist. The price he is willing to pay for the machine or building is dependent upon what he believes future sales returns may provide.

The rule for business, thus, is that running costs determine the price of the firm's products in an open market immediately but that expected future prices determine investment decisions in fixed capital. There is also, of course, the possibility that faulty judgments are made, which makes the investments worthless. It is obvious that it is attractive to these less successful businessmen to seek the help of the state in ensuring higher prices in the future. In order, however, that the economy should develop according to Darwinian principles, prices must be set by the market, and businessmen should be rewarded for their ability to correctly judge its future development.

2.4 Growth and Judgment

Assume that you wish to build a home and that you prefer managing the project yourself without hiring an entrepreneur. You can employ a bricklayer and carpenter, while you yourself may purchase the timber and also mix the cement. You would almost certainly end up paying higher wages than are usual, which would be a personal loss, but not a loss to society as the money would end up in the bricklayer's pocket. Worse would be your lack of knowledge concerning building techniques and the organization of work. There is a good chance that you would build wrongly and that the contract with the craftsmen is not fulfilled as a result of faults in the building plans. These risks could be avoided by employing a competent building master and a qualified architect for the plans. These two kinds of entrepreneurs are paid by you to take over the risks in connection with the supply of your order. The house is thus built for you according to your specifications and under your general directions. Your neighbors perhaps then see the house and wonder if they may not purchase it for a good price. Since you now have reason to think that there may be a market for the house, you sign a contract with the building master and architect to build several more such houses. The building master and architect still stand for the narrow risks in the process of production, but you yourself have accepted the broad risks of finding, in the future, purchasers for the speculatively built houses in the general market.

Time will soon show whether you are suited to be a businessman or not. If you do not immediately lose your invested capital, it is possible that you would become, with a little more practice, a good businessman in the future. On the other hand, if you succeed according to your expectations, then you are in possession of what Marshall called the "telescopic faculty,"[31] that is, a kind of falcon's eye for future market prices. Such a capacity would also include the ability to analyze and successively build up a view of where future market prices would come to lie. With an example from a fishing business, Marshall illustrates how this analytical process could proceed.

Suppose you are a fisherman who reckons that people will come to eat more fish in the future. When the lust for eating fish increases, both you and your competitors stay out at sea longer and work more intensively. Perhaps many fishermen continue to pull at their nets now that times are better, instead of moving off and hiring a trading vessel, as they had otherwise planned. Old fishing boats are repaired and put to work on the cod banks. The weather and wind are left out of the analysis, since you assume that they even out over time. Similarly, it is possible to ignore such effects as how the boom in fish would encourage parents to bring up their children as fishermen. An idea of how large the supply of fish is likely to be when the demand of it increases finally begins to form in your head. The meeting point of these two sides of demand and supply provides your judgment concerning the level of future prices.

In the short run, you see that prices will rise, but when this increase in demand proves stable, boat builders, equipment manufacturers, and seamen will be attracted. Perhaps the shoals of fish near the coast become exhausted, and it is necessary to seek the catch in deeper waters. From this sort of insight, it is possible that you now have some idea as to how production costs will change and how in the longer run prices will fall when all the producers involved have adapted themselves to the larger-scale industry. If now your reflections lead you to believe that future prices will be high enough to cover both your prime costs for products and supplementary costs, the future will seem bright and you may even be tempted to invest more in fixed capital. There is the risk that your reflections are wrong and that you will stand there with large stocks of fish that can only be dumped, so that only the prime costs are covered. It would be possible to end in an even worse situation if trading morals among fishermen do not forbid you from "spoiling the market."

Market judgments, as seen by Alfred Marshall, do not follow any determined pattern. Each businessman has an area where clear-sightedness, talent, and a feeling for business are important. Behind investment decisions lay long and complicated practical judgments with a complex weighing of mutually inter-dependent factors. Marshall considers that there are few good economists who could understand how such practical analyses beyond the realm of any simple rules of calculation actually come about. Marshall's businessman, however, is not entirely left to his own innate resources and judgments, since industrial society has created different institutions that help businessmen with the burden of bearing risks.

3. Increasing Productivity and Distributing Risk

3.1 Expansion to Large Operations

In Marshall's Britain many held the general idea that free trade favored the strong branches of the economy while the weak suffered from imports. During the nineteenth century, much arable land had been converted into meadow, live-stock herds had been reduced, and the area under grain had sunk drastically, and ever fewer people worked directly in agriculture. Following the abolition of the Corn Laws in 1846, the general notion was that food should be purchased abroad in exchange for British industrial products. It was naturally the landowners and farmers who complained about the decline of agriculture, although they did not succeed in waking much response among Victorian politicians, who were more interested in industrial development. On the other hand, the discovery that German and sometimes French machinery was as good and even better than that produced in Britain and that European steel was cheaper awoke a strong reac-tion. Interest in foreign trade was now serious. Free trade and industrialization, nevertheless, remained as the ideal situation even among people who recalled the hungry years of the past and the time when more than half the budget of the worker went for bread. Alfred Marshall's advice to the nation was to continue on the path of industrialization. The production of goods that showed "increasing returns" should be intensified. Businesses should clear the crisis through an expansion toward large-scale production. The question was, however, What would encourage businessmen to undertake such an expansion?

A building carpenter, for example, may work at small odd jobs for private customers. He carefully discusses what is to be done with each customer before accepting the contract. If the carpenter, beyond his handwork, is engaged in managing his small one-man company, he is hardly likely to be paid for this as customers will feel that it is they themselves who stand for the broad risks. The carpenter could certainly gain from being so well organized that he manages to perform more jobs than others, but if he wished to be paid for his management work it was necessary for him to sell his services on the open market. He now successively replaces his own handwork with hired labor and engages himself in the management of the business. The carpentry business hopefully provides an increasing surplus, being the difference between income from sales and the wages and costs incurred. This provides the carpenter with a good reputation so that he can increase his "business connections," which makes it easier for him to obtain capital through loans. The effective manager, held Marshall, is never stopped by a shortage of capital. Since ownership is to a large degree separated from control, it is possible for talented individuals without means to utilize their abilities. The indolent sons of the rich, on the other hand, would be dismissed to make way for ambitious mechanics, clerks, and office boys.[32] The carpentry business, thus, flourishes on loaned capital, and perhaps a foreman is now employed to take over the daily management of work, leaving the carpenter free to pursue long-term strategy. As the business becomes large, it comes into a position where it can, through competition, drive smaller companies out of business in more distant markets. Against the advantages of being near to the building site, there must now be weighed those advantages of large-scale operations in terms of purchasing, marketing, and efficient production. With the increase in the volume of production, there also follows the possibility of developing machines and production processes that can be directly and fully employed. In Marshall's time, machines in established industries such as cotton, wool, and agriculture were usually produced by specialized companies. In fast-expanding branches as, for example, the chemical, jute, and silk industries, it was more usual for companies to produce their own machines. Large companies, moreover, had the possibility of "creating new wants by showing people something which they had never thought of having before."[33]

The large German chemical companies were continuously inventing new processes that they carefully avoided publishing, but instead utilized in production. Small businesses must sell their inventions under the protection of patents, which often provided a poor security despite being both expensive and time consuming.

It so came about that the carpenter became a member of the business class that received its rewards not through ordinary work and technical knowledge but through its talents in "a general art of money making." For the nation, however, the most important increases in productivity would not come about without the development of institutions that reduced the large business risks associated with expansion.

3.2 Standardization as Insurance against Production Risks

Increased productivity assumes technical development. This technical development builds upon a cooperation between scientists who are fascinated by fruitful ideas and the practical men who possess the means to transform such ideas into concrete products and services. In earlier times, technical development had proceeded so slowly that, like a creeping glacier, its progress went unremarked. All knowledge was stored in human memory and originated in instinct. The feeling for rhythm gave rise to repetitive work. Generation after generation of craftsmen produced swords or axes as both effective and beautiful instruments. The modern business, however, utilizes a purposeful standardization both of a general nature, such as that given by watts, ohms, and amperes in electrical units, and of a special nature, such as that employed, for example, in machine and clock manufacturing.[34] Henry Maudslay, who had tired of marking his nuts and bolts, suggested a standard system that had been further developed by Joseph Whitworth. The development of the lathe enabled machine parts to be manufactured to fine tolerances. Machines created machines, and the nature of work had been simplified in a dramatic fashion. The Marshalls themselves, during one of their summer study tours, met a girl who manufactured files after only three hours' training on a file-making machine.[35]

When the dimensions of railway tracks had been standardized, a steel works could securely place its production in stock, knowing that a market for this commodity existed. Andrew Carnegie had noticed the many wooden bridges crossed by railway tracks and had set a team of engineers to work to construct a steel bridge that could be assembled from standard components. These, in turn, could be manufactured in security by small, specialized works. The ammunition factories during World War I adopted standardized production methods on a large scale. With the help of "patriotic sentiments," many shrewd innovations were now realized that had earlier only existed in print as, for example, those of Charles Babbage.[36] Even relatively new branches of industry were standardized. The manufacture of British and American airplanes had been standardized during World War I, although France with its skilled mechanics had resisted taking this step. Large American businesses had begun to hire out standardized machinery for the manufacture of shoes, taking a payment on the basis of the number of shoes produced, which was registered by a meter on the machine. This made it possible for shops to order by telephone special types of shoes from specialized companies and to receive them after a standard delivery time. Even the flour, cocoa, mustard, and paper industries had adopted the production-line technique that enabled production to be regarded as a standardized flow. In the Chicago meat-packing business, workers were integrated into an organization that handled the ongoing flow of animal carcasses. The standardization of production had the further advantage in that quality was often raised. On a production line it was now possible, for example, to produce bicycles of such quality that earlier could have been produced by only the most skillful of craftsmen. Small firms in the building, tailoring, and frame-making businesses all purchased standardized components. In this manner, the advantages of large-scale standardization could even benefit small companies, since the risk that a certain product would not suit other producers or consumers was reduced.

3.3 Exchanges for Reducing Market Risks

Manufacturing companies produced masses of products on speculation; without beforehand knowing who would purchase them and at what prices. Economic evolution had produced two solutions that made this possible.

The first of these began when certain persons specialized in the art of finding a purchaser for a certain stock of goods. When the typewriter had first been manufactured, the stocks would certainly have been overfull if certain "expert agents" had not traveled far and wide in order to provide practical demonstrations of how the apparatus could efficiently replace the pen and thus awake a "latent want."[37] Furniture dealers found new ways of displaying their wares and placed advertisements in the press in order to increase their turnover of stocks. Illustrated catalogues could also arouse latent desires, and ordering by telephone made quicker deliveries possible. Harry Gordon Selfridge's department store, just like the cooperative business at Rochdale, provided examples of how mass production led to a development in marketing. So long as the marketing people did not hinder each other in a competition for an ever higher "national dividend," their activities were all to the good. On the other hand, considered Marshall, it was perhaps going a little too far when marketing psychologists captured attention through ordaining enormous advertisements that overshadowed the equally valuable information provided by small businessmen.[38]

In a manner similar to that of Adam Smith, who had seen that it was possible to increase circulation through utilizing the dormant gold reserves of the tradesmen, Marshall praises the development of modern transport techniques. While the train and steamship made it possible to shift goods quickly from one business to another, within the factory the stock life of goods traveling between different machines was reduced. The stocks of food held by families in their homes had also been radically reduced as a result of transport techniques and the concomitant development of local shops. But the motive for adopting measures that increased efficiency is not exclusively to increase circulation and produce utility for the consumer. The overcrowded homes of the workers had little space for the storage of food; moreover, the drunken father would certainly drink up the whole bottle if it was not rationed out to him by the glass in the public house, at high prices.[39] But the centralization of stocks and the corresponding reduction of volumes held locally were often related to increased availability. When grain was stored during transport in ships and trains, or in the large silos of the railway companies, the small Indian villages no longer needed to maintain their little stocks as barely adequate insurance against hunger.

The second solution of the marketing problem that arose with the increase of productivity is more concerned with transactions in the market itself. For products of a durable nature that were easily described in relation to quantity and quality, and for which there were large numbers of buyers and sellers, there were organized markets known as exchanges. These exchanges actually dealt in commodities that did not yet exist. For wool, cotton, precious metals, or grain, a manufacturer could ensure future delivery prices through a contract with a dealer. In this manner, a businessman who produced for the future could avoid the risk that his raw material prices could suddenly rise or fall in the open market. A miller, for example, who has a contract to deliver flour to a baker at a future date and at a certain price, can count upon receiving at delivery time the price of grain that he and the dealer on the grain exchange had agreed upon. If the miller himself bore the risk, a rise in corn prices would result in losses or a reduction of profits. Other millers perhaps preferred to sell their flour without contracts at the going market price. In order that the mill should be fully employed, however, the miller needs to be assured of future deliveries at the right times. When he buys from a local dealer, he immediately "hedges" his purchasing price through selling the same amount for delivery in the future on just that day when the local dealer has promised to deliver to the mill. In this way, the miller avoids the risk that grain prices sink during the time when he is awaiting delivery. If this were to happen, with the consequent fall of flour prices on the open market, the miller will gain by selling his delivery at the old price. If grain prices should rise, on the other hand, the miller was naturally in no position to profit from the situation. On the contrary, he would lose from the sale of his delivery at a lower price when, in fact, flour prices were rising. A well-functioning exchange made it possible for a producer to reduce risks that arose out of price fluctuations between the time of purchasing and selling. But how well do exchanges actually function?

In the longer run, considered Marshall, the exchanges will come to be run by "able and honest men."[40] Risk-taking speculators, who bid up the prices in Liverpool in order to sell by telegraph when the Liverpool tendency had reached the Chicago market, always came a cropper sooner or later and were excluded by the exchange authorities. This left the sound dealers in the exchange who had the ability to judge future demand and supply situations. The prices and contracts reached on the exchange were spread through telegraph and telephone to manufacturers and influenced the course of production from month to month. The possibility of the exchanges, without large capital investments, to buy and sell commodities that yet did not exist was, according to Marshall, an invaluable instrument in a world where the wheels were continuously turning and business was increasingly oriented toward the future. A well-functioning exchange served to stop unbridled speculation. In Melbourne, Australia, where a speculative wave in land prices had ended with a sudden collapse, the existence of an exchange with the right to deal in "futures" for land would have given warning about all too optimistic expectations concerning price rises. Managers might concentrate on their tasks provided such transactions were handled by experts on a central exchange. The professionalism of exchange dealers was not to be underestimated, for nothing was more dangerous than situations in which amateurs imagined that they were sufficiently well informed to participate in the transactions. It was just these amateurs who were the easy victims of rumor-spreading speculators who used the exchange in the hope of fast profits instead of as an insurance in business transactions. In Marshall's economic world, amateurs could certainly own assets in companies, but control was to be left to the professionals who quietly and sensibly developed industry in the direction of increased production and stable prices. When ownership and control are separated, the distribution of power left knowledge in the hands of the experts.

3.4 Business Solidarity and Investment Risks

When businessmen calculate their profits, they compare their incomes (receipts) against their costs (outlays) for a given period of time. In order to estimate the capital costs involved here, it is necessary to assess the value of fixed capital. Were buildings, machines, and other fixed assets worth the same today as when they had first been purchased?

A businessman who invests in fixed capital could be likened in many ways to a farmer who purchases his land. The price of the land, like the prices of buildings and machines, depends upon the expected rates of return in the future. Those future returns, which the purchasers think they can see, are discounted with the help of a suitable rate of interest to a sum that provides the basis for the valuation of fixed capital assets. Both the purchaser of land and the business investor think in these terms. In the judgment of the future returns on land, the large unknown factor is usually the demand for food. With investment decisions concerning buildings and machinery, there is also the risk that more efficient means of production will result in a fall in the value of these fixed assets. When competitors begin to use more effective machines, the price of the product falls, and those who own older equipment find that their fixed capital has fallen in value. But the market system itself offers a certain security against such investment risks without, for this reason, regulating the level of prices and in this manner creating an inflation in fixed capital. As standardization, together with the contribution of the exchanges, reduces the risks of production and marketing, so "the aggregate volume of production in the neighbourhood"[41] offers a certain security that Marshall terms "external economies."

The medieval prince assembled in his court a diverse number of craftsmen who soon constituted a closely knit community within the protection of the town walls. The circle was expanded by skillful foreigners who could weave, dye, or cast and work metals. From the countryside came those who specialized in the construction of agricultural equipment. When machines replaced the horses in the fields, yet further numbers of mechanics became indirectly dependent on agriculture. Within the towns there developed an industrial society where knowledge was fairly widespread concerning production processes, and trade secrets were few. Children were soon introduced to work, and women were expected to help out as needed in the process of production. It was not only the availability of suitable labor that attracted the entrepreneurs to the towns. The expensive equipment used required a high volume of production in order to ensure a suitable return on the capital employed. A businessman in the town dared to make such investments because he could count upon the demand arising from his industrial neighbors. In the industrial society, a businessman did not need to rely solely upon his management ability and internal economy. Where in modern times an aggressive competition has been exchanged for a helpful solidarity, the external economy contributed toward the stability of capital values. Modern businessmen, like medieval princes, had attempted to establish industrial communities. Here Marshall particularly refers to Titus Salt and George Pullman, who had founded the towns of Saltaire, England, and Pullman, Illinois, respectively, where land prices had risen with the blooming of industry.[42]

So long as business went well, it was easy to ignore external economies and business solidarity, although the advent of crises was the result of a lack of such solidarity. According to Marshall, when investments in fixed capital fall off, when no new railways, machines, and factories are built and there is resulting unemployment, it is not possible to blame the situation upon consumers at the end of the chain. The cause of the crisis rather lies in the lack of confidence among businessmen who have experienced too many "failures."[43] Those who have the means and can invest in fixed capital have become doubtful, and when the capital goods branches are unemployed, orders to their respective suppliers also stop: "This commercial disorganization spreads: the disorganization of one trade throws the others out of gear, and they react on it and increase its disorganization."[44]

Those who had carefully read John Stuart Mill knew that the demand for products was dependent upon the supply of other products. The payments for products were made quite simply in other products, and if businesses in the consumer branch decided to maintain production during crisis situations, confidence would soon return. The attraction of demand would soon be transmitted to the capital goods industries and set things in motion: "[T]he revival of industry comes about through the gradual and often simultaneous growth of confidence among many various trades: it begins as soon as traders think that prices will not continue to fall: and with a revival of industry prices rise."[45]

Where businesses engaged in production for consumers show a responsibility toward industrial society, the first step toward the revival of confidence has been taken.

4. Managerial Problems in Scale Economies

4.1 Business Ethics

Darwin had shown in his doctrine how various species developed useful qualities that were profitable for their own survival. At the same time he held that this development did not necessarily involve improvement or progress. Marshall advocates an expansion of firms that offer "increasing returns" as a means of increasing total production. The average company—the representative individual of the industrial species—would grow with the development of efficiency. A firm could grow either in a gradual manner, expanding from a one-man affair to a limited liability company, or in jumps such as when a printer buys up a bookbinding company. Expansion in certain branches demands large jumps in the amount of capital employed, such as, for example, when the United States Steel Corporation, which amalgamated its mines and open-hearth furnaces, now coupled these directly to the rolling mills in order to make large savings in energy. The large-scale steelwork could use coal gas as fuel and utilize the valuable tar that remains from the manufacture of the gas. Similarly, the large-scale slaughterhouse could sell the bone and horn that accumulate as industrial waste product. The German chemical giant Ludwigshafen and Elberfelt could afford to maintain a whole army of experts who worked to draw commercial gain from waste products. The waste products A, B, and C from dye manufacturing provided a further chemical reaction that produced product D for the development of photographs and product E, which was an ingredient in a further reaction that led to a new dye or a by-product useful for pharmaceuticals, and so on. These giant companies could afford to locate themselves outside the towns and in the countryside where they invested in land and factories and yet succeeded in attracting "educated operatives" who were prepared to renounce the pleasures of the towns and devote themselves to industry.

Marshall, nevertheless, regards the increasing appearance of these "giants" and "monsters" on the industrial scene with mixed feelings: "A race of wolves that has well organized plans for hunting in packs is likely to survive and spread; because those plans enable it to catch its prey, not because they confer a benefit on the world."[46]

Marshall questions, in other words, if the much lauded development of productivity would not tend to lead toward an industrial state of the Prussian variety. Must British democracy be offered at the altar of productivity? The general public and the press, held Marshall, must interest themselves in all aspects of this economic development. At any moment of time there would come a limit where the increase in the size of the company no longer contributes efficiency and economy. In cotton spinning and the weaving of calico, for example, the optimal size of the firm is very much smaller than in the steel industry. The "parrot wise"[47] propaganda that modernity belonged to the large company should be regarded with suspicion. It was equally untrue to maintain that monopolies were always damaging. In order to intervene where necessary, monopolies and large companies should be open to public inspection so that they did not decline into bureaucracies or tyrannies whose privileges rested upon the advantage of increased production that they had long lost.

4.2 Limited Liability and Joint-Stock Companies

When the businessman was transformed from a merchant into an employer without yet assuming the form of the capitalist with stocks, machines, and buildings, the question of ownership, which then becomes a problem in terms of control and management, results in different solutions. In 1862 full freedom to deal in "stock exchange securities" was obtained in Britain, and "special charters" to deal in "joint stock," introduced following scandals such as those that Adam Smith termed the "bubbles" (1700–1720) and the "joint stock mania" of 1825–26, were then dropped.[48] Prior to this, it was those who had invested their capital in a company who had themselves born the responsibility for debts. It was thus necessary every time an interest was secured in a company to obtain careful and detailed information concerning the other participants. The introduction of limited liability gave both small savers and the rich the possibility to leave the administration of their capital to businessmen who pursued an activity of which the investers had no particular, or even necessary, knowledge. At the start of the new period, before small savers had become used to reading stock exchange reports, shares were usually purchased by professional dealers and bankers. There soon developed in Britain, however, exchanges that negotiated long-term financing, as the British banks had only specialized in short-term credits that required a high liquidity. In contrast, in Germany industrial financing was undertaken by the large banks, which had industrialists and other experts on their boards. A somewhat more complex system had developed in America with the bank and "trust companies," which were often controlled by a few magnates such as Rockefeller or Carnegie. These gentlemen not only possessed enormous fortunes, but as distinct from millionaires in the Old World, displayed a "napoleonic faculty in its use."[49] The introduction of the limited liability company certainly made owner democracy possible, but with a skillful handling of the 51 percent majority—shares without voting rights, debenture bonds, and the spread of shareholdings—it was also possible for a firm like the Standard Oil Company to be run for all practical purposes like a private firm. The form of limited liability organization was to a high degree "elastic," but despite this, there arose general problems for which different institutional solutions had emerged in the course of economic development.

A small businessman, such as the carpenter or builder mentioned earlier in this chapter, himself bore the largest part of the risks of business. In limited share companies, on the other hand, there were managers whose job was to control the work, directors with often small shareholdings and little technical knowledge, and many share owners who were the actual and final bearers of risk. Small businessmen themselves know the market and their employees and are aware if and when the latter are idle or shirk their work. The small businessman has the time and the possibility of keeping an eye on each employee, finding the right job for the right person. The small businessman, moreover, could do the following:

> [T]rust in his reading of human character, and his power of detecting unfaith-fulness by sharp verbal inquiries. But the officials of a joint stock company, being themselves trustees for others, can seldom take such risks; and they have very little chance of taking them safely. Their accountant's work for every department must be full and precise; and so arranged as to be part of a system of elaborate checks and counter-checks. Such a system is necessarily wasteful of effort, and hostile to elasticity: and here lies a chief disadvantage under which a joint stock company lies in competition with a private firm.[50]

The small business could naturally become ineffective when the sons of the founder had been sent to university and considered themselves above working in the workshop. But it was yet possible to obtain new blood in the company by letting a promising employee marry the owner's daughter. In the joint-stock company and in "government business" it was certainly possible for a poor but talented person to make a career in management, although creative ideas and organizational experiments were seldom to be found. In large companies where risk taking was spread among officeholders, the single business talent, "selected by the struggle for survival,"[51] could not develop its individual (balance) psychological abilities in important business decision making. Business talent was replaced with the mechanical methods of bookkeeping, which could lead to bureaucratic ossification: "A tendency to ossification of the social organism might therefore be feared as a result of bureaucratic habits of shirking trouble-some initiative, the main benefits of which would accrue to those who had not borne the burden."[52] In the social organism, however, there were two natural counterweights against this danger.

First, the profit motive of managers can be minimized by peer pressure and "collegiate" support. The managers as colleagues meet in conferences and meetings and receive each other's support in the difficult discussions when both board and share owners must be persuaded to accept a change in the organization. Instead of profits, a love of the organization as such would come to be important in the same manner as was the case in the colleges of Oxford and Cambridge. The business would be held together by aesthetic values, as is the case with the landowner who keeps his estate and garden in good order to please the senses.

Second, the stock exchange provided dealers and "promoters" with the possibility of revitalizing the company so that it awoke from its slumber and became profitable again. A "promoter" earned his living through buying up shares cheaply in companies that were then combined into a large company, the shares of which were sold expensively on the stock exchange. The purchase of shares was financed through bank loans, which were underwritten by shares in the future company. The promoters had a clear view of future possibilities that was lacking in the managers of the slumbering companies whose shares they purchased. They used different tricks in order to create a large difference between the sales value of the old share company and the purchasing value of the new amalgamated company. The purchasing value in itself was dependent upon the evaluation of future business possibilities, and such evaluations were naturally influenced by optimistic or pessimistic expectations. A certain guarantee against overevaluations lies in the interests of owners who naturally do not want to attract too many competitors into a branch. Stock exchange matters were reported in the newspapers, and the negative publicity given to dishonest promotors ensured that they were soon driven out of business. The honest individuals who remained received the continued confidence of shareholders to revitalize flagging and ailing companies.

4.3 Cartels and Monopolies

Cournot had already cautioned against monopolies, with the example of how Dutch merchants burned stocks of spices in order not to spoil the market. Where monopolistic conditions prevailed, there was no chance for prices to be driven by competition toward the level of the lowest possible production costs. But it was not always the case, maintained Marshall, that the profit maximization of monopolies was an evil. The "conditional" monopolists, such as John Boyd Dunlop with his excellent bicycle valve or Coats with his sewing thread,[53] acted in a much more cautious manner than the Dutch absolute monopolists from the Spice Islands. Without an absolute monopoly, like a unique gold mine or a health-giving mineral water spring, there always exists a certain risk that competitors could be attracted, even if it demanded high investment costs and large advertising campaigns to overcome consumer resistance. A large monopolistic company could often manufacture products more cheaply than several small competitors, because of the economies of scale. Monopolies could save, moreover, money on competitive advertising and had more resources for further product development. The "farsighted" monopolist, who knew that he could increase supply and thereby lower production costs, was likely to advertise his product just through the means of lowered prices. In this manner, he could influence an elastic demand, sink costs, and while retaining the monopoly goal of maximizing net revenue, yet offer more and cheaper products. The time limit on a patent, considered Marshall, should cover the time it took to develop an effective, large-scale manufacture of the patented product. Through a moderate pricing policy, the monopolist attracted new customers. Railway monopolies, for example, held prices low so that they increased on their short-distance service between two stations. Soon it was possible to install round-the-clock signal boxes and strengthen bridges for fast goods trains. With advantageous rebates, people had even been attracted to build their houses near the railway tracks. But it is also obvious that the freedom of the monopolist with regard to the setting of prices could also have negative consequences for consumers.

A monopolistic company has through its price-differentiating capacity the possibility of eliminating small competitors at an early stage. In the absence of a competitive market with a single equilibrium price, the monopoly company has the freedom to distribute its costs differently with regard to sales to various customers and markets. The price setting of the railways was naturally followed very carefully by freight companies that compared the prices of different transporters. Private individuals, however, did not have the same possibilities of being informed; when the general public felt that the price differentiation was strange, they had small chance of making their voices heard. Marshall thought that the various committees appointed to weigh the advantages and disadvantages in doubtful cases of price setting by producers needed to be more alert to consumer interests. [54]

In the absence of any absolute rules for the distribution of costs in the setting of monopoly prices, it was necessary to consider the matter case by case. Was it right that a railway should take higher fares for short journeys with a high turnover in cargo than for longer stretches? Had the terminal costs for loading and unloading become higher than those of the fast trains where costs had fallen as a result of technology? Was it right to burden cargoes on high-density lines with higher prices than on other lines? Could it be reasonable to calculate passenger costs through dividing the total costs of the train by the number of passengers who traveled on it? Should one not instead calculate the marginal costs of extra carriages? Was it proper to require a nationwide unit price for goods and traffic when such did not exist in the centrally controlled Prussian railway system? What attitude should be adopted toward companies that secured advantages outside the unit price? Were rebates for large quantities justifiable? Was it right that certain firms used railway carriages as storage places? Was it true that their competitors' goods were sometimes delayed? What was to be said for the British model of railway development that encouraged competition on parallel routes around the country? Was it economically justified to nationalize the railways even where military reasons were lacking? Should not large-scale integration with giant stations be undertaken where prices were held low through increased competition from "motor lorries" and the vertical takeoff "helicopters" of the future? [55]

Besides the railways, there were in Marshall's time certain areas of shipping that were increasingly dominated by monopolistic companies that had the means to invest in enormous ships equipped with telegraph and the latest novelties. The

German Hamburg–America line had no less than ten "flag ships" that were prepared to fend off any newcomer of any weight. Several of the Atlantic lines had allied themselves in what the Americans called "conferences" and the Germans "Kartellen," with the official purpose of offering fixed prices for transport. With their united "artillery," these conferences were often sufficient to frighten off any newcomer to the business. At the same time, Marshall pointed out, in shipping there were often price-setting habits that hindered the setting of all too damaging rates. It was, for example, unthinkable to transport "first class goods" according to fourth-class prices. Cartels had also spread to other branches. Rockefeller had in 1882 started an association of shareholders in different oil companies and entrusted leadership to a nine-member committee. Standard Oil had since engaged itself in overbidding its competitors in the purchase of oil and underbidding them with its sale and was busily buying up land that lay in the way of pipeline projects. The Sherman Antitrust Act of 1890 was designed to oppose these "trusts." The response was to create holding companies, which were declared in 1904 to be in breach of the Sherman Antitrust Act. In their battle against monopolies, American lawyers could refer to no single legal definition for the evil that worried them and were forced to cite investigations by committees appointed as watchdogs of the social and commercial effects of trusts and monopolies. In 1903 the Bureau of Corporations was founded; it was transformed into the Federal Trade Commission in 1914.

The early freedom of competition in Germany had led to murderous competition in industry, which had therefore welcomed cooperation among firms in the form of cartels. This cooperation was voluntary, and according to Marshall a cartel needed to comprise 60 percent to 90 percent of a branch in order to be effective in holding the agreed price structure. The cartel also needed to be continuously alert to firms that could find it profitable in the short run to openly flout the price agreements. There were many indirect methods of avoiding the voluntary regulation of prices. Goods could be sold as seconds, or extra service and long credits could be provided for customers. Large customers sometimes attempted to break cartels through laying all their orders with one company that was a member. Other companies then broke the cartel price agreement in the belief that the favored company had provided secret rebates or the like.

To follow the development of a cartel through time was to witness a continuous balancing act where the interests of different companies were weighed against each other. The study of cartels also shows how they could affect industrial investments in a country. The Westphalian coal cartel, for example, had begun as a marketing syndicate. Orders were centralized at the office of the cartel and then transferred to coal producers on the condition that profits would be distributed in proportion to the respective producer's agreed production quota. The steelworks that also owned coal mines were annoyed by the cartel's regulation that required them to debit the official coal price for their own consumption.

They thus left the cartel and began to sell coal cheaply. In order to save the cooperation of the cartel, they were tempted back with the promise that they could use their own coal at a lower price. This, in turn, influenced investments in such "mixed works," since it reduced their energy costs. The steel-only works, which were often better managed, were placed in a difficult situation cost-wise, whereas the coal-only mines had difficulties in selling their product and often resorted to dumping abroad. Steel production nevertheless increased, and Marshall could note that a British company, in competition with the Germans, won an order for the delivery of a gas holder that was manufactured with dumped German steel. The German cartels did not confine their activities to the marketing of products. In the case of local conflicts with labor, they could easily reorganize to minimize the damage. Marshall considered that the holding down of wages by the German cartels had contributed to the political unrest that followed World War I: "There are strong reasons for thinking that the exploiting of the masses of the people by the dominant classes, through the agency of the cartels, made an important contribution to the discontent which broke into violence after the war."[56]

It would seem that there were limits to even the German workers' industrious self-offering!

4.4 Trade Unions

As long as workers were prevented from organizing themselves in trade unions, it was possible for employers, working in cohort, to press down wages somewhat. But the major tragedy, according to Marshall, was the damage it did to the self-respect of workers and their "intelligent interest in national affairs."[57] The important function of trade unions was to strengthen the social standing of workers and in this manner contribute to increased productivity. Among trade unionists it was said that an "aggressive policy is a foolish policy." The rise in productivity that was sought was impossible without the active cooperation of the workers. Indeed, Marshall engaged in discussions not only with businessmen but also spent much time discussing and teaching in the trade unions. Following a visit to the Marshalls' Cambridge house in 1901, a student from a "Working Men's college" reported:

> Then we talked of supremacy—English, German or American—of the causes of economic changes, of wars of our own, of the French and the Germans and of the Americans, of our wealth produced during their troubles, of their advance since; of the relation between imports and exports, between production and importation and the sending abroad of securities and money; of the need for us to improve our methods and our education in things concerning the production of commodities, of phonographs, typewriters, hinge screws, nut and washer bolts, spokeshare irons, eyelethole punches, drug stores and many other things."[58]

Marshall held that the foremost instrument for the trade unions was the establishment of "common rules" for the standardized payment of labor. This was for Marshall, who always emphasized that men and machines were quite different phenomena, something of a problem. Payment for work should include both an element for effort and an appreciation of the "motor force" of such efforts. An equal regulation of wages independent of questions of efficiency in different jobs and firms was to be deplored. It was also necessary to avoid attacks on the use of machinery and other sticks in the wheel of productive development. Neither should trade unions shut out the weak and aged who could perhaps obtain some job from an enterprising businessman at a rate somewhat under the minimum wage. It was obviously the task of trade unions to ensure that workers' wage levels did not lie under an open-market valuation of the productivity of work.

In America, noted Marshall, Frederick Winslow Taylor had introduced a system of wages related to increasing efficiency: "The chief outward token of the new plan is the elaboration of a system of cards so full, and so carefully organized that the central control shall have a firm basis for arranging the details of its work."[59]

Marshall recognized that scientific management had increased productivity in many American companies, even if the method was not quite so original and effective as Taylor and his disciples would maintain. Scientific management was a system of cost accounting that could be so detailed and administratively demanding that it cost more than it was worth. It was, moreover, something that was typically American. In Britain and Germany, the workers had old traditions and the ethics of their crafts. The European worker felt a sense of duty toward his job that was lacking among the immigrants to the United States. But it was, nevertheless, good that Taylor's system made it possible for an anonymous worker in a "monster works" to show his weak and strong sides. The chief of a large company seldom had time to undertake the kind of study trips, made by the Marshalls, in order to observe workers on the factory floor. The modern head of a large company probably lacked the ability to guess—something of which Alfred Marshall was very proud—the wages of a worker within a few pennies after having watched him in full action in the factory. There was, however, a solution to the problem of efficiency that was more suited to the conditions of Britain, a solution likewise suggested by Mill and Walras.

To start a business in the form of a cooperative is a way of organizing surplus energies in the service of production. It was unfortunate that cooperatives did not appreciate the value of good business management. Since they were not prepared to allow their managers to participate in the profits, many cooperatives were badly managed and suffered an early death. Another manner of increasing the productivity of a company is to introduce a system for participating in the distribution of profits within the company. Marshall recommends the introduction of "works committees," which could take up questions such as whether a certain wage was fair for a given job. Daily contact between workers and managers would, moreover, promote an understanding of the common interest. Here perhaps the works committee fulfills the dangerous myth that there was a given "wage fund" that could be portioned out in higher wages if fewer people worked less. This myth led to strikes and the refusal to utilize productivity investments in shifts. When a house is half built, it could be thought that this is the right time for the bricklayer and carpenter to press for higher wages with the threat of stopping work. The economy as a whole, however, does not function in this manner. True solidarity consists in all working in more efficient ways, since the demand for a product—like the demand for labor itself—consists of other products. The citizen needs the right attitude toward the business enterprise, even as the businessman should display confidence in the industrial society. When this confidence is lacking, crisis is standing behind the door. While trade unions are responsible for the solidarity of workers, it rests upon the state to educate its citizens in concrete economics.

5. The State as a School of Ethical Management

In Alfred Marshall's theory of development, it is possible to distinguish a dynamic model of the firm and the entrepreneur—Léon Walras had already in 1873 encouraged Marshall to publish his "diagrammatic illustrations of economic problems."[60] Marshall, however, had no desire to become just another static theorist bound to a certain form. Mathematics was important to him, not as the goal of his endeavors—as was the case with Walras—but as a means of checking his own thinking. Marshall never followed Walras's suggestion to issue a separate publication of his diagrams and formulas, but rather engaged himself over seventeen years in constructing his large *Principles of Economics*, which was based upon "concrete studies of actual conditions."[61]

In Walras's static analysis, the firm appeared as an account (see chapter 6). It was here, at a certain point in time, that the interacting returns on capital, labor, and land met and were transformed into goods to be sold on the product markets. The various factors of production were hired for a given period of time. The firm itself administered no owned or fixed assets. This timeless static situation can be represented diagrammatically as follows:

Figure 1 **Walras's Model of the Timeless Firm**

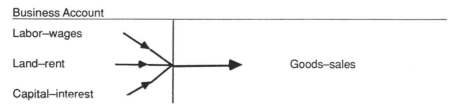

Business Account

Labor–wages

Land–rent

Capital–interest

Goods–sales

Marshall's considerable knowledge of actual business conditions assured him that the flow of economic resources was hardly so "fluid" as the static model assumed.[62] The flow rather was often "viscous," and between the purchase of resources and their sale as products there was also an important time lag. This period between different sets of market transactions should be used by the businessman to perform manufacturing and transport functions. It also happened that it was not possible to find immediately the necessary factors of production, machines that were free for their transformation into products, and customers for such products. Between the transactions in the purchasing and selling markets there was a further period of time concerned with stocks. The introduction of time gave a somewhat different picture of the firm:

Figure 2 **Marshall's Model of the Dynamic Firm**

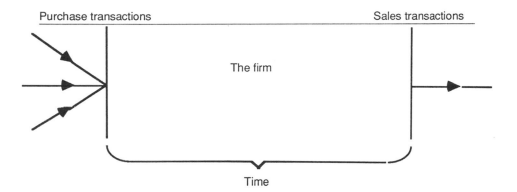

If the businessman succeeded in purchasing cheaply and selling more expensively, the resulting profits became a measure of his success. These purchases and sales were made, according to Marshall's major supposition, under conditions of open-market competition. But the businessman made these purchases and sales at different points in time, and the difference in the prices involved was dependent upon his ability to make judgments about the future. Marshall showed how it was possible for the dynamic businessman to engage specialists to take care of these judgments. They were the province of the dealers in the various exchanges that arose in connection with certain markets. Marketing specialists undertook, for a certain reward, the responsibility of finding customers in the future. The exchanges functioned like insurance companies, but without the usual demands on funds posed by insurance operations. Marketing insurance was rather like an insurance operation that at the same time covered the fairground owner against rain and the cinema owner against fine weather. Whatever the outcome, one pays what the other loses. Marshall dismissed the danger that the exchanges could become controlled by ruthless speculators without security, who would distort judgments concerning the future. The exchanges were rather self-regulating instruments for making judgments about the future, where a process of natural selection sorted out competent judges from the others.

The businessman who wanted to increase the flow of transactions did so through investment in the firm. Since, in Marshall's world, investment was so profitable, there was no difficulty in persuading people to come forward with the necessary capital. The share-issuing company could thus appear where the businessman had now become a manager of resources owned by others. With this, a new dimension was added to the model of the firm. It was not only productive resources and products that were bought and sold, but the firm itself in the form of shares could be traded on the stock market. This stock market, in its turn, was an exchange where specialists in future judgments, the promoters, managed the risks of ownership in return for a suitable reward.

In Walras's static theory of the firm, depicted in Figure 1, profits depended upon the ability of the businessman to cheapen the cost of the inflow. In this accounting model, the differences that arose between input and output were regarded as profits or losses, being the rewards and punishments of entrepreneurial activities. In Marshall's dynamic model, however, depicted in Figure 2, a positive difference could not automatically be regarded as a profit or reward for good management during the given time period. The difference between inflow and outflow here was dependent upon the valuation placed upon investments or assets. If the value of assets had risen, wealth (in the sense of the firm's debts to owners) had increased. To regard this as a profit that could be disposed of by the businessman would be to rob the owners or shareholders in the company. If the positive difference was dependent upon an increase in the value of assets, it was not necessarily a sign that the businessman had managed the daily affairs of the firm (that is, the inflow and outflow of a business pump of a certain capacity) with skill and success. On the other hand, it could be held that the owners, as traders on the stock market, had shown skill in their dealing with the shares of the company (being the activity concerned with developing the capacity of the business pump). But this skill was not rewarded through dealing out the gain as profit to the owners, because such an action would be to distribute the assets of the company. This was rather rewarded when the owners sold their shares on the stock market at a profit. In Marshall's more complex notion of the firm, there appears accordingly a balance sheet. Marshall showed (see Figure 3), moreover, how the daily flows in terms of profits and losses and trading with the firm itself were related in a complex system that acted to reduce business risks and place responsibilities in the hands of specialists.

Despite the fact that Marshall's businessman could delegate much of the risk taking to specialists, nevertheless, he frequently gave in to the temptation of seeking to freeze future prices through monopolistic action. It fell to the lot of the general public, state, and mass media to follow the course of economic events and ensure that the rules of competition were followed. With this element

Figure 3

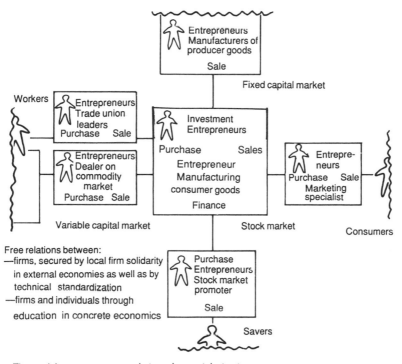

The model assumes open markets and no cartels, trusts or prices protected in some other way.

in place, we begin to recognize in Marshall's understanding of the firm, outlined in Figure 3, our modern business economic models. In the four-sided box we find those groups of people upon whose industriousness and capacity for judgment economic development is ultimately dependent.

In earlier times it was the duty of the church to insure society against the human factors. For Marshall, however, it was rather the duty of the state to raise its citizens from the cradle to the grave in the knowledge and spirit of concrete economics and good management. Citizens should be industrious, and economic well-being meant something other than simply piling need upon need. It was not the "standards of comfort" that should necessarily increase, but rather the "standards of life." His ideal was that of an active life rather than one spent in seeking satisfaction in pleasure. The course of economic development showed that people could voluntarily increase their performance when their conditions of life improved. The greatest error of the classical economists was in failing to recognize the dynamic nature of economic development, where poverty created more poverty and economic development created more well-being. To understand the importance of "the human factors" was to know that people were neither machines nor material for slave drivers or grist for the military. People should invest in people and apply the Kantian imperative to human resource management.

It was the same thing with sensible parents who sought to care for their children's physical and mental development. The good mother stayed at home with her children, while the wise father considered which occupation would provide his children with the best returns in the future. The legal obligation to attend school guaranteed all children the possibility of an education and a taste for activity. The nineteenth century had been a period of educational reform, and Marshall himself was particularly impressed by the German and Scottish school systems. Marshall had worked for the introduction of an examination in economics (tripos) at Cambridge that would free the discipline from its ties with philosophy and history. Human energies were increased through both "better food" and "better education."[63] Students at Cambridge should be educated for public offices and the leadership of large companies. When national identity was so closely connected with economics, employment in industry for a Cambridge student was no longer something of which to be ashamed. But a university education should not for this reason assume a technical content, which was something best left to the firms. Nor were mathematics and the economic doctrines particularly important. What was important, on the other hand, was an insight into the course of historical development, together with the capacity for sympathetic insight into the conditions of working people.

Economic research did not in the first place need desk-bound logicians. Marshall hoped that the new education in economics would attract open-minded natural scientists with a taste for fieldwork and practical case studies. Official statistics were yet too undeveloped to provide a sufficient basis for economic theorizing, and it was necessary—as Marshall himself had done—for researchers to go out and meet businessmen, workers, and shopkeepers in their normal working environments. This was not only a question of understanding the actual conditions of producers and consumers, but also one of gaining insight into the operation of the rules and actions undertaken by states to support and control economic development.

Economics, for Marshall, was never some kind of fully realized theoretical discipline that was the prerogative of a privileged few. Public education, preferably following the German model, would give the children of workers a disposition for work and faith in industry, rather than special skills. Higher education should not be concerned with bookkeeping and the techniques of production but should rather develop balanced thinking and the capacity for judging others. It is perhaps easier to understand what Marshall meant by concrete economics by considering his suggestion for the content of the new Cambridge examination in economics:

(a) The methods of business generally: the modern expansion of jointstock companies, the growth and working of so called "Trusts", railway organization, & c:

(b) Organized markets for goods and for credit; monetary and banking systems; stock exchanges; commercial fluctuations:

(c) Methods of employment, relations between employers and employees, trade unions, & c; methods of tenure of land and other real property, and their social results:

(d) Earnings, nominal and real, of various industrial classes; and the use made of these earnings; housing, the standard of life & c:

(e) The course of international trade, and the mutual interaction of foreign commerce and national industrial character:

(f) Systems of taxation, central and local:

(g) Regulative influences exerted by public authority and public opinion over the economic conditions of life and work and over the supply of water, electricity, and the means of transport and other uses of large public rights:

(h) Constructive intervention of authority in economic matters: Government undertakings.[64]

As Marshall's best-known student, Lord Keynes, was to certify, his teacher always welcomed ideas and regarded both the economy and the discipline of economics as being in a state of continuous development.

Notes

1. Mary Paley Marshall, *What I Remember*, pp. 47–50.
2. Alfred Marshall, *Industry and Trade, A Study of Industrial Technique and Business Organization, and Their Influence on the Conditions of Various Classes and Nations*, p. 3.
3. John M. Keynes, *Essays in Biography*, p. 153.
4. Alfred Marshall, *Principles of Economics*, p. 606.
5. Alfred Marshall, *Industry and Trade*, p. 71.
6. Alfred Marshall, *Principles of Economics*, p. 104.
7. Ibid., p. 576
8. Alfred Marshell, *Industry and Trade*, p. 63.
9. Ibid., p. 111.
10. Ibid., p. 123.
11. Ibid., p. 149.
12. Alfred Marshall, *Principles of Economics*, p. 167.
13. Ibid., p. 563
14. Keynes, *Essays in Biography*, p. 154.
15. Alfred Marshall, *The Present Position of Economics, An Inaugural Lecture Given at the Senate House at Cambridge*.
16. Ibid., p. 16.
17. Charles Darwin, *On the Origin of Species by Means of Natural Selection or the Preservation of Favoured Races in the Struggle for Life*, p. 443.
18. Ibid., p. 60.
19. Alfred Marshall, *Principles of Economics*, p. 379.
20. Mary Paley Marshall, *What I Remember*, p. 23.

21. Alfred Marshall, *The Present Position of Economics.*

22. Mary Paley Marshall, *What I Remember,* p. 19.

23. Alfred Marshall, *Principles of Economics,* p 17.

24. Alfred Marshall, *The Present Position of Economics,* p. 25.

25. Mary Paley Marshall, *What I Remember,* p. 22.

26. Alfred Marshall, *Principles of Economics,* p. 306.

27. Ibid., p. 340.

28. Ibid., p. 340.

29. Ibid., p. 495.

30. Ibid., p. 341.

31. Ibid., p. 566.

32. Alfred Marshall, *Industry and Trade,* p. 359.

33. Alfred Marshall, *Principles of Economics,* p. 234.

34. Alfred Marshall, *Industry and Trade,* p. 201.

35. Mary Paley Marshall, *What I Remember,* p. 43.

36. Alfred Marshall, *Industry and Trade,* p. 224.

37. Ibid., p. 306.

38. Ibid., p. 307.

39. Ibid., p. 798.

40. Ibid., p. 264.

41. Alfred Marshall, *Principles of Economics,* p. 220.

42. Ibid., p. 367.

43. Ibid., p. 591.

44. Ibid., p. 592.

45. Ibid., p. 592.

46. Alfred Marshall, *Industry and Trade,* p. 175.

47. Ibid., p. 581.

48. Ibid., p. 313.

49. Ibid., p. 344.

50. Ibid., p. 324.

51. Alfred Marshall, *Principles of Economics,* p. 255.

52. Alfred Marshall, *Industry and Trade,* p. 325.

53. Ibid., p. 403.

54. Ibid., p. 472.

55. Ibid., p. 497.

56. Ibid., p. 576.

57. Alfred Marshall, *Principles of Economics,* p. 585.

58. Mary Paley Marshall, *What I Remember,* p. 45.

59. Alfred Marshall, *Industry and Trade,* p. 369.

60. Keynes, *Essays in Biography,* p. 184.

61. Ibid., p. 184.

62. Alfred Marshall, *Industry and Trade,* p. 410.

63. Alfred Marshall, "A Plea for the Creation of a Curriculum in Economics and Associated Branches of Political Science," p. 5.

64. Ibid., p. 14.

8

Managers as Officers of the State: The Role of Enterprise in Gustav Schmoller's Prussian Theory

1. The Bismarckian Attack on False Abstractions

In German history the period between 1870 and 1873 is known under the name *Gründerzeit*, the time of the founding of modern business organizations. The Franco-Prussian War had ended with a victory for the Germans, who obtained an agreement from France to pay 5 billion marks in reparations. North German philosophical idealism had realized itself in the notion of the German state under Prussian leadership. Since the building of the railways that had begun in the 1840s, German industrial development had been on the march. The enormous French reparations payments started the rush under the *Grunderzeit*.[1] Some 928 companies were founded with a capital of 2.9 billion marks, which was a half billion greater than the total amount invested in the previous twenty years.

The founding of these new companies was often initiated by the large banks and credit institutions, which pumped new capital into projects that had earlier been self-financing under individual ownership and management. Not all of the new shareholding companies, however, found their origins in this way. The chemist Schering, for example, had begun in 1851 to manufacture iodine in his small pharmacy. Encouraged by the sharp increase in demand from military sources during the war years, and from the expanding photographic industry, he transformed his business into a shareholding company in order to finance further expansion. With the founding of the great giants of German industry—Loewe, Borsig, Siemens, and so forth—the steps had been taken that definitely established large-scale technological organization at a national level. This new industry saw Berlin as its capital and rapidly transformed the city into a shining electropolis.

Not a few of the newly established companies lacked the resources to survive the crisis of overproduction that struck in 1873. The share market crashed as the factories of the Ruhr with large stocks of unwanted products ground to a halt. The *Gründerzeit* swung over into the "grosse Depression," displaying the symptoms of overproduction, falling prices, reduced returns upon investments, the flight of capital, payments difficulities, bankruptcies, and unemployment. The depression reduced the level of wages for workers while increasing the purchasing power of those on fixed salaries such as state officials *(Beamten)* and officers. As the crisis deepened and the "social question" became acute, a serious attack was made on political and economic liberalism. The function of individual entrepreneurship in national economic development was put into question; the notion that the individual company or business should provide the basic unit of modern economy was dismissed. The attack was led by a new generation of young German Bismarckian economists inspired by a historically oriented approach to economics that derived from Hegel's theory of the state and Fichte's *Address to the German Nation.* It also contained a strong sociological element. Large landowners and business interests that were concerned with maintaining protectionist tariff barriers joined the campaign against liberal economic doctrine. With a parliamentary majority of a similar disposition, Bismarck was given a free hand to undertake reforms of a political and financial character in response to the crisis. A "national Wirtschaftspolitik" based on "Solidarprotektionismus" for industrial products took form, and early action involved the nationalization of the railways.[2] The leading role of the nation-state as against the individual entrepreneur and business for economic development was the creed of the new German economists.

On October 6, 1872, a bright young professor from Halle named Gustav Schmoller welcomed an assembly of learned gentlemen to a conference at Eisenach for "Besprechung über die soziale Frage [discussion of the social question]."[3] These economists, historians, lawyers, and directors of statistical bureaus were already derided by liberals for their "Katehedersozialismus." This depended not upon their socialism, Schmoller explained in his welcoming speech, but rather because their political home lay in the middle ground that lacked influence over the reactionary forces that denied the existence of "die soziale Frage" and thereby inflamed the class hatred of the workers. That which united the members of what was to become the "Verein für Sozialpolitik" was the following:

> . . . an idea of the state that differed from both the doctrine of natural rights that glorified the individual and the doctrines of the absolutists concerning an all-embracing state power. Under different historical epochs and cultural conditions, the influence of the state may increase or decrease; but we refuse to regard the state, like the Manchester liberals, as a necessary evil that should be limited to a minimum. The state is the greatest institution for instilling moral habits in the human race. . . . We shall always be true to our inheritance from the German state system, the result of a two hundred year fight by the Prussian

kingdom and its officials for justice, the limiting of the privileges of the higher classes and for the development and emancipation of the lower classes.[4]

Such was the new doctrine that Schmoller now preached to the faithful.

Schmoller had obtained the inspiration for an organized state economy from his home. His father was the financial administrator in Heilbronn, responsible for the railway that was constructed to compete with shipping on the river Neckar. On being sent to the University of Tübingen, Schmoller studied economics in the German tradition of financial administration. Although English liberal ideas had made some impression at Tübingen, there was still something left from the eighteenth-century tradition that was concerned with training the "Kammerbeamte" who controlled the economy of the principalities through a "wirtschaftspolizeilicher Tätigkeit."[5] The lectures of Professor List, for example, managed to blend protectionist notions with ideals of freedom deriving from Adam Smith. Schmoller's doctoral thesis of 1880 was a study of the economic ethics of the German Reformation. Shortly thereafter he was employed in a statistical bureau that gathered data for a "Gewerbezählung," an economic-statistical investigation in Württemberg.[6] Schmoller then wrote a pamphlet concerning this investigation, the purpose of which was to provide a basis for economic planning, and this provided his foremost merit when he was appointed to his first professorship at Halle.

The statistical investigation of Württemberg had revealed among other things the extent of the employment of women and children in the factories of the area. While Schmoller was prepared to admit that industrialization had its merits in attracting the peasants from the local drinking shops to the factories, he nevertheless considered that the large numbers of people involved under the existing conditions of the factories rendered the matter serious. The introduction of the German customs union had increased the level of competition and led to an increasing concentration of various branches of industry in certain areas. Schmoller, however, emphasized that proletarianization could hardly come to dominate economic life. He also noted, but did not consider it particularly interesting, that the ratio of workers to entrepreneurs was in the region of 2 : 1. A later German statistical analysis from 1895 showed that small-firm entrepreneurs constituted some 28 percent of the working population as against the 67.8 percent who were workers and 3.3 percent who were officials [7]

During Gustav Schmoller's active life he witnessed the growth and concentration of German industry in large-firm organizations covering many branches of industry, although the small firm yet remained an important and considerable section of economic life. It was clear to Schmoller that there were still large gains to be made through the rationalization of certain branches of industry to increase efficiency. He pointed out, for example, that while in Germany each spinner handled some 60 spindles, the English worker cared for 104. While such action presumed state intervention, Schmoller's recipe for dealing with economic crises went in the same direction. Unemployed workers were through "advice and deeds" to be transferred to activities that could not be touched by mechanization.

Schmoller was, in fact, much concerned to find an alternative position to both the free-enterprise notions of the Manchester liberals and the notions of the socialists that were growing in popularity. His arguments against liberal ideas were based on denying the relationship that was meant to exist between free enterprise and economic development. This was, according to him, only a myth spread by English pamphleteers who were just children of their time rather than serious scientists. It was not individual initiative and peaceful free trade that had created British economic wealth but rather, as history had shown, that free trade was soon given up in favor of imperial expansion. Britain's empire had increased between the years 1880 and 1912 from 27 to 30 million square kilometers and contained more than 400 million people.[8] The liberal dream concerning the eternal natural rights of all equal individuals created the illusion that nature created economics. But who could imagine that Britain had better natural propensities than Germany? Had not Prussia won the struggle with Austria for the leadership of Germany through an economic development founded upon a number of reforms undertaken by the state? Demand and supply function in a limiting framework of rules, laws, morals, and habits that the liberals with their naive individualism and historical illiteracy simply ignore.

Schmoller's enthusiasm for the socialists was equally limited. Their prophets imagined that it was possible to solve social problems through the application of simple formulas. For example, Ferdinand Lassalle, the socialist who had died in a duel after having connived with Bismarck on a common front against the liberals, imagined that state cooperatives for production provided the ultimate solution of the social question. On the other hand, Marxists believed that the exploitation of surplus value inevitably led to the collapse of capitalism. Schmoller, indeed, reckoned that 280 books on Marx had appeared between the years 1894 and 1904.[9] Strangely enough, it was, according to Schmoller, in the theory of the state that the Marxists made their largest errors:

> The marxist theory of class warfare completely forgets that there exists a state and a state power. This state is the precondition for all higher culture, and it uses its power not only for external defence, but also to maintain the inner peace. Accordingly, it can happen that cultivated people cannot always avoid an unlimited right of the fists [*Faustrecht*], but this is never a case of open class warfare."[10]

Others, such as Johann Karl Rodbertus, blamed all social problems upon the single institution of property; in this they showed an ignorance of both property and other institutions such as the company and the family.

It was clearly necessary, according to Schmoller, for a scientific economics to take up cudgels with both the natural rights theory of the liberals and the utopianism of the socialists. Schmoller held the following:

> The theory of the natural economy rests upon an incomplete analysis of humanity, a one-sided, optimistic natural rights worldview deriving from Epicurus and the rationalism of the Enlightenment. It is naively believed that there is an identity of interests between those of society and the individual; while in an unhistorical manner it is explained that English riches are the result of hunger for profits instead of seeing that such build upon English institutions."[11]

It was entirely clear that human beings had a biology, but economic life was cultural in character. The lust to work and earn profits was explained by the liberals in terms of natural individual egoism, but concrete historical studies showed that human beings are not simple instinctive creatures. They feel not only a lust for food but also for music and art. Moreover, they are pleased by honor, seek good positions at the table, take joy in their families, and enjoy as fulfilled cultural beings "das beglückende Gefühl des Heldentodes für das Vaterland [the wonderful feeling of a Hero's death for the Fatherland]."[12]

Economic action arises not only out of hunger or sexual drive, and economics must take into consideration the cultural needs that provide purposes as well as capturing primitive natural instincts.

The modern calculating business was a cultural achievement that replaced the primitive hunters' search for prey. The Darwinian model of the struggle for survival must be translated into the war ceremonies of the modern state. Competition was never "free" but was always bound by innumerable moral rules. In the German state, it was "the entrepreneurs . . . who were the officers and general staff of the economy."[13]

The English economists lived in a departing age and perhaps imagined that the "Sturm- und Drangperiode" would last for ever. It was not to the individual, profit-hungry capitalist that the future belonged, but rather to a well-disciplined corps of financial administrators and planners at the service of the nation-state.

A major point of Schmoller's historical national economics was to explode the myth that the economy of a country was simply the sum of its individual enterprises. The liberal economists rejected notions such as "folk-income" (*Volks-Einkommen*) as meaningless abstractions. But Schmoller, who was influenced by Hegelian concepts, regarded ideas as having a concrete and material existence and the material world as being abstract. He thus maintained that the "folk" notions are the real and the concrete and that their effects are visible in the ongoing adaptive processes of individual economic action (*Vergesellschaftlichung*) to the social totality. The English, German, Greenland, or Chinese economy is more than the sum of individual enterprises of Englishmen, Germans, Greenlanders, and Chinese.

> And what they have in common that binds these individual economies into a folk or a state is not only the state, but something that lies deeper: the common language, history, memory, habits and ideas. It is the common world of emotions and ideas, it is the mastery of a common imagination, more or less in agreement with psychological instincts; and even more, it is the objectivized common ordering of life, a common ethos that has arisen from the collective psychological basis.[14]

In the final resort, it was the common race with its common psychological instincts and common language that provided the preconditions for the existence of a national economy.

The treasure of a common language that found expression in schools, literature, and newspapers slowly raised and developed the character of the people from its unconscious depths. With this there also develop self-conscious circles (*Bewusstseinskreisen*) that encompass cultural values concerning needs, exchange values, and the use of products and services. These common values cement over and cover the class and racial differences among the population. The primitive instincts are transformed into industriousness, entrepreneurship, obedience, and frugality. Following Hegel, Schmoller considers that the morals, habits, and laws expressed by the state provide a major influence upon the character of work. The existence of safety regulations makes work a healthy activity; compulsory insurance helps to integrate the worker in the people's economy so that he tends to forget himself and work for the common good. The manager is transformed from a moneymaker (*Geldmacher*) into a state official (*Staatsbeamte*). His primitive hunger for profits is transformed into a patient self-discipline and love of order. While the savage pulls down the tree in order to get at its fruit, the modern businessman carefully weighs both goals and means. Courage, justice, and determination are the outstanding qualities from which the new national spirit is created. Where the earlier forms of natural economy were controlled by habits, the new modern business organization is controlled by morals.

In earlier times it was religion that provided the moralizing function, but following the Reformation and the break with Catholicism, an attempt had been made to found morals upon a purely philosophical basis. The technical and social changes that had occurred between 1750 and 1850 had rendered the old morals and legal structures irrelevant and old-fashioned. It was now the case that it was imagined that society had been freed from all morals and habits and that behavior was in some manner spontaneously directed toward a total harmony. But this notion of liberal economics and natural rights philosophy created only an unconscious immorality that could be condemned by all culturally conscious people. Morality in economy is unavoidable:

> When I see a poor woman cheated into buying bad and coloured coffee from some rogue, and at the same time see how this honourable woman can obtain

good products against a good price, I ask myself how low our morals can really sink? Has competition destroyed the businessman's moral habits? I question further if there does not exist a punishment in the paragraphs of the laws concerning food stuffs that can put a stop to this? Or perhaps one should introduce a new paragraph?[15]

In order to spread morality, it is necessary to have both education and a correct upbringing. Schmoller is of the opinion that if this cannot be undertaken by a union of the Protestants and Catholics in a national church (*Nationalkirche*), it would be necessary for the state to take over and coordinate this moralizing function. In medieval times, it was possible to exist without a live feeling for the state because of the strength of the church, but "[t]he modern society cannot survive without a high pitched patriotism and an intense feeling for the state. On the other hand, this feeling for the state is impossible without the state showing justice to those who bear the burdens of the state, pay taxes and provide for the public conscription."[16]

The love of the state was to replace the love of God, and was to be engendered through education, upbringing, and the provision of justice.

Meanwhile, the liberals imagine that it is possible to deal with the problems of ethics and morality "with abstract slogans about economic freedom."[17]

Marx and the socialists blame the lack of morality upon capital. Following in the footsteps of Ricardo, they maintain that the economy is bound to destroy itself. But contrary to Marx, who held that capital created the national state, Schmoller maintains that it was the nation-state that created capital. While Marx explains the class differences among people who were born equal, through property and capital, Schmoller holds that individuals are not so equal in origins as democratic theory implied. The Marxist considers that a business originates in capital and that entrepreneurship is identical with capitalism. Schmoller, on the other hand, explains entrepreneurship with the entrepreneur's personal characteristics. It was the inventive genius of Werner Siemens that distinguished him from the ordinary worker and ensured him success, and capital was only an instrument that made this possible. The railways, postal services, and telegraph are more important instruments when it comes to the development of businesses. When it comes to the question of economic crises, such have nothing to do with capital, but rather depend upon the lack of honesty, the misuse of market information, swindling, extortionist interest rates, and counterfeiting. Not even the French Revolution was to be explained in terms of the false abstractions of capital, but rather was to be understood in terms of the moral decadence of aristocracy.

Schmoller rejects—even as had Mill and Marshall—Marx's pessimism that finds its origins in the work of Ricardo, but his solution in terms of moral regeneration differs radically from the parliamentary ideas of the English economists. Not the least, business enterprise and economy lose their major role as the agents of social change that had been implied in their writings. Schmoller thinks rather in terms of his "Volk" and the new "Reich" with a foretaste of the corporativism that was to mark future developments. At the same time, he reduces economic activity to a question of business technique, and this provides a point of view that had influence far beyond the German borders.

With his major work, *Grundriss der Allgemeinen Volkswirtschaftslehre*, Schmoller sought to provide a textbook that covered the ground of his influential lectures. Besides taking some thirteen years to write, the work marks a departure from his earlier principle of writing only historical monographs. The central issue to be addressed was expressed by him as follows: "[H]ow can humanity develop a state power that stands over parties and classes? How have justice, law and the state developed in earlier times? Which aristocratic, oligarchic and democratic forms have hitherto existed? Which future world historical development can be discerned in these tendencies and institutions?"[18]

The book reflected the dominating attitude toward economics and business in contemporary Germany. It was not without a certain self-satisfaction that Schmoller could consider in his old age that there was no longer any German who would accept the title of a Manchester liberal. Bismarck himself apparently was so impressed by the heavy volumes that emerged from the pens of the "Verein für Sozialpolitik," that he declared himself willing to become a "Kateheder-sozalist" if only he had the time.

2. The Hegelian Thesis—Traditional Enterprise

The mode of thinking developed by Schmoller and his school was essentially historical in character and influenced by Hegelian categories of analysis. Nature had provided southerners with rich soils, and the black people with their breadfruit tree, while the traders enjoyed the natural gifts of navigable rivers. But more than climate, it was culture that explained why people in the north were more industrious than those in the south. The study of races, however, was meant to show that human beings were hardly born equal. The Polynesians, Bushmen, and Hottentots were believed to have underdeveloped extremities, stomachs like animals, the inability to understand very much; in addition, it was believed that they become easily tired when subjected to instruction. Blacks may enjoy the bustle of the marketplace, but it was the higher-standing Jewish nature, suitably mixed with the national consciousness of the Germans, which devotes its life to competition and invention. There were, unfortunately, a few extortist Shylock types still hanging around, exploiting the simple German peasants.[19] If strict caste systems prevented interesting race mixtures from development, it was just as well to keep an eye on the numbers of Slavs and Chinese, writes Schmoller.

The interaction of biology, climate, and geography, however, was held to obtain economic significance only through the medium of culture. A highly developed technology could only lead to economic development if there existed a correspondingly high level of cultural development. From the simple plow of the ox to the waterwheel working with a 15 percent efficiency, on to the 75 percent efficiency of the turbine, steampower, gas, and the petrol motor, there was a path toward an increasingly high level of culture. The diesel motor, the galvanic battery, Edison's bulb, and the electric motor made it possible for the simple silk weaver earning ten marks per month to keep his loom in action. But in the same manner as the aqueducts of ancient Rome presumed an administrative culture in the form of the state, so also does the existence of modern technology with its warships, locomotives, steel mills, and machines presume the existence of the state as the major customer. The further improvement of production and technology demands higher levels of ethical, moral, and legal organization. History has many examples of technologically clever peoples who because of the lack of appropriate moral institutions had vanished from the face of the earth. Concrete knowledge concerning economic development was to be obtained through the study of social institutions, which constitute the body of society, and among these institutions the form of the business is the latest addition.

When human beings left the nomadic stage and became settled agriculturists, when slaves and women became objects of trade and livestock began to be hired out against a natural rent in the form of milk and calves, these events and trends provided the end of the matriarchal family and the origins of the patriarchal familial institutions. The head of the household became judge, priest, director, and financial administrator in one and the same male person; his noble and sympathetic feelings in respect to the responsibilities involved constituted an important ethical advance. The captured slaves and purchased women, together with the free men, built a community where all received their daily bread and were seldom beaten or sold. In this patriarchal group, the children received the love of the mother, while the father provided an example that taught both paternal respect and the history of the family based in the moral development of the institution. When the patriarch died, the group could appoint a new leader and could take care of its own preservation through the following generations.

This "natural house-keeping" was founded upon forced labor in both the pursuit of agriculture and the simple workshops that provided for household needs. The slaves plowed the common land under the control of their masters, because all higher organization, according to Schmoller, requires a division of labor among those who obey and those who give orders. Military service was undertaken by the free males and demanded some 25 percent of the population as against the perhaps 2 percent in modern society. When the men excelled themselves in battle, they were often rewarded with a piece of the common land; when this land was not returned to common usage after the death of the holder, it was converted in this manner into private property. The growth and development of these estates assumed an increasingly businesslike form that involved both administrative officials and servants. The small peasants were now required to deliver their surplus production to the lord of the estate if he did not prefer to extract such directly through imposing his retinue upon the peasant. At the same time, many peasants became specialized as craftsmen, foresters, or charcoalburners who were required to work and deliver their products according to the patriarchal order and the laws established by the courts of the castles. Those who lacked property or inheritance became dependent upon paid labor (*Lohnwerk*) provided by the estate.

These large estates were economically successful when they were managed with an iron hand that ensured their efficiency. In good times, they could provide sufficient production even to meet the needs of slaves and foreigners who were peripheral members of the large household. Slaves occasionally married the daughters of the master, and in many cultures, it was the custom to give them the rights and responsibilities of members after a few years. Where, however, the masters were lazy and wasteful, the conditions of life were much harder for the small peasants, workers, and peripheral members, even if the European estates seldom degenerated into the infernos of thralldom that marked ancient Rome or the colonial plantations.

The disappearance of these large estates with their patriarchal order took place slowly and depended upon developments that demanded other kinds of skills than were to be found within its bounds. The first of these developments was an increased organization of production for distant markets whereby the burden of work placed upon the subjects of the lord of the estate greatly increased. The second involved the measuring and mapping of the lands under the control of the lord so that a wasteful landowner in need of money could then use the land as a security against loans and mortgages. The papers referring to such transactions—like the state loans and share certificates that came later—could be bought and sold, creating a market in fixed property. The value of lands in Prussia in 1870 was some 25 billion marks of which 10 billion was mortgaged. When it was properly used, credit of this kind was like technology and capital, a useful support for business enterprise, but unfortunately not all landowners were culturally mature, and it led to the splitting up of landed estates under the pressure of high interest rates. At the same time as the estates were split, their other assets, such as the dairies, were leased out to provide a return with which to pay the interest on loans. In this manner, the common utilities of the estate were transformed into private property. In the final resort, there was little left of the community of the estate except a shrunken and inflexible tradition. The peasants pursued their activities for their private benefit in isolation from each other, and when times were hard they provided an easy prey for the loan sharks. On the other hand, the land that remained to the large estates was managed in an increasingly routinized manner by the Junkers, who were more often than not military officers, rather than auditors and numerate entrepreneurs. It was not until the users of the land had obtained an education in business economics that they came to understand that it was necessary for them to unite in credit and dairy cooperatives. But even before these new organizational tendencies became apparent during the 1870s, other historical forces had transformed production in the country. When the smallholding failed to provide a sufficient income, the peasant took to handicraft production in the cottage, which was distributed through intermediaries to the towns. Where the peasant lost his patch and lacked the six or ten thalers to purchase a weaving loom, he was forced to join the hunt for paid work, so becoming a worker. In this manner, the old economic institutions and their organs gradually declined and were replaced by new more businesslike forms of economic life.

The German cities had developed over a thousand-year period and were integrated into a European network of trade routes that contributed to their expansion. When, however, the simple peasant came bearing his products to the town market he was faced with a well-regulated and controlled system that determined the conditions under which trade was permitted. Only the freemen of the town or city were allowed to pursue trade outside the weekly and yearly time schedules of the market. The laws of the town forced the traveling salesman to offer his products in the marketplace (*Stapelrecht*) and also to pay a tariff (*Strassenzwang*) to transport his goods through the town. The town council employed an overseer of the market, a controller of weights and measures, and a coiner for the minting of the means of payment. All of them naturally took a fee for the utilization of their services, as also for the hiring out of market halls and places on the market square.

Outside the town gates on the market days, long queues of peasants would assemble bearing their loads of wood, corn, hay, and vegetables. It was forbidden to enter the town before eight in the morning, and no town dweller was permitted to purchase anything before this time. It was, indeed, even forbidden for the town dweller to talk to anyone from the countryside outside the town walls before the market opened. When the gates were opened, the queue of peasants moved forward to take up their allotted places under the watchful eye of the master of the market (*Marktmeistern*). The commerce between town dwellers and peasants then commenced between the hours of eight and twelve. After the stroke of twelve, it was the turn of the shop owners of the town to obtain their supplies from the market. At the stroke of two the whole spectacle was finished, and no unsold goods were allowed to remain in the town. If some rich buyer had purchased a large amount of a product, a needy town dweller could exercise the right to buy a certain portion of this stock at the ruling market price. The clothing manufacturers in the town often had the right of first choice with regard to the purchase of wool supplies, and the same was true for the tanners with regard to skins. The ideal running through all this regulation, however, was that consumers and producers should meet without the intervention of middlemen. Buyers and sellers should meet as groups, in a face-to-face situation.

The ordered routine of the market, however, was not without its difficulties and conflicts. Much to the chagrin of the local hosteliers, for example, strangers had the right to sell drink during the course of the market; moreover, Italian credit merchants could make their appearance at the annual markets for animals, clothing, and linen. In order to extend control over larger stretches of the countryside, certain town councils introduced markets that could last as long as four weeks at a stretch. The growth of suburbs to the towns with a tendency to develop their own local markets that competed with those already established was another problem that persistently worried the town elders. The arrival of strangers among the town dwellers was also a hot question, although those who did not obtain burgher rights could be expelled without warning.

The best method of obtaining burgher rights was to purchase fixed property in the town. But it was also possible for the craftsmen, traders, and workers to obtain such rights through trade qualifications or the recommendation of their particular livery corporation and the payment of fees. There developed ever closer relations between the town councils and their livery companies; these administrative structures tended to become dependent upon the large financiers such as the Medicis from Florence or the Fuggers from Augsburg. In this manner, financial institutions could obtain extensive political power over wide areas of the country. Those trade corporations of the towns (*Innungen*) that developed such close relations to the town councils provided the basis for the formation of the middle classes. Around the year 1300, Paris had about 120 recognized corporations, while Vienna possessed 50, and there were 14 in Frankfurt. The divisions and classifications of the medieval town provided for between 150 and 300 different crafts and trades. The corporations provided the craftsman with an assurance of work for himself and for dependents, which included the apprentices to whom he taught the craft. Each corporation had its own police and apprentices and "eintrittsgeld" were followed. Many of these corporations changed their character through time to become forms of trading associations where the richer masters purchased their poorer brethren's production, which was then resold in distant markets at higher prices.

In all this activity the original ideal of the market economy was being persistently undermined. Between the producer and the consumer there were now often long chains of middlemen and financiers who organized credit and distribution over broad areas of the country. For example, traveling merchants who owned large warehouses and sometimes specialized machinery would deal out handwork to individual households to which they also sold the materials. Caught between high material costs and a low return for their work, a mode of proletarianism came into existence that was much worse than that introduced by the factory system. During the late Middle Ages, this tendency was opposed in some degree through the intervention of the princes and town councils. The prince could well support the rebellious weavers, who were tired of being shut in their part of the town, working to the chimes of the church clock, and not being able to buy wool or sell their products in the local market. The prince would, for example, demand that the merchant provide long-term contracts for the weavers that could ensure a market for their goods over a ten- to twenty-year period. Such contracts were required to be registered in the public records.

From time to time, other kinds of revolts would arise when the weavers in the towns would invade the local countryside and destroy the looms of the peasant households. As the conflicts between town and country increased in severity, the budgets of the town administrations were also being burdened by the costs of fortifications together with military and diplomatic personnel. The social costs, however, were not yet included in the public accounts, since the relief of the poor and the like was managed by independent institutions. As the wars among the towns placed increasing demands upon town budgets, the bankers also increased their power over the indebted town councils. The organization of the towns was weakening; important results of the Thirty Years' War were that the princes established themselves and the territorial state emerged as the most important economic institution.

One of the most important functions of the new principalities was maintaining the peace among the trading towns that had developed a dependence upon distant markets. Venice had extended its area during the fifteenth century as far as Verona; Philip the Brave put an end to the internal wars in Flanders and established free competition among the towns. The princes thus developed central administrations that determined the conditions under which economic life was pursued. Quarrying and salt manufacturing, together with other forms of production, were often effectively and successfully established as princely monopolies. The riches of Saxony, Brunswick, and the Tyrol rested upon the silver mines; Maximilian I of Bavaria financed a large part of his administration through his salt works and monopoly over beer. It was from this period that the techniques of mercantilist economics developed. While businesses that met simpler needs were left in private hands, those involving higher needs that often gave rise to antagonism among the different classes and estates were established as state enterprises. The collection of taxes, however, was always a source of corruption, and this led to the attempt to create an ethically high-standing middle class of state administrators (*Beamten*) that found its satisfactions through a career of service to the state and a salary that derived from direct and indirect taxation. This process of bureaucratization demanded access to information concerning the calculation of both capital and profitability. It was relatively successful in relation to certain enterprises run by the state where the necessary insight existed, but in other cases there were difficulties. A solution was found in devolving certain enterprises upon private persons through the means of granting concession rights. The postal services, for example, were given to a family by the name of Taxi. More often than not, these concessions were granted to Huguenots and other enterprising foreigners who settled in Prussia. At the same time, the state rationalized the confusion of weights and measures and the proliferation of currencies that provided serious barriers to the development of trade and industry within its territorial area. Through the encouragement of both internal and external colonization and the concluding of treaties with other states, the modern national state slowly took form. It claimed authority over millions of people and vast areas of territory, while its budget was now to be reckoned in millions of marks. With the advent of great leaders such as Cromwell, Colbert, Sully, Fredrick Wilhelm II, and Peter the Great, the larger states were organized with regard to both their inner legal systems and outer defense. Before, however, the thesis provided by the old economic orders was integrated into the synthesis of the new national state, it was, in course of history, forced into collision with the antithesis of free enterprise.

3. Antithesis—Free Enterprise

The period between 1750 and 1870 was to be regarded as the era of the false doctrine of free individuals, free businesses, and free markets; whereas the year 1789 was to stand as the symbol for all that was worst in this doctrine. The simplified abstractions of Adam Smith's teachings concerning free markets had reached Germany, but it was obvious, according to Schmoller, that Smith was entirely ignorant of the historical role of the state in Germanic development. Influenced by Rousseau's notions of natural rights, writers such as Schiller and Hölderlin complained incessantly that individuals could not develop themselves freely within the framework of the specializations of the contemporary division of labor in society. If they had known anything of anthropology, however, they would have known that such a freely acting individual had never existed anywhere in history. The world had never been populated by these free and equal human beings as was supposed by the advocates of economic freedom. The notion of equal "individuals" is a utopia, since all persons possess different powers and different personal qualities, which ensure that contracts entered outside the scope and limits of existing law, ethics, and morals could be nothing other than an exercise in power. "Two persons with conflicting interests can arrive at a contract for work [*Arbeitsvertrag*] only if the stronger commands and the weaker obeys or both are forced to make concessions."[20] The liberal economists, moreover, were blinded by a false scientific ideal that they had obtained from the physical sciences.

It was this confusion that led them to explain the question of economic value in terms of the supply and demand of goods, money, and credit, instead of an understanding orientated toward social conflict. From Schmoller's point of view, all value arose from a summation of forces that were eventually psychological in character. These provided social facts that could only be understood through a deep analysis of the attitudes and aspirations of the (*Volk*) masses. Schmoller shared Hegel's view that the liberal free thinkers imagined that they were moved by great ideas only "when they differed from those generally accepted and valid, and implied something strange and new."[21] These unscientific utopists refused to follow the Hegelian tradition in the manner of Schmoller and his school, who regarded social science as "the attempt to understand and depict the state as something in itself rational."[22] The liberals, moreover, had the effrontery to question the productivity of the officials and officers, raising the business to the most important of social institutions.

Schmoller admits, nevertheless, that history has provided reasons for a business-orientated perspective on the world. Out of the patriarchal family and the feudal estate, business institutions had slowly developed through production for distant markets. Meanwhile, in the towns, the development of trade and manufacturing had led to the development of specialized economic institutions. Schmoller's point, however, is to illustrate and emphasize how the division of labor, property concepts, social classes, and the structure of prices dictate the behavior of individuals. The behavior of businesses, thus, must also be explained in terms of institutions that lay outside the businesses themselves. When the territorial state got rid of the old guild and livery corporations, as when the enlightened reformers from Frederick the Great to Stein and Hardenberg during Napoleonic times worked for a freer economic life and for the abolition of the privileges of the Junkers, it was easy to obtain the impression of a drive toward total freedom. It was true, of course, that Hardenberg had been accused of placing the land in the hands of usurious foreigners and allowing the development of a "neumodischer Judenstaat" as a result of his Prussian liberalism, but such complaints were exaggerated. While the time for mercantilism was certainly past, these Prussian reformers never imagined that the goal was to set free market forces. Total economic freedom, according to Schmoller, had existed only in the daydreams of the liberals and the nightmares of the Marxists who feared capitalist anarchy. A man like Stein may have sought after a freer economic life, but he had also been Oberbergrat in the administration of the state mining industry and was well aware of the duties and responsibilities of management toward the state.

Where the liberals had managed in places to realize their utopia in reality, they had succeeded in causing much harm. Their strategy had consisted of falsifying economic history. Trade in the towns had been depicted as being hidebound and inflexible; the ban imposed by the churches on interest payments had been presented as absolute in character, and the more articulated views of the church fathers and monastic institutions were simply ignored. The workers were to be freed from a slavery and mode of life that, after it had been abolished, proved to have been their only defense against lumpenproletarianism. The landowners were depicted as idle drones whose property would only become productive when the interest on land was not refused. The military officers were regarded as unproductive, and there was pressure to reduce the salaries of officials. The complex system of social classes was reduced to abstract groups of landowners, capitalists, and workers, and only those values that arose from the interaction of resources, businesses, and consumers were counted in the form of national income. The business was raised in status to the heart and mind of society; the shareholding company was prized as the most democratic and efficient mode of economic organization. All production of goods and services, whether such concerned agriculture, credit, or insurance, was forced into this one form of business organization. Where the course of development from the old orders had taken this path, according to Schmoller, the results had been little less than terrifying.

When, for example, the rent of land in Ireland had been set free, the Irish peasants were faced with starvation; the social conflicts that arose in these circumstances were so great that competitive rents were abolished in favor of ethically "fair-rents." When the price of bread was set free after the French Revolution, it soared to undreamed heights at the same time as the quality sank. New regulations were introduced in response to the demands of the public. When interest rates were set free in Germany in 1854 in accordance with the recipe of the Benthamites, extortionist rates spread and therewith the growth of antisemitism. In 1878 new maximum interest rates had been introduced. When the printing of money was set free on the advice of seductive bankers, the result was a series of bank crashes. When the liberal-minded small saver practiced his self-help notions through the purchase of shares or insurance, he was soon forced to abandon his liberal illusion through the experience of bankruptcy, and then may have become prey to the even more dangerous illusions of socialism. Against all such misery and mystification it was necessary to take a firm line, as had been the case with the foundation of the German state in 1870. The Iron Chancellor had persuaded Wilhelm I to accept the title of German emperor since he refused that of emperor of Germany, a nation that did not yet exist.

The Great Depression of the late nineteenth century and the appearance of *Grundriss der Allgemeinen Volkwirtschaftslehre* marked the end of the period of the antithesis. Inspired by the corrected version of the history and sociology of earlier economic institutions, a new mode of economic order would take form. This was the Bismarckian-Schmoller synthesis that arose from the contradictions of the old.

4. Synthesis—Corporativist Enterprise and Managers of Morals

The suggestion that most scandalized these German economists, historians, and sociologists was the implication of the liberal message, as they understood it: the institutional structure of society should be demolished in order to free the forces of enterprise; further, this could result in an automatic distribution of income among capitalists, landowners, and workers. It was held that the proof that such would occur was built upon abstract notions and that their ideas concerning competition and values could be rejected after historical studies of the operation of real markets had been undertaken. These showed that the distribution of abilities was very unequal in the real world, that the organization and distribution of power in society was perhaps the most crucial variable, and that the operation of the price mechanism of markets was more of an expression than a determinant of these social realities. It was true, of course, that a ham costing 18 francs had increased in price to 120 francs during the siege of Paris, while the price of a lettuce had risen from 2.5 centimes to 1.25 francs; but why had market prices in Charlottenburg risen in the proportion 1 : 50 when the population had only increased in a proportion of 1 : 13? Moreover, why did people complain so much about prices in free markets when, according to the lights of the Manchester liberals, these prices reflected a natural and moral justice?

Schmoller was particularly anxious to reject any claim by the liberals to have captured the nature of eternal truth and to assign their achievements to the realm of history: "The old ideas of the Manchester school that market prices can be calculated from information concerning the size of supply and demand must be regarded as completely old fashioned."[23]

The period of transition from the old order had shown, on the contrary, that free enterprise had created more problems than it had solved. Moreover, Schmoller emphasized that these problems had arisen in a different form from that dreamed up by the socialists, Marx and Lassalle, and by the social democrats who hated business. These social philosophers argued in the style of the Talmud and obtained their inspiration from the French Revolution and Ricardo, who was a Jew. They condemned the industrial state that they imagined was controlled by a cold and calculating bourgeoisie that made capitalist vampire profits out of the myth that the utilization of property was worth a rent beyond the costs of depreciation. Many liberals had fallen into the same trap and imagined that they could take the pulse of the (*Volk*) economy through measuring the amount of capital. They, moreover, cheered for the raising of prices as the means of exploitation for the assembly of even more capital for the purpose of investment.

The real sociopolitical problem, considered Schmoller, was not that of harnessing the evil and calculating capitalists who pressed the masses toward ever higher consumption as they offered them lower and lower wages until they were forced to participate in a world-encompassing revolution. The real problem was that the free entrepreneur was an emotional, psychically unstable, and morally unreliable creature who was controlled through shortsighted calculations concerning immediate production needs and the daily prices of the market. These sad creatures play in an irresponsible manner with the capital of shareholders and banks. Schmoller would, in other words, dismiss the notion of a robot-capitalist and replace it with one of a depraved and immoral entrepreneur. In Adam Smith's time when businesses were small and many, these moral and psychological shortcomings were equalized by the action of the market. But in the modern large business organizations, and in the share markets, key people with psychological weaknesses can set in action swings of activity that correlated only with the manic and depressive phases of their condition. This managerial madness could result in fateful consequences for society.

The definitive nail in the coffin of liberal economy came with the *Gründerzeit* and the business research reports about it produced by the members of the "Verein für Sozialpolitik." Schmoller's own analysis of the crisis rejected the socialist thesis that depressed consumer demand caused the fall in prices and the large stocks of unsold goods. The consumption patterns of modern economies, he held, had become largely stable. The modern individual did not need to consume large amounts at a single sitting, like the primitive Bushman, in the fear that there would be nothing to eat on the morrow. It was rather the case that the swings of economic activity depended upon changes of demand in the capital goods and raw material markets where it was the business enterprises that were the major customers. Large railway projects, for example, set in trail a chain of demands that soon resulted in economic swings, particularly when suppliers were dependent upon a single source for orders. Between 1860 and 1875, according to Schmoller, the rush to build the European railways had resulted in many crises that could have been avoided if the governments concerned had regulated the rate of building and investment.

A new industry with high profits and good export possibilities soon attracts new investment capital to established companies. Their subsequent expansion provides work for many new businesses that, in turn, increase the demand for capital yet further. The resulting rise in the rate of interest attracts many small savers to the market, while businesses make increasingly unrealistic offers and calculations in the attempt to outdo each other and invest in increasingly risky projects. As the stock of capital available for investment purposes sinks yet further, the rate of interest rises even higher. Where the banking system is centralized, it is not unusual to find that the state itself joins in the speculative wave, although it restricts itself to the more sound companies involved. The limited responsibility of the companies, together with the possibilities of immoral entrepreneurs selling worthless paper or obtaining loans from banks on the basis of false balances and manipulated accounts, only adds to the general frenzy. When the first signs of overinvestment appear in the market, the entrepreneurs dare not reduce prices in order to hold up the sales volume because of their own speculative investments in the shares of the company. Rather, they find a number of small tricks to give the impression of an unchanged level of productivity and profits, and this maintains the flow of investment capital, although at the same time stocks of goods are accumulating. The time perspectives of the immoral entrepreneurs become ever shorter as the crisis develops. In the end, it is a question of holding up prices for a few hours in order that worthless paper can be sold without loss in the share market. It now requires just a single bank or company to withhold payments for the balloon to be punctured and the whole market to fall flat. Mass bankruptcies follow, and the crisis becomes a fact. It takes several years to clean up the mess and for confidence in the future to be restored. The process then begins all over again. The basic causes of the crises, according to this analysis, are to be found in the free-enterprise system and particularly in the institution of the shareholding company with its limited liability. The companies deserved the old saying "Compani ist Lumperi."[24]

Adam Smith had doubted that a company organized after the shareholding principle would find managers who were other than corrupt and lazy bureaucrats. The reason was, held Smith, that they lacked personal responsibility for the whole of the invested capital. Since many kinds of economic activities need large amounts of capital that could only be raised through the sale of shares, it was necessary according to the liberal point of view to give the shareholders responsibility through a mode of ownership democracy in the form of company meetings and elected boards. Following the massive bankruptcies of the depression, a new company law was introduced in Germany that raised the minimum capital requirements and sharpened the internal accounting through the introduction of an *Aufsichtsrat* that was to keep an eye on things in the interest of shareholders. Modes of control of this nature, maintained Schmoller, whether applied to businesses or nations, were really of very little significance. In good times, the company meeting was always a "schlecht besuchte Komödien"[25]—a sparsely attended comedy—where evil-minded directors easily fooled the owners with the help of corrupted board members and accountants. When optimistic socialists such as Owen or Fourier imagined that the solution to business corruption was to be found in radical democracy that made the people into the decision makers through direct elections, they failed to understand that "all mass decision-making is dictated more by feelings and emotions than by reason and knowledge; and that the counting of votes in a divided society always results in the lowest needs, predetermined thoughts and ideas that are the widest spread coming to predominate. Reason tends to diminish even among people of education and character when they are assembled in larger groups."[26]

The major problem of business life is not that of creating a functioning democracy, but rather that of finding good managers. According to Schmoller, it is, indeed, only necessary to study the cooperative forms of business that were so much loved by the liberals in order to understand this. Such forms of economic activity certainly motivate the workers to industriousness but, nevertheless, always end in bankruptcy. This is because the workers lack the insight that they must always be led. They also lack the following insight:

> [H]uman progress is only possible when individual persons or groups according to race, abilities, power and skills are outstanding in the process of the division of labour. When they become political, technical and organizational leaders, fathers of families, generals, landowners, traders, captains and businessmen, they demand power in order that their decisions shall be carried out. When, moreover, their younger sons and relatives are insufficient to man their organizations, there emerges a suffering class of workers in society."[27]

The true managers and leaders are honest and intelligent and are suitable to lead the army of workers, since they are born to command. It is they who master the art of uniting and leading thousands of workers in their factories as is the case at Siemens and Loewe. The German manager is not primarily a moneymaker of the "smart fellow" type so popular in American business life. It is true that a board member may earn anything from a thousand to eighty thousand marks per year, but he is more often a prince or old general with good contacts in the worlds of government and banking. While it is obvious that it is not damaging for the directors and board members to own shares in their companies, the most important point is that the banks choose high-standing leaders who can meet the ethical demands of public life.

All great projects had found their generals, even as the nation-states had their elites. The development of the mining industry, for example, had given rise to a class of competent technicians and administrators who were morally sound. This leadership class had been augmented by those who emerged from the *Bergschulen* (Mining School) that had been founded in the 1700s. With the coming of liberal notions, this duty-bound middle class of responsible administrators had dissolved. The German state must now reconstruct a similar middle class to take control over the modern industrial activities. The great shareholding companies with their "aristocratic" and powerful leaders could provide the ideal model. One could learn from Werner Siemens's manner of taming the natives from Caucasus by providing them with good housing, and by promoting in their women a taste for expensive ornaments and trinkets, so that they were forced to become industrious wage earners in his factories in order to support their new life-style. Even the Social Democrats had now given up their immature earlier ideas concerning radical democracy that made them incompetent for business leadership, and had obtained a corps of their own officials and leaders. When the competent leaders had managed to tame the companies into obedient instruments of their will, it remained only to stabilize the swings of economic life through cooperation pursued in cartels and corporations.

But cooperation among businesses, upon which so much of earlier economic success had depended, had become old-fashioned as a result of the worst propaganda that had been distributed by the Manchester liberals. Schmoller relates how such cooperation was rediscovered when the stagnation induced by the economic crisis forced companies to make radical decisions:

> Why not finish with the general discussions of trade interests, and attempt to grasp the decisive problems—the regulation of sales and competition, common price fixing, care concerning a sufficient profit and interest on capital, sufficient employment for the workers. It had been forgotten that such cooperation had earlier occurred on a large scale. Now one had a strange feeling that it was wrong and that it created monopolies. Therefore such discussions were often held in secret. But need has no law. One acted.[28]

The cartels were able to make agreements on conditions of payments, credit, and production. Minimum prices were established and administered by centralized marketing departments. The German (*Volk*) character, with its well-disciplined masses, was much better suited to these cartels than to individual enterprise, considered Schmoller. The leaders of the cartels, on the other hand, were stigmatized as "Mässigkeitsaposteln" by liberals, because they were obviously less interested in maximizing profits than ensuring a quiet and stable industrial development.

These historically minded economists were always ready to remind the practical men of affairs that sales could be equally well organized in accordance with taxable values as with market prices. Had not Luther, Calvin, Leibniz, Frederick the Great, and even Fichte all called for unfair market prices? Examples could be cited that ranged from the price lists of Diocletian under the Roman Empire to that of the town council of Augsburg from 1276 and Morel's list of building prices in Paris from 1840. There was a clear need to hold a firm hand over prices in areas where the military were quartered and purchased their foodstuffs locally. When the town councils utilized local transport facilities that were drawn by the horses of the peasants or the boats that plied the rivers, they had developed a differential price system that varied from winter to summer. Prices in such cases were often settled by negotiations between the town council and the relevant corporations. Negotiations should be conducted on the basis of underlying ethical principles—such as the equal treatment of all citizens—which could determine contemporary traffic tariffs. Transport companies should be mindful of the fact that when they transport goods from one area where they are cheap to another where they are expensive, they do so upon roads and bridges that have been paid for by the public.

With an almost endless stream of examples and moralizing lessons, the point was driven that prices should be formulated in accordance with moral principles as a result of negotiations among corporative institutions. In this manner, liberal business economics were dismissed in favor of a management technique exercised by an elite that would kindly but firmly lead the masses to a "more human form" of earlier modes of oppression and slavery. Violent swings in economic activity would be avoided through the participation of an enlightened managerial elite in the regulation of business relations, particularly with regard to investment and prices. It is perhaps interesting to conclude here with the observation that for Schmoller and his school, social classes were something that lay much deeper than economics. Economics, in fact, was to be reformulated as an expression of such differences.

It was in this climate of opinion that the first German "economic miracle" took form with its powerful flagships—Siemens, Krupp, Loewe—leading the way, followed by a veritable armada of middle-range and small businesses. The concentration of cartels and large companies did not mean that the size of factory units would be subjected to a corresponding increase. Schmoller had already considered that it was a difficult task to maintain industrial discipline among units employing a hundred workers; for reasons of this nature, the giant companies split production into units that seldom exceeded a thousand employees. The elite of business technicians who succeeded in imprinting punctuality, submission to leadership, and honesty among their work force were nevertheless always haunted by the danger of class warfare that threatened to destroy the structures they had so carefully erected. If the goal of a stable economy was to be achieved, according to Schmoller, it was essential to eliminate all values from the area of business and transform the company into a working machine guided only by the principle of technical efficiency. This notion of a perfect, functioning machine provided the ideological background to modern German-inspired management training that also extended its influence to other areas such as Scandinavia.

The problem of class conflict arose particularly acutely in this context, since the very values inculcated by the discipline of the workplace, together with its sharp structural differentiation into the classes of management and labor, tended to intensify the political conflict. The same fanatical loyalty and discipline engendered and encouraged in working life could also be exploited in the political arena. The danger was that workers would be prepared to march in step under the red banners with the same serious-minded, humorless, and repetitive fashion that marked their daily experience in the perfectly functioning machines of German industry. Moreover, the notion of a perfectly functioning industrial machine was likely to induce the illusion that a perfectly functioning machine at the political level was both possible and desirable and would provide the ultimate solution to all the problems of injustice in society. Equally dangerous for internal order here, it was considered, were the reactionaries who would carve up the working class according to old-fashioned feudal principles.

The solution to the complex of problems that arose here was found in Bismarck's social policy, which involved the creation of new corporations and carefully considered social reforms. Social insurance covering employment, injury, and old age was planned, introduced, and administered by the state. Schmoller's own organization, Verein für Sozialpolitik, engaged much of its energies toward producing pamphlets and holding meetings designed to support these social reforms and state intervention in business life. This *Machtübernahme* was often exercised forcefully as in the example of workers' insurance, and the conditions of work were subjected to increasingly complex regulations administered by appropriate authorities. Police were now required to enforce a wide variety of regulations, from building to hygiene and fire fighting. It is perhaps ironical to note, however, that all this regulation did not prevent the burning down of a large social-political propaganda exhibition promoting public hygiene, before it even opened.

The transfer of values from the places of work to state institutions and corporations, which was the heart of Schmoller's message, had been foreshadowed in Hegel's "Grundlinien der Philosophie des Rechts" as a means of ensuring the victory of middle-class moral values. Schmoller was also of the opinion that the family provided the basic institution for the schooling of children, where the father provided both the example and the stern headmaster and the mother was his loving, self-offering assistant. The socialists who wanted to abolish the family had not read their Hegel sufficiently carefully and had, moreover, forgotten that the provision of public institutions for the care of children would be far more expensive for society than for the family. In order that the new state incorporating its Hegelian monopoly of pure reason should wax and ascend to ever higher levels of culture, it was only necessary to ensure that it did not print too much paper money or take large loans from the bankers. With the monarch leading and the Beamtes taking care of the administration, the modern state would slowly absorb economic life:

> It is a matter of a stepwise social establishment that more and more permeates the daily [*Volk*] economy and develops it far beyond the simple conflicts of power and squabbles of the market, and much further than the institutions with the duty of pouring social oil through insurance and helping a rickety egoistic machine. It is a matter of the beginning of the socialization of the economy from a humanistic, ethical and legislative perspective.[29]

The corporate national state and the economy would merge into a single functioning unit.

Gustav Schmoller was undeniably a considerable authority on the subject of the German state, although he never lived long enough to witness the collapse of its second version and the rise of the third. Nevertheless, his massive attack upon individualism, liberalism, and the basic role of businesses in economic life, together with his alternative proposition of the corporative state, was a strong influence upon the subsequent course of developments in Germany and beyond. He was during his time sometimes attacked by contemporaries for his paucity of theory and vagueness as an economist. The point, however, surely Is that in such a perspective both theoretical and business economics are diluted into the broader and grander streams of historical developments where they could at the most expect to provide technical and administrative help to those who would hasten the judgments of history. Schmoller was not, indeed, forgotten by the men of the Third Reich, who on the centenary of his birth in 1938 wrote the following:

> Schmoller could as little foresee the catastrophe of 1918 as anyone else, and also the beginning of the movement that would lead to the reestablishment of a great German state. Class peace has not been achieved in the form that he hoped. But is it not just those powers and traditions that Schmoller knew were necessary for progress that lie at the back of the new state and the people that we witness today?[30]

There seems little reason to dispute this judgment.

Notes

1. Gustav Schmoller, *Grundriss der Allgemeinen Volkswirtschaftslehre.* Vol. II, p. 485.

2. Hans Rosenberg, *Grosse Depression und Bismarckzeit*, p. 177.

3. Gustav Schmoller, *Zur Sozial und Gewerbepolitik der Gegenwart*, p. 1.

4. Schmoller, *Zur Sozial und Gewerbenpolitik*, p. 9.

5. Schmoller, *Grundrissder Allgemeinen Volkswirtschaftslehre*, Vol. I, p. 88.

6. Carl Brinkmann, *Gustav Schmoller und die Volkswirtschaftslehre*, p 16.

7. Schmoller, *Grundriss der Allgemeinen Volkswirtschaftslehre*, Vol. I, p. 369.

8. Gustav Schmoller, *Zwanzig Jahre Deutscher Politik*, p. 117.

9. Schmoller, *Zwanzig Jahre Deutscher Politik*, p. 128.

10. Ibid., p. 131.

11. Schmoller, *Grundriss der Allgemeinen Volkswirtschaftslehre*, Vol. I, p. 93.

12. Ibid., Vol. I, p. 22.

13. Gustav Schmoller, *Über Einige Grundfragen des Rechts und der Volkswirtschaft*, p. 58.

14. Ibid., p. 44.

15. Schmoller, *Grundriss der Allgemeinen Volkswirtschaftslehre*, Vol. I, p. 58.

16. Schmoller, *Über einige Grundfragen des Rechts*, p. 158.

17. Brinkmann, *Gustav Schmoller und die Volkswirtschaftslehre*, p. 61.

18. Schmoller, *Zwanzig Jahre Deutscher Politik*, p. 95.

19. Ibid., p. 181.

20. Schmoller, *Grundriss der Allgemeinen Volkswirtschaftslehre*, Vol. II, p. 272.

21. Georg F. Hegel, *Grundlinien der Philosophie des Rechts*, p. 23.

22. Ibid., p. 34.

23. Schmoller, *Grundriss der Allgemeinen Volkswirtschaftslehre*, Vol. II, p. 114.

24. Ibid., Vol I., p. 517.

25. Ibid., Vol. II, p. 519.

26. Ibid., Vol. II, p. 555.

27. Ibid., Vol. II, p. 261.

28. Ibid., Vol. I, p. 494.

29. Ibid., Vol. II, p. 417.

30. Arthur Spiethoff, ed. *Gustav Schmoller und die Deutsche Geschichtliche Volkswirtschaftslehre*, p. 348.

9

Self-Management and the Hope for Moral Emancipation: Charles Gide's Social Economy

1. Guns or the Eiffel Tower?

The World Exhibition of 1889 saw the opening of the Eiffel Tower at Paris in the midst of an economic crisis characterized by falling steel prices and problems of overproduction. The previous year had seen a further large project—the Panama Canal—which had been financed through the issuing of state bonds. The Panama Canal company continued into bankruptcy, and the engineer, A. G. Eiffel, was also involved in this. But in the year 1889, which celebrated the 100-year jubilee of liberty, equality and fraternity, the Panama Scandal with its unpleasant anti-Semitic tone had not yet exploded. French industry was pleased with the encouragement provided by the large orders. It was in the shadow of the World Exhibition that the third annual conference of cooperative businesses was held. As at the first conference at Lyon in 1886, it was Charles Gide (1847–1932), professor of political economy, who gave the welcoming address.

The usually shy professor spoke out strongly in favor of the future of the cooperative movement, comparing it to the beacon provided by the newly opened Eiffel Tower. It was this rather than the Tower of Babel that was the goal of the cooperative movement. The Eiffel Tower had restaurants on its first floor that satisfied concrete human material need. On the second floor, there was the newspaper, *Le Figaro*, and a telegraph office from which it was possible to send messages around the world. At its pinnacle was the beacon that each night sent its rays eighty kilometers across the city. The tower to be built would have consumer cooperation as its base and throw its rays even further:

> We would climb even higher and light a beacon to show the way to all those who seek in darkness. Through its shining example the socialistic ideal of

195

cooperativism awaken and touch the mass of people. Such an ideal is like a light house beacon. Its beams can be doused but will be kindled anew by its faithful followers.[1]

If the gaze is turned for a moment from this great tower toward the "galerie des machines"[2] provided by the World Exhibition, there are further lessons to be learned. Everybody knows, Gide went on, that the British cotton manufacturers produce sufficient cloth in their factories to surround the world 120 times. The question that arises is, How is it possible to satisfy real human needs when these textile factories, now struck by crisis, have a sufficient capacity to clothe the whole world? Did this enormous productive capacity correspond to real human needs or did it reflect a process of decline? Could the visitors who crowd around the vast assembly of colossal machines at the World Exhibition contemplate the future with equanimity?

The worker knows that his freedom is hardly likely to be increased by these great machines, except perhaps through unemployment. Producers and capitalists, on the other hand, regard them equally with fear. The machines produce so many goods that they kill off more firms in the market than a Gatling gun or Maxim machine gun killed soldiers on the battle field. They are, moreover, dangerous to life and limb. "It was no pleasure to have anything to do with these formidable machines of our times: the worker risked losing an arm or leg in their cogs, and the manufacturer his fortune."[3]

Charles Gide, who delivered this message, was both an economist and a pacifist, although at the same time he was no dogmatist. His dislike of the weapons industry, for example, did not hinder him from performing his duties as a teacher at the Ecole Supérieur de la Guerre, where he was noted for his ability to engage the students with important and serious lectures.

His perspective had been formed by a lonely childhood in a Calvinist home in the south of France. Of the other children in the family, only an elder brother survived. That brother, Paul Gide, was to become a professor in Roman law. He was the father of André Gide, the 1947 Nobel Prize winner in literature, who often used to visit his uncle Charles Gide when he moved to Paris around the turn of the century. Charles Gide had, in fact, earlier studied law in Paris, where he had moved with his mother. Although more truly interested in drawing, he had at this time successfully defended a thesis with the title, *Le droit d'association en matière religieuse*, in 1872.[4] Two years later he received his *aggregation de droit*, and a career as a teacher of law then stood open to him. This was, however, something for which he was hardly suited.

Perhaps realizing this, his elder brother, Paul Gide, who had watched his struggles with legal studies, had sent him a copy of the collected works of Claude-Fréderic Bastiat, the French liberal economist. The times were suited for liberalism. The French Empire had fallen at Sedan, and Alsace-Lorraine was occupied by the Prussians. The Paris Commune had been suppressed, and the

Third Republic had sworn never again to allow power to fall into the hands of a dictator or dynasty. Different groups—Orleanists, legitimists, centrists, and radicals—fought their battles in a parliamentary context. The church sought to renew the lost faith of the population, and the founding stone of the Sacré Coeur was laid on the hill where the Commune had defied the republic and religion. The works of Bastiat proclaimed the arrival of the era of freedom. The eighteen years of oppression under Emperor Napoleon II were to be exchanged for free trade and free competition, together with a free press and political liberty. The ideal was individual freedom. Charles Gide was appointed to an assistant professorship in political economy in 1874 at the law faculty of the University of Bordeaux. The post had been created following pressure from contemporary liberals. It is possible to imagine the fuss raised when, following a series of lively public lectures on such subjects as "The Sources of the Nile" and "The Mormon Church," Charles Gide began increasingly to attack the liberal ideal of freedom and its roots in political economy.

With the turn of the century, it was time for another World Exhibition in Paris. The city was again cascaded with electric lights from the Eiffel Tower, and a bridge was built in honor of Alexander III, the previous emperor of Russia. The Russian railways were being financed by the French small savers who invested their money abroad when they did not purchase government bonds as a security for their old age. Anatole France provoked the radicals while Sarah Bernhardt drew sighs from the public that laughed at the plays of Eugène Labiche and Georges Feydeau. Charles Gide had returned to Paris in 1898. He was no longer a provincial professor in political economy, but a teacher of comparative social economics. Gide's social economics included a concrete program of business economics for the cooperative movement.

2. Satisfying Real Needs with Concrete Objects

The century had seen an increasing consciousness concerning economic crises. Charles Gide reckoned four economic world crises—1825, 1847, 1857, and 1878—in the course of the century. He noted ironically that the English economist William Stanley Jevons had found a relationship between poor harvests and sun spots.[5] But what was an economic crisis other than a shortage or surplus of things such as corn, capital, money, or credit? A general glut led to a fall in prices where consumer incomes could not absorb the increased production, and where tariff barriers hindered export markets from taking the surpluses. When there was a surplus of capital, it was invested in new mad schemes that certainly increased the relative value of old investments with a secure return in the short run, but also drew these down when the crash came. A shortage or surplus in the means of payment, for example, could lead to violent changes in discount rates, so that firms could no longer meet their payments and went into bankruptcy.

While crises could originate in both surpluses and shortages of goods, capital, and money, Gide held that it was particularly surpluses that most frightened economists. Deep in every businessman's brain[6] was the fixed idea that profits were dependent upon the shortage of products. These businessmen demanded that capital should provide a return in the form of a percentage profit, but this was an abstract fantasy. It was only that which increased the quantity of wealth in the country, held Gide, that was worth calling capital. If someone hired out a carnival costume, for example, it was possible that something was earned, but nobody was a bit richer from such a transaction. Frightened businessmen, with a horror for the accumulation of stocks and falling prices, stopped production in the same manner as the old mercantilists who imagined that it was possible to measure the well-being of the nation by the size of their own profits. Economic transfers and the profits thereof had nothing to do with concrete economics. Genuine business profits, according to the concrete definition, were in terms of "net production": "If a businessman was sufficiently skillful to produce a considerable value with a small outlay, his profits could be very considerable: and this was also good for society because it showed in the difference of values that relatively non-useful things had been sacrificed for relatively more useful things that at least respond to an intensive desire."[7] The true concrete enterprise was to be productive and not merely lucrative.

But Charles Gide did not mean that the concrete firm was productive in the sense of the old Physiocrats, in creating material. Humans could only move the materials of nature around in the course of their work: "It was not dependent upon them, as we know, to create one atom of material."[8]

The shocking experience of the economic crises had often led to the faulty conclusion that mechanization had gone too far. The printing presses had replaced thousands of copyists; modern warships corresponded to 200,000 galley slaves. These and all the other machines had pushed world production to a maximum. This conclusion was, however, by no means the case, maintained Gide. Of the 4.6 million steam horsepower employed in France, no less than 4 million were in water and railway transport. The remaining 600,000 horsepower consisted often of machines that, like the threshing machine, produced the same amount of corn with less labor. If the machines employed in the manufacture of other machines were discounted, together with those used to obtain fuel for other machines, then it was clear that the mechanization of industry had barely begun. The need was also very large. If the 200 billion francs of wealth in France was divided by the number of inhabitants, it provided the figure of 5,000 francs per person. This was so small that it could hardly be believed with John Stuart Mill that the day of harmony and plenty was waiting at the door. It was necessary rather to invest in increased production for the concrete economic welfare of the population. But how was this possible without the dreaded economic crises that so frightened the businessmen?

Assume that all branches of industry expand production at the same rate and that consumers now purchase larger quantities of everything produced. Food would become cheaper and leave more money over for the purchase of cotton materials. A trader who came with ivory to the village market would note with pleasure the bustle around other exchange commodities such as rubber, gold, or ground nuts. The more products available for exchange—the greater the supply—the less was the risk that a producer would lack goods against which to exchange his own supply. The negative effects of overproduction would be counteracted by a free flow of exchange trading. As J. B. Say had expressed the matter: "[T]hat which most favours the debiting [sale] of a merchandise is the production of another." [9] The best security against economic crisis was a highly articulated and many-sided system of economic production.

It was unfortunate that many of the 5 million businessmen and retailers in France did little to promote this flood of wealth. Some 10 percent of the French population had decided to earn their upkeep without concrete work through spending their days minding pleasant shops. Even if it was taken into consideration, maintained Gide, that the seller of material needed to cut the cloth or that the grocer roasted the coffee, these businessmen lived for the most part only by purchasing something in order to sell it. The profits were a transfer that did not increase the concrete wealth of the country. Following the introduction of economic freedom, moreover, so many tradesmen had established themselves in the retail business that they had difficulty surviving. If it was known that there was one baker for every 1,300 of the population in Paris, it was easy to ascertain why bread cost 40 centimes per kilogram when it should really cost only 25 centimes. Charles Gide calculated that the French population paid an annual 7,000 million francs too much for its bread. This sum never went to the working farmer or the miller.[10] Gide was keen to emphasize that the number of businessmen was far too large in France: "[I]t is a veritable waste to maintain one intermediary for every ten persons."[11]

Trade itself did not stimulate the production of wealth in concrete firms, but rather tended to encourage the rationing of products through speculative holdings in stocks. The effects of trade could even have a negative effect on production through destroying or reducing the qualities of goods. People became used to buying poor-quality products, such as, for example, gray-colored salt, and were surprised when occasionally they happened to come across the fine white product direct from the producer. These tradesmen absorbed the purchasing power that should have kept the pump of wealth in action. They diverted resources from where they were needed and were a burden to consumers: "[I]f we shall go through the journey of life burdened by a grocer, a baker, a butcher and a wine merchant, the position of the consumer becomes hardly tenable!"[12] Gide would exchange this leaky hose for one that was watertight. The question then was, How was it to be coupled?

Charles Gide would begin with the consumers and create a direct link with the producers. To do the opposite would be to allow the producer to determine the pattern of demand. The tailor, for example, could dictate next year's fashion and ensure that the quality was such that a new suit did not last for more than one season. It was necessary to ensure that producers could not seduce the consumers through advertising:

> Do you really believe that the consumers' need for absinthe and apéritif have led to these discoveries and their considerable production? No! It is because the manufacturers and traders have covered the walls with posters that repeat a thousand times: Byrrh! Byrrh! Byrrh! or China! China! China! until the consumer is hypnotised.[13]

There were liberal economists with well-formulated arguments who opposed this close coupling to consumers. Consumption, they had maintained, was the destruction of material, whereas production was a creative act. Could it be considered, asked Gide, that alcohol, obscene pornography, and the like were less destructive? Consumption was not destructive, but rather the basis for life itself. The liberal economists then maintained that the producer only worked on behalf of others, whereas the consumer is satisfying egoistic needs. Gide would respond that the stomach's need for culture—from the Christian Communion to the bourgeois family dinner—had always been transformed into a social love affair. Consumption was socially determined and was capable of development. It was but necessary to look at the libraries, music, and study groups.

It could also be objected that the worship of consumerism would lead to luxury and waste. Gide admitted that having large hunting grounds on fertile lands was destructive luxury, but he pointed to other cases where a disproportionate investment in the satisfaction of a small need had led to a development of a generally demanded product. The real destruction of wealth occurs when the consumer is seduced by the producer, when something was damaging for both body and mind. It was only necessary to consider those fine ladies in Zola's novels whose beautiful dresses were made by starving slaves. Should rare birds be exterminated to decorate the hats of these ladies? Should we allow the fashionable magazines to so heat up demand that it led to a fetishistic kleptomania of elegant silks?

It could yet be further objected by the friends of the producers that machines would not be invented if producers merely waited upon the demands of consumers instead of making speculative investments in possible future demands. Consider, for example, the fine white bread that would never have existed if it was not for the large capital investments in milling inventions. This provided a good example of producer egoism, held Gide. Everyone knew that dark bread was much more nourishing and, moreover, could be stored longer. It was the baker rather than the consumer who was served by that white bread, which molded overnight and must be purchased fresh every morning. Finally, it was held by the liberals that the market only existed in order to satisfy consumer needs with useful products. Gide would agree, pointing out that this stood in the works of Bastiat, but he would add that the existing economic order unfortunately did not function in this manner. Liberals who imagined that the existing economic production harmoniously delivered maximum utility needed to reflect that "utility" could only be compared for those several products that met the same need. But how would they explain that a hat was willingly purchased for a larger sum than a loaf of bread? It was not utility, but need that counted. The concept of utility was only used to legitimize the existing order. Needs should be the guide, maintained Gide, and with this he opened the door to consider the objections of the socialists based upon their theory of labor value.

If capitalists pumped wealth directly to the consumers, considered the socialists, it would lower the level of wages. This was because needs were only physiological in character and were dependent upon how hard the consumer, in the role of the worker, labored in the factories. But, objected Gide, it yet needed to be explained how a French worker would survive on a wage level that an equally hardworking coolie lived upon. Value was not determined only by labor, held Gide, and this was obvious from everyday experience. Goods incorporating the same quantity of labor had different prices in the market; those things which nature provided without labor also had a value. Consumer needs were not simply determined by physiology and production but also belong to the world of ideas where they develop out of human imagination through imitation, habit, and cultural inheritance. It was just this innate power of the development of human needs that made it meaningful for Gide to proclaim a new era in economic thought: "le règne du consommateur."[14] In this new "reign of the consumer," political and social freedom were to be complemented by economic freedom. All the shopkeepers and trading parasites of the world should know that their time was now over.

Gide already saw signs of hope in contemporary economic developments. Trade that previously had been productively justifiable when the merchant had transported goods and provided credit was now only lucrative in character. Transport had been taken over by specialized agencies, while the banks provided money and credit. Business transactions were beginning to assume the nature of simple bookkeeping transactions without the intervention of middle men. The importance of trade had been exaggerated, and the time for a return to honest exchange was nigh: "It is not the first time in history that one has seen the remarkable sight of human development progressing towards a pinnacle only to come back after a certain time, to a point close to its original starting point."[15]

In Gide's concrete economy, the line went directly from people as consumers to people as producers without the intervention of middle hands. This was how it must have been for Robinson Crusoe before he found his Friday with whom he could exchange things on the island. He managed to increase his own wealth without crises and in a regular manner through manufacturing in order to satisfy his own orders. We can now turn to see how Charles Gide thought of introducing this exchange of needs through concrete business economics.

3. Self-Management and Economic Growth

Out of our wishes, imaginations, and ideas arose the needs that provide the impulse to work with nature and to produce objects. The savage, who one time found the free gifts of nature for the taking, saved energies that could be devoted to inventing traps and snares. When perhaps a shaggy mammoth fell into a trap, hitting its head on a stone and dying, he got the inspiration for inventing the stone axe. Charles Gide would remind us of the concrete origins of business economy:

> One time long ago, a person on this earth, much poorer than Robinson on his island, resolved the problem of producing the first wealth before any such wealth existed. That was, without doubt, a difficult moment to pass, an impasse on the route to the machine. With only the strength of their hands, these people set the immense wheel of industry in motion. When once it had been set in motion, the most difficult time was over, and all lighter pressures were sufficient to keep the wheel in motion.[16]

In today's situation with its capital and machines we have forgotten how things had really begun. People, moreover, no longer believed they could begin a concrete economic business.

A usual misunderstanding (a "fantasmagorie")[17] was that capital itself is business that gives a return in the same manner as a tree gives fruit or a chicken lays eggs. But the fruit of the tree and the eggs of the chicken only appear because nature had provided the gift of life. It is labor that is necessary to transform the egg into an omelette or to ensure that it hatches to produce capital in the form of another chicken. Labor and nature are necessary inputs in the genuine business. Capital is also necessary, but it could produce nothing if labor and nature were lacking. The produce of the business could either be consumed or utilized to support further production in the future. When Robinson Crusoe pursued his lonely activities on the island, he did so in the first place in order to survive, and then to obtain greater comfort. The contribution of labor and the benefits of consumption were united in the case of Robinson Crusoe in a single individual. When Friday appeared on the scene, a process of the division of labor could begin. Friday at first imagined that Robinson Crusoe might be mad, since he seemed entirely fixated with work as a means to something else. Friday regarded activity rather as a pleasure or sport; but in order to increase production on the island through the division of labor, it was necessary to make a strict distinction between work and pleasure. If the distinction was not maintained, the division of labor would be undermined with all the resulting consequences. More generally, when the borders between pleasure and pain, debit and credit, needs and work, were dissolved, it was no longer possible for persons to keep account of their own activities. Being economically blind, they could no longer work on their own account, becoming instruments in the hands of those more gifted individuals who—like Robinson Crusoe—did not suffer from this handicap. It was thus that wage labor emerged. Charles Gide clearly disliked the idea of wage labor, since it was the means that transformed human beings into the instruments of others. Had not Immanuel Kant taught that we should regard each other as ends rather than means? But the only way out of wage slavery was to understand how labor—as distinct from play—together with nature created the enterprise.

Charles Gide thought that both liberalism and socialism had missed the significance of the dynamics of an economy. Economists from Smith to Jevons had taught that savings and capital were the basic preconditions of business enterprise. Jevons had even maintained that everything began with a well-filled larder out of which the worker borrowed food on interest in order to devote his energies toward the production of the first manufactured object. But was it really necessary for the farmer to have a year's supply of food in stock before he began the cultivation of the land? Was it necessary that ten years' supplies existed before daring to take the first spadeful in digging the Panama Canal? No, all businesses financed themselves in some degree "from day to day."[18] Business was not completely dependent upon advances of capital, and the source of such capital was not merely a passive saving, but rather an active contribution of labor in combination with nature.

The socialists made the same sort of abstract error when they attacked capital, which they believed controlled the pump of wealth. They imagined that workers, following a revolution that confiscated land, mines, factories, machines, houses, and other forms of fixed property, would control the store of capital. The workers believed that the collectivization of fixed property would give them power over the process of production. They failed to note that the movable capital would run out of the land between the fingers of the revolutionary party within a few hours of it taking power. With this, the economic system would lose its lifeblood:

> The real capital that serves to produce all the wealth and instruments of production is called circulating capital in political economy because, like blood, it flows through the invisible canals of the organism of production, causing the boilers to steam, the machines to run, being the breath and life of manufacturing, and without which the great body would be as a dead corpse.[19]

The socialists should give up their dreams of confiscating the capital of the bourgeoisie, declared Gide, in response to statements about the inability of workers to ever save sufficient to purchase all industrial equipment. A business could create itself through a process of self-financing. Let the rich keep their capital, he held, and concentrate instead upon the creation of capital in the future. This was something hindered by both liberals and socialists, who through the encouragement of wage labor stopped workers from becoming businessmen.

So long as workers were instruments in the slavery of wage labor, they would never see their potential as business entrepreneurs. The point of the abolition of wage labor, emphasized Gide, was not that rewards would increase considerably if payments to shareholders and directors went instead to workers. The liberals and socialists had pursued an uninteresting pseudodebate on the question of distribution in terms of how a historically collected assembly of productive resources should be distributed among those who had already done the job. The concentration of the debate concerning distribution upon past results avoided the central question of a concrete business economics—what should happen in the future? Liberals and socialists squabbled over the rules of distribution. Should distribution follow a principle of equality? Would not lazy people take advantage of this? Would it not be better with a principle where all received according to needs? Could this lead to a hysteria in relation to consumption? Should not wages be distributed according to functions where—as the followers of Saint-Simon advocated—people were elected to different posts? On the other hand, should not workers be paid, as Marx wanted, in proportion to the labor expended on the job? In this case, how would the problem of measurement be solved? For Charles Gide, all this was meaningless, as the correct reward for work lay in its results. This was a point of view that he illustrated with the following anecdote:

> I was reminded of the story of the ship's boy who for the first time would climb the main mast: he followed just that advice that I have related: he looked down and set his foot on each peg after having looked ... so increased his sense of giddiness, and the risk of falling became all greater. He was about to lose his grip when the captain took his megaphone and shouted: Look upwards, and you won't fall![20]

The goal of enterprise lay in its results. When the liberals in France propagandized for the limited shareholding company, which could be freely established after 1867, they hindered, according to Gide, the development of a popular consciousness in respect of concrete business economy. This was because the limited share company separated ownership from work, while wage slavery continued and the workers became less orientated toward results. Moreover, it opened further the gap between lucrative speculation and productive work. This provided wind in the sails of the socialists and allowed the trade unions a certain justification for their simplistic and vulgar theory of two classes. When people began to believe that the limited share company, which was perhaps well suited to the needs of building the canals and railways, was the only possible form for a business, it was high time for Gide's alternative model of cooperative business to be pushed forward.

4. Strategy for a Self-Managed Society

4.1 Utopic Models

Charles Gide was fortunate in having known in his youth a remarkable man. Gide was included among the circle of friends who gathered around Auguste Fabre. They would meet, as was the custom then in southern France, at the home of one of the group on Saturday evenings where, by the light of a fire, they would read, discuss, sew, and relate stories to each other. Fabre had much to relate concerning both his own life and the ideas of others. He had several years earlier resigned from his post as head of a silk-weaving firm and taken to wandering alone along the highways of the country. At the town of Guise he had found a job as bookkeeper and "économe" in Jean-Baptiste-André Godin's "familistère." Fabre had now returned to his hometown of Nîmes, having definitely broken with his earlier middle-class background, and becoming a mechanic and founder of one of the town's production cooperatives. But what exactly was a "familistère" or a cooperative, and who was Charles Fourier, who was so often referred to by Fabre as the source of his inspiration? Charles Gide was no doubt already puzzling over such questions when he heard of these new forms of business enterprise that sprang up as islands in the otherwise gray economic oceans. Nîmes was itself something of an intellectual island where Protestants with social interests sought to find practical ways of expressing their faith. It was here, for example, that de Boive, who was rich and half English, together with the bricklayer, Besson, had founded l'Abeille (The Bee) as a cooperative business in 1883. The pair had established a school for teaching concrete economics. It was in this "société d'économie populaire" that Charles Gide gave a lecture in 1885 on what he had learned of Fourier during the Saturday evening gatherings. Gide was perhaps interested in attempting to counteract the influence of Marxism and anarchism, which had made their mark on the working-class movement, "not through workers, but youths who were often students or journalists."[21]

In response to the anarchism of the Russian, Mikhail Bakunin, and the collectivism of the German, Karl Marx, it was time for a purely French version of utopia in the ideas of Charles Fourier. The situation was made even more piquant since the socialist collectivists had propagandized during the workers' congress of 1879 for the rejection of all efforts to establish cooperatives as small bourgeois and sneaking capitalism. The battle was to be fought on the political rather than the economic front, and concrete economics led nowhere. Gide would show in his lecture on a French "socialist debonnaire" and peaceful anarchist that individual ownership was something in keeping with French grass-roots traditions.

In the beginning of the nineteenth century, most French businesses had been founded on the basis of "autofinancement familiale." Friends and relations got together to provide the initial capital. Of the 2,000 or so companies that were founded yearly during the 1840s, only about 5.7 percent were in the form of share companies. It was mutual help of this kind, for example, that provided Louis Renault with the possibility of establishing his company. In other cases, it was a trading company or a local capital market that financed industry. The banks and exchanges had no importance in this respect before the law of 1867 permitted the free establishment of limited share companies. Even trade and guild organizations contributed toward the starting of new industries. It was, strangely enough, diamond dealers who provided André Citroën with the necessary starting capital. Within the textile industry, it was often written into the articles of the company that profits should be reinvested or saved in funds in order to ensure the independence and self-financing character of the company. French industrial traditions, thus, were strongly on the side of autonomous business development.

Independence was also the ideal for the communes that Charles Fourier (1772–1830) had described in his rather bizarre books. They were printed in a variety of types and styles in order to stimulate the reader with their variety and diversity. Fourier had experienced the French Revolution. Employed in the clothing trade before a small inheritance freed him from commercial life, he turned his back on politics and constructed his own world in his writings. He had a hatred of "civilization," particularly the existing structure of economic and moral order that ensured that an apple in a restaurant cost ten times what it did in the nearby marketplace. This observation concerning the prices of apples was considered by Fourier to be of equal importance with Newton's discovery. The consumer was exploited by the tradesman who was personified by Fourier in the figure of the Jew. Commerce stifled human needs, even as the moralists inhibited human passions. People should be freed from a civilization where the workers were forced into slavery and the rich were subjected to frustrations. All coercion displayed a lack of intelligence, declared Fourier, and he promoted the consumer—a gourmet—to the leading position in his phalanstery: "If enslaved people are driven by the whip, free people follow their own palate."[22]

A phalanstery was a community of 1,620 persons, since, according to Fourier, there were 810 types of people, and two of each type should naturally be included in each community. The phalanstery was housed in a gigantic palace where members lived, worked, and slept. The house had great rooms with large glass windows and also contained beautiful apartments. The women should be as free as the men; besides their wedded husbands they had the right to choose a favorite, a suitable number of "posseseurs," and another man to father their children. Married and unmarried persons mixed together, but the number of children should not be so large as to be disturbing.

Each person was to be a member of several working teams that were responsible for the economy of the phalanstery and that provided opportunities for happy working conditions. When work was no longer a question of force, considered Fourier, people's passions would be released, and they would happily flit among different tasks like butterflies during the greater part of the day. The dirty work would become sheer pleasure for the children, who could, thus, satisfy their passion for making themselves filthy. People would have so many different working tasks that their interests would never become fixed in a few professions. When it was time to determine the distribution of the productive surplus, this would not cause problems or conflicts of interest in the phalanstery. According to Fourier, four-twelfths of the profits should go to capital that consisted of three classes of shares: "bancaire" (owned by some outside financier), "foncier" (shares in land and soil), and "ouvrier" (shares owned by those who worked). Each kind of shares had its determined part of the profits accruing to it. A further five-twelfths of the profits went to labor and was distributed according to a complicated system that first divided it among the different work teams and thereafter to the different tasks within each of the work teams. Finally, three-twelfths of the profits went to "talent" in the leadership of the phalanstery.

Fourier's ideal society was described in detail in several books, and all that was now lacking was a rich patron to finance the project. Fourier let it be known that he was at home every day after twelve o'clock when he would be willing to consider suggestions. One bright day soon after, a rich patron walked into Fourier's simple, flower-filled room; it was not long before an estate of some 500 hectares had been purchased for a sum of 1.2 million francs. This was divided into 2,400 shares, most of which were retained by the rich patron himself. Fourier and his patron, however, were soon at loggerheads concerning the details of the plan, and the projected building of the phalanstery was never realized. It was yet the case, related Gide, that faithful Fourierists met in the small house that remained on the estate where they walked in the woods and fished in the nearby river.

In Gide's thinking, Fourier was a remarkable visionary who had foreseen in his strange books the miracles of modern technology in transport and machinery. He had understood that agriculture with its growing of crops and rearing of animals was only a primitive form of an earlier phase of civilization. The future belonged to a world of green fields and pleasant fruit gardens where the arts of the kitchen took a prominent place. The delights of the palate, indeed, provided one of the important areas for product development. Sugar and jams that, according to Gide, were now known to be so beneficial were Fourier's favorite food-stuffs. While there was much that was sound in Fourier's basic ideas concerning producer and consumer cooperatives, maintained Gide, it was unfortunate that they also included much that could not be accepted by reasonable, Christian people. The thirty or so communes that had started in the United States, inspired by Fourier's ideas, had all failed. The causes of these failures, held Gide, lay in the lack of morality and the belief that people were naturally good in nature. But without religion and a sense of duty it was not possible for genuine cooperation to lead to success in business. The idea that work in itself was attractive was entirely confused. If all activity was pleasurable, why was it necessary to pursue rationalization and how was it possible to accommodate technical developments? Work must be regarded as Christian sacrifice or at least a duty toward other people. Without this, the preconditions for any economic calculation did not exist.

It was equally silly to break up the working day into different occupations or series as in the work teams of Fourier's phalanstery. People were not butterflies flitting from job to job, but rather busy working bees going about their special duties. It was the ideas of Frederick Winslow Taylor rather than those of Fourier that appealed to Charles Gide at this point. Even if housing became increasingly expensive and it was difficult to obtain servants, this was not reason for abandoning the institution of the family as Fourier had done in his utopia. People did not want to eat in refectories and sleep in dormitories, but rather they wanted their own small nest in which to bring up their young. It was necessary to warn against the more suspect aspects of the morals of the old rebel, Fourier, who rejected Christianity and loved cats and flowers. Gide discretely remarked that he suffered from "the manias of bachelors, or more correctly, those of all spinsters".[23]

In the last resort, Fourier regarded people as being promiscuous and without morals and as developing through stages to bloom like flowers with all their beauty and ultimate sterility.

4.2 Real Signs of Change

Charles Gide held that the utopists such as Fourier regarded facts as being springboards to the stars: "The facts were not the rock on which the system was based, but rather a trampoline from which the clown throws himself up to the stars."[24]

Gide's lecture on Pytor Alekseyevich Kropotkin and Jean-Jacques-Elisée Reclus attracted many young and enthusiastic anarchists, whom Gide managed to interest in constructive action through lending them books and pamphlets, to the cooperative federation that he and his friends had founded at Nîmes in 1886. He encouraged them to give up their revolutionary chatter and prepare for the long task of infiltrating the old economic order. This demanded certain ideals and goals, and Gide here sought to accomplish more what had been achieved by the earlier cooperative waves of 1848, 1863, and 1877. The task was to transform the firm in the economy to a consumer-guided and worker-owned cooperative. It was necessary, however, to start at the beginning where people learned together how to run a business and freed themselves from the psychological bonds of wage slavery. When the Marxist-inspired socialists argued that the battle should be fought by the trade unions, Gide responded that the trade unions, unlike the cooperatives, were not businesses. The way to a more just society was through the spread of concrete economic knowledge. It was primarily through economic deeds rather than political ballots that greater democracy was to be achieved. Economics was to be learned through starting a cooperative business.

How was all this to be achieved? When Charles Gide was asked to contribute a review of social economy ("économie sociale") during 1900, the year of the Paris Exhibition, he delivered a veritable catalogue of grass-roots reforms. These reforms were intended eventually to make possible the introduction of the new economic system founded on the independent business owned by its workers. While the workers had come some way through their associations, there were problems that must be solved before the era of economic freedom could arrive. The first of these concerned wages.

Wages had undoubtedly risen, held Gide, during the latter part of the nineteenth century. While this may have been partially due to the gold finds in California and Australia, it was also the result of an increasingly mechanized industry. It was, moreover, clear to all but those who were completely blinded by demand and supply models, that the workers' own organizations had influenced the improvement in real wages.[25] In 1890 there existed in France about a 1,000 trade unions with around 140,000 members; by 1900, this had increased to 3,000 with a membership of nearly half a million.[26] These unions had neither the means nor the inclination to display their experience in large exhibitions. Two-thirds of all strikes had been organized by the trade unions, and it was clear from available statistics that the results in terms of wage rises far exceeded the cost of lost jobs. Of some 4,194 strikes between 1890 and 1899, only 44 percent involved a complete stoppage of work. Strikes were, therefore, not entirely of a destructive character. When liberal economists maintained that the market forces of demand and supply alone should be allowed to regulate wages in a mechanical manner without external interventions, Gide remarked that even a good barometer could occasionally show a wrong reading and was set right by a light blow. To strike, however, was but one—extreme—method of knocking the wage barometer. Through organizing themselves into federations, workers could demand collective agreements, fixed wage levels, and limits upon the number of apprentices accepted in certain branches. It was also possible to organize boycotts against employers who failed to cooperate. With a large strike fund behind their backs, the workers were more like the free party to an agreement that the liberal utopians considered should be reached without threat, pressure, or exploitation. At the same time, emphasized Gide, it should not be forgotten that the trade unions were interest organizations that always had one eye upon defending a trade or profession. It could not be expected that they would change the existing economic order. The following is the reason:

> [T]he trade unions are created, according to the legal definition only "for the protection of trade interests." It cannot, thus, create an industrial or commercial enterprise, and if this happened . . . it would lose its character, which the leaders of trade unions are very conscious about, and why they protest against such a transformation.[27]

The sources of economic change had to be located somewhere other than in the trade unions.

Gide was also careful to point out the differences between the militant and Catholic trade unions, the latter often being prepared to cooperate with employers on questions such as wages. Employers themselves were often willing to introduce improvements in conditions and wages on their own initiative. Robert Owen at New Lanark or Jean Dollfus at Mulhouse[28] provided examples of employers who had shown that better wages and shorter working hours could lower the costs of production. A further example was given by the decorating firm, Redouly, which had been started by a certain Leclaire in 1843. The suggestion that the workers should share in the profits of the enterprise had been opposed by the prefect of the Paris police as a departure from the practice of free wage setting: "The workers should be entirely free to fix their wages and should not enter a pact with their chief."[29]

The social economic statistics that were gathered in connection with the Paris Exhibition could, nevertheless, record that some 126 companies in France practiced some form of profit distribution by 1893. This could amount to a wage increase in these cases of between 5 percent and 9 percent. Where experiments of this nature had not been laid aside, it was because they had contributed to better productivity through reducing labor turnover or improving the spirit of the company. One manager would witness: "Never in sixty years of experience had the workers the slightest thought of striking." Profit sharing, thus, could not be considered an entirely utopian form for pursuing industrial activities.

The social economy pavilion at the Paris Exhibition provided a wealth of methods for increasing the concrete value of employment. The glassworks, Baccarat, provided nursery schools, free housing, schools, a pension fund, hospital, child care, and a philharmonic orchestra. Firms such as National Cash Register, Cadbury's, and Lever Brothers, together with many others, offered showers, restaurants, gymnasiums, and workers' clubs. The working day had been reduced to ten hours in France, although in Britain it was often down to nine hours with five on Saturdays. Salaried employees were sometimes given paid holidays; a yeast factory at Delft provided three days' holiday per year for workers. Photographs of American factories showed well-kept gardens and streams. Other employers offered twenty minutes in winter and forty during the summer months for a weekly bath. A certain van Marken talked proudly of how he had introduced a premium system to reward industriousness, capacity, and cooperativeness, which could raise wages by up to 20 percent. At the same time, it was admitted that these premiums had been attacked by the socialists, who objected to being regarded as children in the school classroom. Other changes to be observed concerned the disappearance of the trucking system whereby employers paid their workers in kind or in tokens that could be exchanged for goods in local shops. As late as 1886, the miners at Decazeville had gone on strike in anger over the company's expanding "economat" system whereby workers could obtain bread, meat, and wine on credit against their wages. It often resulted in wage envelopes containing a debit on paydays. When the company planned to expand the system to include clothing, tempers exploded and the strike began with the murder of the senior company engineer. This had led to the building, for the first time, of a socialist deputy group at the Palais Bourbon. A further change to be observed was the disappearance of the internal systems of factory punishments whereby workers could be fired or suffer wage reductions.

The second question raised was that of security. All people were threatened by sickness, old age, and death; workers had also to contend with unemployment and accidents. In the same manner as workers had united to obtain a decent wage, they should also demand insurance against poverty and accidents. Some 16 percent of the population in Germany were already members of some form of insurance fund. The problem that often arose with voluntary insurance schemes concerned the aging of its membership, which resulted in large demands upon its funds. Gide considered that these insurance schemes would necessarily have to depend upon voluntary contributions from rich people until such times as they could be organized on a national level. The German insurance scheme had solved the problem through investing and capitalizing the enormous sums that flowed in annually from obligatory payments. These funds were used not only to purchase state bonds but also to build houses, sanatoriums, and other institutions that increased security. A few individual managers had attempted to show the way in France. Leclaire, for example, had retained a part of the profits so that he could offer such "incredible benefits" as 3.5 francs per day in sickness pay and a pension of 1,500 francs with retirement at the age of fifty.[30] Charles Gide was very much impressed by such solutions since he had reckoned that a pension worth half of a wage would require an annual cost of 15 percent of a worker's wage packet. This was certainly too expensive to be contemplated by the individual worker.

But how then would it be possible to create the economic security that could make the worker into a free economic agent? In the absence of rich benefactors, Gide suggested that consumer cooperatives should be linked to pension schemes so that the dividend provided the means for financing pensions. This, however, would have the disadvantage of reducing the funds necessary for the financing of the cooperatives A further possibility was to allow the insurance associations to pursue business activities in the form, for example, of chemist shops. Only one country, New Zealand, had gone so far as to finance old-age pensions through taxation. Unemployment insurance, considered Gide, was something that could not be contemplated. Of each 100 French workers in 1898, 15 percent were either unemployed or supported themselves by casual labour. It was not to be wondered at that some 1,500 private individuals made a good living by demanding between 5 percent and 33 percent of a wage in return for obtaining a job for a worker. It was for this reason that the trade unions had opened so-called labor exchanges that obtained jobs for unemployed members on the condition that they refuse to accept a wage below the minimum. Beyond this, there was little hope for those who were unfortunate, beyond the soup kitchen and a bit of bread from some church institution. For the aged without means, life was an ongoing misery during Gide's time. Care of the aged did not exist in France.

While the rich saved money in order to speculate, it was the poor people who saved in order to obtain some security. Unfortunately, it was the small shopkeepers and traders who had the possibility of making the most use of the savings funds. These funds, moreover, often tended to invest their money in state bonds on the mistaken understanding, according to Gide, that they offered security. It would be better if these savings funds invested their money in projects of a social nature such as housing, hospitals, libraries, or other useful institutions that could contribute toward increasing the comfort, security, and strength of the workers.

With the safety net provided by the insurance associations and the wage improvements of the trade unions, it was now possible to encourage worker participation in the material well-being of the community. For Charles Gide, thus, the goal became that of participation in the "civilization" that was so hated by Fourier. Beyond wages and security, there lay the whole question of physical and moral education. One did not, however, become an independent entrepreneur through an education in political economy: "For the business leader, the primary condition was not that of understanding political economics, but that of procuring a certain capital."[31] The capital of the workers lay in their knowledge of the trade. The introduction of mechanization, together with competition among craftsmen, had destroyed the system of apprenticeship, which it was necessary to reconstruct with the help of both state and trade unions. It was also necessary to convince parents that they should invest in the education of their children. An economic consciousness should be awakened in the parents even before the child was born. Abroad it was already the case, related Charles Gide, that a humanistic attitude provided expectant mothers with six weeks' leave before giving birth, together with regular care for their newborn children. Moreover, cribs and children's nurses replaced the old women who dosed the children with alcohol and hung them up on hooks while their mothers worked in the factories. Local governments abroad, where the mayors had greater powers, had invested in hygiene. Water and sewerage systems, cemeteries, bathhouses, gas, electricity, and trams all contributed toward the "great hunt for the microbes."After providing examples of investment in human beings, Gide continues: "It is true that this enormous capital provides no great return, but it gives health, and makes savings in human capital that are considerably more valuable."[32]

According to Gide's concrete teachings, investments are only interesting in the degree that they result in new products. The education in concrete economies should, therefore, warn against a tendency to waste resources. The great 1900 Paris Exhibition had actually included a number of groups formed with this purpose in mind. There was represented, for example, a group that had originally been formed in 1830 by students from the Ecole Polytéchnique with the intention of providing a "Sorbonne for the workers."[33] There were also the "idea cooperatives" such as that in which Gide himself had participated in Nîmes, which later provided the basis for a popular university. Catholics as well as Protestants had their own educational organizations; a certain Cave had begun a savings fund for schoolchildren where some 450,000 paid a sous each week into a personal savings account that went toward a collective sickness and pensions fund. By such means, people were to be encouraged to invest in themselves.

It was, however, not only the mind, but also the bodies that needed to be strengthened. The microbe hunters, Calmett and Pasteur, were the popular heroes of the period and even inspired boulevard theater successes. The Paris Exhibition had displayed such novelties as washbasins, showers, toilets, and bidets, which depended upon public water supply. Hygiene was something that should extend to the population as a whole rather than being limited to small children and brothels. Such discrimination in hygienic questions should be forbidden, and men should take the blame for the spread of diseases from the open brothels.[34] Those who hung up notices against spitting in public or created leagues against urinating in public were using economic microbiology to inspire puritanical morality. Vegetarians were certainly friends of animals, held Gide, but they should in the first place be regarded as food economists. They wanted to guide production in the direction of foodstuffs with a greater return on invested resources. When the consumption of alcohol fell, this also led to an improvement in physical condition. Large companies, such as Suchard, Cadbury's, Baccarat, and Creusot, which provided sound and more spacious housing, were making an investment in the quality of their labor force. Since this lay also in the interests of workers, they created in the large towns cooperative building projects that provided good and cheap housing.

But the largest cost in the worker's budget was food, which took some 64 percent of income. The Paris Exhibition had included a communal bakery from Lisbon, a slaughterhouse from Pamplona, a soup kitchen from Berlin, and a school kitchen from Paris. In 1910, Gide himself became a member of a league that used united consumer power against high prices. He related how consumers signed protest lists against price monopolies and obtained rebates from shopkeepers in return for promises to purchase from their stores.[35] He also enthusiastically told about a beer strike against a German brewery. The firm, PiedSelle, had lent capital to workers to found a purchasing cooperative. Such company controlled cooperatives, however, often withheld the dividends so that they could be used in pension funds. The independent cooperatives were, nevertheless, increasing in numbers, and Gide pointed here to the British and German examples. The town of Kettering was almost completely controlled by cooperatives, while Leeds could boast 50,000 organized consumers. Gide estimated that there were some 10,000 cooperative ventures in the world of which there were about 1,500 each in Germany, France, and Britain. In the case of France, this meant that the number had doubled since 1889. Besides the "union cooperatives" that had started at Nîmes, the socialists—who objected to the production investment strategy adopted by Nîmes—grouped their own activities in so-called exchange co-operatives. Where Gide's idea was to incorporate the workers in society through placing the profits of trade into their hands, the notion of the socialists was to obtain funds to pursue political conflict. It was to be used to support socialist candidates and striking workers and for propaganda rather than to create independent economic enterprises. The Belgian socialists went so far as to talk of bombarding "the citadels of capitalism with shells of potatoes and loaves of bread."[36]

From Charles Gide's side, however, consumer cooperation was not a manner of pursuing a conflict concerning distribution between workers and owners in an existing economic order. It was rather the first step toward a uniting of workers and owners in a new business experiment that would slowly, without revolution, infiltrate and replace the existing economic order. Its ideal was a republic of small cooperative enterprises, which could offer an economic equality that was not possible under the ideas of political economy. The goal was independence, and the struggle was in the first place of a concrete economic nature, while politics were relegated to a secondary position.

4.3 Cooperative Reforms

A union of the power of labor, savings, and consumers in the pursuit of security was the grounds for the final combination of ownership and workers in enterprise. Wage labor would cease, and the worker would become a "producteur autonome" who worked for his own account without being employed. The socialists opposed the notion of small-scale enterprise on the grounds that it was inappropriate to the times. They looked on the large companies and trusts with pleasure as providing the best hope for the predicted future collapse of capitalism; socialists did not want to do anything that could undermine such a development. Statistics, on the other hand, showed that small businesses were increasing in number. For many people, work in the home appeared to be a more attractive alternative than wage slavery in the large factories. It was to be regretted that the trader had nestled himself in this area and transformed it into a "sweating system." These traders must be opposed in order to provide small industry with the chance of a human existence. The clockmakers in Berlin, for example, had taken over the marketing operation from the traders and established their own "Magazin Genossenschaft,"[37] a cooperative organization for the sale of clocks. The silk weavers of Lyon had combined to obtain capital for the purchase of modern electric power looms and had been helped by the local government and chamber of commerce. Through different cooperative credit schemes, the risks of starting small businesses could be reduced. The most important point, however, according to Gide, was to create new firms of a free and cooperative character.

One way of achieving independence was for the owner of the firm to "abdicate" and voluntarily transfer both the shares and leadership of the firm to the workers. This had been the idea of Jean-Baptiste-André Godin, who, following an inspiration from Fourier, had systematically planned to transfer his company at Guise to his workers. The company had been founded in 1859. Godin had introduced an unusual form of profit sharing in 1876 that was much admired by Gide, since it provided labor rather than capital with the larger share of the profits. Godin, in fact, did not bother with the relationship between total capital and labor. If the year's profits, for example, were 300,000, while the capital employed was 2 million, and labor 1 million, a proportional distribution would have given 200,000 to capital and 100,000 to labor. Instead, Godin considered that the sum of the annual wage costs (1 million) should be compared with the contribution of the power of capital (that is, the interest on capital, for example, 5 percent or 100,000 francs) during the same period. According to Godin's formula, labor would receive 272,620 francs, and capital only 27,380 francs. The next step in the abdication of Godin occurred in 1880 when he transferred ownership to the workers. Godin was well aware that many workers would prefer not to own their company. Not the least, there were the socialists who did not want to invest in business; but there were also others who felt safer in placing their savings in ordinary shares or state bonds that gave a return without any effort.

In this situation, Godin—quite correctly according to Charles Gide—resorted to compulsion. Each year he simply transferred the workers' share of the profits to capital. This part of the profits was used to purchase the capital from Godin at a nominal value as if it was a normal loan that was being repaid. When Godin died in 1888, there remained the sum of 3,100,000 francs to be paid. Lacking heirs, Godin left this to his workers in his will. When someone died or finished working in the company, ownership of the shares was transferred to a new worker who, after a trial period, had been accepted by the other cooperative owners. This kind of ownership naturally enough was not to be confused with those cases where a worker purchased shares on the stock exchange. He then became a shareholder with a certain right to vote, but he remained at the same time a wage slave without any right to profits in this capacity. Gide visualized the firm as a kind of small republic where everyone had the right to vote, and where labor and nature rather than capital received the larger part of the profits.

Workers must, nevertheless, understand that capital was necessary. This capital should preferably be regarded as a loan where the capitalist was not given an unlimited right to future profits, even where security for such a loan was lacking. The goodwill and competence of the workers should itself provide a sufficient security, Gide seems to have considered. The cooperative, "Ferblantiers réunis,"[38] had adopted special rules that reduced the capitalist to an ordinary lender. The owners of shares were permitted to participate in the company meeting but were not allowed to hold positions on the board unless they were at the same time workers in the company. The return on shares not owned by workers, considered Gide, should be set at some maximum figure. As soon as a company went with a profit, those shares not owned by workers should be compulsorily repurchased. This was about the same manner that Gide considered that the state should act in relation to its obligations in order to reduce the burden placed on future generations. The production cooperative, le Travail, related Gide, had managed to repurchase 6,380 of its 10,000 shares. If capitalists were treated in this manner, he continued, it would no doubt prove difficult to obtain funds from them for founding independent businesses. But fortunately there still existed philanthropists of the kind that once knocked on Fourier's door. A certain banker, for example, had lent a production cooperative half a million francs under such conditions. He was an honorable man with "ideas from another world"[39] and had shortly after committed suicide.

A further method to found a cooperative was to follow the example of two gentlemen who decided to start a bakery. They gave lectures on their project in the local bars during the "green absinthe hour" when they were most crowded, gathering together people who were willing to participate in the scheme. The state had also on several occasions provided capital for cooperative projects, although most of these funds had unfortunately disappeared. The production cooperatives, for example, had received 3 million francs from the state during 1848; during World War I, the cooperative movement received a further 2 million. The state and local governments offered preference to cooperatives in purchasing if they could at least match the conditions offered by private industry. The more that the work of social reform increased, held Gide, the more probable it became that managers would be prepared to abdicate voluntarily:

> It is not impossible that the number of these abdications, more or less forced or unwilling, will come to increase when the costs of employers increased and the profits decreased, and when they feel more threatened by the trade unions and controlled by the state.[40]

Legal changes were also necessary to encourage the founding of independent cooperative enterprises. It cost between 400 and 700 francs for a lawyer to register a cooperative. This was all too high a sum for those heroic individuals who would use their savings to free themselves and others from the rule of the capitalists. It was also desirable that shares should have a nominal value that could be less than the stipulated 50 francs. The law in France that placed a maximum of 200,000 francs on capital for cooperatives reduced their possibility of competing with large-scale industry. It was pleasing, on the other hand, that despite the wild protests from business circles, the consumer cooperatives were freed from tax on their profits. In a strict economic sense, they made no profits, but only provided repayments to their members, although this assumed that they did not make sales to nonmembers.

Consumer cooperatives were, for Gide, a question of obtaining the necessary capital to pursue economic freedom. Through taking over the lucrative retail trade and using the dividends for further investments in wholesaling, it was possible to purchase directly from the producers without the intervention of middle men. The next step was to finance factories. The consumer cooperative, for example, had helped the glass workers of Albi with a loan of 100,000 francs and then purchased their bottles at a price 20 percent above that of the market. If only the consumers united and collectively decided to invest their dividends, the transformation from political economy to social economy would be achieved. Purchasing power would be united with that of labour, and the productive surplus—allowing a suitable sum for depreciation—would come to benefit the workers. It would also put an end to the speculation in shares that was related directly to the ideas of political economy.

5. Emergence of the Modern State and Death of Gide's Dream

Those who read Charles Gide's series of lectures that he made in his capacity as professor of cooperative studies to the Collège de France in 1921 can only be surprised. Gide now considered that the department and chain stores had began to push out the hated small shopkeepers and traders. Trade was being rationalized, and competition took a form where retail prices were being lowered without the traders being forced into bankruptcy. It was just the lack of competition that had earlier given Gide the inspiration to finance worker-owned enterprises through the consumer cooperatives, and with the emergence of the dominance of the department and chain stores, it could be expected that he would attempt to suggest an alternative source of finance. Instead, Gide proposed that the consumer cooperatives should follow the methods of the department and chain stores. The consumer cooperatives, with certain reservations concerning the dangers of bureaucratization, should be encouraged to centralize decision making. It was the central federation rather than the local membership that should now decide where the store was to be situated. It was, moreover, necessary to exchange the enthusiastic amateurs who ran the stores for professionally trained personnel who could run the integrated business as efficiently as the department and chain stores. The spirit of cooperation, briefly stated, was to be replaced by managers with an interest only in profits.

But, Professor Gide, was it not just such the managers who were the devil that you, like all antimercantilists since Adam Smith, would get rid of through social economy and cooperative reforms of the enterprise? The basic idea of social economy was to allow the labor power of production to be freely balanced against the purchasing power of consumers in the market. In order to achieve this, Adam Smith was prepared to abolish the power of the traders. You, Professor Gide, had observed how these traders had established themselves between the factories and the families. These businessmen lived simply off transfers, manufacturing nothing. They destroyed concrete resources, not the least through tempting producers to engage in the speculative manufacturing of goods that could not be sold. So arose the crises with their enormous waste of labor. The traders were recruited from the general pool of labor, so that the greater their number, the fewer were the numbers of productive workers. The traders seduced consumers to purchase things they did not need and so waste their purchasing power.

It was your dislike of abstract economy, Professor Gide, that made you human; your belief in the revival of a concrete economic point of view was the point of your existence. You, who were so shy that you dared not haggle with a shopkeeper, went forth to lecture on cooperative congresses. You saw a final possibility of fighting speculation through making a pact between labor and purchasing power that went behind the back of the evil trader. Your predecessor had sought to encourage labor to take independent action; you yourself thought that the producer could contribute more than profits through increased production. But at the same time, you knew that many of these manufacturers were financed by traders and that they were, therefore, allied to the abstract economy. It remained, as a last effort, to encourage consumers to combine their purchasing power to create a new productive economy. Yes, Professor Gide, you who were so obviously indecisive did not hesitate for a moment to found a cooperative yourself, "La Prevoyance," in Montpellier.[41] You experienced yourself how the traders worked against your business, how they nestled themselves in through the purchase of members' shares in order to spy on your cooperative. You witnessed how the members fell victims to that hateful business mentality, how they resold the cooperative's cheaper goods at a profit in the town, how the richer members always demanded their money immediately if they heard things were going badly. You experienced failure, and this was certainly a hard blow, even if, as you said, bankruptcy was usual in all kinds of business.

But was it this misfortune that caused you to lose your faith in concrete economics? No. You stubbornly refused to stop believing in the possibility of human salvation and in the possibility that people could actually prefer concrete production more than transfer payments and lottery speculation. You saw how the women disliked the careful reporting of prices at home; how they missed the charms and elegance of the large stores; how they left the cooperatives in the hands of the men who seemed to be happy sitting on their unsold barrels of herrings, endlessly talking philosophy. You had lived in the center of Paris during "la belle époque" and knew its luxury and vanity as it was depicted by Zola in his naturalistic novel *The Ladies' Paradise*. You had looked through the utopian phalanstery door where the sterile and promiscuous beauties tumbled with happy gentlemen among the splendid flower beds and well-kept fruit trees. Work therein became so attractive that people worked for its own sake, and the question of whether anything exchangeable—or any product at all—was produced was simply forgotten. Both reality and the utopian vanity would be, through economic salvation, shown the pathway to love and social life. You knew very well that Fourier, like Satan, tempted our lust for abstract actions. He had suggested among other things that the phalanstery should be opened to paying visitors if other sources of money were not available. This form of prostitution, like others, was unproductive. Concrete economy dealt with things that became valuable products. But in the final resort, Professor Gide, you believed in the possibility of transforming individuals into honest, productive creatures who would remove love from the commercial sector where it threatened to ruin the economically rational calculations. It was not doubts about humanity that led you in 1921 to give up all plans for the concrete project for which you had earlier fought. It was not doubts about humanity that made you into the apostle of the modern large-scale commercial cooperative.

You hated trade. But what happened with these profits? In times of low taxation and limited personal responsibility, these profits landed in the pockets of the businessman. He probably invested them in yet more trade, natural resources in short supply, or industry. The state also expanded during your lifetime, and in your *Principes d'économie politique*, you managed to treat the state, quite naturally, in an appendix as some kind of strange and isolated business enterprise. But now the state had become a great business that issued bonds providing a secure interest, a share-issuing company with a guaranteed return. The rise of political democracy provided wind in the sails of a state that would stop the development of a vision of independent economic enterprise. The expansion of the state into greater numbers of departments and works involved an increasing waste of manpower at the desks of the bureaucrats. The state debt waxed accordingly, and your idea, Professor Gide, that this debt should be repaid appeared itself to be more and more utopian.

Then came World War I, a long, drawn-out process that was quite different from the blitzkrieg of 1870. The state printed more and more money, more indeed than either you or Adam Smith could have thought advisable. One ends up punishing enterprising peasants who take 2,400 of the paper francs which the state refuses to back with gold, for a cow that is worth only 900 gold francs.[42] Women and children were held quiet by judicious state contributions to rent and food. The trade now sells not only to people but also to a new consumer, a giant consumer in the form of the state. Prices rise as the value of money falls, and inflation decreases people's purchasing power. The nation's manpower dies on the battlegrounds like flies. It must have been this, Professor Gide, that brought on your resignation and pessimism in the post–World War I period. While the struggle was only against the abstractions of the seductive trader, you could hope for victory in an honest battle of man against man or through a salvation of mankind by means of concrete economy. But you who had transformed so many anarchists into constructive cooperators perhaps began to wonder if they had not been right after all. What can one do against war and inflation that have been pushed forward and supported by a heated majority of the population? Your task became that of a Don Quixote against the windmills, a figure that was doomed to failure. What does one do when abstract economy becomes raised to the status of a general law? Instead of fighting the modern nation-state, you sadly choose to capitulate.

You never attempted to answer such questions, Professor Gide, although we can perhaps reconstruct your resignation with the help of André Gide, your nephew, who provided a literary sketch of your state of mind and your clinging to concreteness in existence shortly before you left this world:

—It was good in Uzès.
—What was good?
—Lemonade.
—Where?
—In Uzès.
—Who has said that?
—No one. I can remember it.
—How can you be certain of it?
—It was I that drank it.
—You have been there recently?
—No, I remember when I drank it as a child.
—They never made lemonade then.
—Yes, I remember. It was rice lemonade.
—Why rice?
—In order to take away the bitter [taste] of lemon, one boiled rice and poured the boiling water over the peeled lemon.
—One does such only for upset stomachs. You were never ill in Uzès so why did you drink it?
—Well, in any case, I know that I drank lemonade and thought it was good. My uncle continued to insist to the end that it was not so bad. It should not be imagined that this scepticism was something that had come with age. It had always been like that. Such were all conversations with my uncle. It was so difficult to be understood by him. Perhaps it depended upon him never having been ill. Perhaps it was because he could not be influenced. Always the same condition, always true to himself. He could only understand people intellectually, could only understand other people's thoughts. He certainly had a capacity to feel, but only feelings of a public nature. The unique and the special were foreign to him. It did not interest him, and I believe that he doubted whether such could be interesting. All such feelings existed somewhere other than in the imagination of the author. He lived among quantities. Even love and friendship had to be depersonalized in order to find a place in his heart; a heart that beat strongly only for the collective.[43]

Notes

1. Charles Gide, *La Coopération—conferences et propagande*, pp. 82–83.
2. Ibid., p. 87.
3. Ibid., p. 88.
4. Charles Gide, *Sa vie et son oeuvre*, p. 3.
5. Charles Gide, *Principes d'économie politique*, p. 369.
6. Ibid., p. 374.

7. Ibid., p. 517.
8. Ibid., p. 111.
9. Ibid., p. 376.
10. Ibid., p. 266.
11. Ibid., p. 192.
12. Gide, *La Coopération*, p. 264.
13. Ibid., pp. 211–212.
14. Ibid., p. 207.
15. Gide, *Principes d'économie politique*, p. 252.
16. Gide, *Sa vie et son oeuvre*, pp. 27–28.
17. Gide, *Principes d'économie politique*, p. 139.
18. Ibid., p. 142.
19. Gide, *La Coopération*, pp. 14–15.
20. Ibid., pp. 76–77.
21. Ibid., p. 11.
22. Charles Gide, *Fourier précurseur de la coopération*, p. 24.
23. Gide, *La Coopération*, p. 280.
24. Gide, *Fourier précurseur de la coopération*, p. 139.
25. Charles Gide, *Economie sociale*, p. 81.
26. Ibid., p. 82.
27. Ibid., p. 107.
28. Ibid., p. 110.
29. Ibid., p. 111.
30. Ibid., p. 250.
31. Gide, *Principes d'économie politique*, p. 514.
32. Gide, *Economie sociale*, p. 240.
33. Ibid., p. 254.
34. Ibid., p. 223.
35. Charles Gide, *Le Juste prix*, p. 222.
36. Gide, *Economie sociale*, p. 181.
37. Ibid., p. 414.
38. Gide, *Fourier précurseur de la coopéraration*, p. 172.
39. Ibid., p 175.
40. Gide, *Economie sociale*, p. 383.
41. Gide, *La Coopération*, p. 168.
42. Gide, *Le Juste prix*, p. 89.
43. André Gide, *Journal 1889–1939*, pp. 1103–1104.

10

The Amoral, Calculating Manager: Rational Decision Making in Gunnar Myrdal's Walrasian Theory

1. Money instead of Things

1.1 From Product to Capital Markets

One way of searching for the meaning of *concrete economics* is to examine the abstract. The Swedish national economist Gunnar Myrdal (1898–1987) had in his youth a view of business that can be described as abstract. This view is interesting because it came to dominate the education of the economists who populate organizations and businesses of both the public and the private sectors in present-day in Sweden. When the young Myrdal understood that the opportunities offered by a career in law were limited, he began instead to study economics under Gustav Cassel in Stockholm. Myrdal soon became one of a small group of economists whom Cassel nurtured toward an academic career. Cassel was of a frugal turn of mind and considered that a small country like Sweden could well manage with a small group of economic thinkers. Their major job at this time was the public criticism of state economic policy, but the younger economists also began to criticize their older colleagues. This criticism took place not only in writings but also in the National Economic Club, which had been founded in Stockholm by the famous and original Swedish economist Knut Wicksell. After retirement from his professorship at the University of Lund, Wicksell had moved to Stockholm. The younger group, led by Gunnar Myrdal and Bertil Ohlin, would later become known internationally under the name of the Stockholm School. In the early days, however, the battle was directed against the domination of the older generation. Cassel himself called Myrdal a "radical socialist of a dictatorial persuasion";[1] another of the older school described him as "father murderer."[2] The attack on concrete economics had begun!

The struggle was mainly directed against the laissez-faire ideal of the liberals, and the weapons used were logic and skeptical philosophy of the kind that had become popular as a result of the teachings of Axel Hägerström, who was professor of philosophy at Uppsala. The old concrete economy was step-by-step replaced by abstractions. First went the theory. Thereafter, largely owing to Ernst Wigforss, a Social Democrat and friend of the Stockholm School, practice was transformed into an economic policy that was imagined to rest on scientific principles. In this manner, the abstract business economics that had its early roots in the work of Gunnar Myrdal was spread in the form of law administrative regulation and finally normative management training.

In the early 1920s, older liberal economists had been concerned with criticizing Swedish public policy pursued during the crisis years of World War I. Economic policy had been administered by people without any knowledge of economics,[3] and this in itself left the field open for political slogans rather than arguments. The economic historian Eli Heckscher, professor at Stockholm, participated in the assessment of the wartime policy.[4] He painted a picture of deep pessimism among businessmen in the early months of the war, which soon changed to wild optimism as orders began to stream into neutral Sweden from the warring nations. Businessmen who had been gripped by panic were suddenly dizzy with the prospects that promised to fulfill their wildest dreams.[5] One immediate result was an overinvestment in large industrial plants. The cause of this overheating of the economy, held Heckscher, lay in low interest rates. It was too easy for businessmen to borrow funds from savers, and the interest payments on such funds were soon eaten up by inflation. The situation was made worse through price regulations on foodstuffs that made it possible to survive on low wage levels and increased the chances of speculative profits. The savers could, with justice, complain of the businessmen's "capitalistic bolshevism."[6] The workers were forced to unite in the battle for better wages and an eight-hour day. As a liberal, Heckscher was deeply disturbed by the manner in which these interest groups, in a time of crisis, created a near mercantilist society "with all greater deviations from the situation that existed of free competition in its older forms."[7]

Where, however, did the deeper roots of the economic crisis lie? For Heckscher it was clear that these lay in the limits placed upon free exchange where demand and supply were no longer balanced in market prices. The mechanisms of the market were distorted through regulation. The worst dislocation, maintained Heckscher, derived from the monetary policy of the state, which he described as "confused." Lacking the control exercised by gold, the central bank could set the printing presses rolling. It had unfortunately overdone this, and the result had been an inflation that had distorted the general level of prices.

Against this argument, Erik Lindahl, one of the younger generation of economists, held that the older generation had failed to notice that the time of the gold standard was past.[8] They still wanted to hold fast with the old method of first studying the exchange value between demand and supply in order to then suppose that the general price level was determined by the amount of money in the canals of the system. In the new era of paper money, however, prices were no longer independent of exchange, and the price level was not the result of a "mechanism of payment." When payments were made in paper and giro-money that were not covered by gold, an economic investigation of the general price level must also include information concerning transactions and exchanges of money. A general price level consisted not only of the prices of food, clothing, and the like, but also the prices of capital goods, shares, and credit. Heckscher's argument was founded on the notion of an equation concerning the volume of money, where the means of payment multiplied by the speed of circulation was supposed to provide the general price level (which could be measured with a price index multiplied by the quantity of each good weighted by its respective price). A transaction involving machines or shares naturally also had a price and quantity at a certain point in time, and it was possible to include such transactions in the formula for the quantity equation. But credit provided by loans, perhaps the most usual kind of transaction in the modern business, could not be captured in terms of price and quantity at a certain point in time. This was because the whole point of credit was to take payment for a difference between money today and money in the future, that is, the difference between two points in time. In a society with an increasing number of credit transactions, a formula that did not include credit in demand could never be expected to balance total supply. This implied, in the first place, that quantity theory was a dubious instrument for guiding economic policy. Second, Say's law on the equality between demand and supply was not relevant to a world of increasing credit. The rejection of Say's law had just led Knut Wicksell, Lindahl's source of inspiration, to a crisis explanation different from that of the liberals.

Knut Wicksell had in his lectures argued strongly against Say's law and consequently also against the liberal thought of a natural balance between demand and supply in free-market prices. If one wished to study the reasons for individual price changes for products, held Wicksell, it was obvious that one paid attention to changes in the demand and supply of the product. But assume now that the prices of all products rose at the same time, and assume further that Lindahl's criticism was correct in that quantity theory gave no possibility of blaming the rise entirely upon an increase in the amount of money. In this case, maintained Wicksell, the change in the price level could depend upon a change in the total demand or supply. Such a thought led to the questioning of Say's doctrine concerning the equality between demand and supply.

Wicksell's contribution led the analysis of the crisis into new channels. The remedy lay not only in monetary policy or a stabilizing of the level of prices, but action must be based upon knowledge of how the total demand could be distinguished from the total supply. Wicksell provided certain guidelines. He classified demand into on the one side, consumption, and on the other side, savings. Supply was also separated into two categories. First, the production of consumer goods for the market, and second, the production of capital goods that were used by business itself. These capital goods would only later contribute to consumer goods. The production of such capital goods demanded resources, and this implied that the business class—which Lindahl described as the decision makers of the economy—chose to invest resources on inner capital development instead of increasing or maintaining the old supply of consumer products. In this manner, the supply of consumer goods on the market could be reduced in relation to demand. Wicksell taught that if the roots of the crisis were to be found, it was necessary to investigate why businesses created capital goods. The solution was to be found in the companies—a conclusion that had already been reached by Karl Marx. Gunnar Myrdal now developed this analysis further but avoided, probably consciously, giving it any openly Marxist character.

1.2 From Exchange Value to the Valuation of Capital

The basic idea of Gunnar Myrdal's doctoral thesis, *Price Development and Changeability* (Prisbildningsproblemet och föränderligheten, 1927), is that the development of prices in national economics must be explained in business economic terms. This was followed in 1931 by a long article in the *Ekonomisk Tidskrift*, which provided a theoretical perspective that made his struggles with his doctoral thesis more comprehensible. When Myrdal published an English translation of his 1931 article under the title *Monetary Equilibrium* in 1939, he took the opportunity to recall the background to his theory of the firm. He also presented and criticized the ideas of Lindahl and Wicksell concerning how total supply and demand could diverge from each other.

   Their view was presented as follows: Assume that interest rates fall so that businesses can obtain capital more cheaply. Assume also that demand and supply in consumer goods markets remain the same as before the fall in interest rates. The value of saved business capital now increases. This value is fixed by businesses through discounting future payment flows at the new rates of interest. It becomes more profitable to save in terms of capital goods than to produce consumer goods. Businesses purchase capital goods, for example, machines and engineering labor, from other businesses. The prices of capital goods rise so that those who are in this sector obtain increased incomes, which they use to increase their consumption. The decrease in consumer goods is thus accompanied by a rise in demand, which leads to an increase in prices. With the rise in prices for consumer goods, business expectations concerning future incomes also rise. This, in turn, leads to further savings in terms of capital goods. In this manner, the economy is set in motion by what Wicksell described as a cumulative process, away from some original equilibrium between total demand and supply of consumer goods. If, on the other hand, there had been an initial increase in interest rates, instead of a fall, the effects would have been the opposite.

The question posed by Myrdal was why managers should react in this manner. What did changes in the rates of interest actually mean to individual managers? Wicksell had held that businessmen compared the rates of interest of the banks with their own "natural" interest rate. This "natural" rate of interest was a measure of the marginal productivity of the business. Wicksell viewed the manager as a kind of knowledgeable technician who knew that capital had become cheaper because he could make comparisons with physical returns. Myrdal's break with this position constituted a definitive step away from concrete economics toward an abstract business economics.

The assumption that businessmen knew the physical rate of return as an interest rate was, according to Myrdal, quite unrealistic and "does not belong to this world."[9] It presumed a Walrasian passivity in business behavior where the entrepreneur managed to combine land, labor, and capital as he simultaneously delivered consumer goods to waiting customers. Myrdal's intention with his theory of the firm had been, in fact, just that of "introducing expectations in the Walras model."[10] It was the strength of Wicksell's position, nevertheless, that businesses were not conceived as calculating in some static point of time but rather were orientated toward some future period of activity. In Walras's timeless world, utility gave value to products and, in the same instant derivation, to the means of production. When, however, Wicksell maintained that businesses calculated the "natural interest" with knowledge of the productive services of capital, he was falling into the assumptions of the classical theory. He also accepted the classical doctrine that defined costs as "not the replacement [in monetary terms] of productive factors, but the productive factors themselves."[11]

Knowledge of "natural interest rates" could possibly exist in a world where a businessman obtained his capital loans in kind, but modern industry did not consist of physiocratic leasing companies. Transactions took place in money. To maintain under such conditions that businessmen knew the rate of return demanded the further assumption that the business used only one productive factor of exactly the same quality as the product it manufactured. Wicksell, moreover, was forced to assume that the relative prices of competing products and other productive factors, together with the relation between product price and prices of productive factors, were given before the idea of a "natural interest rate" as a basis of comparison could be accepted.

All these assumptions, held Myrdal, meant there was something wrong in Wicksell's thinking. The purpose of his theory was to explain the level of prices, but paradoxically his model adopted the assumption that prices were taken as given. The root of the problem and the way forward, Myrdal appears to have thought, lay in this proposition that managers actually knew the "natural" rate of interest as a concrete figure.[12] It was necessary to remove this from the theory of business economics.

It was, moreover, necessary to pursue this effort into general economic theory. In his work *Science and Politics in National Economic Theory* (Vetenskap och politik i nationalekonomin), which appeared in 1930, Myrdal maintained that economic analysis had suffered from the time of the Physiocrats onward from the idea of "natural" values that could be understood and compared with market values. The physical returns of the land had provided the Physiocrats with their concrete theory of value that supplied a standard for the calculation of land rents. Ricardo had introduced labor value as a basis for understanding and judging the prices of products. Capital was evaluated in terms of "waiting," which provided a "natural" explanation for the price of money as an interest rate. Then there was the doctrine of utility value, which attempted to show that "each relation between demand, supply and price must be able to be referred to a deeper relation between desire and nondesire and the means of need satisfaction."[13] Gunnar Myrdal was very conscious that these concrete values were used as judgments concerning what was right and proper in economic life. The profits of a firm, for example, could be judged as being high or low in relation to these values. Economics, held Myrdal, was full of such attempts to "smuggle in terms of social evaluation within the scientific explanation."[14]

Economics at this time in Sweden was closely related to law as a discipline— Myrdal, in fact, took his doctorate in the legal faculty—and the roots of this disposition were to be found in contemporary legal philosophy. Axel Hägerström, the Swedish philosopher of law whose influence was pervasive at this time, had attempted to show that natural rights were in opposition to scientific explanation of the causes of human behavior. Morals and ethics were nothing other than expressions of the views of authority that could never be shown to be true or false. Moral philosophy, in which both law and economics had their origins, should refrain from the attempt to pass moral judgments. It was the case, according to Hägerström, that "moral science cannot be a teaching in morality, but only a discipline about morality."[15]

Hägerström did not, however, regard all research on this subject as being hopeless in principle, but rather that the social sciences should continue in their efforts to obtain knowledge concerning the causes of behavior. This knowledge could never reveal deeper values or prove that certain actions were better than others. Research could never justify values as such but should seek to expose how people made evaluations:

> It is obvious that knowledge of factual evaluations is not at all any knowledge about values. We confirm so far as this goes only certain factual relations, and not at all that something is better or worse.[16]

If it was from Wicksell that Myrdal obtained the inspiration to look for the effects on the capital market of businesses in the consumer goods markets, it was from Hägerström that he obtained the reasons for dismissing utility and labor value explanations of prices. Myrdal's abstract theory of business economics arose when he left the metaphysical problems of exchange value—"metaphysics" being the major evil in terms of Hägerström's philosophy—and sought a scientific appreciation of the business evaluation of capital.

2. The Firm as Abstract Investment, Not Concrete Savings

2.1 The Firm as Monetary Capital That . . .

Concrete economy has been the dominating theme of the economic thought that has so far been dealt with. For the Physiocrats, business was concerned with the transfer of agricultural production (P) to consumption (K). Adam Smith emphasized human labor in production and saw the saving of products (S) as a necessary precondition for enterprise. When the economic importance of a business was to be assessed, Smith introduced purchasing power in exchange with the products of other businesses as a criterion. Ricardo judged the importance of enterprise in terms of labor value and noted how labor was distributed in the firm for the purpose of promoting innovation in machinery. Thus, the new machines that came into existence could provide the same volume of production with less labor power. According to Ricardo, the risk arose of a concentration of consumption in the hands of the business class and a long-term fall in the level of profits. Marx traced the origins of business capital accumulation to surplus value. He considered that consumption (K) was forcibly taxed by managers and through unjust wages and inhuman working conditions. Managers stole capital from the workers. Walras judged the value of enterprise through the utility provided to consumers. The firm became a kind of assembly line where land, labor, and capital were combined into consumer products. The free market guaranteed that costs, in the form of natural rents, corresponded to consumer utility prices.

   With the arrival of repeated crises in the increasingly capitalist industrial countries, concrete economists such as Mill, Marshall, and Gide recommended a revival of the direct relationship between production and consumption. This is the point of the cooperative form of business activity. The crisis depends upon monopoly profits that hinder free exchange and lead to overinvestment in production that lacks consumers since wages were too low. The crises came about because the costing principle for the setting of prices had broken down. Schmoller in Germany drew the conclusion from this that free markets are an evil. Business is something that should be planned by a small elite who control the rate of investment through state banks and centralized wage fixing. The system could be manipulated in such a manner that permits a fast rate of expansion for companies. Gustav Schmoller—who was perhaps the least concrete among these economists—rejected the theory of value and would replace exchange values with those based in the spirit of the German folk. All these thinkers approached the company or business in an economy conceived of primarily as being composed of three important dimensions: produced consumer goods (P); consumption (K); and savings in the form of stocks, equipment, and liquid recourses (S). Wicksell belonged primarily to this tradition. P sank periodically when businesses decided to manufacture productive capital goods that they hoped would increase P when the new factories were completed. The reduction of P produced a disequilibrium with K, which was why prices rose in the consumption markets. At this point, Myrdal held that Wicksell had failed to think through the full consequences of his position, which itself would require a break with this tradition.

Had Wicksell followed this tradition in economic thinking more closely, he would not have been able logically to explain the general rise in price levels. He had defined K as incomes for a period's rental of resources (labor, capital, and land) that produced P during the same period. If P sank during the period as a result of capitalization by companies, market values should, according to tradition, be temporarily raised. That would immediately attract other companies, which would increase P and redress the balance between demand and supply. This was because, in the old tradition, total price rises where monopoly profits were ignored depended upon rises of natural prices as a result of increased productivity when greater utility or higher labor value streamed out from the pump of wealth. Wicksell's good idea implied that the identity between the sales value of the product and the value of the recourses included in the product was disconnected. The principle of costs, as Myrdal calls this identity, had been broken. How did this happen?

Myrdal's solution to the theoretical problem certainly had a political background. He would become the economist for Swedish Social Democracy; during the 1920s, it had been a goal of the Social Democrats to eliminate Marxism from their thinking. The mystery of prices and the broken principle of costs were, thus, not to be explained in terms of the exploitation of surplus value. The complaints of the liberals concerning the opportunistic attitude of the state toward the new powerful interest groups smacked of a hatred for the trade unions. When these liberals placed the blame for the confused monetary situation on the state and demanded stable prices, it was suspected that what they were really after was a sinking of wage levels. The bankers also grumbled that the printing presses filled the wage envelopes but distorted exchange values. The theoretical criticism of quantity theory, in this situation, provided a welcome defense in Social Democratic circles against the attacks of the conservatives. Social Democratic leaders could assure the fearful that they had no intention of introducing socialism. Indeed, Ernst Wigforss openly declared his faith in the future of capitalism and assured that the Social Democrats "are people who did not want to drop the idea that the existing economic system had such force that, if we could only clear the large challenge that we are now experiencing, it can be assured of a yet rather long life."[17]

The time was right for a management theory that neither condemned capitalism nor placed restrictions upon the workers' demands for higher wages. Myrdal's future political influence was possibly grounded in his skill in delivering such a theory without visible political or moral linkage that was well anchored in contemporary national economic and philosophical debate. Instead of following Schmoller in rejecting economic theory and basing values in the spirit of the "Volk," Myrdal reformulated the theory so that it would be suitable for economic planning in the Social Democratic "Folk Home." Central to this mission was a redefinition of the company and the role of the manager—a reformulation that turned managers into calculators.

Myrdal rejects the exchange value theory. Prices had no deeper causes in utility or labor value. Such metaphysics must be thrown out. A firm is worth, held Myrdal, what managers valued it at; since no absolute measure of value exists, it is not possible for external judges to criticize such valuations. In the old theory, where production factors were hired for a period at market prices, a critically minded economist could compare the business's product prices against the cost of recourses. With cost prices as his divining rod, he could track down monopolies. In Myrdal's thinking, however, it was not possible even for the manager himself to set prices in this manner. This is because every company is a unique combination of different capital objects that must be regarded as a whole. Firms could not be reduced to elements and valued at market prices. The firm is separate from the market, and Myrdal held that it was just this that was the original reason for founding firms. In other words, companies were founded because such actions gave capital a value. This value was something that exists entirely in the minds of the businessmen, in the sense of Hägerström's position on values. From its first foundation onward, the firm is subjected to continuous valuation, although this process of valuation can never be fixed in any objective sense.

Myrdal held that all capital in the nation was in the form of firms. The firms were the capital; the capital of the nation could not be divided for evaluation into units smaller than these firms. The attempt of accountants to value different parts of the firm was based upon arbitrary judgments:

> This implies that we, in the first place, are not able to talk of a special "capital" unit less than the company other than in the meaning: capital object. Its value—that of monetary capital—is incomprehensible. In that degree real capital is lasting and sluggish, it has [by the act of founding the company] become hopelessly confused with the other [form of] real capital: the company itself.[18]

To be a manager was identical to being one who engaged in valuations. The creation of capital, all business, had its final causes in the minds of businessmen. This must be the case because it was businessmen who engaged themselves in production, and this required judgments concerning time. Who was to say what prices his goods would fetch in the future? His valuations included experience, judgment, and skill that guided his guesses. This act of guessing is called by Myrdal a "calculation," "plan," or "program."

Thus, the manager guesses how much money he will invest. He makes judgments concerning returns and costs, inflows and outflows of money for his business, in the future. This manager is not for Myrdal a technician, leader, or engineer, but rather someone who is engaged in share capital, which may be his own or loaned. His mind is absorbed with ideas of the power of capital to grow that Gide had described as "fantasmagories." If it works out badly, he builds his financial castle in the air, like the matchstick king, Ivar Kreuger, who provided accounts that met the dreams of shareholders concerning secure growth. Whether we like it or not, he appeared to mean that this was the manner in which capitalism functioned. Before investments had matured into products, before anyone had seen the bills for the development costs or had sold the products on the market, it was not possible for anyone to be certain of the results. An enterprise's *ex ante* plan was initiated before results could be read in the *ex post* bookkeeping of the company accounts. The manager had necessarily bound the capital before he could show any results in figures. Before he could know that he could repay his debts with interest, it was necessary that he obtain loans. Decisions to take loans could not be based on the difference between the physical return on real capital and the current rate of interest as Wicksell had maintained. Managers, in the first place, reckoned in prices rather than the physical quantities of production. Beyond this, through the very act of founding a company or firm, the manager was prevented from meaningful comparisons of capital with anything outside the company. Wicksell's idea of a comparison between capital productivity and interest rates was based in the classical notion that the entrepreneur paid for the "waiting" for the physical return on the capital employed by a capitalist. Myrdal would hold, on the other hand, that the entrepreneur is the capitalist, since the capital is identical with the enterprise. There existed here no Ricardian landowner or the owner of capital distinct from the entrepreneur who knew the physical return of real capital and negotiated a price that was related to productivity:

> Normally, when we in the future talk of the "manager," we denote therewith a person who has control over free capital and with this purchases the means of production, which he—under the risk for future changes—binds together in order to serve a certain production goal. This way of presenting the problem, however, is directed by didactic reasons; the argument is intended to be immediately generalized. From the point of view of general price development, all people are managers. To make business is to make economically important decisions. Whether such decisions concern acting or refraining from acting, the whole complex of risks emerges as soon as different alternatives stand open, and as soon as it is expected that the decision can have importance for the size of future incomes and costs, or for the point in time when such would occur. If we would define "business" [activity], we should do it in this completely general form.[19]

Such a broad and abstract definition of business that transformed everyone into a manager removed the foundations of a concrete business economics.

2.2 . . . Is Valuated by Managers . . .

Myrdal turned his back on the passive firm associated with Walras. According to Myrdal, the managers are the only active agent in economics. The firm is a kind of pump, whose beat directs the different flows of the economy. The heart must be explained from the inside, since no concept of value could serve to interpret the total suctions and pressures in the economic system. The demand for consumer goods (K) is no longer a function of human utility or needs. Out of the assembly of firms comes the stream of wages to the working class. This working class is presumed to exchange money for consumer goods that also stream out from the firm (P). In Myrdal's world market decisions are not primarily made by individual consumers but by the producing firms. It is naturally the case that the demand for the products of an individual company could fall when workers favor other companies, resulting in price rises for more attractive products. But profits and losses for Myrdal are not only market phenomena, they are dependent also upon managerial valuations. This is because it is managers who decide how much should go to wages, production, and capital goods, respectively. Besides the managerial class, there exist in the nation only individuals who consume their wages; they live a kind of hand-to-mouth existence without reflection. They make no decisions or calculations and have no plans regarding the future. As soon as they begin to save money, however, they become members of the managerial class with a calculation or plan. They act in an economic sense and are presumed to have made a decision. The consequence of such is that K decreases while S increases. People who perform such acts are, according to Myrdal's definition, members of the managerial class. But why do they save ? How do they think?

As soon as a person puts money aside, that person's action depends upon a valuation of capital that is based on the faith that there would be a monetary surplus following its amortization. If a worker, for example, valued his labor power, consuming only so much as was necessary to maintain that labor power, he would save such wages as exceeded the amortization of the labor power for a given period.[20] Myrdal emphasizes here again that such an appreciation of amortization could never be based on any measure of physical depreciation or bookkeeping device concerning write-offs. All such decisions are based in valuations. If a worker values himself as a capital asset, he is equally a manager. A manager is constantly engaged in evaluating his capital, making guesses concerning future costs and proceeds, in order to determine the rate of profits in a given period. It is such evaluations that lie behind the decision to save a part of income—to become or to continue as a manager.

In all societies that had proceeded beyond the "hand-to-mouth" stage, such decisions are made. The beating of the entrepreneurial heart, controlled by thoughts of capital evaluation, is the root of capital development. Myrdal, however, considered that the variables P, K, and S were insufficient to explain the operations of the system, and so he introduced a further variable—I for investment—into the economic system.

Adam Smith traced capital to parsimony, something that he considered to be a natural instinct among civilized human beings. It was parsimony that led to investments. Marx provided a distinctly negative picture of the miserly capitalist, while other economists sought to develop savings as a kind of storage of physical values. It is now the value of objects rather than human nature that explains the phenomenon of savings. Wicksell considered that businessmen invested when they knew something concerning the productivity of capital goods. In modern industrial states, however, the manager saves in monetary terms; but the value of money itself is determined by the actions of the manager. Myrdal's businessman, thus, could not compare some kind of natural interest with the going rate of interest on loans, in order to make decisions concerning savings. He rather calculates in future flows of money, inflows and outflows, and has instead some idea or expectation concerning the return on a certain placement of money—an investment. It is the case here that savings do not lead to investment. On the contrary, it is investment that gives rise to savings.

For Gunnar Myrdal, technology is also controlled by the world of thought. The physical volume of production is not a cause but a result of investment decisions. When a business invested, it took in engineers who constructed within the firm the apparatus of production. It was here that a small oasis of concrete economics survived. Calculations were not in monetary terms; rather, it was the physical laws of technology that determined how large would be the number of products the firm would come to offer on the consumption markets. These laws, more usually known as production functions, provided the physical basis that usually led to large-scale operations. A scaling up of a motor often resulted in positive effects; the lengthening of the walls of a building led to a progressive increase in the volume of the building. Technique, however, also provided limits on the scale of production that Myrdal defined in terms of quantity of products per unit of time. A building that was too high would simply collapse.

Myrdal thus sought to trace economic activity to a calculation concerning investments. When a manager estimated the yield of capital and considered this to be higher than the rate of interest, it was the difference between the two that provided the opportunity for profits. It was this profitability that commanded him to invest. He would continue to fill the gap with investments until the expected yield from capital was equal to the rate of interest. The manager, thus, functioned as a maximizer of profits, and we have here the well-known rational actor of modern microtheory:

The most important assumption is, of course, the old familiar one of "rational behaviour." The idea is that there are a large number of private entrepreneurs who act rationally so as to maximize their profits.[21]

But if the yield of capital was equal to the rate of interest, how could it be shown that it was the expected yield of capital that controlled the rate of interest, that it was investment calculations rather than savings that was the motor in the economy? Wicksell had held that the natural return should equal the rate of interest and that savings should balance investment in an equilibrium situation. In Wicksell, these were two independent criteria, since investment decisions could be founded upon concrete physical judgments. But Myrdal rejected all this as metaphysics, holding that the yield of capital and the rate of interest were interdependent. In his efforts to eliminate all savings explanations for the existence of capitalism, Myrdal now stood in front of the chicken-and-the-egg problem with regard to investments and savings.

2.3 . . . Calculating—But How ?

The solution must surely lie in the priority of thoughts over deeds. Managers sought to read the future; the results of any single firm were dependent only on the thinking activities of other managers. If all businesses happened to invest at the same time, the results of the individual business would worsen. Costs would rise with the increased demand for raw materials and fuels. If the manager making guesses about the future only knew how all other managers thought, he would be in a better position to plan his investments within a certain framework of costs and income. But this was never the case, held Myrdal, who based the whole of his theory on the assumption that one firm was never so large that it could dictate market prices. The manager was forced to consider alternative consequences with regard to payments for the same investment. A large part of Myrdal's doctoral thesis was concerned with how different risks in the mental world of managers were assessed in terms of various probabilities. Such were obviously influenced by individual temperament, caprice, and feelings, but howsoever this was the case, it did not affect Myrdal's fundamental postulate that managers think first and act later. This position itself was likely to raise questions concerning the possibility of making calculations about the future. Did not calculations have to do with figures, and did not figures refer to the measurement of something that actually existed? The future was something that did not exist.

In order to avoid criticism of the abstract economy in such terms, Myrdal now introduces the term *quantifiable* instead of the word *measurable*. He finds support for his arguments in Bertrand Russell, who held the following:

We can know that one magnitude is greater than another, and that a third is intermediate between them; also, since the differences of magnitudes are always magnitudes, there is always (theoretically, at least) an answer to the question whether the difference between one pair of magnitudes is greater than, less than, or the same as the difference of another pair of the same kind. And such propositions, though to the mathematician they may appear approximate, are just as precise and definite as the propositions of Arithmetic. Without numerical measurements, therefore, the quantitative relations of magnitude have all the definiteness of which they are capable—nothing is added, from the theoretical standpoint, by the assignment of correlated numbers."[22]

It was, thus, not actually necessary to count anything in a concrete sense in order to reason about the future. Myrdal actually dismisses the question as to whether or not the calculation was actually undertaken by some human agent with the well-known supposition that the manager acted as if he calculated. The real businessman may consider his investments in but a rough-and-summary manner.

When Myrdal traveled to the London School of Economics, he was advised by Professor Cassel to study what the British economists thought about probabilistic judgments. One of these economists, Frank Knight, had forwarded the view that models of business entrepreneurs should be based upon studies of how they actually thought in a conscious manner. Myrdal, however, was not interested in seeking to penetrate the philosophical and psychological problems involved in an analysis of actual managerial behavior, even if such were possible. He rather advises economists to forget philosophy and hold on to the investment postulate with the following words:

> If the mechanism itself for the construction of judgements cannot be brought to full consciousness—or possibly cannot be made completely conscious—it is nevertheless a long step from a position of completely denying that the premises for such judgements that actually come into being do not exist, and that there does not exist any logical relation between premises and conclusions.[23]

The question could arise here as to whether Myrdal's emphasis upon the thinking of managers was worth much more than the older economists' ideas concerning utility and labor power that were now being rejected as metaphysics. Pressed by his own demands for precision, Myrdal gave the following fundamental justification of his view of management:

> Nothing more perplexing is asserted than an entrepreneur, who reckons his debits and credits in quantities of money—not utility or marginal utility—plans and acts so as to obtain the greatest possible surplus, also expressed in terms of money. Why not accept this directly as simply a statement about people's behaviour under capitalist institutions? What concern is it of economic theory, and what does it matter, that there was, and still is, a liberal-metaphysical rationalization which calls this behavioural "rational" in a deeper

sense, in order to lay the foundation for a social apologetics? Just how far does that provide the sort of explanation we require for scientific purposes? Why not start immediately on the same empirical bases as practical "business economics"?[24]

In the final resort, Myrdal's argument was as circular as those he rejected: Managers calculated investments because investments were calculated by managers. There was, however, yet a further reason for the priority of I over S.

Consider the auditing of a business for a certain period of time, showing the profits or losses. Had the businessman concerned been certain of the relevant inflows and outflows, he would have made neither a profit nor a loss. Profits and losses, thus, were an outer sign that he had evaluated his capital positively or negatively. The results show that things had not worked out the way he had expected. The results depended upon his calculations rather than on market prices. The question remains, however: Is this argument not equally circular in character?

If it is possible to determine how I was determined so that S follows, this would provide a decisive proof for Myrdal's thesis. It could then be shown beyond dispute that the capital yield determined the rate of interest. But the capital yield for a period was calculated through discounting the net return (income minus costs throughout its useful life) on a proposed investment at present values. Thereafter, this value was spread to amortization for each year with the same calculated rate of interest. The coming period's amortization was then set in a perceptual relationship to the net return during the same period. The discounting and amortization factors, according to Myrdal, were based on the manager's judgments of future rates of interest on loans. And the yield on capital, which is assumed to determine the rate of interest on loans, becomes accordingly only the rate of interest on loans with which he had calculated. Myrdal's abstract economics concerning the investing entrepreneur rested upon a superstition that was beyond empirical verification. This, nevertheless, provided him with a theoretical concept for explaining the manner in which he assumed the economy was set in motion. Cumulative trends toward booms or depressions could now follow in a Wicksellian manner without introducing any tendency to fall back on a natural exchange value. Managerial decision making had unexpected and long-term effects, and because of this, political economics should be transformed into an economic policy that guided decisions in the desired direction.

3. A Management Theory for the Working Class

Wicksell had regarded a stable price level as a good indicator of an economy free of crisis. Long into the 1950s, his student Lindahl was writing on the need for norms for the level of prices.[25] Inflation was to be avoided if the voluntary savings were not to diminish. Not only the banks, but those on fixed incomes, particularly pensioners, would otherwise suffer from what Heckscher once colorfully termed "capitalistic bolshevism." If business enterprise was grounded upon savings, the demand for price stability was well justified. Only if prices were known to be stable in the future would people dare to lend their savings for business investments in the hope of increased future consumption. It was against such arguments founded in the theory of savings for business enterprises that Myrdal directed his theory of investments.

In the same manner as investments were made in the minds of managers, savings should take place within the walls of the company. Managers decide to lay aside profits for future projects. Otherwise, they loan money fresh from the printing presses without coverage, but with the responsibility of the investment calculation in setting the economic wheels in motion. This convenient theory allowed the Social Democrats to pass a law permitting the state to underbalance its budget and meet the deficit by printing new money. While this reform met with loud protests from exchange value theorists such as Eli Heckscher, the industrial magnate and banker Marcus Wallenberg expressed himself in the following manner with regard to the way in which the younger economists simplified the economic importance of savings:

> The question is finally if the hare will be allowed to run its course, or whether one should do something to link economic development to the right path. The next question becomes then: what can be done? This is a question of practical politics; it has nothing to do with Myrdal's wishes and utopias. Most simply, the situation can be characterized through the alternative: Will I attempt to preserve the present internal price level or will I set loose inflation?
> The first path demands a firm hold on credits and wages; the latter path will produce a blooming and satisfaction for the moment, but will turn sour later. I for my part am a supporter of the first alternative, but fear that the second has many conscious or unconscious supporters which in part would avoid conflict, and in part have (or believe they have) an advantage in that their debts would be lightened through inflation." [26]

Myrdal, however, dismisses Wicksell's demand for price stability as a question of "pure logic." [27] It could be nothing but metaphysical nonsense to demand respect and protection for a class of savers that did not exist. What Myrdal means by this is that what Lindahl calls "the business class," which is responsible for savings, does not exist. It will be useful to follow here how Myrdal abolishes this business class, that is the capitalists, and attaches managers collectively to the greater Social Democratic working class.

If the managers were really capitalists, they would—as Ricardo had assumed—invest in capital and dismiss workers to such a degree that the economy would ultimately collapse. A state policy of monetary inflation would never be able to control the increasing unemployment. With the Swedish Social Democratic electoral victory of 1932, Myrdal left his "skeptical philosophical period" during which he had created his theory. It was now necessary to take firm action to deal with the economic crisis, the opening shot of which Myrdal himself had witnessed as a Rockefeller stipendiary for 1929. A first requirement was to attack the notion of a stable price level.

Myrdal argues that it never is possible to achieve a stable price level in reality, since certain prices in the national economy are always fixed through agreements and responsibilities. These "sticky prices" depend on monopolistic tendencies that a modern economy could neither attack nor ignore. Myrdal's analysis here is obviously directed at the regulation of the labor market. The trade unions could limit the supply of labor power in their battle for higher wages; against the trade unions, the employers, if they were a united class in a Ricardian sense, could respond by limiting the supply of consumer goods. When wages are raised through negotiations, real wages would diminish, since the supply of consumer goods does not increase in proportion to monetary wages. Rising prices and unemployment could be the only result of the struggle between the working and employing classes. To avoid this result, it is necessary to steer clear of the class struggle. This is to be achieved through what Myrdal calls "industrial democracy," which was to become the hallmark of the Swedish Model. Through linking wage negotiations to rationalization and changes in production, the Ricardian effects were to be avoided. The consumption markets would be regulated through collective action, and the risk for any unplanned business activity eliminated, behind the walls of the harmonious Social Democratic workers' "Folk Home":

> Imagine a thoroughgoing settlement of unemployment in the interests of both parties by agreement! This would not only presuppose that the height of wages but also that of demand for labour would be included in the negotiations on the labour market. This would further require that, with respect to their effect on the demand for labour, rationalization as well as commodity monopolies be discussed and regulated in these negotiations.
>
> However, such an extreme industrial democracy apparently lies quite beyond present practical possibilities.[28]

The success of the Social Democratic struggle against concrete economics had by 1939 clearly exceeded anything envisaged by Gunnar Myrdal. The trade unions came to negotiate for higher wages in return for a guarantee of more work. In this process, the engineers and technicians were incorporated into the working class as experts on rationalization questions.

A further unstated agreement naturally was to consume the increased volume of production. If the process of rationalization led to loss of jobs in the consumer industries, those concerned could rest assured that they would be reemployed in the capital goods industries. In order to replace the class of savers that was being abolished, new rules concerning free write-offs were introduced that provided the possibility of transforming profits into new investments. Those who had previously been savers were now forced to participate in direct investment if they were to guard themselves against the losses of inflation. Banks were forced into a closer relationship with businesses. Private capitalism was replaced by company capitalism. The state stepped in to ensure forced savings, which were transferred to businesses to finance investments that provided jobs at negotiated wage rates. Firms could retain not only profits but even that part of wages that was offset for taxes, insurance, and pensions. When the state economists would influence developments in a certain direction, they no longer needed to negotiate with different classes and groups but could act directly through granting and withholding resources to businesses.

The state economists studied national economics and imagined from this that they understood how managers thought. Gunnar Myrdal, who was himself one of the founders of the econometric society, played early with the idea of taking the economic pulse through statistical estimates of business investments. With the large-scale professional training of a younger generation of managers in the investment school of thinking, a further guarantee was provided that the expectations of the state economists concerning business reactions would prove correct. This new generation was encouraged to use statistical material in decisions involving business investments. The businesses themselves were soon run by bureaucrats who were content to receive negotiated wages as their reward. As this transformation of business life took place, they were transformed from savers and businessmen into workers, becoming without fully realizing it members of the worker party.

When John Maynard Keynes visited the young economists in Stockholm, he soon became quite irritated. He believed himself to be radical, but the Swedes insisted on regarding him as being rather traditional. Myrdal maintained that Keynes's work appeared "for us as brilliant and important writings following well known lines, and causing not at all that shock and sense of intellectual revolution that they did in his own country and elsewhere."[29]

Before Keynes had began to wrestle with his "general theory," the Stockholm School had been struggling with the classics. The earlier engineer-led Swedish companies became controlled by increasing numbers of business economists. These were largely members of the abstract school of economics who dreamed from their earliest days about capital yields, welfare, and newly printed paper money. Economists, engineers, and workers were thus reduced to members of the same class, a class without struggle, where dreams became true if all were industriously engaged in production and consumption. It was unnecessary even to inquire about the value of a product or worry about the concrete reality beyond the wage negotiations and the rolling printing presses. Their wallets were full of letters of debt to the state that they would spend their lives attempting to repay. They were born in debt to a life of full employment, committed to business management.

Notes

1. Gustav Cassel, *I förnuftets tjänst, en ekonomisk självbiografi*, Vol. 1, p. 54.

2. Gunnar Myrdal, *Vetenskap och politik i nationalekonomin*, p. 267.

3. Ibid., p. 303.

4. Eli Heckscher, ed, *Bidrag till sveriges ekonomiska och sociala historia under och efter första världskriget*, Vol. 1.

5. Ibid., p. 16.

6. Ibid., p. 25.

7. Ibid., p. 38.

8. Erik Lindahl, *Om förhållandet mellan penningmängd och prisnivå*.

9. Gunnar Myrdal, *Monetary Equilibrium*, p. 48.

10. Gunnar Myrdal, *I stället för memoarer kritiska essäer om nationalekonomien*, p. 18.

11. Gunnar Myrdal, *Prisbildningsproblemet och föränderligheten*, p. 29.

12. Myrdal, *Monetary Equilibrium*, p. 50.

13. Myrdal, *Vetenskap och politik i nationalekonomien*, p. 133.

14. Myrdal, *Prisbildningsproblemet och föränderligheten*, p. 42.

15. Axel Hägerström, *Socialfilosofiska uppsatser*, p. 65.

16. Ibid., p. 55.

17. Bertil Ohlin, *Memoarer, ung man blir politiker*, p. 213.

18. Myrdal, *Prisbildningsproblemet och föränderligheten*, p. 58.

19. Ibid., p. 115.

20. Erik Lindahl, *Penningpolitikens medel*, p. 14.

21. Gunnar Myrdal, *Om penningteoretisk jämvikt*, p. 296; Myrdal, *Monetary Equilibrium*, pp. 204–205.

22. Myrdal, *Prisbildningsproblemet och föränderligheten*, p. 95.

23. Ibid., pp. 107–108.

24. Myrdal, *Monetary Equilibrium*, p. 205.

25. Lindahl, *Penningpolitikens medel*.

26. Torsten Gårdlund, *Marcus Wallenberg 1864–1943, Hans liv och gärning*, p. 548.

27. Myrdal, *Monetary Equilibrium*, p. 128.

28. Ibid., p. 156.

29. Myrdal, *Vetenskap och politik i nationalekonomien*, p. 268.

11

Enterprise as Adventure; or, The Golden Calf Dance in John Maynard Keynes's General Theory

1. Prince Pozzo's World Threatened

John Maynard Keynes, whose father was also a Cambridge logician and economist, grew up in an intellectual environment in the family home on Harvey Road. While never ostentatious, it was "well staffed" and full of lively debate and argumentation.[1] Although his father made himself responsible for his son's early education, this never went to the lengths practiced in the Mill family. There were readings from Dickens and visits to selected plays showing in the London theater. The British Empire appeared richer and stronger than ever; the chances that the younger Keynes (1883–1946) would achieve a responsible position were increased after his acceptance at Eton. Being quick in thought and word, he was popular with both teachers and other children. He read much and already as a twelve-year-old was a recognized customer in the Cambridge bookshops. It was on his suggestion that the calf bindings on Eton's prize books were abolished, since this resulted in objects that were only of interest to book collectors.[2] Nevertheless, in later years, many an expensive volume from the London book auctions disappeared into his personal collection.

He had from early days intended to become an English gentleman, and when older, he could say without flinching that "the Class war will find me on the side of the educated bourgeoisie."[3]

As an educated gentleman, he spent much of his time in polite company. Already at Eton he was known as a good sportsman, and at Cambridge he continued long "toiling at the oar."[4] When he won an Eton scholarship to Kings' College, Cambridge, it was natural for his father to send a few well-chosen bottles to celebrate the occasion. A small supper was arranged for his friends where the menu consisted of "soup, fish, pilaugh, turkeys, partridges, plum puddings, mince pies, paté de foie gras, dessert. . . ."

Most important, however, was to talk well and discuss intelligently. Following his time at Eton, he naturally continued on to Cambridge rather than Oxford, which was never given a thought. He landed in Cambridge literary and philosophical circles that taught the young to express themselves in well-chosen words. He studied mathematics as a hobby, but without any considerable success. Logic and philosophy proved more suited to his temperament.

This was certainly known by the two tall and slim gentlemen who toward the end of his first term at Cambridge knocked upon his door. Lytton Strachey and Leonard Woolf were invited in, and they were soon engaged in an interesting conversation with the young John Maynard Keynes. Keynes passed the test and was soon invited to drink tea with G. E. Moore, the leading Cambridge philosopher of the period, becoming a member thereafter in the secret group called "The Society." Together with the other "apostles," he discussed philosophical problems, sharing the view that their major task was to spread poetic and metaphysical wisdom to the poor, ignorant people who were referred to by the "apostles" as "Stumpfs." G. E. Moore was at this time the leading figure in "The Society," and his work *Principia Ethica* appeared in 1903, the year that Keynes was elected as a member. The book became for Keynes something of an aesthetic and philosophical bible.

G. E. Moore's message was simple and direct. The task of ethics was to find "the good." If, however, something was thought to be "good," it was not possible to prove the case, as such judgments were based upon intuition. It was, nevertheless, necessary to discuss and attempt to convince others concerning the "good" that was being upheld. Sitting before a comfortable fire in the club, a person should give clear reasons for holding to be true the statement that something really was good. But although the good should be the goal of our actions, what was good could never be decided through a scientific proof that defined the content of goodness. This was because, held Moore, the good is good, and therewith the best. The word *good* was a simple and synthetic word that could not be defined through analysis into other terms. It was not like other words, which were amenable to such treatment, and it was necessary to be wary of false prophets who maintained that they knew the nature of goodness. Some of these false prophets would encourage us to stop debating and to stop "looking about us."[5] They believed that goodness was a quality that gave value to actions or objects and included in their rank the "naturalists," who maintained, for example, that physical exertion in work created value or made an object good. Yet others pointed to unseen metaphysical entities such as "will" or "spirit" and considered that these were identical with goodness.

Moore was, in fact, less critically disposed toward the naturalists than toward the metaphysicians, since the latter at least had the advantage of being so wild in their statements as to set our imaginations in motion. In this they did more good than harm through waking up discussion with their wild ideas:

But the wilder they are, and the less useful for Metaphysics, the more useful they will be for Ethics; since, in order to be sure that we have neglected nothing in the description of our ideal, we should have had before us as wide a field as possible of suggested goods.[6]

It was, however, a third group of false prophets, the hedonists, who provided the greatest problem. These economic moralists maintained that pleasure was the only good, and they justified this with the argument that we desire the pleasurable. It was out of such an ethical position that Mill and the other classical economists had developed their rules of behavior. The rational human being in this perspective sought pleasure—not the least in the form of money—and had thus achieved this good when a product had been sold. Moore pointed out that it was "the thought" of pleasure that inspired activity. "The pleasure" in itself—the psychological phenomenon—could not alone constitute the goal of an action, but must at least be followed by a "consciousness" that we actually obtained pleasure. Therefore, held Moore, "the good" just was not pleasure in itself, but possibly the "thought" of pleasure. Goodness was rather a state of consciousness. It was necessary to be careful when calling a means "good" because it sometimes led to good ends, if only because an economic action could also lead to bad results. Goals could not justify means, and no certain rules in this respect could be formulated.

This was considered a radical message in a world permeated by Victorian morals and manners. For Keynes and his contemporaries, it provided a weapon against classical clichés:

We were among the last of the Utopians, or meliorists as they are sometimes called, who believe in a continuing moral progress by virtue of which the human race already consists of reliable, rational, decent people, influenced by truth and objective standards, who can be safely released from the outward restraints of convention and traditional standards and inflexible rules of conduct, and left, from now onwards, to their own sensible devices, pure motives and reliable intuitions of the good.[7]

This was certainly no revolutionary anarchistic doctrine for all its contemporary novelty. Moore considered that certain commonsense rules such as industry, temperance, and the keeping of promises could provisionally be raised to the status of duties.[8] It was also clearly not a doctrine of value nihilism such as was popular elsewhere in Europe at the time. While Moore railed at length against "the naturalistic fallacy,"[9] he did not draw back from a discussion of what he thought to be good in his final chapter, which was titled "The Ideal." For Moore, as for Keynes, it was the beautiful that was the good, "the pleasures of human intercourse and the enjoyment of beautiful objects."[10] The situation would be even better if such people and objects were also related to the truth. But what did it matter if such goodness was male Victorian, honorable, just, or natural?

Concerning Moore's interpretation of goodness, John Maynard Keynes wrote: "It conveys the beauty of the literalness of Moore's mind, the pure and passionate intensity of his vision, unfanciful and undressed up."[11] It was an attack on materialism and a celebration of idealism that went far beyond any practical concerns with mundane affairs. Keynes, indeed, held that "[t]he New Testament is a handbook for politicians compared with the unworldliness of Moore's chapter on 'The Ideal.'"[12]

Thought, passion, and intuition became as respectable in polite circles as pure reason and industry had been earlier. Although Keynes could be persuaded to follow his Etonian friends on a climbing expedition in the Alps, it was not long before he was pining for his discussions in polite Cambridge circles. Like Lytton Strachey—who was to become known for his biting satire on Victorian mores—Keynes moved toward the point of view that nature was absurd. The good was no longer to be identified with enterprise or natural phenomena.

In 1908 Lytton Strachey moved to London; Keynes had already been traveling back and forth from London for several years. The notions of Moore spread to a London circle of writers and artists that went under the heading of the Bloomsbury Group. The possession of a sense of aesthetics became a major preoccupation of this circle, and it was just the lack of such a sense that Strachey was to hold against Keynes: "What irritates me about Pozzo is that he has no aesthetic sense."[13] But Pozzo—as friends called Keynes after a clever and opportunistic Corsican diplomat—nevertheless had a taste for artists and people with beautiful hands. As he wrote of President Roosevelt: "[N]aturally my concentrated attention was on his hands. Rather disappointing. Firm and fairly strong, but not clever or with finesse, shortish round nails like those at the end of a businessman's fingers."[14]

During a long period, his nearest friend was the painter Duncan Grant, who together with the other Bloomsbury talents, which included Virginia Woolf, created a small society where Keynes experienced a realization of Moore's social ideal. Beyond the hypocrisy and materialism of Victorian society, it was possible to seek pleasure in passions that had been purified from naturalistic fallacies in art and life. Effort and struggle were only justified as a means to maintain such intellectual oases of the mind.

The views of outsiders, however, were not always so flattering. Following his acquaintance with Bertrand Russell, who introduced him to Keynes, Grant, and their friend Augustine Birrell, D. H. Lawrence was to write:

> To hear these young people talking really fills me with black fury: They talk endlessly, but endlessly—and never, never a good or real thing said. Their attitude is so irreverent and so blatant. They are cased, each in a hard little shell of his own, and out of this they talk words. . . .
> Never bring Birrell to see me any more. There is something nasty about him like black beetles. He is horrible and unclean. I feel I should go mad when

> I think of your set, Duncan Grant and Keynes and Birrell. It makes me dream
> of beetles; . . . it came full upon me in Keynes and Duncan Grant. And yester-
> day I knew it again in Birrell—you must leave these friends, these beetles.
> Birrell and Duncan Grant are done for ever. Keynes I am not sure—when I
> saw Keynes that morning in Cambridge it was one of the crises of my life.[15]

When Keynes began to study political economy in his spare time, his father's
friend at Cambridge, Alfred Marshall, was very pleased, for he had always hoped
that the younger Keynes would chose economics as his subject. But Marshall
himself was a little too Victorian and colorless to influence Keynes very much at
this time, and the pattern of Cambridge life in discussions and philosophical
argument continued. In the summer, there were car trips to Italy or climbing in
the Alps with a few friends from Eton. In the end, even Keynes's understanding
mother began to fear that the practice of the good life meant little more than
being without useful employment.[16]

It was now time for Pozzo to seek a place in the Civil Service. Despite a
witnessed arrogance, he was placed in the second position on the list, something he himself explained was a result of the other candidates' being "rather
a crew,"[17] and also a result of the contemporary administrators' knowing
nothing at all about economics. Work in the India Office, however, proved
hardly to the liking of Prince Pozzo, and after two years in the bureaucracy,
he was prepared to accept Alfred Marshall's offer of place in the newly
established economics department at Cambridge. The time in London had not
been completely wasted, as Keynes brought back with him a written thesis
that G. E. Moore, Bertrand Russell, and Alfred North Whitehead considered
worth publishing. It was, however, not at first accepted by King's College.
Following an extensive rewriting during a holiday on the Orkney Islands,
where Duncan Grant painted his portrait, Keynes's thesis was eventually
accepted by the college in 1909.

This work, titled *A Treatise on Probability*, was related to Moore's discussion
of the means of obtaining "the good." If we with certainty knew the effects of
our actions, it would be possible to state principles and rules that had the status
of duties:

> But it is obvious that our causal knowledge alone is far too incomplete for us
> ever to assure ourselves of this result. Accordingly it follows that we never
> have any reason to suppose that action is our duty: we can never be sure that
> any action will produce the greatest value possible.[18]

The relationship between goals and means was always uncertain. Despite this,
we act and argue that we have acted in a certain manner. It was the logic behind
such arguments that Keynes examined in his thesis—our manner, given direct
knowledge, of determining the probability that our actions were good. Keynes
sought logical rules for showing that certain beliefs were rational. How, for

example, did an insurance agent, a lawyer, or a bookmaker reason? As a good student of Moore, Keynes rejected all attempts of a naturalistic nature to transform the question of probability into a question of factual observations and the frequency of events. Our actions were not controlled by "events"; rather, our propositions and logic were what gave us reason to believe that certain results of our actions were probable. That this was the case, maintained Keynes, became clear if we investigated how people in general acted. They may often choose to act on the grounds of fewer, more weighty facts than to follow a course having a greater factual basis. Only those who had no experience of life maintained from their ivory towers that the term *rational* should be reserved for people who calculated in figures.

As a lecturer in economics, Keynes was much appreciated. He illustrated Marshall's theories with modern examples, using the example of sugar prices to demonstrate price elasticity, the cotton industry to show the theory of profits, and modern banking statistics to illustrate the export of capital. The more gifted students and colleagues were invited to participate in a discussion club on economic questions where even the shyest of them was encouraged to express his or her views. In these sessions, Prince Pozzo sat curled up on the sofa like a dark, purring cat with his claws concealed in the arms of his dressing gown. He stirred to round off the meeting with a few elegant and well-chosen phrases, puncturing the more pompous contributors where he felt this was required. Beyond his academic duties lay the Bloomsbury Group in London, with its studio parties and interesting exhibitions. The presentation of Matisse, Gauguin, and Cezanne in 1910 had shocked the London public. Keynes's writing at this time concerned the Indian credit system, and he then became a member of an investigation to reform the Indian banking system. At this point, unfortunately, World War I began.

Keynes was now to be seen traveling up Whitehall in the sidecar of a motorcycle on his way to the Treasury to work on the financing of the war. His friends in the Bloomsbury Group refused to bear weapons. What did it matter if the Germans arrived here? questioned Lytton Strachey, expressing an attitude later adopted by other members of the Bloomsbury Group. The main point was that the good life dedicated to beauty and pleasant relationships should continue and that talented persons should retain a certain modest unearned income that gave them the possibility of devoting time to the important things in life.

Pozzo's participation in the war was somewhat lightened for members of the Bloomsbury Group when he discovered an auction of Degas's private collection in 1918. Having convinced the Treasury of the need to save the cultural treasures of France, he received lists of works to be purchased from his Bloomsbury friends: "We have great hopes of you and consider that your existence at the Treasury is at last justified. . . . I think a feast off our pig will be one of your rewards."[19]

Pozzo could return as a Bloomsbury cultural hero after successfully bidding for the masters of the impressionist school. Perhaps for a while this achievement lightened the atmosphere, which for Keynes was heavy with the feeling that civilization was threatened in its very existence. Virginia Woolf was writing years later, in 1928: "I fancy sometimes the world changes. I think I see reason spreading."[20] Keynes's view of developments was somewhat darker.

As a British delegate to Versailles in 1919, Keynes's fears for the future received a firsthand confirmation. Clemenceau, Wilson, and Lloyd George appeared to Keynes to be playing something of a tragicomic opera as a prelude to the definitive failure of human civilization. Clemenceau seemed to be bent upon crushing Germany under the burden of war debts in order to turn the clock back to 1869. While Keynes could admire the French tiger, who always managed to cover his claws with gloves, Keynes was, nevertheless, critical of the wisdom of this course. Wilson, however, appeared not only distasteful but lacked any consistent theory behind his declared Fourteen Points.[21] He, moreover, appeared to be some kind of Presbyterian pastor calculated to raise the hackles of economists. Lloyd George—also known as "the goat"—was more diplomatically sensitive to the needs of others but was unable to contribute anything to the peace that would create a basis for the preservation of European civilization. The Allies, Keynes held, had not founded their position on economic realities, and Germany would never be able to fulfill the obligations of war damages that were now imposed by the Versailles Treaty. Keynes resigned his position in the Treasury and wrote a book on the dangers involved in the peace treaty:

> The danger confronting us, therefore, is the rapid depression of the standard of life of the European populations to a point which will mean actual starvation for some (a point already reached in Russia and approximately reached in Austria). Men will not always die quietly. For starvation, which brings to some lethargy and despair, drives other temperaments to the nervous instability of hysteria and to a mad despair. And these in their distress may overturn the remnants of organization, and submerge civilization itself in their attempts to satisfy desperately the overwhelming needs of the individual. This is the danger against which all our resources and courage and idealism must now cooperate.[22]

More clearly than most, Keynes had seen the writing on the European wall and felt the impending forces that could be released in the pursuit of the peace.

2. Saving Civilization by True Enterprise

2.1 Bread and Business

Art and love made life worth living, and artists had a value in themselves. The duty of the economists was to provide the resources that made the practice of the free arts possible. Keynes sought to be one of these "economists, who are trustees, not of civilization, but of the possibility of civilization."[23] But even a trustee of the possibility of civilization, thought Keynes, needed to possess the means of economic independence, although this was difficult since teaching at Cambridge took so much time. He turned down the offer of becoming director of the London School of Economics and also that of the chairmanship of a bank. Accepting several minor duties as a financial expert to an insurance company, he managed at the same time to create a small private fortune through currency speculations on the exchanges. When he had cleared up his daily correspondence and financial affairs in bed each morning, he was free for the rest of the day to devote himself to more important questions. How, for example, would it be possible to create employment for the suffering masses so that they would feel less inclined to threaten civilization during their involuntary leisure time?

The time of crisis had arrived, and its hallmark was that of unemployment. Keynes authored a stream of liberal-minded propositions for dealing with the situation. His intuition was that a world so full of machines, raw materials, and transport equipment must certainly have places for more people in its factories. He was gripped by "the paradox of poverty in the midst of plenty."[24]

The government should rather promote the development of industry and the building of houses than merely pay out funds in unemployment benefits. He warned of the ideological consequences of the crisis with the shadows of communism and fascism on the horizon. People were no longer content, as they had been in the previous century, with low wages and a distorted distribution of incomes that provided most to those who could afford to save most. The time was over when "[t]he duty of 'saving' became nine tenths of virtue and the growth of the cake the object of true religion. . . the virtue of the cake was that it was never to be consumed, neither by you nor by your children after you."[25]

The workers had in the course of World War I lost their faith in authority. They required no G. E. Moore to reveal the duality in the morals of industriousness and savings.[26] Even the faith of the middle classes in capitalism was threatened. A small dose of inflation was sufficient to wipe out their savings and transform in their eyes the heroes of capitalism into parasitic profiteers. "We worked to make cannons for you," the melody ran, "and then we were consumed as cannon fodder. If you want our confidence and would that we should refrain from voting for the Fascists and Communists, give us jobs in your companies. Let us consume for ourselves. Give us work and we shall both consume your products and vote for you in parliament."

2.2 More Adventure!

Keynes considered that if business or its economic advisers were directly to respond to this challenge, the revolution would soon be a fact. A third generation of managers was unfortunately both weak and stupid.[27] They founded their liberalism on a classical economy that had two unsatisfactory means of dealing with the problem of unemployment. One of these was to convince the unemployed that they would soon find work if only they went out and searched—that they, in other words, were suffering only from frictional unemployment on a path between two jobs. Alternatively, economists had advised the unemployed to beg the trade unions to lower their wage levels. They maintained that the unemployed were really refusing to accept jobs that businessmen could offer. The businessmen needed to have a certain level of profits, and therefore wages had to be lowered under the strike levels fixed by the unions. Keynes thought that such arguments were little better than a slap in the face for the unemployed, whose reaction would be in terms of Marxism and hatred of industry.

In his famous work, *The General Theory of Employment, Interest and Money*, which appeared in 1936, Keynes sought to provide a new, but yet liberal and more hopeful, answer to the reigning problems. No one who had with their own eyes witnessed the crisis in America in 1932 could seriously maintain, as had the classical economists, that people lacked jobs because they refused to work for lower real or monetary wages.[28] Nor did the root cause of unemployment lie in the so-called fact that the factories already and for all time had a sufficient supply of labor. Business should not be judged from the perspective of old-fashioned economists who knew no better, warned Keynes. Such voices easily gave the impression that firms were at fault when in actual fact the problem lay in national finances. It was necessary to investigate this question to understand what hope lay in the future.

Keynes began his exposition by postulating, on the one side, the concrete economics of the enterprise, and, on the other, the abstract nature of the financial aspects:

> Consumption—to repeat the obvious—is the sole end and object of all economic activity. Opportunities for employment are necessarily limited by the extent of aggregate demand. Aggregate demand can be derived only from present consumption or from present provision for future consumption. The consumption for which we can profitably provide in advance cannot be pushed indefinitely into the future. We cannot, as a community, provide for future consumption by financial expedients but only by current physical output. In so far as our social and business organisation separates financial provision for the future from physical provision for the future so that efforts to secure the former do not necessarily carry the latter with them, financial prudence will be liable to diminish aggregate demand and thus impair well-being, as there are many examples to testify.[29]

If managers could not provide jobs, this depended upon too little of their products being consumed. The factories, workshops, and machines stood idle when the prospects for sales were poor. The more people followed Adam Smith and his school in saving money, the more quickly prices could fall, resulting in reduced production and increased unemployment.

If no one saved for investment in new industry, business would certainly waste away, leaving poverty in its place. But, on the other hand, the more that was saved, the greater the risk for this sort of crisis because "a greater proportion of income [is] being saved as real income increases."[30]

In order for firms to provide jobs, there must exist markets to compensate for the decline in the propensity to consume that occurred with rising incomes. One such market was that for capital goods. This market consisted of goods that were sold to other firms: machines; semimanufactures; buildings; and raw materials— all of which in the final resort led to the production of consumer products in the future. Increased investment in the capital goods market could compensate for declining or static demand in consumer goods, but this also led to the hope that people would in the future have the means to consume more in order that the invested capital would give the expected return. This dilemma was expressed by Keynes as follows: "Each time we secure to-day's equilibrium by increased investment we are aggravating the difficulty of securing equilibrium to-morrow."[31]

New jobs were created through investments that demanded ever greater returns. But this had nothing to do with the intentions of managers in a moral sense, and was rather a result of the functioning of the economic system. It was to this that Keynes now turned.

2.3 Casino instead of Adventure

Let us assume that we know how large a proportion of income people choose to consume. We can then easily calculate the effects of an investment in terms of how the wages that flow from buyers to sellers are reflected in the markets. If nine-tenths of wages are consumed, the multiplier effect, given certain simplifications,[32] shows that an investment provided ten times its original working effect in the economy as a whole. But this is unfortunately offset by the "casino effect," which characterized modern economies, resulting from the investments of businesses that, in the longer term, should provide the means of solving the unemployment crises.

Keynes regretted the passing of the adventurous entrepreneur who had once provided the mainstay of economic development. Keynes hoped for his return. The adventurous entrepreneur had been replaced in the modern economy by the business manager, aided by financial and exchange experts. In earlier times, businessmen had invested their own money, but now they borrowed from largely ignorant savers on the exchanges. There would probably never have been an industrial revolution without this adventurous entrepreneur whose concrete economic activities depended upon his lust for adventure combined with knowledge of the market and a nose for business. Business capital in the modern world was raised by people who did little more than make a desktop calculation concerning prospects over the next few years. Often they omitted to make any judgment concerning the investment itself, concentrating entirely upon attempting "to guess better than the crowd how the crowd will behave."[33] In the gap left by the lack of the true adventurous capitalist, held Keynes, we must accept the pharaohs with their pyramids or the bishops who loved to build cathedrals as a means of solving the problem of the lack of investment.

We should, nevertheless, be on our guard concerning the activities of the exchange sharks who did not understand that enterprise implied "the activity of forecasting the prospective yield of assets over their whole life."[34] But these exchange sharks believed, instead, that speculations in mass psychology or sociological guessing games concerning the attitudes of people, exchanges, and markets provided a sufficient guide for long-term investments: "When the capital development of a country becomes a by-product of the activities of a casino, the job is likely to be ill-done."[35]

The casino effect was that which, particularly in boom periods, raised the level of expectations concerning the returns on investments. In earlier times, of course, many business adventures had proved failures; but these entrepreneurs had been driven by a sense of adventure in their projects. How would it be possible, for example, to explain the phenomenon of the gold mines from the point of view of desktop calculations of chances and effects on employment? In earlier times, it was unusual to calculate investments, but today a price is set for the shares of a company whether or not this is approved by the entrepreneur. The businessman was forced to place a figure on his activity, despite its being possible to show that this was logically impossible.[36]

The problem of unemployment certainly demanded real adventurers, but the problem did not lie with these people in the modern world so much as with the structure of financial institutions. Concrete economic adventuring was something quite different from the cold calculations of the modern world of finance:

> In former times, when enterprises were mainly owned by those who undertook them or by their friends and associates, investment depended upon a sufficient supply of individuals of sanguine temperament and constructive impulses who embarked on a business as a way of life, not really relying on a precise calculation of prospective profit. The affair was partly a lottery, though with the ultimate result largely governed by whether the abilities and character of the managers were above or below the average. Some would fail and some would succeed. But even after the event no one would know whether the average results in terms of the sums invested had exceeded, equalled or fallen short of the prevailing rate of interest; though, if we exclude the exploitation of natural resources and monopolies, it is probable that the actual average results of investments, even during periods of progress and prosperity, have disappointed the hopes which prompted them. Business men play a mixed game of skill and chance, the average results of which to the players are not known by those who take a hand. If human nature felt no temptation to take a chance, no satisfaction (profit apart) in constructing a factory, a railway, a mine or a farm, there might not be much investment merely as a result of cold calculation. . . . Enterprise only pretends to itself to be mainly actuated by the statements in its own prospectus, however candid and sincere. Only little more than an expedi-

tion to the South Pole, is it based on an exact calculation of the benefits to come. Thus if the animal spirits are dimmed and the spontaneous optimism falters, leaving us to depend on nothing but mathematical expectation, enterprise will fade and die; though fear of loss may have a basis no more reasonable than hope of profit had before.[37]

The origins of the problem of unemployment were to be found in these wild fluctuations in expectations in the financial markets such as Wall Street. The casino was more attractive than the true concrete economic adventure, and Keynes toyed with the thought of imposing taxes and other costs to limit the worst of excesses. The financial exchanges provided little stimulus to the consumption of goods and services but rather were engaged in a speculative activity in which piles of paper changed hands several times a day. Such speculative investments were seldom undertaken with a view to long-term economic development but rather were inspired by insider information and the prospects of short-term profits. If people were forced to choose between consumption or long-term investment, which bound their funds perhaps for their lifetime, such a choice would no doubt frighten many investors who confidently expected to be able to sell their paper at any time. It would, however, provide one solution to the threat of unemployment deriving from the dance around the golden calf.

2.4 The Golden Calf in the Casino

For the classical economists there existed two kinds of dual-natured economic activities: production and consumption, and savings and investment.

Keynes maintains that the roots of the problem lay in a third possibility—liquidity. Both individuals and businesses obviously need a certain stock of money in order to meet ongoing payments. But the more uncertain they feel concerning future returns, the more liquid resources they store up for future use. They do this to ensure that they will have money available in the uncertain future. The problem with these stocks is that they reduce consumption in both the present and the future, since they are not aimed at any precise plan of consumption, even in the longer perspective. This storage of money by the hoarder is thus "to pile up claims to enjoyment which he does not intend to exercise at any definite time."[38]

This form of liquidity, which reduces consumption, is something that is based in the wish of people to feel themselves secure, if not rich. At the same time, however, it undermines the major purpose of economic activity in consumption. When money is simply stored for its own sake, a transformation occurs from concrete economic action to an abstract, self-serving goal. The demand for liquidity at its worst is a form of lust for power, and the worst sinners here are not individuals but companies that set aside funds to maintain their fortunes. At least a third of the savings in the modern state consist of collective funds. Keynes, indeed, located the most important cause of the 1929 crisis in "the extreme financial conservatism of corporate finance in the United States."[39]

The financial caution displayed in write-offs limited both consumption and investments. This was the case particularly after a period of expansion when businesses had made large investments, which they proceeded to write off without replacements. In this manner, businesses become power factors by virtue of their reserves rather than because of their contribution to concrete economy. The preference for liquidity—and this is the point of Keynes's theory—has fateful consequences for investment in businesses.

The manager who with the best will would increase employment is often forced to borrow his funds, and this forces him into the position of attempting to calculate the return on his investments. He reckons out the net gain from future costs and income as a percentage of the cost of the investment. This is called the marginal efficiency of capital or "the rate of return over cost,"[40] and this must be higher than the rate of interest in order for the manager to be able to borrow capital. The classical economists had assumed that the rate of interest was the equilibrium price for the demand for investment capital and the available supply of savings for this purpose. But for Keynes, the rate of interest was no guarantee at all that a balance exists between savings and investments. The rate of interest rather is a norm that controls investment, arising itself in a manner other than through investment activity. As he expresses the matter:

> I would, however, ask the reader to note at once that neither the knowledge of an asset's prospective yield nor the knowledge of the marginal efficiency of the asset enables us to deduce either the rate of interest or the present value of the asset. We must ascertain the rate of interest from some other source, and only then can we value the asset by "capitalising" its prospective yield.[41]

A manager who complains that he cannot create employment since he is unable to borrow the necessary capital would have been dismissed by the classical economists as being ineffective. His business was not sufficiently well run, since the bank rate showed that other firms gave a better return on the capital employed.

But all this is nonsense, according to Keynes. The rate of interest shows only what people are prepared to pay today for a certain sum of money in the future. The rate of interest is internal to money itself. If the return of a business lay below the rate of interest, this could depend on there being other borrowers such as governments and exchange speculators who diverted resources to other nonproductive ends. Keynes seeks to encompass this dance around the golden calf, this abstract economic aspect, by his concept of liquidity preference. The victims of this preference are the workers who become unemployed in increasing numbers. The more the world becomes industrialized and the more capital exists in the form of factories and installations, the lower the rate of return of long-term investments in business. But at the same time, the preference for liquidity could hold up the rate of interest. That the rate of interest did not fall was the result to be expected when a product—in this case money, which it was the privilege of the state to produce—could not be produced in sufficient quantities to meet demand.

Keynes summarizes his discovery in the following manner:

> Unemployment develops, that is to say, because people want the moon; men cannot be employed when the object of their desire (i e money) is something that cannot be produced and the demand for which cannot be readily choked off. There is no remedy but to persuade the public that green cheese is practically the same thing as to have a green cheese factory (i e a central bank) under public control.[42]

Those who had come to the same insight as himself, held Keynes, had been silenced as dangerous inflationists by the pervasive weight of the classical economists. But he was not frightened of committing heresy against the sacred authority of the past. The mercantilists' fixation with gold, as the church's prohibition against taking interest, could be interpreted as intuitive solutions to the problem of employment caused by high interest rates and a low rate of return on business investment. The mercantilist would hold down the rate of interest through large stores of gold and silver. In the absence of a clear logical theory (that is, Keynes's own discovery of the dependence of the rate of interest on the amount of money and liquidity preference) these insights had been unfortunately been lost "in the underworlds of Karl Marx, Silvio Gesell or Major Douglas."[43]

Gesell, for example, had suggested that the rate of interest should be lowered through weighting it with an artificial storage cost. This would be achieved through a legal monthly stamping of all notes in the economy. The thought was not silly, said Keynes, but Gesell had forgotten that people could always find something other than monetary notes in order to satisfy their demand for liquidity. The dance around the golden calf could never be completely eliminated, but since we lived in such a permeated monetary economy, it was time that we learned to control the rate of interest in order that wealth should not be transformed into poverty. Without this control over the rentiers and speculators, the entrepreneur could come to die, even as he had done in Mandeville's saga concerning what happened in the beehive when the knaves became honest and thrifty.

3. Prince Pozzo's World Saved

Keynes's General Theory could provide only hope for those who stood in the unemployment lines outside the factories. The entrepreneurs of the business world were in the final resort optimistic adventurers "who are certainly so fond of their craft that their labour could be obtained much cheaper than at present."[44]

If they were given the opportunity to build new factories and installations to provide employment, they would certainly take it; they would, moreover, do it in a more efficient manner than could be expected from a system of state ownership. The major problem was the financial limitations imposed upon the plans of the managers, something that had its origins and support in the doctrines of the classical economists. These dangerous economists were established in large organizations and corporations that suffered from the disease of the collective hoarding of liquid resources. The wide influence of the classical doctrine was spread through educational institutions to the younger generation, who thus learned to calculate the value of investment projects from the perspective of existing interest rates fixed by the banks. Projects that failed to meet this hurdle were simply rejected. Otherwise viable businesses could go bankrupt simply under the weight of capital costs. The dance around the golden calf had produced a golden rule: "[C]apital has to be kept scarce."[45]

And the result of this was fewer jobs and reduced production while productive resources lay idle. The rate of interest determined a certain level of investment and employment; as soon as these variables increased, it led to increases in the rate of interest—supported by the doctrine of economic expansion. Rentiers, in such circumstances, were afraid that inflation would eat up the capital savings. When investment increased, moreover, long-term returns on capital fell, so that managers had difficulty in paying off the original rate of interest. It was perhaps not so surprising that the rentiers in big business try to convince others that there is no room for expansion. The only remedy is to abolish these "functionless investors,"[46] who stand in the way of business fulfilling its social functions.

If large businesses were freed of the pressure of rising interest rates, they would seize any opportunity offered and dare to embark on socially motivated projects that create employment. The visible tendency of business to "socialise itself"[47] should be exploited in the cause of "full employment." In the 1800s, business attempted to keep wages low, expecting to make a killing with cheaply manufactured goods once free trade became a reality. If this continued chase for markets abroad is not to result in a new crisis, it is also necessary to increase home consumption. It is, therefore, in the interest of business to find a balance where its own workers are themselves consumers and where returns on investment, not necessarily keeping pace with skyrocketing interest rates, give entrepreneurs a reasonable compensation for the risks they take when increasing production until there is full employment of the working population.

In his reflections upon the theory, Keynes warns against a too mechanistic interpretation. Such misuse of economic theory is dismissed by him as pseudomathematics, basing itself on pretentious and meaningless symbols. Against the background of the manner in which later economists attempted to systematize his thoughts, it is interesting to recall his own point of view in the matter:

> The object of our analysis is, not to provide a machine, or method of blind manipulation, which will furnish an infallible answer, but to provide ourselves with an organized and orderly method of thinking out particular problems: and, after we have reached a provisional conclusion by isolating the complicating factors one by one, we then have to go back on ourselves and allow, as well as we can, for the probable interaction of the factors among themselves. This is the nature of economic thinking.[48]

It was not to be believed, for example, that it is possible to increase the amount of money and, via liquidity preference, maintain a lower rate of interest together with, through capital returns, an increased investment that, via the propensity to consume, provides a definite result concerning the increased employment to be expected from the monetary policy maneuver. Keynes means that he has provided an outline of major economic variables, but how such could interact in detail is unknown because "there may be several slips between the cup and the lip."[49]

It would be necessary, however, for the wise statesman who would release business energies to influence both consumption and investment. Taxation policy could influence both liquidity preference and the propensity to consume, whereas interest levels could encourage technology and training that support capital investment.

Something of a utopian vision of the future sometimes appears in Keynes's writings:

> If I am right in supposing it to be comparatively easy to make capital goods so abundant that the marginal efficiency of capital is zero, this may be the most sensible way of gradually getting rid of many of the objectionable features of capitalism. For a little reflection will show what enormous social changes would result from the gradual disappearance of a rate of return on accumulated wealth. A man would still be free to accumulate his earned income with view to spending it at a later date. But his accumulation would not grow. He would simply be in the position of Pope's father, who, when he retired from business, carried a chest of guineas with him to his villa at Twickenham and met his household expenses from it as required.[50]

This is the Keynsian version of Mill's zero-growth society of the future. But he himself, and his beloved Bloomsbury circle, lived in the era of capital accumulation. Had not his own economic independence been won on the speculative exchanges?

Keynes probably saw himself as an intellectual investor rather than an opportunistic speculator. Pozzo was not a market shark, but rather a Renaissance prince who carefully considered his capital placements, and provided business with the means to pursue the long-term good. In other circumstances, no doubt, Prince Pozzo would have been content to have received a return on his money that was the fair return for the risks of enterprise such as would have been in accord with his own theories. As it was, his winnings provided him with the means of consuming beauty in the form of Cezanne paintings and holding a pleasant court for his friends at the Café Royal.[51] There was time for philosophical discussion with Ludwig (Wittgenstein), who replaced Moore as the court philosopher. Prince Pozzo was charmed by the fine arts and particularly the Russian Ballet of Diaghilev and the ballerina Lydia Lopokova. The only thing Prince Pozzo regretted in his life was that he had not drunk more champagne.

Such a life-style, filled with nostalgic longing for a departed paradise of a preindustrial society, no doubt served to irritate many economists. The logical exposition of his theories celebrating the good manager and entrepreneur providing a future for capitalism no doubt irritated many others. The similarity between the state of full employment policy of companies and the medieval livery guilds was so obvious that many economists of the classical school preferred not to talk of business in this context. Others began to take Lord Keynes more seriously, so that Prince Pozzo's ideal state moved beyond utopia to the realm of concrete economy. The static society, according to Pozzo himself, would take but a generation to institutionalize:

> On such assumptions I should guess that a properly run community equipped with modern technical resources, of which the population is not increasing rapidly, ought to be able to bring down the marginal efficiency of capital in equilibrium approximately to zero within a single generation: so that we should attain the conditions of a quasi stationary community where change and progress would result only from changes in technique, taste, population and institutions, with the products of capital selling at a price proportioned to labour, etc. embodied in them on just the same principles as govern the prices of consumption-goods into which capital-charges enter in an insignificant degree.[52]

This was the ideal state of Prince Pozzo. And as an economist with such sympathies, he became a noble lord in the very homeland of orthodox economy—even chairman of its chilly economic association! Is the circle of thinking in political economy really complete now?

Notes

1. Roy Harrod, *The Life of John Maynard Keynes*, p. 1.
2. Ibid., p. 47.
3. John M. Keynes, *Essays in Persuasion*, p. 324.
4. Harrod, *Life of John Maynard Keynes*, p. 58.
5. George H. Moore, *Principia Ethica*, p. 20.
6. Ibid., pp. 121–122.
7. Harrod, *Life of John Maynard Keynes*, pp. 80–81.
8. Moore, *Principia Ethica*, p. 157.
9. Ibid., p. 13.
10. Ibid., p. 188.
11. Harrod, *Life of John Maynard Keynes*, p. 80.

12. Quentin Bell, *Bloomsbury*, p. 78.
13. Harrod, *Life of John Maynard Keynes*, p. 180.
14. Ibid., p. 20.
15. Bell, *Bloomsbury*, p. 48.
16. Harrod, *Life of John Maynard Keynes*, p. 119.
17. Ibid.
18. Moore, *Prinicipia Ethica*, p. 149.
19. Harrod, *Life of John Maynard Keynes*, p. 226.
20. Bell, *Bloomsbury*, p. 59.
21. John M. Keynes, *The Economic Consequences of the Peace*, p. 37.
22. Ibid., p. 213.
23. Harrod, *Life of John Maynard Keynes*, p. 194.
24. John Maynard Keynes, *The General Theory of Employment, Interest and Money*, p. 30.
25. Keynes, *The Economic Consequences*, pp. 17, 18.
26. Ibid., p. 17.
27. Keynes, *Essays in Persuasion*, p. 327.
28. Keynes, *The General Theory of Employment*, p. 9.
29. Ibid., pp. 104–105.
30. Ibid., p. 97.
31. Ibid., p. 105.
32. Ibid., p. 116.
33. Ibid., p. 157.
34. Ibid., p. 158.
35. Ibid., p. 159.
36. John Maynard Keynes, *A Treatise on Probability*, p. 28.
37. Keynes, *The General Theory of Employment*, pp. 150, 161–162.
38. Ibid., p. 131.
39. Ibid., p. 128.
40. Ibid., p. 140.
41. Ibid., p. 137.
42. Ibid., p. 235.
43. Ibid., p. 32.
44. Ibid., pp. 376–377.
45. Ibid., p. 217.
46. Ibid., p. 376.
47. Keynes, *Essays in Persuasion*, p. 314.
48. Keynes, *The General Theory of Employment*, p. 297.
49. Ibid., p. 173.
50. Ibid., p. 221.
51. Harrod, *Life of John Maynard Keynes*, p. 209.
52. Keynes, *The General Theory of Employment*, pp. 220–221.

12

The Socio-Economic Doctrine on Ideal Enterprise and Good Management: A Summary of Concrete Economy from Quesnay to Keynes

1. The Balance between Fiscalism and Capitalism

1.1 Business Firm between State and Company—Summary

Beyond the details and nuances in the various doctrines concerning enterprise and management from Quesnay to Keynes, there lies a truly radical message. The firm is, for the concrete economist, the only weapon against national imbalance. The business is, in other words, an instrument for dealing with the crises and conflicts that result from imbalance. Driven to its limit the message is this: only through the enterprise are wars and civil disturbances to be avoided. This is because the doctrine of the enterprise provides the only radical rule away from the state fiscalism and company capitalism that create national imbalance. When left-wing politicians, for example, the social democratic students of Gunnar Myrdal, advocate a strong fiscal state to replace the logic of company capitalism, such a proposal is, from the point of view of concrete economics, pseudoradicalism. On the other hand, it is necessary to reject the alternative right-wing proposal that the fiscal state should be reduced to a company in order to reconstruct capitalism in the future. The concrete economist knows that the fiscal state and company capitalism function with the same logic.

It remains as the conclusion to this work to clarify certain of the central issues in the doctrine on ideal enterprise and good management. This involves also showing how the fiscal and capitalist enemies of the business enterprise function and what real business does for the nation. From Quesnay to Keynes, economists have taught that the business enterprise carries out productive activities. It is first necessary to explain what distinguishes such activities from other possible kinds of activity. Production is for economists a solution of difficult conflicts caused by fiscalism and capitalism. Two examples from Quesnay and Keynes follow.

What does the ideal enterprise look like? A modern example of the pure doctrine of the enterprise can now be given. The function of the business is to create a balance in a situation of national imbalance. An enterprise in balance should have a tight management. Conflicts and crises are caused just by imbalances, which, in turn, depend upon leakages in the management. In a business firm, there is always a risk that leakages arise as a result of technical mistakes in productive activities. But such leaks do not create serious crises. The dangerous leaks are purposely caused by middlemen. These middlemen strive to obtain managerial control over concrete economic resources. The doctrine of the ideal enterprise is directed against such middlemen, whose methods of fiscal and capital control have reigned during the 150 years between Quesnay and Keynes. We first meet the fiscal middleman as a tax farmer or trader with the right to pursue leakage in the form of a company. This is followed by a difficult liberal time for the fiscal middlemen. The demand is raised for tight management by the established forces of society. But in the shadow of the development of the exchanges, they return to the scene once more. The middleman is now a company capitalist with the shareholding company as the means of leakage. Against the business with the tight leadership now stands the middleman organization with a leaky company leadership. Gustav Schmoller's Germany provides an example of how middlemen succeeded in bringing about the transformation from business enterprise to company organization for the whole nation. Two modern middlemen strategies were utilized.

But how does the doctrine of the business propose to plug these leaks? Two strategies for achieving tight management are presented here. These are followed by ten principles for managers who would lead according to the tenets of the doctrine of the ideal enterprise. Several interviews with active managers who follow such principles serve to illustrate these principles. For these people, the way out of the crisis is a difficult balance between the cliffs of fiscalism and company capitalism. Finally, it is shown that the doctrine of the ideal enterprise has its limits. The concrete economists do not mean that all is enterprise. On the contrary, the essence of life has little to do with economics. But without a balance between production and consumption and between investment and saving, we can never obtain the peace and energy to engage ourselves in life's higher non-economic values. The business enterprise of the doctrine provides this balance. Its surpluses are given generously to a free art and a free love without demands for state taxes or capitalistic interest.

Let us now look at what all this means. Let us get the differences among enterprise, state, and company straight.

1.2 Productive Action

To avoid the guillotine, the aristocrats should found agricultural firms. Such was the advice of the Physiocrats against revolution. Adam Smith encouraged the idle retainers of the court to seek honest work; that was also his advice concerning bureaucratization. The early economists were concrete philosophers of enlightenment who would convince all, however ignorant or evil, to stop contending and instead turn to *nature* in order to produce *things.* They directed themselves primarily to the propertied class and those in service whom they would convert to productive enterprise. The Physiocrats' lessons for the rich landowner and the poor peasant lad, Antoine, were intended to transform them into the productive *owner* and *worker.*

The rich man was to learn what constituted bad ownership. To own property meant more than the right to the title; and those who claimed this right without utilizing their property were responsible for creating shortages and poverty. Such activity was not productive but *destructive.* In the eyes of these economists, thus, the rights of ownership were dissolved in such cases. Those who had broken the doctrine of business enterprise had no defense against others who might squat on the property for productive purposes. Ownership for the concrete economist means a duty to *administer nature well.* In the business, the owner represents the interests of nature. He knows what returns may be expected but also the needs for maintenance. The good owner's business is an investment in nature.

In the spirit of the Enlightenment, people should return to nature rather than be regarded as included within it. The enlightened populace returns to a technical encounter with nature in the form of a business enterprise. The Physiocrats would convince Antoine of his duty to repay the gifts of life and the caring of his parents through work in an agricultural enterprise. This work resulted in the production of *things rather than services.* Adam Smith would both sack the court retainers and free the slaves. The retainers could not act productively in the production of things, while the slaves, fattened by the slave owners, lacked the will to work as a result of having no sense of responsibility to the past or future. It was when people built families that they came to talk and act for others in the business enterprise. It was here that the pursuit of empty symbolic activities and services ended and productive activities in the form of work that resulted in objects for consumption began.

When the owner not only bears a title to property but also administers it and when the worker manufactures things rather than services, production is balanced against consumption and savings are invested in nature. This balance demands that people meet nature directly in the business enterprise. The doctrine of the business enterprise willingly encourages such a meeting. John Stuart Mill understood that the Malthusian population catastrophe was caused by an imbalance where people were prevented from deciding in small agricultural enterprises the number of mouths to be fed from the harvest of the soil. The economists' teachings on the business enterprise are a manifesto that challenges workers and owners in all countries to unite in an encounter with nature. Then arise productive activities in the business enterprise.

1.3 Warnings at Versailles

Despite all the sensible lectures, the manifesto was not adopted. All organizations were not transformed into businesses according to the commonsense lessons taught by the economists, and this applied even to intelligent and good people as well. Now economists like David Ricardo, Karl Marx, Gunnar Myrdal, and John Maynard Keynes began to study these purposefully antienterprise forces. Keynes's General Theory gives us a clear picture of the capitalistic financier, whom he saw as the chief enemy of enterprise. Myrdal's thesis is a social democratic observer's view of the possibility of infiltrating the enemy's capitalistic logic. These economists may be said to begin and end with a warning of the imbalance that would arise if the enemy is victorious. First we heard Quesnay's warning about the danger of imminent economic imbalance at Versailles, and at the end we heard Keynes repeat the same warning call.

The Physiocrats blamed fiscal policy for the crisis in France. The farmers' businesses were taxed both on the harvest and on the labor by tax-greedy bureaucrats. The privileged traders levied further tax on the rest of the harvest at the customs. Mirabeau warned of a "heureuse revolution" that could result if this tax pressure was not eased, which gave rise to an imbalance between production and consumption on the farmed fields. The imbalance between savings and investment was aggravated by the "careering casinos" of Versailles, where noblemen frittered away the savings. We ought to realize, as John Stuart Mill did, that the Physiocrats did not hold up rationalizing of agricultural production through "la grande culture" as the only solution for the crisis. Not at all. The crisis was the result of taxation, and the ideal enterprise if it followed the doctrine should primarily be an effective weapon against fiscalism. In 1920, Keynes warned the Allies against their hard demands on Germany for war compensations out of its mines and factories. The workers and owners in Germany who had first been bled for the pursuit of the war would now be bled again by a capitalistic-minded Clemenceau for whom the war was obviously a question of a loan to be repaid with interest. For Keynes, however, the peace gave hope for a new and peaceful mode of business enterprise in Europe. The German workers and owners had been organized by the company bureaucrats into cartels and driven by the military bureaucrats as cannon fodder into the war. Further problems in the form of the reparation payments could only encourage them to follow the revolutionary example provided by the Russians. Drop the notion of reparations, advocated Keynes, and regard the war instead as an investment in the freeing of the German people from the power of the state and company bureaucrats. Let them rather unite in productive activities so that the costs of the war would provide a voluntary return to peaceful enterprise.

Photograph 1 **Åke Öberg**

Would it have been possible for the Physiocrats to save France from the consequences of taxation in the revolution of 1789? Would concessions on war reparations in 1920 have hindered Hitler from leading Germany into a new bloodbath? We will never know the answers to such questions, although we do know that Leon Walras considered his contribution to the theory of enterprise to be worth the Nobel Peace Prize. The doctrine of the ideal enterprise has always contained the belief that it could cure the conflicts of imbalance. Let us now follow the diagnoses of the crises as they were implied in the warnings of Quesnay and Keynes.

1.4 Tight or Leaky Management

When the economy flood was taxed in kind, the threat of war and revolution followed. This was, in clear language, the warning of both Quesnay and Keynes. It was, thus, these leaks that caused the imbalance. The Physiocrats wanted a doctrine of the enterprise that in the free union of administering owners and workers who produced things stopped the leakage in the management of the economic flow. The above photograph demonstrates that such a business is not a utopia. It represents a tightly managed enterprise.

The photograph from a French vineyard was taken in the Beaujolais district in 1982. It pictures a pipe through which the newly pressed grape juice flows. Half of the production runs into the owner's reservoir, while the other half flows into the barrels of the workers. As on a physiocratic estate, the landowner an-

Figure 1

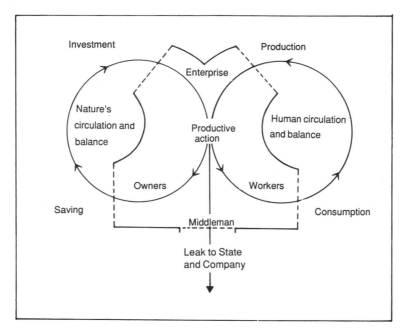

swers for all investments in land and buildings, while the tenant is responsible for all movable equipment. Why install such a tight management where the whole of the production flows in kind to the owners and workers? Previously the wine had flowed into the store of the wholesaler, and it was he who sold the product to the consumer. Now the marketing is undertaken by the owners and workers together. Previously the Beaujolais district had been known for its poverty, but today everyone has heard of the "Beaujolais Nouveau" as the area has bloomed into a physiocratic model farm. With the tight business leadership, the leakage to middlemen was stopped. That is the concrete function of good management. But management can never, on the other hand, eliminate business risks. The direct confrontation of people with nature can also result in misfortunes that fail to provide those things that had been hoped through their work. The harvest can go wrong, and the sun may be covered by cloud. But when the leakage has been stopped (see Figure 1), the flow of resources runs undisturbed into the circuits of nature and people.

The doctrine on the enterprise from Quesnay to Keynes was in reality a 150-year-long plea for tight management. The nation could only be saved through plugging the leaks. The first concrete economists thought that the leakage was of a technical nature. The Physiocrats called, in the main, for better techniques of production through, for example, the use of horses that would increase the efficiency of human labor and increase the flow in the pump of wealth. But Adam

Figure 2

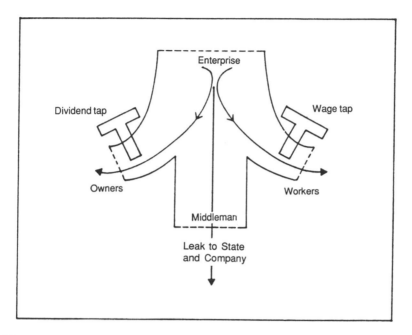

Smith already saw that the purely technical diagnosis of leakage was naive. It failed to take into consideration that leakage was purposefully created by the political enemies of business enterprise. Management, therefore, should not be regarded as a purely technical responsibility. The doctrine of the business enterprise demanded *active* managers who could foresee leakage and reveal the disguised intentions of middlemen. The duty of leadership is to hinder the transformation of the business enterprise into a company organization with a leaking leadership by way of the monetary taps of dividends and wages and thus control the economic flow in kind (See Figure 2).

In Figure 1 we saw how a middleman, who was lacking in Photograph 1, managed to squeeze in between owner and worker in order to become in Figure 2 an "entrepreneur" in that word's original French meaning: a person who takes, "prend," what exists "entre" or between. Alfred Marshall preferred, in fact, to refer to the ideal manager as an "undertaker," possibly to avoid the connotation of the true businessman with the middleman. In the physiocratic view, the middleman was someone who should be sacked by the aristocratic estate owner who administered his estates properly. In Marx, they appear as "managers" and "overseers," being the bureaucrats of the factories; with Charles Gide, the middlemen have become shopkeepers who prefer lucrative to productive activities. Figure 2 shows how the middleman strives to increase the leakage at the cost of workers and owners. In a genuine enterprise, the reduction of the flow to workers (that is, wages) and owners (that is, dividends) would imply, via the principle of balance, a reduction in investment and production. Owners and workers who keep their autonomy of action would quite simply leave the leaky business and let it sink with the middlemen on board. It is this that the middleman would prevent at any price. He must transform a balanced enterprise into a controlled company organization without a sense of balance. Such a company organization lacks the economic democracy of the business enterprise where owners and workers themselves control the economic flow. In an organization, a middleman can increase production without increasing consumption. In the plain moral language of concrete economics, this means *compulsion*. The middleman forces workers to produce without a just exchange in consumption. He can even increase investment without increasing savings. This is defined as the *exploitation* of nature. When he saves without investing, *accumulation* results. While the middleman himself produces nothing, he nevertheless consumes. This is the economic definition of *theft*. The middleman, thus, breaches the doctrine of the business enterprise. *Compulsion, exploitation, accumulation*, and *theft* are four economic crimes of which theft is the least weighty. This is because the thief at least, according to John Stuart Mill, returns into circulation that which he has stolen from the stores of wealth. But the other three crimes lead to a form of property that involves a *destructive action*. The following short rhapsody of the alleged crimes of the middlemen during the 150 years from Quesnay to Keynes shows how it works.

2. Fiscal and Capitalist Enemies of the Business Enterprise

2.1 The Fiscal Middleman

The genuine business enterprise should, according to the doctrine, be self-financing. Adam Smith praised the fundamental instinct to save, while Gide held that daily small savings made it possible to invest in increased production without resort to outside capital. When John Maynard Keynes, however, examined the history of the large British trading companies, he discovered that they were *not* self-financing. These organizations probably had the pirate Sir Francis Drake and his gold treasure to thank for their initial capital.[1] But all plundering expeditions under royal patronage were not equally successful. The banker Lorenzo di Medici, for example, lost the 52,000 florins that he loaned to Edward IV to finance the War of the Roses.[2] When the treasure hunts of war failed, the payment of the state debts became a large problem. If the prince himself had pursued the project, he was left with only his power to sell; this power was exercised in the taxation of his subjects' enterprises. The power of taxation was often sold in the form of an office, so that the tax farmer in this manner took the payment of the state debt under his wing. Where the peasant failed to hide his harvest and labor power, it was seized by the tax farmer in kind. Adam Smith placed himself almost on the side of the tax dodgers and showed a strong distaste for the leakage caused by the tax collectors. Before the tax collectors managed to infiltrate the business enterprise and transform it into a company organization under their own control, much of the nation's economic flow certainly ran into underground streams. The "black" economic enterprise certainly worried the fiscal powers that were, and it made them feel uncertain. It is related how suppliers to the court of James I always charged double price to guard against the risk of not being paid. Queen Elizabeth I was reputed to have put off her own funeral because of the lack of funds in the state treasury; it was considered by many that the revolutionaries who stormed the Bastille in 1789 could have been stopped with a single salvo from the king's soldiers if only they had been paid on time. But when the fiscal power of the state faded away, the kingdom dissolved almost automatically.

The princes, however, did not limit their fiscal activities only to their home markets but even sold trading privileges and power over foreign peoples to aid the state finances. So arose the trading companies of which the first in England in 1553 was named "the mysterie and companie of the Merchant Adventurers for the discovery of regions, dominions, islands and places unknown."[3]

The inspiration was hardly that of managing a landed estate or an efficient pin factory in the spirit of Adam Smith. Smith, indeed, did not consider these companies to be a form of business enterprise at all. With the infamous South Sea Company[4] scandal in mind, he was willing to suspect all companies of bluff and false transactions. The repayment of the debts for the failed wars for the Spanish throne threatened by 1720 a very unpopular raising of the English land tax. In order to avoid the dangers of increasing the internal tax pressure, Parliament gave a certain Blunt the right to sell shares in the South Sea Company in return for obligations. This company would, under the protection of the English Crown, conduct trade in a part of the South Pacific that, by the way, happened to be under the rule of the Spanish throne. No ships actually sailed in order to obtain by force the means to repay the state debts. Blunt, nevertheless, made fine business. He would ingraft the state debt in the stock of the company and, through complicated loan transactions, raise the price of his own shares in order, when the rate was highest, to pursue conversions. Blunt finally stuck a hole in his own financial bubble when trying to stop other swindlers who competed with him for capital in the smoky taverns and coffee houses where the price lists of bluff companies were displayed.

Thus, the demand for the services of the middleman was created by the existence of *state debts*. The leakage of the tax farmers and the traders was a mode of *fiscal oppression of business enterprise* against which the Physiocrats encouraged a nonviolent "heureuse" revolution inspired by the doctrine of the business enterprise. *Tight business management* should stop the supply of the leakage. A reduction of the state debt should reduce the demand for the unproductive services of the middleman.

2.2 The Hunt for Fiscal Middlemen

The demands of the bourgeois middle class for "freedom" were directed against the middlemen. With the economists in the lead, they demanded concrete freedom for both economic and trading activities. The most important kind of freedom, however, was that of the citizens *to control their own taxation.* It was unjust to confiscate production in the enterprise. According to Adam Smith, people had the right to the concrete product of their labor in kind, and production was to be fairly exchanged in consumption. The scale of economic justice was the balance of the economic enterprise, and this balance had been upset by the state debts.

Among the economists from Quesnay to Keynes, we find many variations upon this theme of saving enterprise from the fiscal middlemen. Mill considered that the state could be financed through its free purchase of land from existing owners, which would allow the introduction of the efficient management of agriculture. Beyond this, the state only needed to find the means to *free people* from the chains of ignorance. Léon Walras suggested that the state should retain the whole of the rent from land and with this finance all its activities without imposing taxes on business. With the limiting of state expenses, the need for loans would decrease. The middlemen who looked after this financing would become functionless, and they would be forced to take up honest production of things in order to consume. The career as a bureaucrat in the service of the state would no longer be attractive to the ambitious children of the workers, while the heirs of the owners would no longer find it attractive to move to the towns where they frittered away the money obtained from mortgaging their property in the courts or exchanges. This was the inspiration that moved the original concrete economists with their hope that the doctrine of the business enterprise would be fulfilled. John Stuart Mill imagined that the age of harmony stood just before the door, and Charles Gide attempted to hold the door ajar. Finally, we met John Maynard Keynes, who in nostalgia yearned for a return of a departed era. Today this intellectual tradition is still upheld in, for instance, James Buchanan's antistate theory of public choice.

The achievement of harmony, however, implied the free combination of workers and owners to chase off the middlemen. The business enterprise would then bloom, and the middlemen would be forced to withdraw like black sheep to the far horizons of their world of exchanges. The leaks would be repaired. When the workers in the home market had need to consume, the local owners could place more of nature at their disposal. If the owners themselves saw the possibilities for investments, they encouraged the workers to populate the area with children who were prepared to engage themselves in the business. The balance was thus reconstructed. Production favored consumption, and savings meant investment in the care and maintenance of nature. The good owner invested himself in the process of production. He would never again, as with Mill's home workers, allow middlemen to control supply and increase leakage through higher prices. In the same manner, Gide advised the workers to prevent the middlemen from obtaining control over the factories and to buy out the good owners. Economists now saw that one of their important tasks was to provide concrete examples of ideal business forms that would encourage others to follow. It was not only in the vineyards that it was necessary to establish tight business leadership, but also in the mines and the fishing fleet, where half the catch went in capital costs and the remainder to the crew. The teachings of Leclaire, Godin, and Babbage showed how associations between owners and workers could be formed. In these associations, if we are to believe Charles Gide, such a harmony could develop so that even owners, after having educated workers in good management, finally abdicate their power.

When the middlemen were driven out of the business enterprise, it yet remained to chase them out of the marketplace. The Physiocrats already suspected the leakage and misuse of power associated with transport and distribution. They wanted impartial functionaries in the pipeline that joined the business to the market. In the same spirit, Gide and Marshall praised the mechanizing of the system of payments and the technical means of communication as a guarantee that the natural flow of products would remain untouched by the dirty fingers of the middlemen. Walras had hoped that it would be possible to transform the entrepreneur from a middleman to a good functionary in the midst of the wild marketing of the economic flow. Gide, Mill, and Walras suggested a pincer action called cooperation, where owners and workers regained control over the leakage on the market, returning it to productive activities. Gide considered that through this means it would be possible to stop the leakage that was used to pursue political interests and obtain power in Parliament, something that undermined honest work and development of true economic democracy.

It was unfortunately a concrete economic fact that the possibilities of satisfying all needs through production were sometimes limited. Land was scarce, and the grapes were dry. When such natural monopolies arose, it was important to ensure that the unavoidable price rises involved did not benefit only a small group of middlemen. Walras suggested, as did also Mill and Marshall, that enterprises of this character should be nationalized. In order to ensure that the functionaries employed here did not fall for the fiscal temptation to gain from the leakage, these nationalized enterprises should be under competent and continuous observation by the press. For these economists, it was the journalists who were the true auditors.

So long stretched the ideas that the reader met in the first eleven chapters of this book. But what happened in practice? It is certainly claimed that the British state debt remained constant from the close of the Napoleonic Wars to the beginning of World War I.[5] It then increased tenfold, ending the era that John Maynard Keynes came to miss so much. During this long period of low state debt, many ideas concerning economic enterprises were transformed into concrete activities. But, nevertheless, the citizens with their calls for freedom and economic democracy had not succeeded in driving out the middlemen, although they had caused vexation in financial circles. Other opportunities were available, such as when the democratic states of Pennsylvania and Maryland in 1839 simply refused to tax their citizens.[6] Those who, in the lack of the royal projects of earlier times, now attempted to increase their capital through participating in romantic revolutionary enterprises forgot that the reason for revolution was to get rid of that fiscal state power that guaranteed the interest payments on their capital. Each citizen in a nation should be responsible for his own debts; no hero of freedom worth the name would set the people in debt on his account. The secure state was but a memory, and a belief in the new clothes of the emperor was worth a good laugh. People laughed at those who had been fooled by the Scott MacGregor into buying shares in the land of Cazique that did not exist and at those who lent money to the Greeks to free themselves from the Turkish occupation. One such loan was so well administered by a certain Lord Cochrane that but a few pennies emerged for the support of the Greeks and then several years too late. But, nevertheless, it was possible for someone like David Ricardo to earn a fortune as a middleman for state loans on the London Stock Exchange.[7] It was here that resources leaked from owners whose belief in the doctrine of the business faded and who sought to secure their old age through becoming rentiers. It was on the *exchange* that middlemen now created new leakage—an exchange that opposed the doctrine of the business enterprise through seducing owners of their property, something that led to the destruction of business enterprise. The middlemen who had been driven out of businesses and markets created in the London Stock Exchange a new temple. No broker or jobber there knew anything about the production of goods. The exchange was no free market of the kind that Walras had described. An eyewitness related how a stranger who attempted to arrange his affairs without the aid of the middlemen was first tricked into buying shares in the Wall of China, then had his hat knocked off and the newspaper he was reading burned, and finished up lying in the gutter. [8] It was not long before all who were not professionals were forbidden from entering this "open market."

2.3 Middlemen as Company Organizers

The return of the middleman was thus prepared on the stock exchange. In the first place, the exchange was nearly entirely engaged in matters concerning the state debt. It then began to sell shares in canal and railway companies that controlled transport to the markets. What leaked into the hands of the exchange disappeared from the productive flood of economic enterprise. Genuine productive businesses are self-financing and, according to Marshall, seldom lack sufficient capital. Even the transport companies were often locally financed before seeking parliamentary permission for "incorporation," which gave the right to own the land where the canal or railway would be sited. Capital, according to the doctrine of the business enterprise, is never an initial problem for those who would *begin* a business. Capital is an instrument for control over the business, a method to transform an enterprise into a middleman company organization.

The new leakage probably began when the owners gave up active administration for a passive ownership.

Karl Marx and Charles Gide described this first step most clearly. In the first place, the wage tap (see Figure 2) was created through which owners paid monetary wages to workers instead of paying them in kind with part of the product (see Photograph 1). Production *in natura* was now completely controlled by the owners who distributed it further to the shops to which workers were sent to spend their monetary wages. In the shops, they were met by Gide's trader who took high prices for bad products. Meanwhile, in the factories, Marx's managers squeezed hard on the wage tap; the workers could observe how those things they produced had become so expensive that they were no longer available on their home market, but rather were sent to the "finer" quarters of the town or exported. The business had now been transformed into a *compulsory organization* where production was not balanced by consumption. *Theft* was common in the market where bureaucrats now consumed without themselves producing anything. The leakage flowed away from business enterprises into the coffers of foreign states and railway monopolies in whose stocks and shares the owners now chose to accumulate.

During the closing years of the nineteenth century, however, the Victorian owner began to purchase shares in manufacturing companies on the home market. It was here that the second step toward the company capitalistic leakage logic was taken, although it had already been described by David Ricardo. Ricardo had, indeed, invested what he had earned as a middleman in a landed estate; it is known that the swindler Blunt had hopes of a similar placement of his funds that guaranteed shortage.[9] As a passive landowner, sitting on an asset that was guaranteed to be in short supply, it was, according to the logic of land rents, possible to claim an increasingly large portion of the harvest in kind. This was possible without being bothered by the administrative duties that would normally fall upon a good owner. Mill had shown how this passive ownership had caused hunger in both India and Ireland. It seems certain that he would have opposed any extension of the same logic to industry where Victorian gentlemen purchased shares in businesses with the leakage they had obtained from their own companies. Mill had considered that real wealth consisted of equipment and machines in productive service. Now, however, the middle class was tempted to purchase shares with the prospect of control over production and market dominance. As distinct from agriculture, which at least provided Ricardo with rent in the form of barrels of physical corn, the middlemen installed a *dividend tap* (see Figure 2) . The middlemen, not the shareholders, became the lords over the concrete economic flow in kind.

The owners were first tempted to play on the exchange. They often managed to get themselves into debt and were forced to sell their firms to middlemen. These latter thus bought out the administering owners, replacing them with passive shareholders. Economists from Quesnay to Keynes have always emphasized that no business could begin as a shareholding company. Good administrators and productive workers were advised to avoid involvement with the organizers of shareholding companies. The shareholding company came into existence when the middlemen purchased their way in and took over monetary control of an economic flow that already existed.[10] In the same manner as Marx's manager looked after the wage tap, it was now the task of the company director to look after the tap through the medium of the shareholders' meetings, which were once described by Gustav Schmoller as being "poor comedies." But the share company that hinders the balance of a business is not merely a comic form of swindling as in the time of the South Sea Company. In the theories of Wicksell, Myrdal, and Keynes, it becomes the very source of the crises of imbalance. It poses a serious threat to national security.

The businesses that have now become shareholding companies create large industries whose investments lead the economic flow on even longer round-about routes before reaching the consumers. Charles Gide doubted whether these accumulated investments led at all to consumption. He saw in these large companies an industrial race where people and natural resources were concentrated in ever larger units with a threatening potential of productive overcapacity. Great reserves of material and labor had already been condemned by Adam Smith, who wanted to reduce the gold reserves in businesses, together with Mill who considered that the trade unions' protectionism was a danger to the economy. The productive capacity was not actually utilized but served rather as a kind of industrial Maginot Line to frighten off genuine businesses that would manufacture consumer goods and compete through productive activities. Company wolves in business clothing proudly displayed the "model works" and let it be understood that if others threatened to enter the market they would push the button and drown them in the subsequent flow of products. This passive threat amounts to exploitation and constitutes a destructive activity. With their power over shortage and supply, even in the midst of the enormous wealth of industrial society, the company middlemen milk the economic flow to obtain interest payments and taxes. They stand at the source, and neither owner nor worker can as in earlier times of fiscal domination hide from their predacity. The modern middleman, nevertheless, is forced to resort to tricks to hide his bloodletting and as well to prevent a complete collapse of the nation's economy. It is interesting to examine these strategies, but first I will discuss an example of the takeover of power.

3. Leaky Management as Applied Abstract Economy

3.1 A Historical Example

In 1870 it was time to build the German Reich. "But how and with what?" wondered the anxious statesmen who knew that the German middle-class citizen preferred to purchase foreign railway shares rather than exchange his leakage against German stocks. After the victory of Sedan, however, there arose a nationalist feeling that directed the stream of leakage toward the newly established Berlin exchange. And so began a gigantic operation to finance the new state that would bring the middlemen to power and cleverly deprive the German workers and owners of control over the economic flow. It happened in four stages. The first step was getting the owners of businesses to play on the exchange. Their leakage was taken over by the share-issuing bankers, many of whom were of Jewish origin. Their agents traveled up and down the land in search of cheap businesses to transform into share companies. Collapsing factory buildings and cold chimney stacks became "Gründungsobjekten." A timber man could become a building entrepreneur, and a boy who played with his chemistry set became a chemical engineer. But even well-established businesses were bought up, although sometimes good administrative owners resisted the temptation and chose, like the locomotive manufacturer Borsig, to continue production and investment themselves. If the doubtful security offered by certain "Gründungsobjekten" came to light, the bankers were there as convenient legal scapegoats. Lumpen pogroms served as an outlet for the aggressions of those ruined; the process of company building could proceed relatively undisturbed. The capital of the middle class was thus taken over by the large companies, and the businesses that were ruined were purchased cheaply.

The next step was to squeeze the wage tap. The campaign against free enterprise was taken up by the universities. The dangerous and damaging implications of the doctrine of business enterprise were extolled in thick volumes by the state-serving professors such as Gustav Schmoller and his colleagues in the Verein für Sozial Politik. When modern students at the business schools read the theory of organizations, it should be kept in mind that this subject was founded in the sociological masterpieces of these German professors who used them as the heavy artillery of the state against the doctrine of business enterprise. When the German worker was forced to produce in these great organizations, the question of economic leakage was masked under "the social question." The privations of the workers were naturally blamed upon free enterprise, and it was not long before the company directors could throw off their masks and openly accept the jubilations of the "Volk" while dressed in the uniforms of the state bureaucrats. They now had the mandate of the "Volk" to lead and control the economic flow. The wage tap was screwed downward through first setting prices as "taxes"—as the term was—in the cartels. The quality of production for the home market was reduced, while at the same time exports were dumped abroad. When the workers discovered the imbalance between production and consumption, the middlemen, with the benign help of the universities, managed to turn their rage against the shareholders. The middlemen themselves, who completely controlled production, used to refer to the poor beer produced by the new giant brewery as "actienbier" or "dividend soup." First they closed off the wage tap, and then they played on the myth of class warfare to blame the matter on the owners. But the real class that needed to be opposed was the middlemen's growing middle class of bureaucrats.

The third step was taken when the middlemen turned to the dividend demands. Schmoller praised his state-loving German shareholder who was satisfied with a low return on his money. The middlemen now controlled the whole flow of the economy in kind and could use this position for the further purchase of small competing companies. The German state raised itself as a well-shielded medieval castle to which increasing numbers sought their way for a secure career as a state-serving middle class. The fourth and last stage arrived with Bismarck's final solution of the problem of business. The funds of the companies were sucked into the state coffers through compulsory state insurance; this last stage was accompanied by large doses of moralizing concerning social welfare. The German citizen was reduced to little more than an industrious taxation object in peacetime and a brave soldier in war. The whole of the economic production now flowed through the pipeline of the middlemen, being freely at the service of the goals of fiscal and company capitalism.

3.2 Social Control of Values—First Leaky Strategy

But why do not owners and workers unite to throw out the middlemen who have their fingers on the wage and dividend taps? The concrete economist's answer is that the middleman has succeeded in undermining the sense of balance of both owners and workers. Through the use of social control, he has broken their unity to reign alone over the concrete economic resources.

In the doctrine on business enterprise, it is the workers' sense of balance that accounts for the division between production and consumption. Workers produce in order to consume and consume in order to continue the production necessary for the maintenance of life. The business is an instrument for the maintenance of the life circle of workers and families (see Figure 2). But the sense of balance is undermined when the relation between production and consumption is cut. The worker's instrumental view of the business is exchanged for a subjective and moralizing viewpoint. Production, which without its relation to consumption is meaningless, is given a fictive value in itself. The middleman, thus, is interested in replacing the doctrine of balance with one concerning values. In the chapter of Léon Walras's abstract economics, for example, we find such a theory of values for consumers.

Walras postulates that consumption controls the economic flow. The purpose of consumption is not anything concrete but rather "utility," which is a value that can only be experienced subjectively by the consumer. The purpose is absolutely not that of obtaining oats for the horse in order that it shall manage to draw the load. Nor is this incomprehensible "utility" allowed to be an abstract "nothing." Walras, on the contrary, would explain everything with his "utility" and so lands in the middle of that morality that Mill, Moore, and Keynes would eliminate from economics. This was because in such a subjective world it was not possible to ask the pragmatic question "why?" Where this was the case, it was easy to be deceived. It was, therefore, not cynicism that caused the economists to advise keeping morality out of economics. They rather wished us well, hoping that we should not be deceived to become the robot producer or automated consumer in the organized company of the middlemen.

In Myrdal's works, we find a similar theory for ensuring that the middlemen are not disturbed by the shareholders in the company. The owners' sense of balance consists in deciding on the basis of what the amount saved is likely to yield in consumer products when it is invested in production. An owner who is in control of his sense of balance could be imagined to object strongly when he discovered how middlemen save without investing in production. An administering owner dislikes those destructive strategic investments that serve to limit rather than increase consumption. With the aid of Myrdal's theory, a middleman could influence a technically competent and administrating owner to become little more than a calculating bookkeeper dreaming about an abstract "profit maximization." Such an owner does not save in order to obtain a natural yield but rather money as value in itself. He is a master of just the geometrical method that Mill held was useless for the analysis of concrete economic affairs. He is the prize pupil of the business school in the subject of business technique, although he has never set his foot within a workshop. That is why the discipline remains an empty shell. Shortly stated, he leaves control over the economic flow to the middlemen themselves.

If owner and worker should wake up from the indoctrination provided by the theories of values, it seems certain they would seek to do something to tighten up business leadership. It was to avoid this possibility that Schmoller taught the importance of listening to the elite (read middlemen) who were the bearers of culture and experts in the usage of the German language. The middle-class philosophers and professors are the propagandists for the abstract economics of the middlemen. The concrete economists, on the other hand, would see the craftsman and farmer as their ideals. A further method of maintaining the division between owners and workers is to spread the myth of the class warfare. Its purpose is to make the owner suspicious of the wages of the workers and the workers suspicious of the dividend to the owners. The result is that owners and workers both seek the support of the middlemen in their struggle with each other. In this manner, they come to support the fiscal state and company capitalism that originally created the demand for the leakage for which they blame each other. And the middlemen stand quietly by at the source of the economic flow while the obscure, metaphysical ideologies function to divide the members of the middlemen's organizations into an upper-class and lower-class with the middlemen's middle-class as arbiter.

3.3 Write-Offs and Funds—Second Strategy

When both workers and owners have been harnessed by values and divided by social control, the company can take over the financing of the state. By the turn of the century, institutional savers were increasingly taking over the stocks issued to cover the debts of the state. It was no longer just the Victorian middle class who purchased these obligations, but the banks and insurance companies. Behind these "savers" often stood other companies.

When Colbert was given the task of reducing the debt of the French state, he cast a sharp eye toward the insurance business.[11] Perhaps he was thinking of King Ferdinand of Portugal who already in the fourteenth century introduced the compulsory insurance of ships. Life insurance was a usual source of finance; in the trail of the South Sea Company there sprang up insurance companies together with the state lotteries that were used to help out the state treasury. Insurance, thus, is an old and well-proved source of finance. When the concept of insurance met up with the shareholding company, the idea of write-offs arose, which helped to create large funds of organized savings. It was just such funds that Keynes blamed for the reduction of purchasing power that caused economic crises. The write-offs were legitimized with the notion that the company should retain funds in order, as it is said, to insure the company's own value. That which was retained under this heading reduced wages and dividends to owners. And that which determined the size of these funds was not prices, but the costs of the equipment and installations of the company. These came to cost just what the company had the possibility of writing off. In Myrdal's theory of the firm, there is a clear description of this circular argument for the legitimatization of leakage. The result was that the companies could control an even larger proportion of the economic flow; this, in turn, was legitimatized by an industrial state that, in Keynes's apt formulation, found it "expedient to use entrepreneurs as collecting agents."[12] The companies themselves, thus, became "collecting agents" for their own account and for the servicing of the state.

4. Leakplugging Management—Concrete Economy Applied

4.1 Balance and Action

The doctrine of the business enterprise from Quesnay to Keynes contained advice for opposing the development of the middlemen. In the first place, it was necessary to free both workers and owners from the values and social control that had become commonplace. The worker was split: on the one side, he was meant to be a consumer who only dreamed of "utility"; and on the other, a producer who worshiped the god of employment. The owners were also split into high-flying consumers and abstract, calculating "profit maximizers." The remedy lay in recreating the relationship between production and consumption and that between savings and investment. Only then can the organization return to being a balanced business enterprise with an objective judgment and active individuals.

Marshall taught that we are all equipped from birth with a sense of balance. Mill taught that our sense organs gave us the weights that we then used on our balance scales. Smith held that it was only through physical activity that our senses obtained the means for making such decisions concerning balance. Sense data, according to Smith, involved a physical registration through experience, and this could *not* be obtained through studying symbols. In order to make balanced judgments, it was necessary that we ourselves had undertaken enterprising actions. No other person could with symbols, whether in figures, letters, or verbal means, communicate to us the sensations that were the data on which our balance depended. Each human being must himself have the experience out of which such balance emerges. That which we experience, moreover, could not be communicated to others with symbols in a satisfactory manner. Economic knowledge is personal and tacit. We must give our fellow human beings things that they, in their turn, can experience for themselves. To undertake productive actions, thus, is inseparable from both direct learning and the communication of knowledge. Marshall considered, for this reason, that the school could never replace actual experience in a business. Mill, on the other hand, went so far as to hold that the encounter between human beings and nature in the enterprise was the only source of knowledge.

The doctrine of the business enterprise supposes, accordingly, the existence of individuals and their objective realities. The concrete economist is no materialist, skeptic, or subjectivist. Marshall preferred to talk with practical men about concrete economy. In order to understand their works, he made no deep philosophical analysis of their sayings or writings, but rather traveled to their businesses where he could observe what was happening with his own eyes. Language is only a certain reflection of actions: first come the actions, and then the symbols. To maintain the opposite is, with Schmoller, to prepare the way for social control. To hold that culture is prior to nature is to indulge in what John Stuart Mill liked to term German metaphysics. This is the path to the abstract economics that would shield us from the experience of nature and thereby undermine our sense of balance. In the end, we are unable to believe in our own senses and are prepared to do whatever the elite wishes.

Charles Gide's advice to the consumer was simple: "Forget the subjective utility!" Hold fast rather with the natural needs that can be balanced against production; those needs that cannot be satisfied through production are not of a natural character. Gide encouraged consumers to sober up and free themselves from drugs such as alcohol, which distorted their sense of balance. He also rejected the idea that production could have a value in itself. This was the reason that he attacked Fouriers's utopia where work was held to be a pleasure in itself. Production must be coupled to consumption so that people themselves produce as their families grow and needs increase. If workers and owners are reduced to consumers, the middlemen can allow their demand to raise prices on those things whose production they control through the organized company. Gide held that people should demand autonomy, themselves taking responsibility for their needs through creating new enterprises. Workers and owners were thus to be saved from Walras's consumer subjectivism.

Owners should as soon as possible be taken out of Myrdal's accounting school and, in the spirit of the Physiocrats, returned physically to their businesses. Keynes had suggested a "marriage" with lifelong faithfulness between the shareholder and his company. Owners should not be the passive recipients of rents and interest, but rather should work for an increase in production when consumer needs exist. Within the business enterprise, he should study the pages out of nature's book, learning how natural yields and technical possibilities provided opportunities for manufacturing things in harmony with nature. He then becomes a balanced administrator who saves in order to improve the production of consumer products.

The *workers* should be awakened from their idiotic guild and union slumber. Adam Smith already criticized the guilds that lengthened the apprenticeship times as a means of regulating wages. Gide emphasized that trade unions could, through use of their monopoly power, obtain a larger slice of the economic cake but that they would never succeed in baking better and larger cakes. Instead of more bread, the worker was fed on a diet of moralizations that undermined his sense of balance. In returning to the workshop, he can open his mind and, in the study of the division of labor, balance his intervention in nature against those things that his work creates. Marshall considered that it was the function of the trade unions to return to workers their sense of self-confidence in their own abilities and help them develop an individual sense of balance through a consciousness of costs. As soon as trade unions established general rules concerning production, it threatened this individual sense of balance. The trade unions, moreover, were almost entirely concerned with wage demands, although Adam Smith had already emphasized that workers should receive the result of their labor as "fixed and realized" in production, like the wine that ran into the peasants' barrel during the grape harvest (see Photograph 1). This is because a sense of balance demands a physical perception of the reality obtained by making things instead of selling time for money.

When workers and owners have passed through the concrete treatment of the business doctors from Quesnay to Keynes, they will not so easily lose control over the economic flow in their business enterprises. It will become very much more difficult for the middlemen to create leaks when the business leadership becomes tighter.

4.2 Risk and Flow

In a concrete economic enterprise, the owner knows the physical effects of his investments, and the worker knows what his productive working activity gives as a result in things. But it is, nevertheless, still possible for things to fail, since nature plays many tricks with human beings. It is risks of this kind that, according to the doctrine of business enterprise, result in things going wrong. This view of risk, however, does not justify those large write-offs and funds that the middlemen create with the argument that they want to insure the value of the company. Risks refer to human beings who cannot be infinitely insured against such events. People are truly mortal.

The doctrine of the business enterprise encourages all people to resolve their conflicts with production. The national imbalance will be resolved if we with silence and open minds turn to nature in order to perform work that gives things as a result. All must attempt it for their own benefit. This is the attitude that Mill called "self help." In the first place, activity, then words. But our attempts can fail, in which case we all have the right to each other's sympathy and help.

Sympathy and help should relieve human need and not that of companies. It should first and foremost be given inside the family; and those who lack families can build familylike associations for mutual help. It was in this manner that the first insurance associations came into being in the time of ancient Rome.[13] Marshall's "external economy" is really a mutual support association for administering owners. Gide advised workers to build associations for mutual security. He emphasized that the members themselves should administer the reserve fund that they maintained as "first aid" in cases of emergency. He strongly advised against allowing a share-issuing company to take care of the insurance. Use of a share-issuing company resulted in an overinsurance, since such companies hid through the use, among other things, of standardized tariffs that were fixed by cartels and insurance pools. Keynes's thesis on probability expresses the doubts of a concrete economist that statistical methods could be used to compare the risks for different people in different enterprises. According to Keynes, each person has an objective knowledge of the probability that his particular action would provide a certain result. But this objective and concrete knowledge is, nevertheless, of such a personal nature and so bound to a certain situation that it could not be summarized as a figure that could be compared with the figures for other situations and people. Only routine activities that did not require insurance could be calculated by the means that the insurance companies employed to justify their prices. The prices of insurance policies, thus, were really arbitrarily fixed. The insurance companies provided the middlemen with great possibilities to milk the economic flow through high prices without risking criticism on objective grounds.

How large, according to the doctrine of the business enterprise, should be the reserves of a business? The Physiocrats considered that it was sufficient to maintain a store against bad harvests, together with—at the most—a gold coin or two that was hidden from the clutches of the tax gatherers. Adam Smith wanted to reform the currency system just in order to reduce the gold reserves held in businesses. To retain the means for guarding against harvest price changes was regarded by the Physiocrats to be completely reprehensible. In a similar manner, Keynes considered that entrepreneurs should not speculate in other people's valuations, neither on the market nor in the exchange casinos. The doctrine of the business enterprise would forbid funds from being set aside as an insurance against changes in values. There then remains an objective need·for insurance that would cause the middlemen to turn pale. When our business project fails, we need, beyond a friendly and sympathetic acceptance, a bowl of soup, a roof over our head, and a warm blanket. Release the remaining write-off funds, and let them flow to the benefit of consumers in the economic circuit formed by people and nature.

4.3 Ten Principles for Tight Management

The idea of tight business leadership can be summarized in the following ten principles that presumably would have been acceptable to economists from Quesnay to Keynes, but with the exception of the advocates of the more abstract versions of economic doctrines. For each principle of tight leadership there is a middleman's counterprinciple. The active business manager must work in the field of tensions between the principles of concrete and abstract economics:

The Tight Business Manager's Concrete Principles	The Leaky Middleman's Abstract Business Principles
1. Business action is productive.	1. Business is also a symbolic and destructive activity.
2. Production demands the free union of owner and worker.	2. Business is led by the middle class.
3. Production is risky.	3. A business is security.
4. Production is the flow of things.	4. Business includes also services.
5. Activity occurs through voluntary engagement.	5. To make business involves organizing.
6. Business finances itself and also art and love.	6. A business begins on borrowed capital, and it can then make loans to the capital market.
7. Risks can only be shared.	7. Through insurance and write-offs, funds can be created that shield the business against risks.
8. The function of the market is the exchange of things.	8. Production is a function.
9. Individuals have an objective sense of balance.	9. Individuals have socially based subjective values.
10. Business is not money.	10. Moneymaking is the hallmark of good business.

The *first principle* is an encouragement always to lead needs into production. Consumers should not be stopped at the gates of the business but encouraged to engage in productive activities. This involves avoiding the purchase and sale of services and the reduction of all strategic stocks that serve destructive purposes. The *second principle* rejects the myth that business enterprise demands a middle class. The middle class is a middleman interest group with the task of splitting owners and workers who need to unite in the business enterprise. The *third principle* encourages all to seek to meet nature in their business enterprise and not to seek security through guaranteed interest or taxes. The *fourth principle* draws a lesson from history. In earlier times, workers were forced to sell their labor for a minimum of consumption possibilities. Today their children take revenge when they, as bureaucrats, steal from businesses and consume without themselves producing. Avoid services so that we also avoid theft and compulsion. The *fifth principle* implies that people should not be set in debt in order that they can be forced to work through interest and tax payments. The *sixth principle* refers to what economists have always taught: The share-issuing company is not a form of enterprise. Companies that are financed with leakage can never begin new enterprises but only "swallow" the existing ones. To begin a new enterprise is a long, self-financing process. Never expect speedy miracles. The *seventh principle* is directed against the constant attempt of the middlemen to save without investing and by this, under the flag of insurance, financing the state debt. The *eighth principle* emphasizes that business is about production and that close attention should be paid to this interaction with nature. But the middlemen create leakage through holding sociological playgrounds in marketing. The *ninth principle* would remind all of their independence and dignity in the face of the manipulations of values and ideological social control exercised by the middlemen. Finally, the *tenth principle* would remind us that money is the language of economics and that a language—in the doctrine of concrete economics—must always be a reference to some reality. If we can only think of business in terms of money, the language of money loses its meaning because such a language must refer to something other than itself. Owners and workers must, therefore, control the real economic flow in kind through tight management. In a company economy where the control of nature is separated from the handling of finance, money becomes an incomprehensible language game where the situation is further confused through inflation and changing exchange rates.[14]

4.4 Management Leak-Pluggers in Action

The photograph reproduced earlier in this chapter shows that the business model of the Physiocrats from 1750 still exists today. We shall now listen to contemporary voices of people who have attempted to stop the leaks in business leadership during the crisis years for European business in the beginning of the 1980s. They live according to the doctrine of business enterprise, even if this is somewhat unarticulated. These managers often live dangerously. To follow the doctrine of business enterprise involves setting in question both the fiscal state and company capitalism. It is a difficult balancing act where the attempt must be made either to reduce the costs of the state or to increase the efficiency of the economic flow from local industry.

Thierry comes from the French town of Roubaix. His story rings with the messages of Mill and Gide. As a modern Physiocrat, he discovered and administered local housing that had been left unused. He now sought insight to the auditing of the local government to find funds that could be returned to the economic flow:

> The project began ten years ago in an old quarter where there were 16 houses that had once been occupied by textile workers. These houses had only one source of water among them. This had knitted the little community together, providing a meeting point where people came to discuss and learn to know each other. The authorities decided to demolish the quarter, and they began with closing off the water. The project got underway when people formed a long chain from the town fountain to the houses in the quarter.
>
> It is necessary to begin with the concrete problems of people. The passive model must be broken. All people have a lot of ideas about what to do with their lives. But technocrats and politicians live in another world. What ordinary people want to do with their lives is too simple for the technocrats and politicians. Neither do the trade unions have much understanding. They strive rather for global solutions, and so soon as someone does something on the local level and in a small scale, he is decried as being an enemy of the working class. One becomes a victim of their democratic centralism.
>
> We began with the houses. The first step was to occupy the houses and control their renovation. We obtained our own architect who went around and talked to householders concerning how the quarter should be restored. Our plan for the quarter finally won over that of the town planners. We decided that rebuilding should proceed on a house to house basis. We now undertake the maintenance and cleaning ourselves. Cleaning and hygiene provide a good first job for those who are socially handicapped or unemployed. These 21 persons meet once a week to plan their own work. We used to say that they belonged to "the fourth world." We took over the cleaning when our caretaker had a nervous breakdown and took a job in industry. When a flat became vacant or someone wanted to move, we gathered to discuss the question of distribution together. It was thus decided collectively where one should live, and this resulted in that people with problems were not clumped together. One knew if someone would come home drunk at 2 A.M. and create a disturbance.
>
> The second step was to teach ourselves to understand the economy of the local government and town, to make the budget comprehensible. There was very much money to be found if one could only penetrate the figures. Money for health, social help, economy and education. We have learned how to get access to these funds. But it is also necessary that one can clearly account for what the money has been used so that people can understand what has happened with the funds. We have, for example, travelled around to other towns in order to study their projects.

There are now several businesses in the quarter, a printing press and a cooperative building firm, together with a cooperative restaurant and a number of individual businesses. The project is a way of life, but we found our position on the problems of ordinary people. We are not students or intellectuals.

In Berlin there is a small shop where youngsters are given practical training in the retail trade. This is a modern version of business education such as can be found in Marshall and Gide. But in the background there still lurks something of Schmoller's moralism in the abstract dream that work is something "good in itself":

> I began as a teacher in a trade school. We started this project five years ago, and we finance five people and have two trainees. The first idea we had was to sell coffee from Nicaragua as a means of helping the people there. In the course of a week, we sat down and read everything we could about the coffee trade and rang all the coffee exchanges in the world. We then opened the shop. One of us was also an arranger of concerts, and through this experience had learned much about business and organization.
>
> The goal was to give training through an interesting work. We did not want to train through normal educational methods. When no-one clears mathematics in school, the teacher thinks he must create motivation. This we did not want. We did not want some pedagogic method, only interesting work. We like to experiment and improve the shop. Our aim is not money, although we want sufficient to cover our costs. If it is money one wanted, it would be better to work for IBM. Good work gives good training. The problem is that work becomes boring. One must get up in the mornings to open the shop otherwise the customers become angry. Certainly there is new music and new concerts, but the organization easily becomes a routine. How does one maintain joy in work?

The next voice comes from an Austrian experiment in business, providing an answer to the moralizing tones of the Berliners in the spirit of Mill, Moore, or Keynes. Keep morals and duty out of economics. Let the business enterprise become the area of the sense of balance. Throw out all attempts at social control:

> You are sorry for the lack of joy in work! I hope you have related to your trainees that life is not only work. Even group work becomes boring. Work is not the only thing in life. But this is really the problem of the left in hoping to realize their dreams through work. Marx and his children believe that they become happy when they work and help others. They do not work for themselves, but rather for Nicaragua. I believe it is a mistake that one should give to people all the time. An old Christian idea. Ask people instead what they want and what they can do. Then give them tips. Tell them to stop talking and do something instead. No, it is a mistake to imagine that one achieves anything through political work. It is too altruistic. Go to church instead. I know what I am talking about as we worked for five years with a pure communism among us, but now are we also egoists. In order to be social, it is necessary at the

same time to be egoistic. We now give courses and save money to invest in our own school and our own house. We are not capitalists, but nevertheless middle class in our private lives. We are a hundred adults and fifty children, having a school and a farm of about 20 hectares. Some of us are married and others not. We raise our own children, and in the summertime give courses for people who come as visitors. We want to enjoy life. We are not helpers, but are happy to show people that we live well. Come here, we do "good things." People become curious then and can identify themselves.

Through examples like this, it can be seen that the doctrine of the business enterprise is spread in "leagues" reminiscent of the style of Mirabeau's tastes. The active managers do not allow themselves to be cheated into becoming "collecting agents" for the state or to create leakage that supports idle rentiers. They know that the application of political economy in practice means to economize politics and not the reverse. Finally, a voice from a "new-old" business leader in the middle of a contemporary economic crisis. He comes from a group called "War on Want," which was founded in the 1950s to fight poverty through enterprise:

We are 25 employed in London, Newcastle and Manchester. There are then the local "War on Want" groups with about 10,000 members who help the organization with contributions. We make financial campaigns for projects. Recently, for example, we collected 40,000 dollars for El Salvador. We made a similar project for Bangladesh. The yearly turn over is about 3 million dollars. Three quarters goes to projects and a quarter to publications and information about projects. A large problem today is that there are too many advisory consultants for beginning business enterprises as a means of dealing with economic stagnation. All these people struggle for funds. Our problem is to avoid all middle hands and see that those people who need money obtain it directly.

We think that cooperation is a good form for enterprise, although not *any* kind of cooperative. In India it was not unusual for cooperative forms to lead to an even greater exploitation of the poor workers. It is also important to obtain the confidence of those groups one would support. In Britain, we work with people from the West Indies, and when we come with money they want to know where it has come from. They do not trust whites in general, and it takes a long time to develop a mutual confidence. We also do not draw back from conducting campaigns against things we consider damaging. We supported, for example, a campaign against those who would sell powdered milk to mothers in developing countries. But also often in Europe, businesses often create a dangerous working environment. It is the large organizations that have the money and possibilities to control the activities of businesses. Our organization will not support hierarchical forms of enterprise. Our job is to change people's social situation within different businesses. One example is the campaign we drive to obtain jobs for unemployed women. We help them by looking after their children, attempting to convince employers to take on women who perhaps do not have precisely the right qualifications, and conduct discussions concerning their concrete situation.

5. Art and Love beyond Business

John Maynard Keynes never doubted that the only function of the business enterprise was that of *consumption*. The enterprise was an instrument for meeting concrete needs through the production of consumer goods; as long as there existed needs, the business enterprise would continue to produce. Keynes was certain, moreover, that businessmen did not require very high profits in order to engage themselves as entrepreneurs. Mill considered that Englishmen would produce without the carrot of profits. Profit maximization is an abstract idea of the middlemen who would help to assure themselves of their source of leakage and create shortages through continuously binding resources in industrial capacity. Gide considered, and quite rightly too, that owner-cooperatives give priority to consumption rather than to investment, and Keynes would have agreed this was the right approach. The middlemen, on the other hand, warn of "stagnation" and demand more and more investment. The doctrine of the enterprise is not so interested in the middlemen's financial transactions. Its task is production rather than the financing of the state or company capitalism. When need is fulfilled, the business can close, after, what Marx would have called, the "necessary work." The surplus can be used in terms of free time, on art and in love. Not until more children are born will there be any need for increased production. No one need be lured by the middlemen's flattery about "work for its own sake" or the "beauty" of work.

Outside the factories people discuss the good and the beautiful. When artists and courtesans resign and want to turn their passions into salaried jobs, they can be offered a sandwich, that which Keynes called "unearned income" and a promise of a regular job if inspiration and passion begin to run low. If there is surplus, it is better to donate it to the cause of art and love than, with tax and the purchase of shares, feed the monster company capitalism, which will sooner or later eat up the genuine enterprises. What the artists and courtesans choose to do with our gifts is their business, as long as they do not turn into "useful" bureaucrats who bother us continuously with their (dis)services. And thus the economists from Quesnay to Keynes teach us where to draw the line of tolerance between concrete economics and the good, the beautiful, and the free spiritual life. To know its limits is the doctrine's noblest characteristic, a characteristic that makes it less useful for the purposes of maintaining social control as is the case with the theories of organization and the state that botanize in our mental life.[15] Where faith and aesthetics begin, there ends concrete economics, and so does this study in the doctrine of the business enterprise and its moral philosophy of management.

Notes

1. John M. Keynes, *The Applied Theory of Money*, in Keynes, 1930
2. Anthony Sampson, *The Money Lenders*, p. 28.

3. Victor Morgan and William Thomas, *The Stock Exchange, Its History and Functions*, p. 49.

4. John Carswell, *The South Sea Bubble*.

5. Morgan and Thomas, *The Stock Exchange*, p. 79.

6. Sampson, *The Money Lenders*, p. 35.

7. Morgan and Thomas, *The Stock Exchange*, p. 49.

8. Ibid., p. 161.

9. Charles Kindleberger, *Manias, Panics and Crashes*, p. 85.

10. Pierre Guillet de Monthoux, *Läran om penningen* .

11. Otto Bucht, *Försäkringsväsendets företagsformer från antiken till våra dagar*, p. 27.

12. Keynes, *Treatise on Money*, p. 174.

13. Bucht, *Försäkringsväsendets färetagsformer från antiken till våra dagar*, p. 20.

14. Ibid.

15. Pierre Guillet de Monthoux, *Action and Existence—Art and Anarchism for Business Administration*.

Bibliography

Bell, Quentin. 1968. *Bloomsbury*. London: Futura Publications Ltd.

Berlin, Isaiah. 1965. *Karl Marx His Life and Environment. 1963*. London: Oxford University Press.

Boson, Marcel. 1951. *Léon Walras fondateur de la politique economique scientifique*. Paris: R. Pichon & R. Durand-Auzias.

Brinkmann, Carl. 1937. *Gustav Schmoller und die Volkwirtschaftslehre*. Stuttgart: Verlag W. Kohlhammer.

Bucht, Otto. 1936. *Försäkringsväsendets företagsformer från antiken till våra dagar*. Stockholm: Kooperativa förbundets förlag.

Carswell, John. 1960. *The South Sea Bubble*. London: The Cresset Press.

Cassel, Gustav. 1940. *I förnuftets tjänst, en ekonomisk självbiografi*. Volume I. Stockholm: Bokförlaget Natur & Kultur.

Cournot, Augustin. 1938. *Recherches sur les principes de la theorie des richesses*. Paris: Marcel Rivière.

Daire, Eugene. 1846. *Physiocrates*. Paris: Librarie de Guillaumin.

Darwin, Charles. 1906. *On the Origin of Species by Means of Natural Selection or the Preservation of Favoured Races in the Struggle for Life*. London: Hutchinson & Co.

Ephemerides du citoyen ou bibliothèque raisonnée des sciences morales et politiques. Vol. 111. 1769. Paris.

Frängsmyr, Tore. 1977. *Svärmaren i vetenskapens hus*. Lund: Raben & Sjögren.

Funck-Bretano, Frantz. 1936. *L'Ancien regime*. Rio de Janiero: Americ Edit.

Gårlund, Torsten. 1976. *Marcus Wallenberg 1864–1943, hans liv och gårning*. Stockholm: P.A. Norstedt & Söners förlag.

Gemkow, Heinrich. 1967. *Karl Marx eine Biographie*. Berlin: Dietz Verlag.

Gide, André. 1948. *Journal 1889–1939*. Paris: Gallimard.

Gide, Charles. 1889. *Principes d'economie politique*. Paris: L. Larose et Forcel.

———. 1900. *La Cooperation—conferences et propagande*. Paris: Librairie de la societé du recueil général des lois et des arréts.

———. 1904. *Economie sociale*. Paris. Librairies de la societé du recuiel général des lois et des arréts.

———. 1924. *Fourier précurseur de la coopération*. Paris: Association pour l'enseignement de la cooperation.

———. 1941. *Le Juste prix*. Paris: Presses universitaares de France

1933. *Charles Gide sa vie et son oeuvre*. Paris: Recueil Sirey.

Guillet de Monthoux, Pierre. 1981. *Vulgärkantianische Unternehmenslehre*. Munic: Verlag N. Leudemann.

———. 1987. *Läran om penningen*. Stockholm: P.A. Norstedt Forlag.

———. 1991 *Action and Existence—Art and Anarchism for Business Administration*. Munic: Accedo Verlag.

Hägerström, Axel. 1939. *Socialfilosofiska uppsatser*. Stockholm: Albert Bonniers förlag.

Harrod, Roy. 1951. *The Life of John Maynard Keynes*. London: Macmillan & Co. Ltd.

Heckscher, Eli, ed. *Bidrag till Sveriges ekonomiska och sociala historia under och efter första världskriget*. Stockholm: P.A. Norstedt & Söners förlag.

Hegel, Georg, F. 1952. *Grundlinien der Philosophie des Rechts*. Stuttgart: Frommanns Verlag.

Hilton, Boyd. 1977. *Corn, Cash, Commerce, the Economic Policies of the Tory Government 1815–1830*. Oxford University Press.

Keynes, John, M.. 1920. *The Economique Consequences of the Peace*. London: Macmillan and Co, Ltd..

———. 1930. *A Treatise on Money*. Volume II. London: Macmillan and Co. Ltd..

———. 1931. *Essays in Persuasion*. London: Macmillan & Co. Ltd.

———. 1933. *Essays in Biography*. London: Macmillan and Co. Ltd..

———. 1973. *The General Theory of Employment, Interest and Money*. London: Cambridge: Cambridge University Press.

Kindleberger, Charles. 1977. *Manias, Panics, and Crashes*. New York: Basic Books.

Levy-Bruhl, Lucien. 1899. *Lettes inédites de John Stuart Mill a Auguste Comte*. Paris: Felix Alcan.

Lindahl, Erik. 1929. *Om förhållandet mellan penningmängd och prisnivå*. Uppsala universitets årsskrift. Uppsala: AB Lundequistska bokhandeln.

———. 1930. *Penningpolitikens medel*. Förlagsaktiebolagets i Malmö Boktryckeri.

———. 1930. *Spelet om penningvärdet*. Stockholm: Kooperativa förbundets bokförlag.

———. 1957. *Spelet om penningvärdet*. Stockholm: Kooperativa förbundets förlag.

Malthus, Thomas. 1798. *An Essay on the Principle of Population as it Affects the Future Improvement of Society with Remarks on the Speculations of M. Godwin, M. Condorcet and other Writers*. London.

Marshall, Alfred. 1885. *The Present Position of Economics: An Inaugural Lecture Given at the Senate House at Cambridge*. London: Macmillan and Co..

———. 1886. *A Plea for the Creation of a Curriulum in Economics and Associated Branches of Political Science*. Printed pamphlet.

———. 1919. *Industry and Trade, A Study of Industrial Technique and Business Organization and of the Influences on the Conditions of Various Classes and Nations*. London: Macmillan and Co.

———. 1979. *Principles of Economics*. London: Macmillan Press Ltd.

Marshall, Mary P. 1947. *What I Remember*. Cambridge: Cambridge University Press.

Marx, Karl. 1977. *Das Kapital, Kritik der Politischen Ökonomie* –Vol. 1. Berlin: Dietz Verlag.

———. 1979. *Zur Kritik der Politischen Ökonomie*. Berlin: Dietz Verlag.

Mill, John S. 1872. *System of Logic Ratiocinative and Inductive*. Vol. 2. London: Longmans, Green, Reder and Dyer.

———. 1879. *Autobiography*. London: Longmans, Green and Co.

———. 1909. *Principles of Political Economy with some of Their Applications to Social Philosophy*. London: Longmans, Green and Co..

Mirabeau, Victor. 1769. *Les économiques*. Amsterdam.

Moore, George, H. 1960. *Principia ethica*. Cambridge: Cambridge University Press.

Morgan, Victor and Thomas, William. 1962. *The Stock Exchange its History and Functions*. London: Elek Books.

Mossner, Ernest, and Ross, Ian, eds.. 1977. *The Correspondence of Adam Smith.* Oxford: Clarendon Press.

Myrdal, Gunnar. 1927. *Prisbildningsproblemet och föränderligheten.* Uppsala: Almqvist & Wicksells boktryckeri.

————. 1930. *Vetenskap och politik i nationalekonomien.* Stockholm: Kooperativa förbundets förlag.

————. 1931. "Om penningteoretisk jämvikt." In *Ekonomisk tidskrift.*

————. 1939. *Monetary Equilibrium.* London: William Hodge & Company Ltd..

————. 1972. *Vetenskap och politik i nationalekonomin.* Stockholm: Rabén & Sjögren.

————. 1973. *I stället för memoarer kritiska eaaäer om nationalekonomien.* Vänersborg: Bokförlaget Prisma.

Ohlin, Bertil. 1972. *Memoarer-ung man blir politiker.* Stockholm: Bonniers förlag.

Quesnay, Francois. 1756. "Fermiers." In Daire, ed., 1846 *Physiocrates.*

————. 1757. "Grains." In Quesnay, *1969 Tableau economique des physiocrates.*

————. 1765. "Dialogues sur le commerce et sur les travaux des artisans," in Daire, ed. 1846. *Physiocrates.*

————. 1969. *Tableau economique des physiocrates.* Paris: Calmann-Levy

Rae, John. 1895. *Life of Adam Smith.* London: Macmillan & Co.

Ricardo, David. 1973. *The Principles of Political Economy and Taxation.* Guildford: Dent & Sons Ltd..

Rosenberg, Hans. 1967. *Grosse depression und Bismarckzeit.* Berlin: Walter de Gruyter & Co..

Sampson, Anthony. 1981. *The Money Lenders.* London: Hodder and Stoughton.

Schmoller, Gustav. 1890. *Zur Sozial und Gewerbepolitik der Gegenwart.* Leipzig: Verlag Dunker & Humblot.

————. 1904. *Grundriss der Allgemeinen Volkwirtschaftslehre,* Vol 1, 11. Leipzig: Verlag Dunker & Humblot.

————. 1904. *Über Einige Grundfragen des Rechts und der Volkwirtschaft.* Leipzig: Verlag Dunker & Humblot.

————. 1920. *Zwanzig Jahre Deutscher Politik.* Munich and Leipzig: Verlag Dunker & Humblot.

Smith, Adam. 1904. *An Inquiry into the Nature and Causes of the Wealth of Nations.* London: Methuen & Co.

Smith, Adam. 1979. *The Theory of Moral Sentiments.* Oxford: Clarendon Press.

Spiethoff, Arthur, ed. 1938. *Gustav Schmoller und die Deutsche Gesichtliche Volkswirtschaftslehre.* Berlin: Verlag Dunker & Humblot.

Sraffa, Piero, ed.. 1951. *The Works and Correspondence of David Ricardo.* Cambridge: Cambridge University Press.

Walras, Léon. 1896. *Etudes d'economie sociale.* Lausanne: F. Rouge Editeur.

————. 1900. *Eléments d'économie politique pure ou la théorie de la richesse sociale.* Paris: R. Pichon and R. Durand-Auzias.

————. 1909. *La Paix par la justice et le libre echange.*

————. 1969. *Les Associations populaires de consommation, de production et de crédit.* Rome: Edizioni Bizzarri.

Warnock, Mary, ed. 1962. *Utilitarianism.* London: Collins Fontana.

Index

Abstract theories
of economic freedom, 177, 184, 186
of middlemen, 275, 280
of Myrdal, 222–39
of Ricardo, 65, 71
and sense of balance, 277
of Walras, 274
Advertising by producers, effects of, 152, 200
Aesthetics, in Bloomsbury Group, 244
Agriculture. *See* Farming
Alexander III, 197
Apprentices
in early trade corporations, 182
need for, 212
training period for, 40, 278
Artists, value of, 244, 246, 247
Association businesses, experience with, 108–10

Babbage, Charles, 109, 151, 269
Baccarat glassworks, 210, 213
Balance
and equilibrium theory of Walras, 117, 129, 135
between fiscalism and capitalism, 259–66
and imbalance caused by middlemen, 266
investment and saving in, 260
and opposition to middlemen, 276–78
production and consumption in, 260, 277–78
and production in agriculture, 19–23
psychology of, 145–46

Balance *(continued)*
in supply and demand, credit transactions affecting, 224
Bank Restriction Act of 1797, 47
Bankruptcy, causes of, 115
Banks, cooperative, for credit and loans, 134
Bartering, 35
Basic needs
agricultural production of, 19
and problems of survival, 28
produced by workers, 32–33
Bastiat, Claude-Fréderic, 196, 197, 201
Beamtes, as state administrators, 183, 193
Bentham, Jeremy, 90, 91, 92, 97
Bentham, Samuel, 92
Bernhardt, Sarah, 197
Birrell, Augustine, 244–45
Bismarck, Otto von, 172, 174, 178, 186, 192
Bloomsbury Group, 244, 246
Bookkeeping
and bureaucratic ossification, 158
developed by Walras, 130–31
Buccleuch, Duke of, 25, 27, 37
Buchanan, James, 268
Bureaucrats
as consumers while producing nothing, 271, 281
middle class of, 274
Business enterprise
as balance between fiscalism and capitalism, 259–60
and capitalistic bolshevism, 223, 237

Working time *(continued)*
  and wage payments, 81
Works committees, for determination of
  wages, 163–64
World War I, 246
  economic policies in, 219, 223
  unemployment after, 248

World War I *(continued)*
  and Versailles Treaty, 247, 262
Write-offs for businesses, effects of, 253,
  276, 280

Zero-growth society of Mill, 103–4
  Keynesian version of, 256

Pierre Guillet de Monthoux is a professor at Stockholm University where he is responsible for the doctoral program in management. He frequently teaches in France and Germany and has held research positions in Germany and the U.K. He has published works on the socioeconomics of money, the role of Kantianism for European industrial organization, and the theories of organization in European anarchism. He is currently exploring the aesthetics of entrepreneurial action in modern and postmodern societies—a project that combines investigations of both art practice and art theory form a socioeconomic point of view.